THE WORLD'S GREATEST
UNSOLVED MYSTERIES

ALVA PRESS

This 2002 edition published by
ALVA PRESS
A division of Book Sales, Inc.
114 Northfield Avenue
Edison, New Jersey 08837

The material in this book has previously appeared in:
The World's Greatest Unsolved Crimes
(Hamlyn, Octopus Publishing Group Ltd, 1984)
The World's Greatest Mysteries
(Hamlyn, Octopus Publishing Group Ltd, 1994)
The World's Greatest Trials
(Hamlyn, Octopus Publishing Group Ltd, 1986)
The World's Most Infamous Murders
(Hamlyn, Octopus Publishing Group Ltd, 1994)
The World's Greatest Crimes of Passion
(Hamlyn, Octopus Publishing Group Ltd, 1990)
The World's Worst Atrocities
(Bounty, Octopus Publishing Group Ltd, 1999)
The World's Greatest Serial Killers
(Bounty, Octopus Publishing Group Ltd, 1999)

ISBN 0 7858 1483 3

Printed in Great Britain by Mackays of Chatham

Front cover picture acknowledgments:
Princess Diana (Photo B.D.V./Corbis)
Kurt Cobain (S.I.N./Corbis)
Lord Lucan (Hulton Getty Picture Collection)

Contents

Crimes
Without Call

Who was R. M. Qualtrough?

William Herbert Wallace was a drab, colourless, boring man who lived a drab, colourless, boring life. He was thrifty and hardworking, mild mannered and a little snobbish, soberly dressed and utterly, utterly respectable. His idea of a night out with the boys was his regular fortnightly visit to a local cafe to take part in chess tournaments. A swinging party at home with his mousy wife, Julia, usually consisted of the couple playing duets on violin and piano.

Herbert's meek and unassuming manner was greatly appreciated by his employer, a solid dependable insurance company who employed him as a collector and agent. In 15 years in their employment he had proved to be utterly trustworthy. He was diligent and he never pushed for promotion.

His admirable personal qualities and those of his shy little wife made them ideal neighbours in their neat terraced house in Wolverton Street, Anfield, Liverpool. He was never known to show outbursts of exuberance or bad temper.

In fact, the jury at his trial decided, Herbert Wallace had all the characteristics of a sadistic brutal murderer.

His wife had been battered to death so violently that her brains had spilled out on to the floor. She had died at the hands of a man who deliberately laid a meticulous trail of false clues to throw the police off his scent.

There was no real evidence to connect her husband with Julia Wallace's death. In fact he had a near-perfect alibi. But then Herbert Wallace was a man who ordered his life with pedantic attention to detail.

He was too good to be true. The jury's verdict seemed to be that Wallace was so absolutely ordinary that he had to be capable of great evil . . .

In spite of flimsy police theories which hardly stood up

to defence cross-examination, in spite of a complete lack of motive on the part of the accused man, in spite of a summing-up by the trial judge who virtually begged the jury to acquit him, Wallace was found guilty of his wife's murder.

He sat impassively in the dock when the verdict was returned. It was this same lack of emotion which had led him there in the first place. 'I am not guilty. I cannot say anything else,' he whispered plaintively to the court as the judge prepared to pass sentence.

The judge, Mr Justice Robert Alderson Wright, showed more distress than the convicted man. But he had no option under law. Shaken by the jury's verdict, he donned his black cap and passed the only sentence open to him: to be hanged by the neck until dead.

And the mystery man who actually bludgeoned Julia Wallace to death heaved a deep sigh of relief. He had got away with the perfect murder.

The first sign that Herbert Wallace's humdrum life was about to be shattered came with a telephone call from a complete stranger to the City Cafe in North John Street, Liverpool, at 19.15 on Monday 19 January 1931. Herbert Wallace was due at the cafe that night to exercise his rather mundane skill as a chess player. He was taking part in a tournament aptly named 'The Second Class Championship'.

But the 52-year-old insurance agent was not there to take the telephone call. A waitress answered the phone and passed it to Samuel Beattie, Captain of the chess club, who explained that Wallace had not yet arrived. Did the caller want to phone back later?

The voice on the other end of the line asked to leave a message for Wallace. The caller identified himself as 'R. M. Qualtrough' and requested that Wallace should call on him at his home at 25 Menlove Gardens East, Mossley Hill, the following night to discuss some insurance business. Beattie wrote the message on the back of an envelope.

4

About the same time, Herbert Wallace was setting off from his home at 29 Wolverton Street to catch a tram to the City Cafe for the chess club meeting.

The Wallaces had been married for 18 years, after a two-year engagement in their home town of Harrogate, Yorkshire. Herbert had a worthy, but lowly paid, job as political agent for the local branch of the Liberal Party. When the meagre party funds could no longer support his salary, he moved to the quiet suburb of Anfield in Liverpool.

Julia, five years younger than her husband, set about making their new home in Wolverton Street neat and tidy, just like their lives. In her earlier years she had spent some time in the genteel studies of music and painting, and a small upright piano took pride of place in the parlour of their trim terraced house. As Herbert settled in to his new job as a collector for the Prudential Insurance Company, the childless couple could afford little luxuries like the £80 which Mr Wallace had spent on a microscope.

He prided himself on being a diligent amateur scientist. He even lectured part-time in chemistry at Liverpool Technical College and often he and Julia would spend the evening in the little laboratory he had built just off his bathroom, examining slides on the microscope. At the age of 50, Herbert had even started to learn the violin and accompanied Julia on the piano.

His job paid him an annual salary of £250 and the thrifty couple lived quietly within their means. Herbert had a bank savings account of £152 and Julia had her own modest savings of £90.

As Herbert Wallace wrote in his diary: 'We seem to have pulled well together and I think we both get as much pleasure and contentment out of life as most people.'

The only times he left Julia alone were his visits to the chess club and his lectures at the technical college. But when he stepped out that night to catch his tram to the cafe, there was a nagging worry in his mind. There had been a spate of burglaries in Anfield in the past few weeks and Wallace often kept large sums of his insurance company's money at home. 'Don't open the door to any strangers while I'm gone dear,' he reminded Julia as he left.

Samuel Beattie never actually saw Wallace arrive at the City Cafe but shortly after the phone call he saw him seated, taking part in a game, and he passed on Qualtrough's message.

Wallace seemed puzzled by the telephone call. He did not know any Mr Qualtrough. The address was on the other side of the sprawling Liverpool suburbs, quite outside his normal insurance sales territory. On the way home from the club that night, he quizzed other members about the location of Menlove Gardens East. Which tram should he take to get there? How long would the journey take?

The following day Wallace set out, regular as clockwork, on his appointed rounds in Anfield, collecting a premium of a few pence here, paying out a claim of a few pounds there. He returned home punctually for his lunch at 14.00, went back to work for the afternoon and finished in the evening at 18.00. While Julia prepared tea, Wallace went upstairs, washed and changed and filled his jacket pocket with insurance quotation and proposal forms.

At 18.30, their meal over, Julia Wallace answered a knock at the door. It was the milk boy, 14-year-old Alan Close. He handed Mrs Wallace a pint container of milk and she took it into the kitchen to empty the contents into her own jug, returning to the front door to give the boy the dairy's can. That was the last time she was seen alive.

About 15 minutes later Herbert Wallace left the house. He walked a few hundred yards and boarded a tram in Belmont Road for the first leg of his journey to meet the mysterious Mr Qualtrough. At 19.06, after travelling a mile and a half, he switched to a second tram in Lodge

Lane. His behaviour was unusual for the normally reserved Herbert Wallace. He chatted amiably to the tram conductor Tom Phillips about his high hopes of selling a big insurance policy at his destination. At 19.15 he arrived at Penny Lane and switched to a third tram to complete his five mile journey. He asked conductor Arthur Thompson to let him off at the stop nearest Menlove Gardens East.

'Don't know it,' Thompson admitted. 'But we stop in Menlove Avenue. Just ask around, it's bound to be near there.'

For the next half hour Wallace tramped busily around the streets of Mossley Hill. He found Menlove Gardens North. He found Menlove Gardens West and Menlove Gardens South. But no Menlove Gardens East. He knocked on the door of Mrs Kate Mather at No 25 Menlove Gardens West and she told him there was no Menlove Gardens East. He remembered his Prudential Insurance supervisor, Joseph Crewe, lived nearby and found his home and knocked on the door. He got no reply.

He met Police Constable James Sargent on his beat in nearby Allerton Road and was advised to go to the local post office to check a street directory for Mr Qualtrough's address. Wallace agreed. Then he remarked on the late hour.

'Yes, almost eight o'clock,' the policeman agreed. There was no directory available at the post office and Wallace found a newsagent's shop. He pestered the owner, Mrs Lily Pinches, into checking the names of customers on the shop's newspaper delivery round, explaining his errand to her in great detail. No, she confirmed, there is no Menlove Gardens East.

Wallace gave up and went home.

He arrived back at Wolverton Street shortly before 21.00 and his neighbours, John Johnston and his wife Florence, saw him struggling with the handle of his back door. Finally he managed to get the door open and went inside.

7

The Johnstons were still watching as Wallace emerged a few moments later and calmly invited them in. 'It's Julia,' he explained flatly. 'Come and see, she has been killed.'

Within minutes the police were summoned. Julia Wallace was dead. Her skull had been battered by ten separate blows, any single one of which would have been fatal. There was blood everywhere. A total of £4 was missing from the little cash box in the kitchen cabinet. She had been killed, the forensic experts decided later, between 18.30 and 20.00 that night.

Herbert Wallace appeared to be almost unmoved by the sight of his dead wife. Later that night he left the murder house and moved in with his brother's family a few miles away. The detectives, meanwhile, moved in to 29 Wolverton Street. And the tongues wagged furiously.

Why had Herbert Wallace talked of his business so freely to tram conductors and total strangers in his quest to find Menlove Gardens East? Had he deliberately drawn the patrolling policeman's attention to the time? And who was R. M. Qualtrough, whose call the night before had lured him away from his home? If the address in Mossley Hill never existed, did R. M. Qualtrough exist?

On 2 February 1931, a week after the body of Julia Wallace was buried in Anfield Cemetery, Herbert Wallace was charged with her murder. Cautioned by the police, he said simply and sadly: 'What can I say in answer to a charge of which I am absolutely innocent?' The press headlines had become so sensational and strident that when the trial opened at St George's Hall seven weeks later, even the prosecution made little objection to a defence request that no residents of the city of Liverpool should sit on the jury.

The prosecution made much of a key piece of evidence. They had traced the source of the call from 'R. M. Qualtrough'. By sheer chance, the call to the City Cafe the night before Julia Wallace's murder had to be routed through a telephone supervisor because the coin mechanism in the public phone box had been faulty. The call and the defect were duly logged. The call had come from Anfield 1627, a kiosk in Rochester Road, only 400 yards from Wallace's home.

Of course Wallace was not at the cafe to receive the call from 'Qualtrough', prosecuting counsel Edward Hemmerde, explained triumphantly. For the same reason, 'Qualtrough' couldn't phone back later to speak to Wallace after he arrived at the chess club, because Herbert Wallace was 'R. M. Qualtrough'.

Wallace, Hemmerde claimed, had made the telephone call himself then sprinted for a tram and arrived at the cafe to receive the message he had phoned through as 'Qualtrough'.

His pestering inquiries of tram conductors, the policeman and the residents of Mossley Hill the following night were all part of the plan to establish his alibi, the prosecutor insisted. And Wallace's unflurried demeanour when he returned home and found his wife's body was the action of a man who already knew murder had been committed.

Herbert Wallace's defence counsel, Roland Oliver, outlined his case simply. His client had not committed the murder and it was not for the defence to prove who had wielded the murder weapon. Wallace was not 'Qualtrough' and the defence did not need to establish the identity of the mystery man. Wallace made a fuss of finding Menlove Gardens East, he explained, because it was a break from his usual routine, a chance to earn the unexpected bonus of a sale. He was displaying an emotion that was rare for him: excitement. He had only reverted to character when he found his wife's body. He became placid and introspective. Wallace had no motive for killing his own wife.

By all the rules of criminal law, Roland Oliver was absolutely right. The police had no evidence, only suspicions. Herbert Wallace had to be presumed innocent. But on the fourth and final day of the trial, the jury took only an hour to reach their verdict: Guilty.

It is almost routine for a judge to express his agreement with a jury's verdict in a complex, tasking case. Mr Justice Wright, however, did not even offer them a word of thanks for their efforts. He pronounced the mandatory sentence of death by hanging.

The defence lodged an immediate appeal and a week after he should have been hanged Wallace was taken from the condemned cell to London, to appear at the Royal Courts of Justice in the Strand. Far from the hysteria and prejudice of Liverpool, three judges sifted through the hard evidence against Wallace. After a two-day hearing they retired for 45 minutes and pronounced their verdict: Appeal allowed, conviction quashed.

Wallace left the courtroom free – but spiritually broken.

Two days later when he returned home, Liverpool police pointedly announced they would not be re-opening their investigation into Julia Wallace's murder. The cruel implication was not lost on Wallace's hostile neighbours and his workmates. The insurance company gave him a desk job to try to shield him and a year later he retired on a pension.

In February 1933, just over two years after the death of his wife, Herbert Wallace became ill with a recurring kidney disease and died in a local hospital. Five days later he was buried in Anfield Cemetery beside his beloved Julia.

So who murdered Julia Wallace? Who was R. M. Qualtrough? There were only 14 people in the whole of Liverpool with the name Qualtrough and the police interviewed and cleared them all. In the atmosphere of outrage which followed the murder, Liverpool police reached the single-minded conclusion that Wallace was guilty. Squads of detectives armed with stop-watches and timetables spent days riding on trams and walking briskly around Anfield trying to demolish his timing of events.

Herbert Wallace had his own suspicions. In the long nights of lonely agony after his wife's murder, he wondered which of his small circle of acquaintances knew he was due at the City Cafe that fateful night and left the tantalising telephone message for him. Julia, he knew, would only have opened the door to a familiar face. Even facing the hangman's noose, shy Herbert Wallace could not bring himself to scream in righteous anger and point a forceful finger of accusation.

He apologetically mentioned the names of two men to the Liverpool detectives investigating the case. Both men were in their early twenties and both were former employees of the insurance company. At different times, they had both parted company from the insurance firm after cash shortages were found in their accounts. On separate occasions, they had filled in for Wallace on his rounds when he was ill. They knew all about his social routine, about his chess club meetings. And they knew that on some Tuesday nights, as on the night Julia was murdered, the cash box in the kitchen could hold as much as £50. Indeed when they stood in for him they had been inside his home and had handled the cash box. Julia would have readily opened the door to them, knowing they were former colleagues of her husband.

Police records show that detectives only interviewed one of these men – and even then accepted without question his assurance that he had an alibi for the night of the murder.

The police concentrated all their energies on the man they wanted . . . the mousey little insurance agent whom everyone so desperately wanted to believe was a murdering monster.

Advertisement of Death

The voice on the telephone was smooth, fluent and persuasive . . . and instantly Josephine Backshall was cocooned in a web of friendly familiarity. She knew the caller's voice well and had been longing for him to ring. After all, he was helping her to earn £100, a big enough sum of 'pin-money' to make a world of difference to the family budget.

There was nothing in the least shady about the job as a part-time model that Josephine was beginning to enjoy. In fact, the thought that the small advertisement she had placed in the local paper could be misconstrued in anything like an unseemly light had never crossed the mind of the houseproud, 39-year-old mother-of-three, who sang for the local church choir and was a leader of the town's Brownies troupe. And the idea that there could be anything sinister about the man who answered her advertisement and, in a 'trial session', had photographed her on the front lawn of the family's tidy, middle-class semi-detached home in Maldon, Essex, would have seemed too outrageous to contemplate.

The man, she told her husband Mike, seemed like a 'good sort'. And, as she spoke to him again on the 'phone, she realized that what he was offering her would be her biggest job so far: £100 for a day's work – probably, she thought, modelling for something no more glamorous than a cheap cosmetics firm.

The caller talked on, cool, collected, giving the impression of a very pleasant personality. A meeting was arranged for that evening and, after kissing her husband goodbye, she walked through the front door of their spruce home for the last time.

Three days later, at about 12.00 on Friday, 1 November,

1974, she was found strangled to death.

Her body had been dumped in a shallow pond by the side of a lonely lovers' lane. Her hands were bound in front of her with a length of cord strapped tightly to her wrists. An identical cord was lashed to her neck.

Josephine Backshall, the church-going good neighbour who enjoyed an innocent life of simple pleasures, was killed because she put her faith in a confidence trickster. She trusted a mystery man whose identity the police have spent more than 100,000 man-hours trying to discover, with not a single clue to put them on the trail of a quarry whose disappearance has made the Josephine Backshall case one of Britain's most perplexing unsolved crimes.

No fewer than 40 detectives were assigned to the case in the first year of one of the biggest, yet most baffling, investigations of its kind. More than 19,000 members of the public were interviewed. All of them had either the Christian name of Peter or Dave, or the surname of Thomson or Johnson. It was a combination of those names that fitted the clues that Josephine had given her family and friends. It was to them that she had spoken of the man with the camera who was setting her up not, as she believed as a part-time model, but as a victim of brutal murder, even the motive for which has never been established.

Thousands of car registration plates were later pain stakingly checked and rechecked by police trying to find the killer's car – possibly a blue Ford which was seen pulling away from the Fountain public house in Good Easter, Essex, on the night Josephine kept her fateful rendezvous with her killer.

Detectives established that Josephine and the man she so easily trusted did stop for a drink – one half-pint of beer each – at the Fountain about an hour after she had left her home. He was presumed to have picked her up nearby and taken her there after a 'business dinner' at a Chinese restaurant – an assumption based on the fact that forensic experts discovered the remains of Chinese food in her stomach.

Publican's wife Joan Jones became the last witness to the rendezvous of a killer and his victim when she saw the couple in the Fountain's saloon bar. 'I caught only a fleeting glance of him,' she says. 'He was a tall man. His head touched a line of beer mugs hanging over the bar. He never actually seemed to face me and, on reflection, it seemed almost as though he was trying to not let anyone get too close a look at him.'

Mrs Jones identified Josephine from a cine film containing family holiday shots which detectives showed her. 'I remembered her at once,' she says. 'She was an attractive woman. She had sat in the corner of the bar with the man and had seemed totally at her ease.'

For months, police kept details of the Fountain meeting secret in the hope that the killer would retrace his steps. It was a forlorn hope.

The only other potential lead detectives had to go on was a 'French connection'. A keen-eyed policewoman found a cosmetics sample in Josephine's bedroom which was one of a very limited batch which had been imported from France prior to a sales drive. Could the killer, detectives pondered, have been using Josephine to model this new range?

Inquiries again, however, came to nought – as did a scrupulous check on every photographic studio in both England and France from which a killer might have been tempted by Josephine's original advertisement, which read:

'Lady, late 30s, seeks part-time employment. Own transport. Anything considered. Previous experience: banking. Able to type.' Underneath was her home telephone number.

It was the sort of advertisement often used to skirt the

law as a method of offering sex-for-sale. A senior officer on the case later described it as 'positively naive'. He added:

'We all know what the phrase "anything considered" is taken to mean. The great irony and tragedy of this case is that any innuendo couldn't have been further from the truth. Mrs Backshall was a God-fearing woman – and that sort of interpretation of her advert simply wouldn't have occurred to her. It seems more than likely that her own innocence – a rare attribute in this day and age – may have, tragically, led her to set herself up as a victim of murder.'

Other senior officers have described the Josephine Backshall case as the 'most frustrating' they have ever worked on. But, as far as has been possible, they have managed to piece together this diary of death:

A few days after Josephine placed her ad, a male caller telephoned to offer her work 'modelling for cosmetics'. An appointment was made for a week later, 15 miles from Josephine's home, at Witham, Essex. The man never showed up. He 'phoned the following day, rearranged the appointment, and again failed to appear. Two weeks later, the 'phone range once more – and Josephine happily arranged yet another meeting.

This time, the couple did meet. The 'photographer' took a series of pictures of Josephine on the front lawn of her home during the day. By that stage, Josephine's husband had begun to believe her part-time job would come to nothing and, ironically, expressed mild doubt as to the authenticity of the cameraman who was promising his wife tidy sums for what seemed simple work. Josephine allayed those fears, saying that the man seemed perfectly genuine and, indeed, a 'good sort'.

The telephone rang again on Tuesday, 29 October 1974 and the last, fateful meeting was arranged. Josephine left the family home in Norfolk Close, Maldon at about 18.00, driving to Witham in her red Ford Cortina, registration number BVW 374L.

Detectives have established that she was seen at Witham's Collingwood Road car part between 18.30 and 19.00. A passer-by told them her car may have broken down, because he saw her looking into the engine with the bonnet raised close to the car park entrance. Some time before 19.00, however, she must have met her killer.

There is a time gap between then and three days later, when a telephone line worker made the gruesome discovery of her body in the ditch at Bury Green on the Essex and Hertfordshire border.

The killer had left no clue behind. Chief Superintendent Jack Moulder, who still keeps the Josephine Backshall case file open, can only say: 'Someone, somewhere must know him.'

The Green Bicycle Murder

The tragic death of pretty Bella Wright would have been written off as a fatal road accident if it had not been for the shrewd curiosity of a young country constable.

For when 21-year-old Bella was found dead on a quiet road near the village of Stretton in Leicestershire, with her bicycle lying on the grass verge, it added a terrible weight to the complaints of the locals who cursed the reckless and speeding drivers in their peaceful little communities.

The dead girl's face was deeply gouged and matted with blood. Gravel from the roadway was embedded in her face where she had pitched forward from her bicycle and struck the ground. She had obviously been run off the road by some ruthless motorist, the villagers insisted. It was July 1919 and clattering motor cars were not yet a commonplace sight in the quiet countryside. Their drivers, according to popular rural opinion, terrified the farm animals and were a mortal danger to peaceful cyclists and rambling pedestrians.

A cursory examination of Bella's body by a local doctor seemed to confirm that opinion. He concluded that something had caused Bella to lose control of her bicycle, throwing her into the road where she died of loss of blood and head injuries.

The local constable, however, had some nagging doubts. He went to search the scene of the road accident for any further clues to showing exactly how Bella had met her death.

As he poked around the grass verges on either side of the narrow road, the constable found the blood-spattered body of a dead carrion crow. But there were no tyre marks near the bird. He turned its body over with the tip of his boot and continued his search. A few feet away, where Bella's bicycle had lain, he found another object which caught his attention. It was a spent bullet, pushed down into the soft earth by the imprint of a horse's hoof.

A fresh examination of Bella's body showed the grim truth about her death. In the swollen blood-stained tissue below her left eye was a bullet hole. Hidden in the tangled mass of her hair was an exit wound. Bella had been shot clean through the head.

The police search switched from the pursuit of a hit and run driver to the hunt for a cold-blooded murderer.

The night before Bella died she had been on one of her frequent cycling jaunts, riding to the village postbox to send a letter to her sweetheart, a young sailor aboard a warship which was stationed 240 km (150 miles) away in Portsmouth. The pretty brunette who lived with her parents had many male admirers, but she only flirted with them. Her deepest affections were reserved for the sailor she hoped would soon ask her to marry him.

Bella had finished a long tiring night shift as a mill hand in a factory in nearby Leicester when she returned home on Saturday 5 July and slept until late afternoon.

After a quick meal when she woke she cycled off briskly to post her letter, telling her parents she might pay a visit to her uncle, a roadworker, who lived not very far away.

When Bella arrived at her uncle's cottage two hours later, she was not alone. As she went inside the cottage a sallow-faced man waited outside for her, seated astride his green bicycle.

Bella's uncle, George Measures, teased her about her strange companion. She smiled: 'Oh him, I don't really know him at all. He has been riding alongside me for a few miles but he isn't bothering me at all. He's just chatting about the weather.'

When Bella was ready to leave for home an hour later, her uncle glanced through the window and saw the man with the green bicycle was still waiting outside. 'Oh, I do hope he doesn't get boring,' Bella laughed coyly. 'I'll soon cycle fast enough to give him the slip.'

The man with the green bicycle grinned happily at Bella when she left the cottage and pedalled his bicycle to join her as they rode off together in the warm summer evening's air.

An hour later a farmer driving his cattle along the peaceful Burton-Overy road, found Bella's body. An inquest on the dead girl returned a verdict of 'murder by person or persons unknown'. The vital witness, the man with the green bicycle could not be traced.

But his bicycle was found, seven months later, when a barge skipper on a canal outside Leicester found that a line trailing from his boat had snagged on a piece of junk on the canal bed. The junk brought to the surface was the frame of a green bicycle. Policemen who probed the muddy canal bottom soon uncovered a gun holster and a dozen revolver cartridges.

One of the serial numbers of the bicycle frame had been hastily filed off. But another identifying number inside the saddle support led police to the local dealer for the bicycle maker and then to the identity of the man who had bought it ten years before.

The owner of the bicycle was railway draughtsman Ronald Light, a moody shell-shocked veteran of World War I with a fascination for guns. He had been invalided out of the Army and had lived in Leicester until six months after Bella's murder.

When police traced 34-year-old Light he had left his home in Leicester he shared with his widowed mother and taken a job about 100 km (60 miles away) as a school teacher in Cheltenham. He was arrested and brought back to Leicester to be charged with the murder of Bella Wright.

His trial began at Leicester Assizes in June 1920 and from the opening speech of the prosecution the circumstantial evidence was stacked mercilessly against Ronald Light. Witness after witness identified him as the man with the green bicycle and a young maidservant from Light's own home told how he kept firearms and ammunition in the attic.

The prosecution amply proved that Ronald Light had been the mystery man who cycled off with Bella just before her death. Light himself admitted filing the serial number off his bicycle and throwing it, with the holster and cartridges, into the canal a few weeks after the murder.

The only arguably weak point in the prosecution's case was the lack of motive. Bella had not been sexually assaulted or robbed. Even though Light denied killing her, claiming that they parted company at the village crossroads, the irrefutable testimony seemed certain to lead him to the gallows.

One other piece of evidence seemed to cloud the case, almost irrelevantly. The bullet found by the village constable had several marks on it. The marks were caused by it passing through the dead girl's skull and the crushing effect of the steel-shod horse's hoof which had ground it into the earth. There was even one mark which might have been caused by a ricochet.

When Ronald Light gave evidence in his own defence, he seemed at first to be damning himself. He admitted trailing around after Bella on his bicycle on the night of her death, pestering her for the use of a spanner and a pump because his own cycle had developed a loose wheel and a flat tyre.

He told the jury of his own sad and tortured mental history: how he cracked up after three years of savage war in the frontline trenches, and how he was classified as a shell-shock victim and sent back to England in the closing stages of the war for psychiatric treatment.

But the effect of his testimony on the jury was electric. In a firm clear voice, without a trace of hesitation or emotion, Light told the court: 'I was an artillery gunner in the trenches from 1915 to 1918 when I was sent home a broken man. I kept my holster and ammunition because they were wrapped in a bag attached to my stretcher when they took me from the front. The Army kept my service revolver.

'When Bella Wright was murdered I knew from newspaper reports the next day that she was the girl I had been with just before she died. I knew the police wanted to question me.'

Staring blankly and coldly into space, Light admitted: 'I became a coward again. I never told a living soul what I knew. I got rid of everything which could have connected me with her. I was afraid.'

The jury looked at the gaunt face of the anguished war veteran before they retired to consider their verdict. They returned three hours later and pronounced him 'not guilty'.

As Light walked from the court a free man, the sharp-eyed constable who had turned her death into a murder investigation, blamed himself for one flaw in his inspired detective work . . .

The body of the dead carrion crow in the field. He had kicked it aside with hardly a second glance.

Had the bloodied crow also been blasted by a bullet from the same gun which killed Bella Wright? Had the same bullet ripped through the crow in flight and found a second, innocent human target? Could the bullet have ricochetted from a tree and ended Bella's young life?

Without the evidence of the crow and perhaps of further bullets and footprints at the scene, no one would ever know. But it was not beyond the bounds of possibility that an amateur marksman had been taking potshots at the sinister black shapes of the carrion crows in the field beside the country road.

Was there somewhere a thoughtless gunman who knew his wild shooting had killed an unsuspecting girl and who had fled from the scene to keep his terrified secret? A gunman infinitely more cowardly than the shell-shocked, broken ex-soldier Ronald Light.

The Enigma of Nuremberg

The teenage boy who appeared from nowhere, staggering through the streets of Nuremberg, Germany, on Whit Monday 1828, acted as if he was injured or drunk.

He walked unsteadily up to a complete stranger, a local cobbler, and gave him a letter addressed to the Captain of the 6th Cavalry Regiment, then stationed in the city, and mumbled repeatedly: 'I want to be a soldier like my father was.'

The cobbler helped the boy to walk with difficulty to the police station where the lad waited until the cavalry officer was summoned. At the police station the letter was opened and the senior police officer and the cavalryman read the poignant and bitter message.

The letter explained: 'I send you a boy who is anxious to serve his king in the Army. He was left at my house on 7 October 1812, and I am only a poor labourer. I have ten children of my own to bring up. I have not let him outside since 1812.'

With cruel indifference, the letter added: 'If you do not want to keep him, kill him or hang him up a chimney.'

The letter was unsigned and the police and the army officer sadly assumed that the 16-year-old boy, abandoned as a baby, was still unwanted. The scrawled message seemed to explain his peculiar behaviour, unable to walk properly on feet as soft as a baby's and with an infant vocabulary of only a few words. But the lad could write his own name in a firm, legible hand – Caspar Hauser.

The jailer in Nuremberg was fascinated by the boy and kept him in a room in his own quarters where he could watch him through a secret opening. It took him only a few days of careful observation before he decided that Caspar was neither a born idiot nor a young madman. With loving patience, the jailer, using sign language, taught Caspar to talk, noting how quickly and eagerly the boy began to learn new skills.

Within six weeks the burgomaster of Nuremberg had been summoned to the jail to hear the first halting details from Caspar of his wretched life.

All Caspar could remember was being kept in a small cell, about 1.8 m (6 ft) long, 1.2 m (4 ft) wide and 1.5 m (5 ft) high. The shutters on the window of the cell were kept permanently closed and he slept in threadbare clothes on a bed of straw. He saw nobody and heard virtually nothing all the years he was there, living on a diet of bread and water he found in the cell when he awoke each day. Sometimes, he revealed, the water tasted bitter and made him fall asleep. Every time this happened, he woke up to find his hair had been cut and his nails trimmed.

After years of isolation, Caspar recalled, a hand reached into his cell from behind and gave him a sheet of paper and a pen. The hand guided him each day until he could write his name and repeat the phrase: 'I want to be a soldier . . .'

One morning his cell was unlocked and he was taken out into the street, into daylight and the company of other people for the first time in his life. It was the first time, too, that he wore shoes.

In the confusion of unfamiliar sights and sounds, Caspar remembered nothing until he found himself in Nuremberg with the letter in his hand.

The boy's story touched the burgomaster and the people of Nuremberg and soon young Caspar was 'adopted' by a Professor Daumer who began the task of educating the teenager into the ways of the world around him.

In a few months Caspar was transformed from a stumbling retarded child to a bright intelligent young man. With his mysterious background creating a buzz of excitement in his new home town, he became a much sought after guest in the homes of curious philosophers and wealthy intellectuals. And Nuremberg society soon began to remark on Caspar's startling physical resemblance to the members of the families of the grand dukes of Baden, the rulers of the province. Rumours abounded, the most popular being that Caspar was of noble birth and that his childhood isolation had been heartlessly planned to prevent him succeeding to power as a Baden prince.

At the time of Caspar's birth, two of the princes of the Baden family in direct line of succession had died in mysterious circumstances. The people of Nuremberg were convinced that Caspar Hauser was an unwanted son of the royal family, born to the Grand Duke Karl and his wife the Grand Duchess Stephanie.

Grand Duchess Stephanie had indeed given birth to a child sixteen years earlier, but she never saw the baby. Scheming palace doctors had told her that her baby had died soon after birth of cerebral meningitis, a diagnosis confirmed by a post-mortem examination.

And when Grand Duke Karl became seriously ill in 1829, he had no son and heir to succeed him.

Caspar, by that time, had been in Nuremberg for a year, living with Professor Daumer and growing in reputation as a personable, intelligent young man of distinct ability and culture.

As the Grand Duke's health failed, in October 1829, Caspar's already bitterly unhappy young life was almost ended. He was attacked and stabbed by a masked assailant in the basement of Professor Daumer's house, but he survived his wounds.

The following year the Grand Duke died and the royal succession passed to another line of the family, the sons of the Countess of Hochberg.

A few months later an eccentric English nobleman, said by many to be a friend of the Hochberg family, appeared in Nuremberg to petition to courts to become Caspar's guardian in place of Professor Daumer. Philip, the 4th Earl of Stanhope, won his court plea in spite of local opposition. And so, out of public sight, another period of isolation began for the wretched Caspar. He was taken away from his new found friends in Nuremberg on Lord Stanhope's orders and lodged with a surly Protestant pastor in the town of Ansbach, 20 miles away.

With Caspar safely out of the way, Lord Stanhope lost interest in his new foster son, leaving him to his miserable existence with Pastor Meyer.

On 11 December 1833 Caspar, then 21 years old and working as an apprentice bookbinder, was returning to his dismal lodgings through a park when he was stopped by a stranger. The man asked his name and when Caspar replied, he stabbed him repeatedly. Badly wounded, Caspar staggered back to Pastor Meyer's home. But the preacher never informed the police, cruelly taunting Caspar that he had inflicted the wounds himself to get attention. Three days later Caspar Hauser died in agony.

Hearing of his death, the Grand Duchess Stephanie was reported to have broken down and wept, sobbing that she believed the young man had really been the son she was told had died in infancy.

But none of his friends or the German courts could ever prove the background of the boy with no history and no future. They could never solve the riddle of who had locked him away for the first 16 years of his hopeless life, or who the mysterious assassins were who finally succeeded in killing him.

The boy who came from nowhere was buried in the churchyard at Ansbach. On his tombstone was the simple epitaph: 'Here lies Caspar Hauser, enigma.'

Sherlock Holmes' Real Case

It was a murder case worthy of the cold, calculating detective powers of Sherlock Holmes. An elderly widow had been battered to death by a brutal murderer who had rifled through her files of personal papers and who had, inexplicably, stolen just one cheap brooch from her valuable collection of diamonds and other gems.

A tall, dark-haired man of about 30 had been seen by witnesses walking calmly away from the murder house in Glasgow. It had not taken long for Scottish policemen, acting under the pressure of public outrage, to arrest a suspect who was tried for the murder and sentenced to hang.

Twenty-four hours before the convicted man, gems dealer Oscar Slater, was due to meet the executioner, his sentence was commuted to life imprisonment. Although his life was spared, he still faced a grim existence of hard labour in prison until his dying day. Yet there were some lingering doubts about the case . . . fears that Oscar Slater was no more than an innocent scapegoat.

But who could prove his innocence? Who could sift through the evidence with enough authority and thoroughness to overturn the verdict of a powerful court backed by the full might of the Scottish legal system? Sherlock Holmes, that's who – in the form of the creator of the fictional detective, author Sir Arthur Conan Doyle.

Conan Doyle was disturbed by the case of Oscar Slater when he read of the murder investigation and conviction in the scholarly legal work *Notable Scottish Trials*. The book outlined how, on little more than suspicion and circumstantial evidence, Slater had been found guilty of murdering 82-year-old Miss Marion Gilchrist at her home in Queen's Terrace, West Princes Street, Glasgow, on 21 December 1908.

Miss Gilchrist had lived the life of a virtual recluse in her home, attended only by a young maidservant, 21-year-old Helen Lambie, and seeing only rare visitors, mainly relatives. The spinster's only pleasure in life seemed to come from the loving care of her collection of diamonds, valued at £3,000.

On the night her mistress died, Helen Lambie had followed her usual practice of leaving the house around 19.00 to buy the evening newspaper. Miss Gilchrist remained inside, secure behind the double-locked doors of her home. The outer door, leading to the street, was held only by a latch which could be opened by a cord from inside the apartment if Miss Gilchrist recognized a visitor at the street door.

A few minutes after Helen left, downstairs neighbour Arthur Adams heard the noise of a heavy fall from the apartment above and went to investigate. The outer door was open but the double-locked apartment door was still secure. As he stood there puzzled, Helen returned with the evening paper and the couple unlocked the door and went in. Just as they entered the apartment, a tall, well-dressed man walked calmly past them and into the street. Inside, Marion Gilchrist was dead in the living-room, her skull crushed.

While Adams went to raise the alarm, Helen Lambie ran the short distance to the home of Marion Gilchrist's niece, Mrs Margaret Birrell, and told her she had recognized the man who had walked from the apartment. But the niece, in a burst of outrage, told Helen Lambie she must be mistaken and she must not 'smear the man's reputation' in any statement to the police.

The police took only five days to produce some results to still the public outcry which followed the murder. They learned that gem dealer Oscar Slater, who lived not far from the murdered woman, had pawned a brooch of about the same value as the missing one. They also discovered that he and his young French mistress had fled from Scotland aboard the liner *Lusitania* using assumed names.

Police pursued the couple to New York where Slater was arrested and, protesting his innocence, agreed to waive extradition formalities and return to Glasgow.

At his trial the witnesses, with some hesitation, identified him as the mystery man. Slater, a German Jew, claimed: 'I know nothing about this affair, absolutely nothing.' But the jury found him guilty by a majority verdict. Slater suffered three weeks in the condemned cell before his reprieve.

The few doubts about Slater's innocence were carefully noted in the book which Conan Doyle read and it was enough to arouse his interest. He began to examine the case with the same fresh uncluttered mind that he had devoted to his fictional super-sleuth, Sherlock Holmes of

Baker Street.

Three years after the trial, after careful study of the transcripts of the court proceedings and correspondence with witnesses, Conan Doyle caused an uproar with his book, *The Case of Oscar Slater*. In the same calm style as Holmes, he punched gaping holes in the prosecution case.

The brooch which had first drawn suspicion on Slater had been pawned three weeks before the murder. Slater, Conan Doyle pointed out, had fled with his mistress under assumed names because he wanted to give the slip to his domineering, grasping wife. Slater's own lifestyle, as a gambler and womanizer, had probably prejudiced the puritanical Scottish jury against him.

Conan Doyle demolished the conflicting evidence of witnesses, some of whom claimed that the mystery murder had been clean-shaven, others who said he was bearded. And, drawing on his own forensic expertise, he pointed out that when Slater's entire wardrobe of clothes was seized in his luggage aboard the *Lusitania*, not a single trace of blood was found on any of them.

The 'Sherlock Holmes' investigation produced immediate demands for a re-trial or public inquiry. But the wheels of justice grind slowly. It took 18 years before Oscar Slater was released by the newly appointed Scottish Court of Criminal Appeal on the technicality that the judge at his trial had misdirected the jury. Slater was awarded £6,000 in compensation.

But Arthur Conan Doyle never published the final chapter of his important murder investigation. 'Sherlock Holmes' had proved Slater's innocence. But had he ever uncovered the real identity of the killer of Marion Gilchrist?

Shortly before he died in 1930, Conan Doyle revealed to a friend:

'I knew I had a difficult enough job in getting Oscar
Slater freed. That was the most important objective I

had to achieve. If I had tried at the same time to lay the blame for the murder on the real guilty man, it might have prejudiced Slater's chances of release.

But I believe I know the identity of the real murderer, a man who was protected by the police because he was a prominent citizen who desperately wanted something from the private papers of Marion Gilchrist. He has gone unpunished. But it is more important to me that an innocent man is free. I am satisfied.'

Dead Men Cannot Talk

The liner *Georges Phillipar* was one of the best designed cruise ships afloat when she was launched by her French builders from the slipway at St Nazaire in 1930.

It took almost two years to fit out the 17,300 tonne (17,000 ton) ship to carry up to 1,000 passengers in sumptuous luxury in richly panelled cabins with comfortable, efficient air conditioning. And no expense was spared to guarantee their safety, with an automatic sprinkler system and the latest fire-fighting appliances.

Yet the fire which broke out on D Deck on the liner's maiden voyage, a round trip to China, spread with devastating speed, killing 53 passengers and sending the pride of the French liner fleet to the bottom of the Red Sea.

The commission of inquiry in Paris which later investigated the sinking of the *Georges Phillipar* could find no firm evidence that faulty electrical design had caused the blaze, or that the fire had been accidental. They left only a tantalizing, inconclusive hint . . . that powerful international assassins had turned the liner into a floating firebomb just to kill one VIP passenger, a crusading French journalist.

Freelance writer Albert Londres had joined the *Georges*

Phillipar in April 1932 in Shanghai for the return leg of its maiden voyage. He had spent almost a year in Indo-China on a gruelling and dangerous assignment and his carefully guarded notebook was crammed with information which would have caused public outrage against the profiteering industrialists of London, Paris and Berlin.

Millions of readers throughout Europe were waiting and wondering what scandalous subject the best-selling author would choose for his next devastating report. In his first book, *The Road to Buenos Aires*, published only three years before, he had exposed the vile white slave trade of young women from the brothels of Marseilles and Hamburg to South America. It earned him the undying hatred of the French and German vice kings.

Undeterred, Londres went on to expose a similar traffic in young European girls to the houses of pleasure in Shanghai, and followed this up with an investigation of the terrorist group who had assassinated the King of Yugoslavia on French soil.

Now he had completed his damning examination of the deadly arms trade in the Far East, where the Japanese Imperial armies were gearing themselves for an expansive war of aggressive and the bandit Chinese war lords were slaughtering their own countrymen in their bloody battles to gain control of vast areas of China and Manchuria.

Word quickly spread among enthusiastic European publishers that Albert Londres was on his way home with a manuscript that would light a fuse underneath the European millionaire arms suppliers, the Merchants of Deaths.

Londres was safely installed in his cabin, working on the notes for his new book when the liner docked briefly at Saigon, the capital of French Indo-China, and took aboard more travellers, mainly French colonial officials and their families. With a complement of 800 passengers, the liner called at Singapore, Penang and Ceylon, en route for the Red Sea, the Suez Canal and the French Mediterranean port of Marseilles.

On the night of 15 May as Londres worked alone in his cabin, the other passengers gathered on deck for a dinner dance in the sultry evening air, admiring the twinkling lights of the Arabian coast and waving to the crew of the Russian tanker *Sovietskya Neft* which passed less than a mile astern.

Around midnight the master of the *Georges Phillipar*, Captain Anton Vicq, retired to his cabin, bidding goodnight to the last of the dinner-dance revellers who stayed on the starlit deck, sipping chilled champagne.

Two hours later he was roused by the officer of the watch who warned him that a passenger cabin on D Deck was ablaze. When he made an examination in portside Number 5 cabin, Captain Vicq noted that 'It was not a local accident, but a fire appearing to become general and widespread.'

As he retreated along the deck corridor to the sound of the alarm, Captain Vicq was confronted by Nurse Yvonne Valentin who screamed that her cabin, Number 7, was also engulfed in flames. Between the two, in cabin Number 6 on D deck, writer Albert Londres was unaware of the drama.

Trying vainly to contain the blaze, Captain Vicq ordered all portholes to be closed and stopped the liner's engines. Within minutes the flames had spread to the bridge and the captain gave the order to abandon ship.

As the lifeboats were lowered the radio operator broadcast a frantic series of SOS messages. But his transmission was cut suddenly short when his radio failed and power from the generator ceased. Following his well-rehearsed emergency procedure, the radio operator reached for the sealed locker which held an ample supply of spare batteries – the batteries were missing.

As passengers wrapped wet towels round their faces to

fight their way through the blinding acrid smoke, Captain Vicq and his crew calmly organized the evacuation of the ship. All floating furniture which could be used as life-rafts was heaved overboard and terrified passengers were helped over the stern of the liner into the warm still waters of the sea.

The brief burst of pleading on the ship's radio had been enough to summon a rescue flotilla to its aid, including the Soviet tanker, two British steamers, a Japanese cargo ship and two other ocean liners.

The task of saving the souls in the lifeboats and clinging to the rafts was carried out speedily and most of them were soon aboard the mercy vessels. The stricken liner burned for three days in a column of flame which could be seen for 60 km (40 miles). When the *Georges Phillipar* finally heeled over, she sank within two minutes.

But no trace was ever found of the body of Albert Londres who had been trapped in his cabin between the two sources of the sudden, unexplained fire.

Survivors reported that they had last seen him crawling through his cabin porthole, his precious manuscript held tightly under his arm. The man who knew too much was officially logged in the disaster list as drowned.

His notebooks and manuscripts drifted away in the ebb and flow of the Red Sea's tides. And seven years later, the wealthy and ruthless arms dealers, unhampered by the spotlight of Albert Londres's unfinished investigation, saw their staggering investment in munitions bear fruit when all of Europe was plunged into war.

Disappearing Dorothy

Judge Jules Forstein telephoned his wife one October evening in 1950 to let her know he'd be delayed at a political banquet. 'I don't expect to be too late,' he said. 'Is everything all right?'

There was a reason for the question. The judge seldom left his wife and children alone because of an incident at the house five years earlier. But on this occasion Dorothy was cheerful and she assured her husband that everything was fine. 'Be sure to miss me,' she said.

Mrs Forstein had lived in a state of panic for five years, dating from the evening of 25 January 1945. That day, after leaving her two children with neighbours she had shopped briefly in a supermarket and then walked home alone to the three-storey house in a Philadelphia suburb. As she entered the house, someone leaped out of the small alcove under the front stairs and attacked her in the darkness. She had time to scream only once.

The police crashed through the front door of the Forstein home to find her lying in a pool of blood. She had a broken jaw, a broken nose, a fractured shoulder and concussion.

There was money and jewellery in the house, but nothing had been taken. The motive was murder, said police. The attacker had entered the house without leaving fingerprints or disturbing the locks on doors and windows. And there was no clue as to how he had left the house, either.

Judge Forstein had an unimpeachable alibi for the time of the attack. And Mrs Forstein had no known enemies. The intruder could have been an enemy of her husband's but months of investigation turned up no suspect.

Though there was a slow physical recovery, Dorothy Forstein never recovered emotionally from the beating. She make a frequent ritual of checking and rechecking the extra locks that had been put on doors and windows. She constantly sought the companionship of relatives and neighbours and sometimes during parties she would retreat into deep silence.

But she was getting better, Judge Forstein reassured

himself when he returned late from the banquet that evening five years after the attack.

Inside the dimly lit house, the first thing he heard were the screams of his two small children, Edward and Marcy. He found them huddled together in a bedroom, crying convulsively. 'It's mamma,' they told him. 'Something was here and took mamma away.'

Sick with fright, Forstein searched every room of the house. There were her purse, money and keys, but Dorothy Forstein was gone.

Through bursts of tears, Marcy told him what had happened. She had been awakened by terrifying sounds in the night and had run to her mother's bedroom. Through a crack in the door, she saw her mother lying face down on the rug with a shadowy figure crouching over her. 'She looked sick,' the little girl wept.

The intruder had then picked up her mother and thrown her over his shoulder with her head hanging down his back. He saw the child watching and said, 'Go back to sleep. Your mother has been sick, but she'll be all right now.'

When the police arrived, they confessed themselves baffled. There were no fingerprints anywhere, and it seemed incredible to them that any man balancing a woman on his shoulder could have left the house without grasping something for support. Why had no one tried to stop him when he walked down a busy street carrying an unconscious woman in pyjamas? And how did he get into the Forstein home through the multiple locks on the doors and windows?

The police checked every hospital in Philadelphia, as well as rooming houses, rest homes, hotels and the morgue. The search yielded no information about Dorothy.

Whoever had abducted the judge's wife had taken her away for ever. Dorothy Forstein left behind her only the haunting memory of her last words: 'Be sure to miss me.'

Mystery at Wolf's Neck

It was a bitterly cold evening in January 1931 when bus driver Cecil Johnstone saw a fire on a desolate moor at Wolf's Neck between Newcastle upon Tyne and Otterburn in Northumberland. He stopped to investigate. What he saw was almost unbelievable. On fire was the car owned by his boss's daughter, Evelyn Foster. Beside it lay Evelyn, badly burned but still alive.

Johnstone drove her to her home at Otterburn, where she told her parents and the police that she had been attacked by a man who had set fire to her car. She died the following day and left behind her one of the strangest crime stories of the decade. If indeed it was a crime at all . . .

Evelyn Foster was 28 and the daughter of Mr. J. J. Foster, who owned a garage at Otterburn. She had her own car, which she ran as a one-cab taxi business.

At 19.00 on 6 January 1931, she arrived home and told her mother that a man who had got out of a car at nearby Elishaw wanted her to drive him to Ponteland, near Newcastle, to catch the bus home. She said the man had looked respectable and gentlemanly when she picked him up at the Percy Arms Hotel.

The next time her mother saw her was when she was brought home dying of burns later that night by her father's bus driver, Johnstone. And this is the story she told her mother and a doctor, nurse and policeman who had been called to the house . . .

After she had driven through the village of Belsay, about 8 km (5 miles) from Ponteland, her passenger suddenly asked her to turn back. She had turned round and was driving back when the man hit her in the eye and took over the wheel. He stopped the car at the top of the hill at Wolf's Neck and started 'knocking her about'. He then put her into the back of the car and raped her.

The man then took a bottle or tin out of his pocket and threw something over her. She just 'went up in a blaze'. She then felt a bump as the car was going over rough ground. Evelyn told her mother: 'I was all alight. I do not know how I got out of the car. I lay on the ground and sucked the grass. I was thirsty.'

Her last words were said to have been: 'I have been murdered.' And it really looked as though she had been murdered – until doubts began to surface at the inquest.

To begin with, nobody other than Evelyn saw a stranger in the village that evening. Her father admitted that he had not seen the man. And the owners of the Percy Arms pub, where Evelyn was said to have picked him up, said that no stranger had been in the bar and they had heard no talk about a taxi to Ponteland.

The pathologist who conducted the post mortem on Evelyn, Professor Stuart McDonald, said there were no external injuries on the body apart from the burns. There was no trace of evidence of bruising on the face to suggest that she had been knocked about and there was 'no sign at all' that she had been raped.

Doubts were also cast on Evelyn's suggestion that she and the car had been set on fire before it was driven off the road on to the moor. There were signs of burned heather where the car was found just off the road – but no sign of burned heather by the side of the road itself.

In his summing up the coroner, Mr P. M. Dobbs, told the jury they could rule out suicide. The only two points they had to consider were: Was Evelyn Foster murdered? Or did she set fire to the car to obtain insurance money and set light to herself accidentally?

It took two hours for the jury to reach a verdict. It was: wilful murder on the part of some person or persons unknown.

Later, the police took the unprecedented step of declaring that, in their view, the 'murderer' did not exist. The Chief Constable of Northumberland, Captain Fullarton James, declared in a newspaper interview that the verdict of the inquest was against the weight of evidence and Evelyn Foster had not been murdered.

Gradually, the mystery of Wolf's Neck dropped out of the news – until just over three years later. At the beginning of 1934, a Yorkshire groom, Ernest Brown, was sentenced to death at Leeds Assizes for the murder of his lover's husband. In a 'confession' on the scaffold he is reported to have said either 'ought to burn' or 'Otterburn'. But he died seconds later.

Did Brown murder Evelyn Foster? Or did he know something about her death? The answer is unlikely ever to be known.

Otterburn?

Cowering in the lonely farmhouse on the Yorkshire moors, Dorothy Morton and her nurse-companion knew that something was wrong. It was past 3 o'clock in the morning and they were still fully dressed, waiting for Mr Morton's return. He should have been back hours ago from his trip to Oldham where he had gone to buy horses. The groom had been acting strangely all evening, and Mrs Morton had special cause for concern. Ernest Brown, the groom in question, had been her lover and was a violent man consumed with hatred for his employer. The two women heard creaking on the stairs. What was going on? Where was Dorothy's husband?

The creaking ceased. But at 03.30 the crackle of flames could be heard outside. Mrs Morton pulled back the curtain and saw that the garage was ablaze. Hurriedly, she rushed to the telephone to summon help, but as her fingers grasped the received no buzzing tone greeted her ears. The line was dead. Someone had cut the wire.

In stark terror, the two women fetched Mrs Morton's child and, with blankets under their arms, they fled from the house. The rest of the night they spent huddled under a hedge watching as the fire raged. In due course, the groom appeared on the scene and rushed to the house, calling, 'Mrs Morton! Mrs Morton!' Neither of the women called out in reply, but stayed in the shadows as he ran to release the startled horses. Some time later, the local fire brigade arrived to try and deal with the conflagration but it was daylight before the blaze was brought under control, and by that time quite a crowd had gathered. One person, though, who never arrived to view the damage was Mr Morton himself. The missing husband had been in the garage all the time – slumped in the passenger seat of the Chrysler saloon from which his charred remnants were eventually recovered.

The Moors' Garage Fire of 1933 came as the climax to a four-year drama. The dead man was Frederick Ellison Morton, prosperous managing director of a firm called Cattle Factors Ltd. His wife, Dorothy, was a beautiful woman with hazel eyes and fine, athletic build. She was especially fond of foxhunting, a pursuit which she enjoyed on the horses her husband kept. It seems that she was not averse to bedroom athletics either. And when in 1929, Ernest Brown was hired as a groom she found that they shared more than an interest in horses. The groom became Mrs Morton's lover, and a triangle took shape.

Ernest Brown was a personable man and a stylish dresser when not in his corduroys. He was by no means ill-educated either. But there was a streak of violence in his nature which soon came to disturb Mrs Morton. At the trial, she was to state that she learned to dislike him, only continuing the liaison through fear. Through threats, Brown forced his attentions on her and she rarely complied willingly.

The Mortons moved to Saxton Grange in the West Riding early in 1933. Mrs Morton had a 2-year-old child, and the nurse-companion, Ann Houseman, lived in. Ernest Brown was put up in quarters of his own – a little wooden cottage not far from the farmhouse. His servile status rankled and, in the jargon of the day, he had 'ideas above his station'. When, one day in June, he was asked to mow the lawns his fierce pride got the better of him. Ernest Brown threw up the job and quit the Morton household.

Mrs Morton's respite from her love did not last long. Within days, Brown was back at the farm demanding reinstatement. As Mr Morton was away on a business trip, the groom insisted that his wife phone him. He stood over her as she made the call – with his hands about her neck, threatening to strangle her if she failed to persuade her husband.

Ernest Brown was reinstated – but not in his old post of groom. The man who had refused to mow the lawns was taken back only as an odd-job man. This was a bitter humiliation, and afterwards Brown seethed with hatred for Frederick Morton, a vindictive hatred in which jealousy and maimed pride jostled side by side. 'I will clout the little bugger one of these nights', he told a worker at the farm. On another occasion he threatened to ruin Morton's business: 'I can wreck this place and I shall do it.'

Brown nursed his resentment through the summer. And things were made worse when he learned that Dorothy Morton had taken another lover. This man was never identified at the trial, but Mrs Morton admitted his existence. The mystery man was referred to as the 'phantom lover', though his was an all-too fleshy reality.

On 5 September 1933, the tensions snapped. While Frederick Morton was buying horses in Oldham, Brown came into the farmhouse demanding to know what Mrs

Morton had been doing that day. She admitted that she had gone bathing with 'Mr X' and this threw him into a fury. During the quarrel, Brown struck Dorothy Morton to the ground and that evening began the sequence of events which culminated in a night of terror.

At 21.30, Dorothy and the nurse heard gunshots outside, and a hail of pellets rattled at the window. Soon after, they came upon Brown in the kitchen. He claimed to have been shooting at rats. At 21.45, there was a telephone call for Morton, which the nurse answered in the hall. She told the caller that her employer was not there but would soon be back, suggesting he call again at ten. Brown was loitering in the hall for no apparent reason and soon afterwards went into the kitchen to fetch a game knife. The caller did try to ring back at the appointed time – but he never got through. At some time before ten, the line had been cut.

Later, Brown appeared at the farmhouse again with a shotgun in his hand. He told the nurse that he wanted to see Dorothy, but the girl refused to let him meet her mistress alone. Eventually, Brown went away, leaving the two women frightened and anxious in the house.

At 23.30, Mrs Morton and the nurse thought that they heard a car coming. Assuming it was Frederick Morton, they went downstairs to wait for him. But he never turned up. Instead, when they opened the door, they found Brown again who told them, 'The boss has been in and gone out again.'

Gone out again? Brown's sinister prowlings had them seriously disquieted and when it became clear that he did not intend to leave they kept him talking about everyday matters. It was midnight before Brown finally left. There remained the long vigil until 03.30 when sounds of an explosion announced the fire.

When help came to the scene of the conflagration, Brown told a bystander, 'By God! If the boss is in there, he will never be seen again.' And later he provided his own version of events for the police. The ex-groom said that Morton had indeed driven back that night, arriving at 23.30, in a drunken state (or 'clever side up'). Brown had left him racing the engine of the Chrysler in the garage where a second car was parked. The fire, he assumed, must have started through the Chrysler backfiring.

A plausible enough theory at first glance. But the police were to discover more sinister features in the case. There was the telephone wire, cut clean through with a knife. There was the emerging story of Brown's liaison with Dorothy. Above all, there was the grim mass of incinerated flesh which had been Frederick Morton.

Practically nothing remained of the managing director. When the gutted Chrysler was withdrawn from the debris, the victim's body could only be identified through two bunches of keys and a unique platinum diamond ring. Amid the charred remains, only one tiny scrap of scorched flesh still survived in recognisable condition. It was a portion from the stomach – and found to be peppered with shotgun pellets. From the concentration of wounds, forensic scientists determined that Morton had been shot at point blank range. He had not died drunk in an accident fire – he had been murdered before the flames started. As the prosecutor noted when the case came to trial, 'If ever Fate played a murderer a dirty trick, it did so here. Had the wound been in the upper part, it would never have been discovered.'

Brown was the obvious suspect. To the end he protested his innocence, but the evidence against him was overwhelming. Apart from motive and opportunity, bloodstains were discovered on Brown's clothes and shotgun. The clinching detail was the game knife which the ex-groom had taken from the kitchen. From corresponding marks on the blade and wire, it was determined that the knife had severed the cord.

The precise time of the murder could not be determined, but the prosecution contended that Brown probably shot his employer as early as 9.30, then concocted the story about 'shooting rats'. He had rained bullets at the window in case either of the two women had heard the sound of gunfire. As for the later sounds of a car arriving, it should be remembered that there were two vehicles in the garage.

The best the defence could do was to try and shift the blame, by implication, to the unnamed 'phantom lover'. The accused was asked, 'Is it your idea that some other lover of Mrs Morton's who disliked her husband shot him and set the place on fire?' Brown replied, 'It may well be.'

But it was a hopeless case. Ernest Brown was found guilty and hanged at Armley Prison, Leeds, on 6 February 1934. The only mystery surrounding the affair derived from the murderer's last words – but a big and tantalizing mystery it turned out to be. When masked and pinioned on the scaffold, Brown was asked by the chaplain if he wanted to make a confession. From beneath the hood, the condemned man's voice uttered three syllables: either 'Ought to burn' or 'Otterburn'.

Did he mean to imply that he ought to burn, as his former employer had burned? Or was he confessing to a sensational unsolved crime committed at Otterburn 100 miles away?

It had been an extraordinary incident – another 'blazing car murder'. In January 1931, 28-year-old Evelyn Foster had been found on a moor in a burning taxi belonging to her father's firm. In her agony, the dying girl described how she had picked up a fare near her Otterburn home. The man was heading for Ponteland, but during the journey he threatened and sexually assaulted her. She claimed he poured fluid over her from a bottle, and having set the vehicle ablaze launched it careering off onto the moor.

Evelyn Foster died of her injuries, the inquest reporting

wilful murder. But it was suggested that the girl might have accidentally immolated herself while trying to burn the car for the insurance money. The police, in fact, issued a statement after the inquest, to the effect that no murderer had ever existed.

Were they doing her an injustice? And if so, was Ernest Brown the killer? Evelyn Foster described her assailant as a rather stylish dresser, and said that he had a slight Tyneside accent – details applying to Ernest Brown. The ex-groom was a man of violent temper, not above threatening his mistress to achieve forced intimacy. At the time of the Otterburn incident, he was still a groom in the Morton household, and his job involved travelling about the country to attend horse and cattle sales.

Was he a double murderer? We shall never know. Seconds after uttering his last three syllables Ernest Brown jerked into eternity.

Spring-heeled Jack, the Demon of London

There was but one topic on the lips of the people of London in 1838 . . . the identity of the mysterious fiend who pounced on young women at night and whose appearance left most of them too terrified even to give a cogent description of their attacker.

At first, tales of this devil-like figure had been treated as hysterical nonsense. But reports, mainly from people crossing Barnes Common in south-west London, continued – and in January 1938 this strange creature received official recognition.

At London's Mansion House the Lord Mayor, Sir John Cowan, read out a letter from a terrified citizen of Peckham describing a demonic figure. Other complaints flooded in from people who until then had been too afraid of ridicule to report their encounters with the creature who had become known as Spring-heeled Jack.

South London barmaid Polly Adams had been savagely attacked while walking across Blackheath. Servant girl Mary Stevens was terrorized on Barnes Common. And an unnamed woman was assaulted in Clapham churchyard. Eighteen-year-old Lucy Scales, a butcher's daughter was attacked in Limehouse. Jane Alsop was almost strangled by the cloaked creature in her own home before her family were able to beat off the attacker.

The description the Alsops gave of the mysterious fiend made him sound inhuman. Jane said: 'His face was hideous, his eyes were like balls of fire, and his hands had icy claws . . .'

Her description was to be echoed repeatedly by other terrified and presumably hysterical victims. But police and public did not dismiss them. Even the Duke of Wellington, although nearly 70, armed himself and went out on horseback to hunt down the monster.

Reports of attacks persisted for several years, not only in London now, but from all parts of the country.

In February 1855 the inhabitants of five south Devon towns awoke to find that there had been a heavy snowfall in which mysterious footprints had appeared overnight. The footsteps ran along the tops of walls, over rooftops, and across enclosed countryside. The hoof-like footprints were attributed by many to Spring-heeled Jack.

In 1870 the army organized a plan to trap him after sentries had been terrorized at their posts by a horrific figure who sprang from the shadows to land on the roofs of their sentry boxes or to slap their faces with icy hands. Their plan failed.

Spring-heeled Jack was last seen in 1904 in Liverpool, leaping up and down the streets from the pavements to the rooftops, disappearing into the night, this time for good.

The World's Last Airship

It was a monster of the skies, a wonder of technology and engineering. The giant airship *Hindenburg* was more than 245 m (800 ft) long and stabilized by a tailfin as high as a ten-storey building. Its four powerful diesel engines gave it the power to cruise effortlessly above the clouds at 36 metres per second (80 mph). The airship could carry 100 passengers through the atmosphere for a week in a style as opulent as any ocean liner.

When all the 16 bags inside its 22.8 m (75 ft) diameter frame were filled with hydrogen, the airship would wrench itself away from the ground with a lifting force of 239 tonnes (235 tons), enough to raise a modern jumbo jet. Admittedly the properties of hydrogen gas, lighter than the surrounding air, which gave the *Hindenburg* the lift to soar into the sky, brought the risks and dangers of explosion. But with more than a quarter of a century of hard-won experience, the Zeppelin Company was confident that no mishap would endanger their new flagship. They knew that the hydrogen in the gas bags, more than 230,000 cubic metres (7,200,000 cubic feet) of highly inflammable gas, would erupt in a devastating explosion if it was ever ignited. But the design, they said, was flawless. Only an act of God, or deliberate sabotage by a madman, could damage the *Hindenburg*.

And when the *Hindenburg* was consumed in a fire-ball over New Jersey on 6 May 1937, killing 13 of its passengers, 22 of its crew and 1 ground control worker, both the American Government and Hitler's Nazi regime conspired to cover up any clues to what may have been the biggest crime in aviation history.

While the fledgling airliners of the 1920s and 1930s were

plagued by bad weather and mechanical breakdowns trying to operate services between towns only a few hundred miles apart, the monster airships of Germany appeared regularly over the skyline of Rio de Janeiro and New York.

They had become known simply as Zeppelins, after their brilliant but eccentric designer, the Graf Ferdinand von Zeppelin. Born into a noble Prussian family in 1838, he was an adventurous 23-year-old when he obtained an introduction to US President Abraham Lincoln during the American Civil War and joined the Union Army as a 'guest' cavalry officer.

But the young soldier soon became bored by the slow pace of the war and joined a civilian expedition to explore the sources of the Mississippi River. On a scouting mission at St Paul, Minnesota, he took his first ride in a tethered balloon to survey miles of countryside in one brief flight.

If only balloons could be powered and steered, he enthused, what a perfect gun platform and bombing weapon they would make, soaring safely over the slogging infantry and cavalrymen on he field. His vision of giant balloons or dirigibles as weapons of war never left him but he stayed an earthbound cavalry officer until the end of his military career at the age of 52.

Within a few years of retiring, he had applied for a patent for an airship and began experimenting with the designer, Dr Hugo Eckener, an experienced sailor and meteorologist, at their little workshop near Lake Constance in southern Germany.

By 1909 Zeppelin had formed the world's first airship passenger service, Deutsche Luftschiffahrts Atkien Gesell-schaft – DELAG. Operating flights between Berlin, Frankfurt, Hamburg and Dresden, his airships carried 32,750 passengers on 1,600 flights in five years without a single accident.

Then came 1914 and the Zeppelins went to war.

The Zeppelin raids over England caused little material

damage but they raised panic among the population of London. The sight of the dreaded airships caught in the searchlights, cascading their bombs on to the capital, brought Londoners out into the streets, screaming and shaking their fists impotently in the air.

But within two years the British air aces in their tiny biplane fighters were more than a match for the Zeppelin monsters. In their hydrogen bags the Zeppelins carried the seeds of their own destruction. It took only one hit from the newly developed ZPT tracer bullets coated in burning phosphorus, to turn the airships into flying holocausts.

Graf von Zeppelin died in 1917, just as it was proved that his airships were too vulnerable to gunfire to be machines of war.

But Dr Hugo Eckener struggled through the post-war economic ruin of Germany as chairman of the Zeppelin Company, dreaming of a peaceful future for the airships as transatlantic transports.

In July 1928, the world's most advanced passenger airship, the *Graf Zeppelin*, made its maiden flight on the 90th anniversary of the old Count's birth. Three months later, with 20 passengers aboard, it made its first transatlantic voyage to New York where Eckener and the crew were treated to a ticker-tape welcome. In the next five years of operation on regular services to North and South America, the *Graf Zeppelin* established an unrivalled airship mastery of the skies.

The prestige of this achievement was not lost on the new Nazi masters of Germany. Eckener was not popular with the new regime. Before their rise to power he had made radio broadcasts in Germany condemning their brutality. But with the Nazis controlling the purse strings of German industry, including the Zeppelin Company, he was powerless to stop the traditional black, white and red livery colours of the Zeppelins being repainted with the swastika, the symbol of Hitler and his Nazis.

Eckener, a stubborn 68-year-old, was defiant when he was summoned before Dr Joseph Goebbels, the Propaganda Minister, in 1936 when his newest airship, the biggest, fastest and most powerful, was unveiled.

The airship must be called 'Adolf Hitler', he was told by the Nazi minister. 'No,' Eckener replied. 'I warn you the sight of the swastika on our airships is already provoking hostility when we dock in the United States. If the new airship is called "Adolf Hitler" it will be the target for hatred and sabotage.'

Eckener won the day, but Goebbels decreed that in the German press and on radio the new airship would not be referred to by its Zeppelin Company name, *Hindenburg*. In the Nazi press it was referred to by its works design title – LZ 129.

When the *Hindenburg* began its regular services from Frankfurt to the Lakeheath Naval Air Base in New Jersey it received a rapturous welcome. But as the trickle of persecuted refugees from the Nazis reached a flood-tide on America's shores, Eckener's fears of flaunting the swastika proved to be well founded. In August 1936 more than 100 American demonstrators, posing as celebrating visitors, boarded the German liner *Bremen* as she lay at a pier in New York and sparked off a riotous protest against Hitler involvement in the Spanish Civil War.

Security was stepped up at the liner berths and at the *Hindenburg*'s hanger across the river at Lakeheath. The American government was concerned by reports that the *Hindenburg* had even been the target of riflemen who had fired potshots at the Zeppelin from atop the Manhattan skyscrapers and from the open fields of New Jersey.

The German ambassador in Washington had received a great number of threatening phone calls and letters from opponents of the Nazis who were determined to destroy the *Hindenburg* and keep the swastika out of

American skies.

Aware of the serious blow to their regime's prestige if the *Hindenburg* was sabotaged, the Sicherheitsddinst, the security élite of Hitler's SS, began to conduct searches of the *Hindenburg*'s hangar in Frankfurt, and the airship itself, before each flight.

On Monday 3 May 1937, Colonel Fritz Erdmann, the new chief of Special Intelligence for the Luftwaffe, was ordered to SS headquarters in Berlin for a briefing on the *Hindenburg* flight due to leave that day.

Erdmann and the two junior officers who were to accompany him in civilian clothes on the flight to America were startled by the briefing given to them by SS Sturmbannführer Major Kurt Hufschmidt. He told them: 'We have reliable information that an attempt will be made to destroy your flight. The sabotage will come by bomb, probably after the *Hindenburg* has arrived over American soil. This attack is designed to make the Fatherland look vulnerable in the eyes of our enemies: disloyal Germans, Jews and troublemakers in the United States.'

The SS man also revealed that in March 1935 a bomb had been discovered in the main dining saloon of the *Graf Zeppelin*, hidden underneath a table by one of the passengers. The bomb had been defused safely.

He also told of a Gestapo search of a Frankfurt hotel room for a mysterious passenger who had just arrived from America on a *Hindenburg* flight. The man had travelled on a forged Swedish passport and although he eluded the Gestapo, they searched his room and found detailed technical drawings of both the *Graf Zeppelin* and the *Hindenburg*.

Erdmann was given a rundown on suspect passengers who were making the flight with him. They included: a German couple, both journalists, who were known to have a Jewish writer as a friend, a young photographer from Bonn whose cut-price fare had been arranged by a senior Zeppelin executive since sacked for having Jewish ancestry, a 36-year-old American advertising executive who was known to be a spy for US intelligence, and Joseph Spah, a 35-year-old music hall entertainer from Douglaston, Long Island.

Spah was a comedian and acrobat who travelled on a French passport and had an American wife. But to the humourless SS man he was a suspect because his music hall act, popular in parts of Berlin, was known to contain jokes against people in authority.

At the departure hangar in Frankfurt, all passengers and their luggage were thoroughly searched. Security men confiscated all the young photographer's flashbulbs, fearing they could be used to start a deliberate fire. They also X-rayed a small Dresden china souvenir doll brought on board by Spah.

But the Luftwaffe intelligence officer accepted the assurance of the *Hindenburg* captain, Ernst Lehmann, that the two married journalists were both personal friends who were writing his biography. And Captain Lehmann insisted that the American spy working for the advertising agency had been under close surveillance and posed no threat. The intelligence officer accepted his explanation.

Joseph Spah, according to the captain, was no more than a nuisance. He had brought along a frisky young German shepherd dog which was travelling with him in order to become part of his new act at Radio City Music Hall in New York. The dog travelled in the freight compartment at the rear of the airship and twice Spah had been found unsupervised in that area, away from the authorized passenger lounges. But they accepted his explanation that he must personally feed the nervous young dog during the two-and-a-half-day journey.

Colonel Erdmann reassured the captain: 'Any of our passengers sabotaging the *Hindenburg* on this voyage would be committing suicide. I think the attempt will come after we have moored at Lakeheath. Then it will be the responsibility of the ground staff to ensure the safety of the airship.'

But according to many investigators and historians, a bomb was already on board. An incendiary device, wired to a darkroom photographic timer powered by two small batteries was hidden inside the explosive hydrogen atmosphere of Gas Cell Four, near the tail of the *Hindenburg*.

The *Hindenburg* was due to moor at Lakeheath at 06.00 on 6 May. But the night before it ran into strong headwinds over Newfoundland and the airship radioed it would not arrive until 18.00. The *Hindenburg*'s docking was always made precisely at 06.00 or 18.00 to allow definite working times for the ground crew.

A small reception committee waiting at Lakeheath for the *Hindenburg*'s arrival took advantage of the postponement to go off for dinner in the nearby town of Toms River. They included broadcaster Herbert Morrison, who was preparing to record a commentary on the airship's mooring for the listeners of station WLS in Chicago.

By mid-afternoon on 6 May the *Hindenburg* had passed Long Island sound and the sight of the giant airship with its glittering swastikas brought traffic to a halt in Manhattan. As it crossed the baseball stadium at Ebbet's Field in Brooklyn, the game between the Brooklyn Dodgers and the Pittsburgh Pirates was suspended while players and spectators alike gaped in admiration at the pride of Hitler's Germany.

Just before 16.00 the airship arrived over Lakeheath, but Captain Lehmann set a southerly cruising course to ride out the stormy winds for two hours until the ground crew mustered for his appointed time of arrival.

At 17.22, the *Hindenburg* was being advised by ground control to keep circling ahead of an approaching storm front. And it was then, it is believed, that a timer on the detonator of the fire-bomb hidden in Gas Cell Four was set – for two hours hence.

An hour later Lakeheath radioed: 'Advise landing now' and the airship headed for the airfield. At 19.05 the *Hindenburg* crossed the south fence of the airfield. As 92 US Navy men and 139 civilian workers prepared to reach for the mooring lines which would be dropped from the *Hindenburg* to secure the airship, radio reporter Herbert Morrison could see cheerful passengers at the open promenade deck windows waving at him.

At 19.22 the *Hindenburg* lowered the mooring lines and gave one last burst of her engines to line the airship up with the 61 m (200 ft) mooring tower.

If the airship had been on schedule, all the passengers would have disembarked and it would have been floating at the mooring mast with only a skeleton crew . . . But the timer on the bomb had been set to the original schedule.

At 19.22 there was a puff of flame and a fire-ball 122 m (400 ft) across erupted from the linen-covered framework of the *Hindenburg*.

Herbert Morrison had been describing the scene as the airship docked:

What a sight it is . . . a thrilling one . . . a marvellous sight. The sun is striking the window of the observation deck on the westward side and sparkling like glittering jewels on the background of dark velvet. Oh, oh, oh . . . it's burst into flames. Get out of the way please. Oh my, this terrible – it's burning, bursting into flames, it's falling. Oh, this is one of the worst, oh, all the humanity . . .

His voice trailed off in tears.

When the film from the newsreel cameras which recorded the fire-ball were processed, it showed that it took only 34 seconds from the first explosion of flame until the glowing framework of the *Hindenburg* hit the ground. The millions of cubic feet of hydrogen had flamed off in less than a minute, although the blaze of engines, fuel oil and framework lasted for hours.

The crew men on the ground, holding the mooring lines underneath the burning giant, scattered and ran for their lives.

One of them, Allen Hagaman, tripped over the rails surrounding the mooring tower and the glowing framework of the airship crashed down on him. He was identified the next day by the scorched remains of his wedding ring.

But in the few seconds as the *Hindenburg* fell from the sky, there were miraculous escapes as passengers and crew leaped from the crashing airship, or simply stayed inside the burning wreckage until it settled on the ground and ran to safety through the white-hot hoops of the *Hindenburg* framework. Joe Spah was one of those who survived. He jumped more than 9 m (30 ft) from the burning airship and, with his acrobat's training, landed apparently unhurt. Luftwaffe intelligence colonel Fritz Erdmann, who had predicted an attack would come after the *Hindenburg* had landed, perished in the flames. Of the 36 passengers, 13 died. Of the 61 crew members, 22 died.

In the commission of inquiry that followed, German experts were invited to join the investigation as 'observers'. Most of the commission's discussions were 'off-the-record' talks between American government officials and high ranking German diplomats.

Documents now filed in the National Archives in Washington show that the American and German technical experts agreed not to consider sabotage as a cause of the disaster – at least in public.

The archives show that senior officers of the American Departments of Commerce and the Interior warned the commission solicitor Mr Trimble Jr that 'a finding of sabotage might be a cause for an international incident, especially on these shores'. The commission ignored a written report by Detective George McCartney of the New

York Police Department bomb squad, who analysed the wreckage and reconstructed technical details of a fire-bomb which he believed had been placed in Gas Cell Four. And the chief of the Luftwaffe, Hermann Goering, ordered the German technical advisers to the commission not to cooperate with any avenue of investigation that hinted at sabotage by any member of the crew.

After a month-long hearing, the commission reached a conclusion backed by both the Americans and Germans. The hydrogen fire-ball had been sparked off, they claimed, by a freak spark of static electricity, an unfortunate phenomenon not seen before and not seen since. Hermann Goering concurred: 'It was an act of God. No one could have prevented it.'

But behind the scenes in Germany, the Gestapo were ruthlessly interrogating the families and friends of every one of the *Hindenburg* crew and passengers. Their suspicions eventually focussed on 25-year-old Eric Spehl. As a rigger on the *Hindenburg* he was one of the crew responsible for checking the gas bags for leaks.

Spehl had been a devout Catholic, never a fervent supporter of the Nazi regime. And he had one great weakness, a passionate love for a divorced woman ten years older than himself who had become his mistress.

Gestapo agents, who checked the gossip with Spehl's neighbours in Frankfurt, found that the young man had gone through a traumatic meeting with his mistress's ex-husband just before the *Hindenburg*'s last voyage. The man had come to Spehl's flat. He was an artist, he was haggard and half crazed with fear. He was on the run from the Gestapo and needed money to escape.

Spehl gave him all the money he had . . . and then tipped off the Gestapo. The Nazi torturers arrested the artist and crushed his fingers one by one in a vice until the bones showed through his knuckles. Spehl was reported to be infuriated by the sight and still seething with anger when he boarded the fatal *Hindenburg* flight.

The Gestapo searchers in Frankfurt ripped Spehl's apartment to pieces. They could find no sign of his mistress, who had fled the city. And they could find no trace of Eric's beloved new gadget for his photographic darkroom, his two-hour timer.

Neither could they interrogate Eric Spehl. He died, horribly burned, in the emergency field hospital set up at Lakeheath, beside the glowing embers of the world's last great airship.

Crimes of
Our Time

The Computer as Crook

The unsolved crime is usually hailed as the perfect crime. It is a misnomer. More often than not, a crime remains unsolved thanks to a combination of poor planning, coupled with good luck on the criminal's part and sometimes helped by a faulty police investigation. The really perfect crime is never reported. It remains unsolved because it is unrecognized and undetected as a piece of villainy.

And in the criminal's quest for illegal perfection, many have found a willing new accomplice who never gets nervous about being caught and punished, who has no criminal record, leaves no fingerprints and never demands a share of the loot . . . the computer, an electronic brain without scruples or morals, is the perfect partner in crime.

At the beginning of the 1980s it was estimated that there were 300,000 large computers at work in businesses in the United States, Europe and Japan, juggling enormous amounts of cash and commodities every week. Unlike human clerks and bank tellers, with all their frailties and temptations, computers never get their sums wrong and do not possess sticky fingers to dip into the till.

The decision of the almighty computer is final, whether it is sending a demand for payment to a customer who is vainly disputing the bill or releasing vast amounts of hard cash on invoices it has cleared for payment. The computer is above suspicion.

Small wonder then that it has not taken long for criminals to realize the potential of getting the computer on their side. For the computer's infallibility is a double-edged sword. If crooked information is fed in at the start of the process, impeccably crooked instructions are produced at the other end and no one doubts the orders the machine gives them.

That is what electronic whizz-kid Jerry Schneider discovered when he became a millionaire by defrauding the master computer of the Pacific Bell Telephone Company in Los Angeles in 1972. Schneider's crime is still unsolved, only he knows exactly how he fooled the electronic brain. The computer records reveal nothing.

The 21-year-old high school graduate was struggling to form his own telephone equipment supply business when he discovered secret codes which allowed him to tap into the computer controlling the stocks in the warehouse of Pacific Bell in California. Using his own modified computer terminal at home, Schneider persuaded the electronic stock controller he was a legitimate installation contractor for the phone company and he began to order costly wiring and exchange equipment from the warehouse.

The computer accepted his instructions and despatched its expensive goods to locations all over Los Angeles, often to the pavements beside manhole covers where the delivery drivers dumped the bulky crates of electronics, assuming another crew would arrive later to install the equipment. They did not wait to see this operation.

Schneider, with his own truck painted to resemble the phone company vehicles, would hijack the equipment, then return home to tap into the computer once more and give it orders to wipe the whole transaction from its electronic memory.

With his giant rival supplying all his equipment free, Schneider's business boomed until he foolishly refused a pay rise to one of his employees, who then tipped off the police. Even after his arrest officials of the phone company refused to believe that Schneider had milked their warehouse of $1 million worth of equipment in less than a year. If their computer insisted there was nothing missing, they were not prepared to argue with it. Only after police investigators physically went round the warehouse, totalling up the stocks with old-fashioned pen and paper, did the phone company admit their losses.

But Schneider spent only a few weeks in prison. The phone company dropped charges against him after he gave them a secret briefing on the electronic loopholes in their system.

On his release from prison Schneider set himself up in a new business, as one of America's highest paid computer security consultants, revealing the secrets of his unsolved crime for fat fees and searching the electronic brains of his clients' machines for similar loopholes which can let crooked computer operators steal by remote control.

As Jerry Schneider said:

'Many of my clients had already been robbed blind without realising it. They had lost millions of dollars through computer manipulation and the culprits can never be traced because the electronic evidence of their crimes has been wiped out.

Who needs to take the risk of leaping over a bank counter with a sawn-off shotgun when they can sit in the comfort of their own home and rob the bank of even more money just by using a telephone and a computer terminal?'

In the United States, FBI officials estimate the average haul in armed bank robberies amounts to $10,000 a time. But the average electronic bank fraud is enriching crooks by $500,000 a time with only a tiny percentage of the microchip embezzlements uncovered and solved.

In 1980 it was estimated that unsolved computer crime in the US and Common Market countries was producing a haul of £200 million a year and growing fast.

New York police are still searching for the amiable young man who pulled off a childishly simple computer fraud when he signed a loan agreement with a local bank for $20,000 to buy himself a new car. The bank's computer paid the car dealer and the vehicle ownership papers were safely stored in the bank's filing cabinet as security for the loan. A few days later the proud new driver received his loan repayment book, with 12 monthly coupons to be processed by the computer as he coughed up the installments over the next year.

The young man ignored the first 11 coupons and posted the twelfth with a money order to the computer when his first installment was due. Then he waited.

There is nothing as blind as an infallible machine. The computer recognized only the magnetic ink code on the coupon as the twelfth and final installment. With unfailing efficiency it sent the car driver a glowing letter thanking him for paying off the loan. It also posted him the owner- ship documents to the car and a printed assurance that he now had an outstanding credit rating at the bank.

More than a month later a puzzled bank official went to visit the new customer's address in search of an overdue installment. His apartment was empty and the gleaming Cadillac had already been sold to a local car dealer who had happily, and legally, accepted the computer's decision that the car was paid for and owned by the young driver who wanted a cash sale to pay for a 'heart operation' for his ailing father. The mysterious driver was never traced despite strenuous efforts to do so.

Another stunningly easy fraud netted $350,000 in one week for the pretty blonde 'divorcee' who opened her own account with $200 when she arrived at a bank in Miami, Florida. She was planning to buy herself a luxury home near the beach, she explained, just as soon as her divorce settlement came through from her husband. The bank happily issued her with a cheque book and a book of paying-in slips with her own personalized account number printed in one corner in magnetic ink characters.

They never noticed her stop at the counter as she left, when she scooped up a handful of blank paying-in slips in a tray for the convenience of customers who had forgotten to bring their own personalized books.

Somehow (and no one has ever publicly explained the mystery) the young blonde printed her own account number in magnetic ink at the bottom left hand corner of all the bank slips. A few days later she reappeared at the bank and slipped her own specially doctored paying-in slips to the tray at the counter.

For the next five days, busy customers who had forgotten to bring their pre-printed paying-in slips reached for the apparently blank forms on the tray and paid their earnings and savings into the bank. The computer was programmed to direct the pen-and-ink slips into a storage basket for manual sorting. But it instantly recognized the magnetic ink numbers and faithfully credited all the money to the divorcee's account. When she returned a few days later she found her 'dream home' and she was accompanied by a burly male friend with a security attaché case.

She cleaned out all but a few hundred dollars from the account, scooping up a kitty of £150,000 which had been built up for her by unsuspecting customers who kicked up hell at the end of the month when their statements showed their hard-earned cash had not been credited to their accounts. The blonde and her friend were never seen again.

A more ambitious crook used his innocent girlfriend as his unwitting accomplice when he robbed the computer of a bank in Washington, DC, in 1981.

The dapper middle-aged businessman boasted that he was a furniture manufacturer from San Francisco and would soon be bringing new jobs to Washington when he had found a suitable site for his new factory. The bank welcomed him as a potentially valuable customer when he opened his account and told them to expect a very large deposit to follow from his company account in San Francisco.

True to his word, a few days later the San Francisco bank made an electronic transfer of $2 million to Washington. The furniture manufacturer promptly presented himself at the bank, collected the money in a cashier's draft and set off 'looking for development land'. When he failed to reappear, and when the hard cash never arrived from San Francisco, bank investigators started to track down the source of the computer transfer of money.

After months of searching they finally traced the electronic message to one computer terminal at the bank in San Francisco, operated by a group of three female employees who all denied any knowledge of the transfer. But they did tell the investigators that a fourth woman had left her job at the bank only a few weeks before, broken-hearted after an unhappy love affair.

The woman was traced and told in tears how her middle-aged boyfriend had promised to marry her after returning home briefly from Washington to assure his friends and family that he had made his fortune in California. The boyfriend was a great fun-loving practical joker, she explained. He had even persuaded her to send a telex to a bank in Washington crediting him with $2 million as a prank to impress his friends and relations.

The telex message was the only souvenir the bank has left of the fraudster. Their computer had paid out without the need to see the cash or count laboriously through piles of crisp banknotes as a bored, under-paid human teller would have to do. To the computer, a burst of electronic bleeps over a telephone line was as good as money in the bank.

But the prize for the most sought after computer conman of the new electronic age must surely go to the New York genius who was able to tap his way into a municipal computer which controlled no cash, no valuable stocks, no sensitive information.

The AM Tote 300 computer at Belmont racetrack is just an adding machine which is supposed to total up the amount of money bet on each day's racing to an accuracy within a single cent.

Since revenue from the Tote betting tax contributes to the income of the City of New York, that figure is a matter of record. Each day New York newspapers publish the figure. It is simply a statistic which varies each day according to the amount of business done at the racetrack.

The final sum from the impartial computing machine is taken for granted as accurate even by the down-to-earth businessmen of the Mafia. And that daily betting total is the heart of the Mafia's illegal bookmaking enterprise, the numbers racket. The Mafia's persuasive street salesmen offer a daily lottery ticket where a gambler can choose any three digits which he or she thinks will form the vital last three numbers of that day's betting total at Belmont.

The chances of getting the numbers right are 999 to 1. But the organizers pay out odds of only 500 to 1, making a profit on half the $3 million New Yorkers bet on the racket each week.

On 30 September 1980, a crowd of 20,000 gamblers spent a day at the races and bet a total of $3,339,916. The following day the Mafia bookies paid out $250,000 to lucky holders who had chosen the winning number as 916.

A few days later the auditors handling the racetrack's accounts announced that the computer had mis-totalled the amount by $3 and altered the last three figures to 919. The Mafia bookies who had already paid out on the earlier figure, made the splendidly warm-hearted gesture of paying out again on the new total to enhance their reputation as nice honest guys to do business with.

Then the auditors completed an overhaul of the Tote 300 computer and checked its totals against actual cash deposits paid into the bank. In six months the Tote 300 had given the wrong betting total 80 times. Its simple adding machine memory had been accepting any last three numbers fed into it by a crooked computer operator who clicked its electronic register to any numbers he chose.

The Mafia had been conned out of $20 million.

A Sadistic Revenge

'Only a few evil sadists will carry with them to their graves the knowledge of whether her body was alive or dead when they set her on fire.'

The words come from the man known as the White Rat of Uganda: self-styled 'Major' Bob Astles, the British acolyte of one of the most barbarous tyrants the world has ever seen, Idi Amin. They refer to a gentle old woman with dual Israeli-British citizenship who unwittingly became caught up in the now legendary Israeli commando rescue of a hijacked aeroplane and its hostages at Uganda's Entebbe Airport in 1976.

Dora Bloch, aged 73, was one of 105 hostages freed by the bullet in one of the most daring, audacious military swoops of its kind in modern, peacetime history. Freed, tragically, only for an instant . . . because she was hurt during the armed sortie and was left behind to recuperate in a Ugandan hospital.

The Ugandan capitulation after the Entebbe raid was absolute. So, it soon became clear, was Amin's lust for revenge. And the pathetically frail object of that revenge appears to have been Mrs Dora Bloch.

It was only later that clues began to emerge about what really happened to this grandmother, whose only wish when she boarded the 747 Jumbo jet was to see again her relatives in Tel Aviv.

In 1980 a British journalist smuggled a message into Uganda's grim Luzira Prison, where Amin's British aide Astles was being held, following the flight of the tyrant and the country's liberation by troops sent in by neighbouring Tanzania.

In a letter smuggled out to the newsman, Mike Parker, Astles told how he had tracked down Mrs Bloch's grave at a time when Amid was denying to the world that his secret police had slain her.

Rumours in the country had been rife that Mrs Bloch had been tortured to death in the notorious State Research Bureau outside Kampala, along with thousands of others – enemies real and imagined – who had simply vanished after being abducted there.

Astles, however, told Parker in his smuggled letter that he confronted Amin after discovering Mrs Bloch's jungle grave. He wrote:

'Then, all hell let loose, I was summoned to see Amin – and he was in one of his most horrendous rages. His eyes glared with terrible anger.

I knew I was going to be in trouble for asking questions, but I wasn't going to back down. I said to Amin "Bring me the body of Dora Bloch."

And then I was brought down to earth. It was flung at me, by Amin, that I had had a part in her killing. How could I have done? At the time, I was on leave in London.

I came back to Uganda because it was the only life I knew. And I vowed to Mrs Bloch's niece, Mrs Ruth Hammond, in a meeting at her London home, that I would discover what had happened to her aunt.

The truth is that I was working with Israeli Intelligence – but nobody knew at the time.'

'The truth' as propounded by Astles may be anything but fact. Nevertheless, documents recovered since Amin's overthrow – some of them from the so-called State Research Bureau – reveal that Mrs Bloch was dragged screaming from Mulago Hospital, Kampala, after being admitted there as a patient only hours after the successful commando raid on Entebbe Airport.

It was later claimed that she had been taken there for treatment after being unknowingly left behind by the Israeli troops. But subsequent statements from witnesses suggest that she was far too weak to travel and, for the sake of the safety of the rest of the liberated hostages, she was left behind in the hope that Amin would allow her to be treated and then released on her recovery.

It was not to be. Astles said:

'She was a suffering, pathetic old woman. But the State Research police were incensed by the Israeli attack. They wanted immediate retribution.

I have been told many stories about her death. But I was informed by a member of State Research that she was kicked and pummelled to the ground after being dragged from her hospital bed.

Her body, I was told, was finally set ablaze. And only a few evil sadists know whether she was alive or dead when they set her on fire.'

Astles added chillingly:

'Animals from the State Research Bureau were openly bragging about the white woman they had killed. They were boasting of how she had been buried after being beaten and burned and it was an easy job to find her unmarked grave – at a place called Nakapinyi.

I arranged to go there with a friend, but somehow our secret got out. My friend was thrown into jail. And I, too, would have been imprisoned by Amin if I'd made any attempt to get to the body.

Despite my demands, Amin refused to acknowledge that Mrs Bloch had been killed on Ugandan soil. He kept telling the outside world that the "missing" Mrs Bloch was being searched for. But all along he knew the truth.

I think, in all honesty, that he was ashamed that his State Research Bureau had killed her. He would never admit that she died the horrible death that she did on his orders. And, despite my demands, he adamantly refused to let anyone else try to appease her mourning family by finding her body.'

Mrs Bloch's grave was, in fact, finally unearthed by Ugandan police in May, 1979. Her bones were identified by top Israeli pathologist Dr Maurice Rogoff and flown to her homeland for burial. A grave had been prepared for her in Jerusalem by one of her sons, Bertram, and at last she was laid to rest.

Bob Astles told reporter Mike Parker: 'The sorry way in which Dora Bloch died will serve forever as an indictment of Idi Amin. Her killing was needless – a sordid act of revenge by people against whom this fragile person was totally defenceless.'

Piracy 20th Century Style

There is nothing romantic about pirates. In the days of sail they were bloodthirsty killers. In the present day they are just as deadly, just as ruthless, just as merciless. The main difference is that in the days of Blackbeard and Captain Kidd, pirates usually ended their careers on the gallows or in Davy Jones's locker. In the 20th century, however, they get away. Their crimes almost always remain unsolved.

Piracy has become a renewed menace around the world, the most blighted regions being the Caribbean, the West African coast and the Far East. Many ships leaving Singapore for the open seas now frequently take on armed guards to protect them from attack by pirates, who mainly operate from nearby islands with high-speed boats.

In the Philippines, the British captain of a container ship dropped anchor to ride out a storm, and thought he and his crew were safe from danger. But under cover of darkness pirates drew alongside in a fishing boat, threw up grappling hooks and hauled themselves on board the container ship as it lay in Manila Bay. The bandits forced their way to the captain's cabin, pointed a gun at his neck and demanded money. Captain Arthur Dyason refused, and moved as if to parry the gun. The pirates opened fire and the captain died.

A horrifying massacre was carried out by pirates in the Tawitawi Islands, about 500 miles north of Manila. The passenger craft *Nuria* had dropped anchor in a calm bay when two crewmen and two stowaways jumped the crew and passengers. Wielding weapons taken from the armoury, they herded everyone to one side of the ship and stripped them of their valuables. Then they opened fire. In a hail of shots 11 people were killed – then callously thrown overboard. Panic ensued and 20 others dived into the sea and were drowned.

Meanwhile the four pirates transferred to two fishing vessels manned by accomplices. Twenty people survived the ordeal, and the pirates, thought to be natives of the region, were never caught.

In 1981 the International Maritime Bureau was established at Barking, Essex, to deal with and collate evidence of crimes committed at sea. Many of the cases the bureau deals with involve insurance fraud. But increasingly, cases of piracy are reported to the investigators. In one of its first reports, the bureau stated with alarm that fierce tribesmen armed with knives and poison-tipped arrows were hired to protect ships from pirates off West Africa.

But it is the Caribbean that is, as ever, the world centre of piracy. In five years, between 1977 and 1982, it was estimated that 1,500 people had been killed by pirates.

The yacht *Belle Esprit* limped into Nassau in the Bahamas with 50 bullet holes in the hull. The captain, Austin Evans, had beaten off an attack from five speedboats and was eventually rescued by a police spotter plane. Within weeks, pirates raided three sailing boats heading for the Bahamas. They threatened the lives of those on board and robbed them of cash and supplies.

William and Pat Kamemer of Fort Myers, Florida, were murdered when they stumbled across an ocean drug transfer in the Exumas Islands. Walter Falconer and a companion vanished without trace along with their yacht, *Polyner III*, in the 76-mile stretch between Bimini and the Florida coast. After relatives offered a reward word filtered back that both men had been killed and the yacht hijacked to South America.

Peter Beamborough and Michael Collesta fought off four attacking boats near the Williams Islands. They reported afterwards that they sailed their 12m (40ft) yawl *Snowbound* to safety in a hail of gunfire. British businessman Michael Crocker died aboard his 9m (30ft) yacht *Nym*, strangled by an armed intruder.

The reason for most of these attacks is the booming and seemingly unstoppable drugs trade. Whereas the currency of the pirates was once gold, it is now marijuana, cocaine and heroin. The route is from South America, through the Caribbean islands to the Florida coast. Mother ships carrying up to 62,000 tonnes (60,000 tons) of marijuana have been seen anchored outside territorial waters, waiting for darkness and the arrival of dozens of small vessels to transfer the cargo to hidden inlets and coves. Some victims have unexpectedly witnessed drug transfers at sea. Others have been attacked and killed, so that their vessels can be used as drug carriers.

In the Cayman Islands the police chief advertised six aircraft for sale – all confiscated from smugglers. He said: 'It doesn't stop the trade. It simply means that more yachts and planes will be stolen to replace them.'

The Colombian drug network is held responsible for most of the sea attacks, but many of the islanders are joining in the pirate operation.

Grafton Iffel, head of the Bahamas CID said: 'There are 700 small islands spread over 100,000 square miles. With limited resources it is an area impossible to control.'

American yachting magazines now openly warn readers: 'Take weapons with you – the bigger the better.

Display them when other boats come near. Link up with fellow yachtsmen in harbours and buy the best radio equipment you can afford.'

Captain Mike Green who sailed off the Florida coast for more than 20 years, said:

'Fear is replacing leisure here. Nobody listens to fabulous fishing stories any more. The talk is of bullets across the bow and high-speed runs for safety.

The message to yachtsmen who want to fulfil a life's ambition by sailing these waters is simply – don't. It is no longer safe. These seas belong to the smugglers and the pirates.'

Double Dealing at the Dogs

The most spectacular swindle in the history of greyhound racing was pulled off at London's White City track on 8 December 1945. The perpetrators, who were never caught, got away with more than £100,000, a fortune at the time.

The swindle became apparent to the race fans as they watched the last event of the day. The second favourite, Fly Bessie, led at the first bend, closely followed by Jimmy's Chicken. Then, to the amazement of the 16,000 crowd, the dogs began to swerve drunkenly and lose ground. One by one, they started stumbling . . . all except the rank outsider, a white hound called Bald Truth. He streaked home 15 lengths ahead of the second dog, with the favourite, Victory Speech, trailing in fourth.

No one was more amazed than Bald Truth's owner, Colonel B. C. 'Jock' Hartley, wartime director of the Army Sports Board. The dog had only been brought in as a late substitute and his £2 bet on it was prompted more by his heart than his head. He sat speechless as fans shouted and growled and track officials delayed making the official announcements. But there was nothing they could do.

Number 4 went up in lights; Bald Truth the winner. Bets would be paid.

As far as Scotland Yard was concerned, however, the affair was far from over. Chief Inspector Robert Fabian was called in to investigate the coup, which had followed a series of minor frauds at tracks around the country. Slowly the pieces of the puzzle were fitted into place. The swindlers had used a dope called cholecretone, untraceable in pre-race examinations, but which had an alcoholic effect as the dogs heated up during a race.

Investigators decided that the culprit had crept into a disused kennel used to store straw and timber. Then, when all eyes were on the track during the penultimate race, he had crawled out, fed drugged pieces of fish to all the dogs except Bald Truth – the only white dog in the field – and returned to his kennel until the coast was clear. Meanwhile the rest of the gang were placing bets with bookies all over the country and on the course, bringing the price down from 33-1 to 11-2 by the start.

But that was all renowned sleuth Fabian of the Yard could discover. Despite the Greyhound Racing Association's offer of a £1,000 reward, the culprits were never caught.

A Fatal Flight

Two planes carrying 116 passengers mysteriously vanished in the Andes – and investigators believe both craft may have been hijacked.

Saeta Airlines Flight 11, with 59 passengers on board, left Quito, Ecuador, on 15 August 1976 on its 45-minute flight to the mountain city of Cuenca. It vanished without trace.

Two years later Saeta Flight 11 left with 57 people bound once again for Cunca. It passed over the same relay station as its 1976 namesake then vanished. Intensive searches found no signs of the aircraft or their passengers. But at a special hearing in Quito, five farmers and a teacher gave sworn statements that they saw the second flight suddenly veer from its normal southerly course and head north-east.

Major Carlos Serrano, president of Saeta, one of Ecuador's three domestic airlines, supported the theory that the two Vickers Viscount planes had been hijacked. He said drug smugglers may have been involved. 'They are the perfect planes for them,' he said. 'They fly long distances, land on short runways and with the seats removed hold up to 12,000 pounds of cargo.'

Searches for the two planes involved the Ecuadorean Air Force and army patrols, a United States Air Force C-130 search plane and a helicopter with sophisticated laser reconnoitring devices. None of the searches were successful. And Commander Reinaldo Lazo, the United States Military Liaison Chief, said the C-130 crew had reached no conclusions after either of the week-long searches.

James Kuykendall, the Ecuador representative of the United States Drug Enforcement Administration, said his agency had found names of people with narcotics trafficking records on the passenger lists of the missing aircraft. He said his agency had no idea what had happened to the flights.

Saeta's Major Serrano, however, is more certain. He believes the passengers were pressed into service harvesting marijuana. The missing included 74 men, 36 women and 6 children – ranging from farm workers to doctors and lawyers.

Guillermo Jaramillo, a Quito lawyer whose 39-year-old son Ivan disappeared on the second flight, organized a committee of the grieving families to probe the mystery. Together with Saeta, they offered a $325,000 reward for information – without success.

Crimes of
Avarice

Conviction Without the Corpse

Life as the wife of a high-powered newspaper executive gave Muriel McKay all the trappings of suburban luxury – elegance a million miles removed from the street-wise world of the popular press in which her husband had made it to the top. Her world revolved around a genteel neighbourhood where every home had been built with the wealthy in mind and through whose letterboxes you would hardly expect to find the daily diet of sin, sex and sensation which was the trademark of husband Alick's downmarket journals of mass-appeal. But on the evening of Monday 29 December 1969, the McKays' world was turned, ruthlessly and without warning, upside down . . .

Alick McKay, number two to newspaper tycoon Rupert Murdoch and deputy chairman of the huge-circulation *News of the World*, returned home shortly before 20.00. From the outside, everything looked normal at St Mary House in Arthur Road, Wimbledon, south-west London. It was only after he had rung the doorbell a second time and discovered that the front door was unlocked – alarming in itself since the couple had agreed to take special care following a burglary a few months previously – that he began to realize that something was seriously wrong.

His worst suspicions were confirmed as he stepped into the hallway. Muriel's black handbag was lying open with its contents strewn halfway up the flight of stairs; the telephone had been hurled to the floor; on the hall table was an opened tin of plasters, a bale of thick twine and a rusty, wooden-handled meat-cleaver. Instinctively, Alick picked up the cleaver and raced upstairs, yelling his wife's name, fearing the intruder or intruders were still in the house.

But Muriel McKay, and whoever else had invaded the family home, had gone. Within minutes, Alick, trying to remain calm, discovered that several items of jewellery, including an eternity ring, a gold and pearl pendant, three bracelets and an emerald brooch, and a small amount of money were missing from Muriel's handbag. His mind racing, Alick ran to a neighbour's to see if anyone had heard or seen what had happened. No one had, and from the house next door he phoned the police.

In similar cases the police approach is generally low-key at the outset. Every possibility has to be examined and, in most cases, the most tangible one is that the person missing has put himself or herself on the missing persons list voluntarily – by simply walking out. And, in an over-whelming number of cases, if there is a culprit to be found, then it is more often than not the spouse who is 'left behind'.

But any thoughts that this was such a case were soon dispelled when, at 01.15 on Tuesday 30 December, the telephone rang at St Mary House. A detective who answered the call beckoned Alick to take the phone as he hurriedly picked up an extension. This was the chilling conversation that followed . . .

Caller: This is Mafia Group 3. We are from America. Mafia M3. We have your wife.

McKay: You have my wife?

Caller: You will need a million pounds by Wednesday.

McKay: What are you talking about? I don't understand.

Caller: Mafia. Do you understand?

McKay: Yes, I have heard of them.

Caller: We have your wife. It will cost you one million pounds.

McKay: That is ridiculous. I haven't got anything like a million.

Caller: You had better get it. You have friends. Get it from them. We tried to get Rupert Murdoch's wife. We couldn't get her, so we took yours instead.

McKay: Rupert Murdoch?
Caller: You have a million by Wednesday night or we will kill her. Understand?
McKay: What do I do?
Caller: All you have to do is wait for the contact. That is for the money. You will get instructions. Have the money or you won't have a wife. We will contact you again.
The line went dead as the caller rang off.

Further evidence arrived with the morning post, in a letter sent 12 hours previously from Tottenham, north London. Inside, in faltering handwriting on a piece of blue, lined paper, was a pathetic message. Alick McKay recognized at once the writing of his wife: 'Please do something to get me home. I am blindfolded and cold. Please cooperate for I cannot keep going. I think of you constantly and the family and friends. What have I done to deserve this treatment? Love, Muriel.'

The Muriel McKay case had begun to escalate into a major investigation. And with it came the attendant media 'circus'. As the McKay family closed ranks in the house at Arthur Road, one story upon which the press pack thrived was a call to Gerard Croiset, the world-famous Dutch clairvoyant who counted among his more spectacular successes the accurate pinpointing of the graves of murdered schoolchildren in Britain's notorious Moors Murders case. Croiset's unique powers enabled him to point to an area on a map which was, although largely ignored by police at the time, to prove of great significance: the border of Essex and Hertfordshire, some 40 miles outside London.

By the time a full week had elapsed, however, the police, who by then had a 30-strong team of detectives working full-time on the investigation, were still perplexed. Not one positive lead had emerged, despite the usual combing of underworld contacts and a check of hundreds of jewellers to discover whether Mrs McKay's missing possessions had been 'fenced'. The newspapers were running headline stories such as 'The Case That Does Not Add Up', and the crank callers and con-men, one of whom was later fined for trying to extort money from Alick McKay, were hampering what few inquiries could reasonably be made.

By 6 January every Metropolitan Police officer had been issued with a full description of Muriel McKay, her photograph had been posted on 'Wanted and Missing' boards at police stations throughout the country, Interpol had been alerted and a special watch was being kept on all entry points to Australia, the McKay's country of origin.

The breakthrough came a fortnight later. A large envelope posted from Wood Green, north London, contained another letter from Muriel, which read:

'I am deteriorating in health and spirit. Please cooperate. Excuse writing, I'm blindfolded and cold. Please keep the police out of this and cooperate with the gang giving Code M3 when telephoning you. The earlier you get the money the quicker I can come home or you will not see me again. Darling you can act quickly. Please, please keep the police out of this if you want to see me, Muriel.'

Also in the envelope was the ransom demand for one million pounds.

Three more telephone calls from the so-called M3 group came the following day. As the kidnap gang issued a series of demands, rendezvous points and instructions, Alick McKay desperately pleaded for some form of proof that his wife was still alive.

The gang responded with a further letter, accompanied by three pieces of material – one from the green woollen two-piece outfit Mrs McKay had been wearing, another from her black top coat and a snip of leather cut from one of her shoes. From the fourpenny stamp on the envelope, police scientific experts were able to remove a thumb-print. It did not belong to Mrs McKay. Much later it was matched to the thumb of a man called Arthur Hosein.

Police began to plot the ransom handover. It was to be made in two stages – apparently of £500,000 a time. But only £300 of the money, borrowed for the operation from Alick McKay, was to be genuine. The rest would be duds.

A series of attempted drops of the 'ransom money' followed over the next few days, resulting in some farcical mix-ups. The tolerance of the kidnap gang was wearing thin. And to the police, the gang's indecisive, amateurish handling of the actual ransom forced them to consider the possibility that the kidnappers were 'first-timers'.

The crucial day was Friday 5 February. A final call from the gang: 'If you do not drop the money, she will be dead. You must trust M3. We deal with high-powered telescopic rifles. Anyone trying to interfere with the cases – we will let them have it.'

An elaborate plan was agreed whereby, after a sup-posedly monitored journey by tube-train and taxi, the money was to be dropped off by a hedge close to a garage on Bishop's Stortford road in Hertfordshire. This time the plan went like clockwork, with police 'staking out' the drop, ready to swoop on whoever collected the ransom.

It transpired that no one did. But the police, mercifully, had their first stroke of luck. A Volvo 144 car – registration number XGO 994G – was spotted twice circling the drop-off point. It was the same vehicle that had turned up on an earlier, abortive delivery run. It belonged to Arthur Hosein.

Hosein, a Trinidad-born immigrant tailor, had, he believed, finally found his niche in English society when, in 1967, he purchased for the modest price of £14,000 Rooks Farm in Stocking Pelham, Hertfordshire. Two years after he moved in with his German-born wife Else, his younger brother Nizamodeen joined them. They were, from the start, a bizarre family, constantly at odds with their rural neighbours.

Villagers remembered how quickly Arthur became known as 'King Hosein', because of his incredible arrogance and boasts that it was his intention to become 'an English gentleman and a millionaire'. It was patently clear, even then, that he exerted an eerie, Svengali-like influence over his younger, easily-dominated brother. Arthur would talk expansively of his 'estate' – and if Nizamodeen ever dared remind him of the more mundane reality of failing, neglected Rooks Farm, he would be severely castigated.

Despite his Walter Mitty existence, however, Arthur did realize that his dreams of vast wealth were unlikely to be fulfilled were he simply to rely on his ailing smallholding. Then, two months before Christmas 1969, an idea for actually making that million took root in the brothers' minds.

They were watching television when they saw what they believed to be the answer to all their problems: the affluence of Rupert Murdoch. The press tycoon was a guest on the popular David Frost show, talking of his newspapers' involvement in the exposé of the notorious Christine Keeler sex-and-politics scandal. References were made to Murdoch's beautiful blonde wife Anna, as well as the sort of enormous sums his newspaper, the *News of the World*, was willing to part with in exchange for exclusive stories.

A crude, but seemingly foolproof plan was hatched to abduct Anna Murdoch and hold her to ransom for one million pounds. The plan was put into operation just after the Christmas break. Only it was Muriel McKay, the wife of Murdoch's second-in-command, who became the target, purely by accident when the bungling brothers got the addresses of the two executives mixed-up; they followed Rupert Murdoch's Rolls-Royce which was being used by the McKays while Murdoch was away.

At 08.00 on the misty morning of 6 February, a squad of

20 detectives, armed with a search warrant obtained by Chief Superintendent Smith of Wimbledon police in west London, walked up the short driveway to the house at Rooks Farm in Stocking Pelham. They told Arthur Hosein's wife Else, who answered the door, that they were making inquiries about a cache of jewellery which had been stolen in London 39 days previously.

At first, Arthur Hosein remained cool enough to cast doubt in the searchers' minds as to whether he might, indeed, be their man. His wife, who seemed understandably irritated at having so many men trample around her home, also showed no signs of stress. And Arthur himself, when questioned about the missing jewellery, calmly replied: 'I know nothing. I earn over £150 a week. I do not deal in stolen property. You can look where you like.'

Look the detectives did. Methodically, painstakingly they began their search of Rooks Farm. It was only a matter of minutes before a vital shred of evidence – the first of many – came to light. From an upstairs bedroom, a young detective constable emerged with some blue and yellow slips of paper, cut into the shape of flowers for the Hosein children, which were identical to scraps found at one of the earlier ransom drop-offs.

A writing pad, on which could be made out the indentations of words that had been written on a previous page, was taken away. Experts later matched the indentations to one of the pathetic letters Muriel McKay had been forced to write by her captors. More sinisterly, a shotgun, the double-barrels of which had been sawn down in the fashion now favoured by criminals, was discovered. Moreover, it had recently been fired. Later, a key witness was to say he had heard a single shot ring out from the direction of Rooks Farm several days earlier.

The mounting evidence then took a nightmarish turn – one which was to lead to the most grisly of theories and seal forever the mystery which surrounds the Muriel

McKay case. Police discovered a billhook, recently used to slaughter animals, in the farmhouse. At the time of this sinister discovery, Arthur Hosein casually commented: 'I borrowed it from a farmer friend. I wanted to chop up a calf. It was Nizam (Arthur's pet name for his brother) who did the chopping. We fed it to the dogs and put the bones and head with the rubbish.'

The information was not, perhaps, sinister itself. But allied to the fact that the Hosein brothers had recently sold a number of pigs at market, and that traces of bone were found in the fire at their house, police began to ponder the dreadful theory that Muriel McKay may have been murdered . . . and then fed to the pigs.

Had they ever been able to trace the livestock the brothers sold, they might have found the traces of cortisone – a drug Mrs McKay had been prescribed by the family doctor – which would have proved the unthinkable. But the body of Muriel McKay never was discovered. Exactly how she died, where she died and when she died remains unsolved. The considerable efforts of the police to elicit a full confession from the Hosein brothers proved – and still prove – futile.

The brothers were found guilty of the murder of Muriel McKay, even in the absence of her body. The massive weight of circumstantial evidence which the police collected against them was compounded by the matching of Arthur Hosein's fingerprints to those not only on the letters from the 'M3 gang' to the McKay family, but also on a copy of the *Sunday People* newspaper which, ironically, the brothers had dropped in the drive of the McKays' house when they staged the kidnap.

During three days of intensive interrogation at Kingston Police Station in Surrey, the true characters of the Hosein brothers emerged. Weak, easily-dominated Nizamodeen cracked quickly, and twice tried to take his own life. At one stage, when asked where he was on the night of 29

December 1969, he replied in a state of panic: 'Oh, my! What has Arthur done to me? Where did Arthur say I was? I was with my brother Arthur.' Later, he threw his arms around a detective's shoulders and sobbed: 'Kill me. What have I done? Arthur always gets me in trouble. Kill me now.' Nizamodeen's defence lawyers even found it difficult to communicate with him. In deep shock, he completely refused for six weeks even to discuss the murder case with them, until finally they persuaded him to study statements made by the prosecution witnesses.

In contrast, Arthur, while never confessing to the murder of Mrs McKay, put on a show of bravado. Described by one senior officer as 'an aggressive psychopath', he would sit in the interview room dictating statements at a ferocious pace. At one stage he boasted to his interrogator that he intended to write a book about the McKay case and turn it into a film, starring Richard Burton as the policeman in command and Sammy Davis Junior as himself. Arthur's bombast and apparent unconcern at the charge of murder he was facing astonished detectives.

Even during their trail at the Old bailey eight months after their arrest, the brothers played out their completely contrasting roles. Nizamodeen, pale and trembling, could barely be heard giving evidence in the witness-box, even with a microphone strapped around his neck. Arthur, on the other hand, was full of himself as ever. Having convinced himself he would be acquitted – a belief he confided to cellmates and police alike – he launched into an astonishing diatribe when convicted by the jury, yelling at the judge, Mr Justice Sebag Shaw: 'Injustice has not only been done, it has also been seen and heard by the gallery to have been done. They have seen the provocation of your lordship and they have seen your immense partiality.' Unmoved, the judged passed life sentences on both brothers, with further 25-year and 15-year sentences of imprisonment on Arthur and Nizamodeen respectively for the other charges relating to Mrs McKay's abduction.

During the months between the Hoseins' arrest and their trial, the police continued their desperate, fruitless search for the body of Muriel McKay. One inmate who shared a cell with Arthur while on remand claimed that he had told him that the body was disposed of in a reservoir. Police drained the huge site Arthur had named but, again, to no avail. The story was dismissed as having been either another instance of Arthur's many fantasies or an attempt by his fellow prisoner to swap phoney evidence for some sort of remission deal.

Eventually the police were forced to abandon their search – leaving forever three vital, unanswered questions. They are still unsolved: how was she murdered, when was she murdered and where was she murdered? Was she, it is still suggested, the victim of an indescribable fate and fed to the pigs of Rooks Farm? Only two men know the answers: Arthur and Nizamodeen Hosein.

In a final, heart-rending postscript to one of Britain's most perplexing, unsolved cases, the *Sun* newspaper published a statement from Alick McKay the morning after the trial of the Hoseins ended. It said:

'One can accept death in the ordinary way. It is something which has to be faced and one has to adjust one's life to take account of it.

But in these circumstances, one is unable to accept the explanation of death without finding a body, although I am convinced Muriel is never coming home again. I must face this situation of course and face my life as best I can.

I suppose I do not want to know the brutal facts really, and yet I must always ask, how did she die, what happened to her, where is her body?

However much I try to escape the tragedy and hurt of it, I suppose I really would like to know the answers . . .'

Doctor Death

An 84-year-old retired doctor died in July 1983 in the genteel Sussex seaside resort of Eastbourne. His passing might have warranted no more than a paragraph in the local paper, but for one thing . . . The doctor, John Bodkin Adams, was believed by many to be a man who literally got away with mass murder. And it was only upon his death that newspapers could safely produce their dossiers on the astonishing case, in which Adams was tried at the Old Bailey for the murder of one of his patients, Edith Morrell, a 72-year-old widow. If he had been convicted he would have been charged with further murders. Two other charges had been prepared and the Crown believed it had sufficient evidence to prosecute three other cases.

Early in the investigation one of the policemen involved, Scotland Yard Detective Chief Superintendent Charles Hewitt, believed Adams killed nine of his elderly patients. He later increased his estimate to 25, believing that Adams had probably 'eased' many others out of this world after influencing them to change their wills in his favour.

But none of this came to light at the Old Bailey. Adams was acquitted after a classic courtroom duel between the then Attorney-General, Sir Reginald Manningham-Buller QC, and a brilliant defence lawyer, Geoffrey Lawrence.

Lawrence disliked his client intensely but he fought tigerishly, turning the Attorney-General's over-confidence against him in a brilliant tactical coup which is still re-called and admired by lawyers. Manningham-Buller was certain he would destroy Adams once he had him in the witness-box. Lawrence simply told Adams to exercise his right to remain silent – and thus avoid cross-examination. It was that, the police and prosecution believed, that saved him from the rope. For with the linchpin of the Crown's case snatched away, the jury took just 45 minutes to find him not guilty.

The trial was such a disaster that the Director of Public Prosecutions lost confidence that a conviction on any other charge could be procured. So he announced there would be no further action.

What the jury never knew – and could not in law be told – was that the police had investigated the deaths of a further 400 of his patients. They had also exhumed the bodies of two of the women who had not been cremated. They had prepared cases on the deaths of nine patients and had evidence pointing to the murders of many others.

The police knew that over his 35 years of practice in Eastbourne, Adams had been the beneficiary of 132 wills, amassing £45,000 in cash – worth ten times that today – antique silver, jewellery, furniture and cars, including two Rolls-Royces, from the bequests of dead patients.

So was John Bodkin Adams merely a plausible rogue or was he the most cunning mass murderer of the century?

He was certainly the most fashionable doctor in Eastbourne, a town where the elderly could spend their last days peacefully in genteel retirement. He had arrived there virtually straight from medical school in his native Northern Ireland and built up a good practice with the cream of the town as his patients.

He was an ugly man, only 1.7 m (5 ft 5 in) tall and weighting almost 114 kg (18 stone), with a pink fleshy face, small eyes and thin lips and a rolling chin that sagged over the celluloid collars he wore. But to his elderly women patients he was charming. He caressed their hands and combed their hair.

However, the picture painted by the year-long investigation by Mr Hewitt, then a sergeant, and his 'governor' Detective Chief Superintendent Bert Hannam of the Yard's Murder Squad, was this:

Adams made his victims dependent on his drugs. They craved his morphine and heroin and became addicts. He influenced them to change their wills in his favour. Then they died.

His method, the police claimed, was not startling, shocking or gory. He eased them gently out of life with an overdose of drugs.

Scotland Yard's investigations showed that of all the patients for whom Adams signed death certificates, he explained an improbable 68 per cent as being due to either cerebral haemorrhage or cerebral thrombosis.

Even before the war there was gossip that Adams did his rounds with a bottle of morphia in one pocket and a blank form in the other. In 1936 he had been the beneficiary in the will of Mrs Alice Whitton, to the extent of £3,000 – a substantial amount then. Her niece contested the will in the High Court but Adams won and kept the money.

The tongues continued to wag into the mid-1950s. But it was not until 1956 that police investigations actually began and the evidence started to build, much of it circumstantial.

There was the case of William Mawhood, a wealthy steel merchant, who was such a long-standing friend of Adams that he lent him £3,000 to buy his first house. As Mawhood lay dying, Adams asked his wife Edith to leave the bedside for a moment. She heard Adams say: 'Leave your estate to me and I'll look after your wife.'

Mrs Mawhood rushed back into the bedroom. She said later:

'I grabbed my gold-headed walking stick and struck out at the doctor and chased him around the bed. He ran out of the room and as he dashed down the stairs I threw my stick at him. Unfortunately it missed, and broke a flower vase. I shouted to him to get out of the house. It was the last I wanted to see of him. I certainly would not tolerate the idea of Adams trying to get into my husband's will.'

There was the case of Emily Mortimer, whose family had a strict tradition, designed to keep its fortune intact. Whenever a Mortimer died, the bulk of the estate was divided among the surviving members of the family.

Adams persuaded Emily to break the tradition. In the year she died, she added a codicil to her will, transferring £3,000 worth of shares from the family to the doctor. Shortly before her death, she changed the will again so that Adams received £5,000 and members of the family were cut out. Adams signed the death certificate – the cause of death 'Cerebral thrombosis'.

Police discovered the case of the two old women who were persuaded by Adams to let him sell their house and move into a flat for the good of their health. He then refused to hand over the money from the house sale until forced to do so by a writ two years later.

Statements from local solicitors and bank managers on the doctor's insistent concern with the wills of his patients revealed a host of questionable activities. Visits to banks with patients to change details of wills already made; telephone calls to solicitors insisting on their immediate attendance to change or draw up a new will; a comatose patient who signed his altered will only with an X; wills changed on several occasions so that the deceased were cremated instead of buried as originally stipulated; and 32 cheques for the doctor amounting to £18,000 drawn on one old lady's account in the last few days of her life – and with highly suspect signatures.

Odious as such unprofessional behaviour was, it was not evidence of intent to murder. There was, however, plenty of other evidence . . .

Clara Neil-Miller was an elderly spinster who had lived in genteel retirement with her sister Hilda for 13 years. When Hilda died she left everything to Clara. When Clara died, 13 months later, she bequeathed the bulk of her estate – £5,000 – to Adams.

Three years later the police exhumed both bodies and the post-mortem showed that Clara had died of pneumonia, not coronary thrombosis as Adams had put on the death certificate. Then one of the other guests in the rest home for the elderly where she died told the police:

'Dr Adams was called to Miss Clara the night before she died. She was suffering from influenza. He remained in her bedroom for nearly 45 minutes before leaving. I later became worried as I heard nothing from the room. I opened the door and was horrified by what I saw.

This was a bitterly cold winter's night. The bedclothes on her bed had been pulled back and thrown over the bedrail at the base. Her nightdress had been folded back across her body to her neck. All the bedroom windows had been flung open. A cold gush of wind was sweeping through the room. That is how the doctor had left her.'

Police found that, in addition to the £5,000 bequest, Clara had, in the weeks before her death, made out cheques for £300 and £500 to the doctor. The purpose was not clear. It could not be for medical treatment as, apart from the flu, she was not ill. Nor did she receive much in the way of medicines.

Adams had a financial interest in the rest home and sent many patients there. A potential key witness was the woman who ran it, Mrs Elizabeth Sharp. Ex Detective Chief Superintendent Hewitt recalled:

'Mrs Sharp was on the point of talking when we left Eastbourne for a week's conferences with the Attorney-General in London. She was the witness we needed. She knew much of what went on between Adams and his patients. She knew where the bodies were buried and she was scared and frightened. When we left, she was about to crack.

One more visit was all we needed, but when we

were in London she died. When we got back to to
Eastbourne and heard the news, she had already been
cremated on the doctor's instructions.

I always had a feeling, but no positive clue, that
Adams speeded her on the way. It was too much of a
coincidence when she died.'

Then there was the case of Julia Bradnum, a strong and
healthy 82-year-old until one morning when she woke up
with stomach pains. The doctor was called and remained
in the room with her for five minutes. Ten minutes later
she was dead.

Her body was also exhumed but it was too decomposed
to show much more than that she had not died of the
cerebral haemorrhage Adams' certificate claimed.

Only a few weeks before she died Adams had brought
her a new will. He said something about her other will not
being legal, she later told a friend, Miss Mary Hine. 'She
asked me if I would witness the new one,' Miss Hine said.
'Dr Adams pointed to a spot on the paper where I was to
sign. I turned over the paper to see what I was witnessing,
but Dr Adams put his hand on the writing and turned it
back.'

Another of the doctor's patients was Harriet Maud
Hughes, aged 66, whom Adams had started to treat only
three months before her death of 'cerebral thrombosis'.
She spoke of changing her will in his favour. A few weeks
before her death, she became ill but then recovered sufficiently to go to her bank with the doctor, who asked the
bank manager in her presence to make him the executor of
her will. Afterwards, she told her domestic help: 'You
should have seen the bank manager's face. He was most
surprised at my choice of executor.'

After her death it was discovered that she had added
two codicils to her will. The first that she should be
cremated. The second, added a month later, left £1,000
each to a Mr and Mrs Thurston, acquaintances of Dr

Adams. After the death, the police discovered Adams received 90 per cent of the bequests – giving the Thurstons 10 per cent for the use of their name.

Then there was the case of James Priestly Downs, a wealthy retired bank manager and widower who in his last days tried nine times to sign his will while in a drugged state. On the tenth occasion he signed it with an X. Adams guided his hand. The will left the doctor £1,000. All Mr Downs was being treated for was a fractured ankle. After a fortnight of the treatment, however, he was in a coma. A month later he died.

Annabelle Kilgour was a widow who had been ill for several weeks and was being looked after by a State Registered Nurse, Miss Osgood. One night Adams arrived and said he would give an injection to help her get a good night's sleep.

The nurse was astounded as she watched the doctor give what she regarded as being greatly in excess of the normal dose. 'This will keep her quiet,' he said, and left.

It did. She immediately fell into a coma and died the next morning. When Adams arrived, the nurse told him: 'Mrs Kilgour is dead. You realize, doctor, that you have killed her?'

The nurse later told the Yard men: 'I have never seen a man look so frightened in all my life.'

Once again Adams gave the cause of death as cerebral haemorrhage. In her will, Mrs Kilgour left the doctor a sum of money and an antique clock.

Margaret Pilling, a member of one of Lancashire's richest cotton families, was suffering from nothing more serious than flu when Adams was called to her. Within a fortnight she was practically in a coma. But her family insisted she should go to stay with them.

Her daughter, Mrs Irene Richardson, said later:
'At first we thought she was dying of cancer and that the doctor was being kind by not telling us. But we

held a family conference and decided we were not satisfied with the treatment. Whatever her illness, she was definitely being drugged. Her condition was deteriorating rapidly.'

We took a house for her at Ascot, near one of her relatives. Within a fortnight she was on her feet and at the races. Had I not taken her away, I am quite satisfied she would have died.

But the case that really clinched the matter, as far as the police were concerned, was when Bobbie Hullett, a friend of the Chief Constable Richard Walker, died. Mrs Hullett, a vivacious woman of 49 widowed four months earlier, was not even really ill.

Late in 1955 her husband Jack, a retired Lloyds under-writer, became ill. 'Thank God I have a good doctor,' he told one of his nurses. When he was stricken by a heart condition one night in March the next year, the 'good doctor' sat on his bed and injected a dose of morphia. Seven hours later Jack Hullett died. In his will he left Adams £500. The residue went to Bobbie, who was shocked and grief-stricken. Friends rallied round – none more so than Adams, who prescribed drugs to help her sleep. In four months she was dead.

Perhaps in the beginning the sleeping drugs were a wise practice. But as the weeks passed the dosage was not cut down. The domestic staff said later: 'She staggered downstairs most mornings as though she was drunk.'

One of her closest friends was comedian Leslie Henson. He said: 'Her death shocked me greatly. My wife and I saw her turning into a drug addict. We invited her to our home to get away from everything, but she rushed back after 24 hours to get to her pills again. We saw her disinte-grating mentally through them.'

After her death another of her friends, Chief Constable Walker, began to make a few discreet phone calls. It was established that two days before Bobbie fell into the coma from which she never recovered, she gave Adams a cheque for £1,000. He immediately drove to the bank and asked for a special clearance. Within hours the amount was credited to his account. At the time, Dr Adams' bank accounts had £35,000 in them. With his investment holdings amounting to as further £125,000, he was not exactly in urgent need of money.

At the inquest, Adams was severely criticized by the coroner for his diagnosis and treatment. A number of penetrating questions were asked. Why had he not told his co-doctor, called in as a second opinion, of his patient's depressive medical history? Why had he failed to get proper daytime medical attention for her or had her put in a nursing home? Why, after 34 years as a doctor, did he take the advice of a young house surgeon in administering a new drug? Why had he failed to call in a psychiatric consultant? And why had he persisted in his diagnosis of a cerebral catastrophe after a pathologist had suggested it might be poisoning?

The doctor replied: 'I honestly did what I thought was best for her.'

The coroner was unimpressed. 'There has been an extraordinary degree of careless treatment,' he said.

And that was the moment that Chief Constable Walker called in Scotland Yard.

So what went wrong? Why, in the face of all this evidence, was John Bodkin Adams not charged with other offences? Why did the prosecution choose to concentrate on the case of Edith Morrell, the 72-year-old widow of a wealthy Liverpool shipping merchant?

One prosecution lawyer said afterwards: 'We chose it because it was such a clear and obvious case of murder that I should have thought no jury could have regarded it in any other way.'

But Mr Hewitt says:

'Adams was allowed to escape because the law made an ass of itself. I will never forget the conference we had with Manningham-Buller in the Attorney-General's office at the House of Commons. Bert Hannam and I felt sick with disbelief when he announced he was going for Mrs Morrell. It was madness when we had so many better cases, with more specific evidence – and, what's more important, with bodies.

Mrs Morrell had been cremated. This meant we could not use evidence of the best forensic scientist of the day, Dr Francis Camps. But Manningham-Buller was so arrogant he would not listen to his junior counsel, Melford Stevenson and Malcolm Morris, or Mr Leck of the Director of Public Prosecutions' office.

He knew the doctor was a worried man and he would destroy him in the witness-box. But it never happened because Manningham-Buller never considered for a moment that Adams might not be called to give evidence.'

Adams came to trial on 25 April 1957 – six years after Mrs Morrell's death. Prosecution witnesses testified that over a period of six weeks, Adams had prescribed a massive dose of more than 4,000 grains of barbiturate and heroin for Mrs Morrell.

The British Pharmaceutical Association's recommended maximum daily dosage was a quarter morphia grain. But in the last day of her life Adams injected into his barely conscious patient 18 grains of the drug, they said.

But Geoffrey Lawrence managed to discover the nurses' daily record books which gave a more accurate account of the medicine Adams prescribed than the memories of the nurses themselves. Then came his master stroke of not putting Adams into the box.

Three months after his acquittal Adams appeared at Lewes Assizes and pleaded guilty to 14 charges, including the forgery of National Health Service prescriptions and failing to keep a record of dangerous drugs. He was fined £2,400 and ordered to pay costs. In November that year he was struck off by the General Medical Council.

On 22 November 1961, at the age of 62, he was re-admitted to the medical register, an event which went largely unnoticed. Only the Home Office retained some doubts: his licence to dispense dangerous drugs was never returned.

His practice in Eastbourne picked up again, although never to its previous size. In 1965, a grateful patient left £2,000 to Adams in her will.

Shortly before his death Adams was interviewed at his Eastbourne home. He refused to talk about his personal life. 'I don't want any more publicity,' he said. 'I have had too much of it. God knows, I have.'

The Nazis' Gold

War is the ideal cover for crime. World war provides an even more effective diversion. While the Nazi war machine fanned across Europe in World War 2, a criminal operation was carried out on the most colossal scale . . .

Quite simply, Adolf Hitler and his generals set about systematically stealing the untold wealth of conquered countries in an orgy of blatant crime-for-profit. Like 20th-century pirates, they planned to make themselves rich in plunder at the expense of their victims. They stole not only the few miserable possessions of the millions of Jews they sent to the death camps. They literally stripped sovereign nations of their entire wealth – billions and billions of pounds in gold and diamonds and works of art. From the treasure houses of the former Czars, deep inside Russia, to the art galleries of Paris and the bank vaults of Rome, the Nazis stole and stole and stole.

Even decades after the end of the war, many governments still refuse to admit the extent of the fortunes stolen from them by the Nazis. Intelligence experts on both sides of the Iron Curtain estimate that as much as £50 billion worth of gold is still unaccounted for and that hundreds of Nazi crooks and their families are leading lives of luxury on the proceeds of the biggest robbery in history.

Much of the missing billions is still probably hidden inside Germany, sunk out of reach at the bottom of lakes or in the depths of collapsed mine shafts. Fortunes in gold were certainly channelled through Swiss bank accounts into the coffers of South American governments who charged £5 million a head to give sanctuary to fleeing Nazi criminals at the end of the war. But stunned and sickened by the debris of the war, grimly completing the task of counting the toll in death and destruction, the Allied forces gave a low priority to tracking down stolen cash and bullion. By the time they started trying to recover the astronomical sums of wealth stolen by the Nazis, the fortune had vanished into the creaking remains of the international banking system. Stolen Nazi gold is undoubtedly the basis for many of the multi-national businesses which flourish today.

In their panic-stricken flight, however, many Nazis found the sheer bulk of their loot impossible to move and they literally dumped billions by the roadsides of Europe. Even now those caches of casually hidden treasure are being uncovered. In June 1983 workmen renovating the well of an abandoned monastery in northern Italy, near the Austrian border, found the shaft blocked by heavy metal chests. They finally raised them, and counted 60 tons of gold, worth more than £540 million at 1983 prices.

An embarrassed Italian government then admitted publicly for the first time that the Nazis, their wartime Allies, had emptied the Central Bank of Rome in 1944 and had made off with 120 tons of gold. The scramble to prove ownership of the gold brought a counter-claim from neighbouring Yugoslavia that the bullion was just part of the reserves from their own national bank in Zagreb, looted by Nazi occupying forces and loaded into a convoy of trucks to be driven back to the Fatherland.

Throughout the history of warfare, victorious soldiers have plundered and looted their vanquished opponents. The looters have ranged from humble infantrymen who 'liberated' enemy wine cellars to high-ranking officers who commandeered whole castles for their private estates. Their motto: To the victor belong the spoils.

For Adolf Hitler's Third Reich, however, there was to be no petty thieving. With Teutonic thoroughness, the thefts were to be carried out on a grand scale, meticulously planned and on the direct orders of the Führer himself. Organized bank robbery was as much a declared war policy of the Nazis as the conquest of Europe and the mass murder of the Jews. The formation of an official looting department in the Nazi government was born out of Hitler's smouldering resentment of his fellows.

As a brooding teenager, Adolf Hitler moved to the Austrian town of Linz in 1903, after the death of his father in their home town of Braunau, some 20 miles away. He struggled through school, ignored by teachers and disliked by his fellow pupils, nursing only an ambition to become an artist. When his mother died in 1908, Hitler, then 19 years old, felt free to leave Linz and take his meagre talents to the glittering Austrian capital of Vienna. He marvelled at the city's splendid galleries and museums and his first call was on the Academy of Fine Arts where he applied for enrolment as a student. The Academy examiners were unimpressed with his barely competent portfolio of drawings and recommended he try for training elsewhere, perhaps in the less demanding profession of apprentice draughtsman.

For the next few years, until he left for Munich in 1913, Hitler seethed with anger as he scraped a miserable living in doss-houses, selling his poorly painted watercolours to bar-room patrons who pitied him because he looked so ragged and pathetic. The experience left him with a sense of humiliation which remained with him for more than 20 years, until he became the all-powerful Führer and annexed Austria into the Greater Germany. That is when Hitler became master of Vienna – and had his revenge on the city he despised.

As he planned to launch war on the rest of Europe, so Hitler also planned his artistic revenge on the cultured city of Vienna. In March 1938, while basking in a rapturous welcome from the citizens of the drab town of Linz, his adopted home, he summoned the director of the town's provincial museum, Dr Karl Kerschner. 'I will make Linz the art capital of the world,' he promised him. 'It will have the finest treasures all of Europe can provide. I will make those ungrateful peasants of Vienna feel they are living in a slum.'

Then Hitler, the failed artist, began to sketch out his amateur architectural plans for rebuilding the city, centred around his dream of a Führer museum which would be crammed with paintings and sculpture, tapestries and rare books, and all the golden treasures he could loot from the four corners of Europe. He sent for his squat, blood-thirsty deputy, Martin Boormann, and instructed him: 'Wherever German tanks roll, I want them to bring back to Linz all the treasures they can carry.'

And so was formed Sonderauftrag Linz – the Linz Special Mission – history's only example of a select gang of gold bullion robbers, diamond, jewel and art thieves, armed with bombers, tanks, high explosives and carte blanche to murder on behalf of their Government. But before the looting gangs bothered to turn their attentions to the treasure houses beyond Germany's boundaries, they first set out ruthlessly stripping the fortunes of their own tortured Jewish population.

While Hitler ordered vaults to be built inside the air-raid shelters of Munich as temporary store-rooms for the Linz collection, his special squad began to 'confiscate' the belongings of Jewish families. Their first target was Baron Louis von Rothschild, the richest man in Austria. Rothschild was arrested by the Gestapo and interrogated by Hitler's roving art and bullion assessor, Dr Hans Posse of the Dresden Art Museum.

Baron Louis was stripped of all his possessions, as a colossal ransom to allow him and his family to leave the country and escape from Nazi persecution. His priceless collection of gold coins was seized, together with all his valuable works of art including paintings by Van Dyck, Holbein, Tintoretto and Gainsborough.

Fortunes fell into Nazi hands even before their armies began to cross the borders into the Netherlands, Belgium and France. As fear and panic spread through the wealthy and well-to-do classes of Europe, Jews and non-Jews alike, homes and possessions were sold at give-away prices and the dwindling assets of great merchant families began pouring into the banks of neutral Switzerland.

Martin Bormann was one of the Nazi hierarchy given the task of trying to harass and bully the Swiss bankers into handing over the accounts of clients whose funds had been earmarked for seizure by the German government. Scornfully oblivious to the wrath of the Nazis, the bank managers of Geneva and Basle stood firm. They would not even discuss the identities of their clients. Ironically, a few years later, that lesson was not to be lost on the Nazi leaders who had cursed the tight-lipped Swiss money men.

As Hitler's war machine rumbled through Europe, with the Führer's hand-picked vultures following in their tracks, the section leaders of Sonderauftrag Linz were swamped. They could no longer cope with the tidal wave of treasure which began piling up in the Munich air-raid shelters. They were furiously building new offices to house the records of their glittering hoard when the most glittering prize of all fell into their hand – Paris.

Enough gold and works of art had already been allocated to the Linz project to transform the town many times over. And now the untold wealth of the Louvre, the Palace of Versailles and the vaults of the Bank of France were at their mercy. Even veteran looter Hans Posse was overwhelmed. So another unit was established specially to supervise the pillage of Paris. Art expert Alfred Rosenberg was given his own top priority organization to strip France of its national heritage and to transport the country's wealth back to Germany.

Rosenberg, son of an Estonian shoemaker, set about his task with gusto, hampered only by the overwhelming greed of the obese Luftwaffe chief Hermann Goering. The air marshal could not resist setting out to build up his own personal fortune, diverting train loads of looted art works and gold to his own private estate, Karinhall, near Berlin.

For four years the Nazi leaders stole everything they could lay their hands on. From Russia came the treasure of the palaces of Emperor Alexander and Empress Catherine. While German infantrymen died of starvation and exposure trying to capture the cities of Stalingrad and Leningrad, the looting sections plundered a total of 427 museums and banks, transporting their booty back to Berlin in fifty special trains each month.

The bank vaults of Poland and Czechoslovakia were stripped and two thirds of the national wealth of Belgium and Holland were stolen. By 1944 it was estimated that the Nazis had plundered a staggering total of £15 billion from occupied countries, worth about twenty times that amount at present-day prices. Goering's own personal fortune was built on his share of 21,903 objects of art shipped back from France.

Then the tide of war turned against the Nazis. Hitler's dream of his Imperial Museum at Linz began to crumble as Allied bombers hit deeper and deeper into the heart of Germany. With defeat staring them in the face, the Nazis scrambled to dispose of their loot. The salt mines of the remote Austrian village of Alt Ausee were crammed with art treasures and gold; the Hohenfurth monastery, just inside the Czech border, was filled with diamonds and the castle of Schloss Neuschwanstein, near Fussen, Bavaria, packed with bullion. For the demented Führer there was no hiding place where he could scuttle for safety. But those of his accomplices who thought they could save their own skins met in Berlin to form the secret organization Odessa, devoted to financing the escape of the most wanted men in Europe. At their disposal were billions of pounds. War criminals like Bormann, death camp doctor Joseph Mengele and extermination leaders Adolf Eichmann and Walter Rauff began to bless the secrecy of Swiss banks. Using the same well-oiled banking system which had helped to protect some of their victims a few years earlier, the Odessa men funnelled gold through secret accounts to buy themselves new identities and safety in South America. Vast ranches and villas throughout Argentina, Bolivia, Paraguay and Chile were established on the stolen wealth of the men who were never caught, whose crimes are still unpunished. Odessa spent recklessly to finance its fugitives, but it is certain that pockets of Nazi gold still lie undiscovered throughout Europe.

In 1982 Danish naval divers trying to locate sunken Nazi gold in Lake Ornso, in central Jutland, came under sniper fire. The theory police came up with at the time was that it was from a former Gestapo informer who feared the hoard might reveal details of his collaboration in looting Danish banks.

During the final collapse of Germany in May 1945, the most bizarre bank robbery in history took place as American and Russian troops raced each other into the heart of Berlin. The Americans were ordered by General Eisenhower to storm the Reichsbank in Berlin, blow the vaults and transport the contents by jeep and truck back behind American lines for safekeeping. The troops responded enthusiastically, but some £200 million in gold and negotiable Swiss securities went missing on the journey back to American headquarters. Three and a half decades later, in April 1979, three men in Ontario, Canada, were jailed for trading in some of those missing war-time securities. It is also estimated that American soldiers and stragglers from the Germany Army helped themselves to £90 million in gold bullion, foreign exchange and jewels from the bank. Not a penny was ever recovered and not a single soldier charged with robbery.

But South America was not the only final resting place for missing Nazi gold. In the United States and Europe the fortunes of respectable business empires thrive today on the proceeds of Nazi looting during World War 2. Yet the wartime Allies have decided that the scandalous details of history's most massive unsolved robberies will never be published. At the headquarters of the British secret service and the World War 2 Records Division of the National Archives in Washington, the files holding the names of the worst criminals and the details of their crimes will remain Most Secret until well beyond this century.

The Unpaid Debt

They called him Mr Big – the playboy gambler who could fix anything from a roulette wheel or stud poker game to the World Series baseball tournament. He lived a life of luxury and thought nothing of betting $4,000 on odd or even car number plates passing his hotel-room window. He won and lost fortunes on horses and cards; he bought and sold cops, politicians and financiers and was rarely seen without a beautiful showgirl on his arm.

Even on the day he was gunned down – 4 November 1928 – he was trying to talk his way out of an $80,000 gambling debt. But that debt, the one thing Arnold Rothstein could not fix, led to his shooting outside Park Central Hotel, New York.

Police were certain Rothstein knew his killer. Only half an hour before the shooting he took a telephone call in a Broadway restaurant. As he left, he told the head waiter: 'George McManus wants me.' Yet Rothstein died in hospital two days later, from a bullet wound in the stomach, without naming his killer. The only thing he did on his deathbed was to make a will – providing generously for his wife Carolyn, for Ziegfeld Follies showgirl Inez Norton (she got more than $100,000) and for friends.

Perhaps the oddest aspect was that the police had plenty of clues – an overcoat, four glasses and revolver – yet they failed completely to get a conviction. The owner of the overcoat was another gambler, George McManus. The glasses and revolver were covered in fingerprints, some of them almost certainly those of known hoodlums. Only McManus was charged with the murder. He pleaded not guilty and was acquitted because of insufficient evidence. That was the end of the police investigation. Nobody else was charged and the case went on the 'unsolved' files.

There was talk at the time that McManus and his henchmen had 'nobbled' the cops. The then police commissioner was soon swept out of office. It is also possible that the police may have taken the view that since Rothstein was part of the underworld, his killer had done society a service . . .

In his 46 years Rothstein had become the 'King of the Gamblers'. He hobnobbed with gangsters such as Al Capone, Dion O'Bannion and Big Jim Colosimo and wagered around $10,000,000 on games of chance. He once backed Jack Dempsey to beat Jess Willard in a world heavyweight fight and won $200,000. He picked up $300,000 when he backed Gene Tunney against Dempsey. And in what he described as the 'biggest gamble of my life' he won almost $300,000 when a horse called Sidereal won at the Aqueduct track, Long Island, on Independence Day, 1921, at odds of 30–1.

Poker was another of his passions – and it was this that was to cost him his life. He sat in on a stud poker game with George McManus and other gamblers including 'Titanic' Thompson, so-called because of his reputation for 'sinking' opponents. At the end of two days and nights Rothstein owed $150,000. His biggest creditor, Nathan Raymond, to whom he owed $80,000, was in no mood to wait for his money. Rothstein had never welshed on a bet in his life. But this poker debt was to prove the exception. One underworld theory was that Rothstein had suspected he had been cheated, though he never made any accusation. It would certainly explain his reluctance to settle up – for he had assets to cover the debt many times over.

Over the next few weeks the gangster-gamblers put the squeeze on. But still Rothstein refused to pay up. Then on that fateful Sunday night in November, Rothstein went to Room 439 at Park Central Hotel to make his excuses to McManus.

The theory is that there was a lot of whiskey drunk and a lot of shouting – then McManus or one of his henchmen pulled a gun. Rothstein tried to wrest the gun from his killer, but in the struggle it went off and Rothstein fell to the floor. McManus and his gang fled, throwing the gun out of the window. Somehow Rothstein then staggered down two flights of stairs to the street. Police believe that Rothstein was murdered in the heat of the moment. Only one shot was fired – and gangsters intent on murder, they reasoned, usually pumped their victims full of lead.

But they are just theories. And George McManus, the

one man who could have proved or disproved them, died in New Jersey in 1940 of natural causes.

The Black Widow

For a woman who did very little farming, widow Belle Gunness ate very well. While her neighbours in La Porte, Indiana, raised crops, Belle planted bodies and produced a bumper yield of dollars.

Once she had been Mads Sorenson's wife – but thanks to a stein of beer she gave him in their home on Lake Michigan, their marriage did not last long. The beer was generously laced with strychnine, and the self-made widow had Mads cremated before the insurance investigators knew what has happening. The company objected, but the policy brought her $8,500.

She had no trouble finding a new husband. At 31, Belle was still an attractive woman. It was an attraction that was to prove fatal for real estate promoter Peter Gunness of La Porte. Belle married Gunness and had three children – two girls and a boy – and a domestic life with which she was satisfied till the day the money ran out.

One day in December 1902, Gunness told Belle he was down to his final asset: a $10,000 insurance policy that would have to be cashed. He had invested everything in real estate options near a railroad that had never been built. Belle helped him find the policy and went with him to the door. As he turned to kiss her goodbye, she raised a meat cleaver and smashed it into his skull.

Gullible police accepted her story that Gunness had slipped on the icy pathway and had split his own skull against the doorstep. But the insurance underwriters were more suspicious and there was an investigation that lasted for months before Belle could cash her second husband's cheque.

Belle then began to publish advertisements in the lonely hearts columns of a Minneapolis newspaper. The bait was her sumptuous 12-room house on a 75-acre farm 'adjoining a boulevard'. And even more tempting to greedy or lonely men were her personal charms. She picked through the replies with care. She wanted men without relatives – but with plenty of cash.

George Berry of Tusca, Illinois, came first, in July 1905. He had obediently brought his life savings, $1,500 in cash. But he was puzzled by the sight of Belle, who had now become fat, walked with a waddle and had a growth of hair on her lip. She decoyed him from the station to her farmhouse with assurances that she was only the beautiful widow's maid. And while he waited patiently for the beauty to appear, she approached him through a side door with a well-honed axe in hand.

In the next year the farm had three other visitors all with their nest-eggs in hand. None were to leave.

In 1908 the black widow's pit claimed two more bodies. One was Andrew Helgelien, who wrote to Belle from Aberdeen, South Dakota – but chose to conceal the fact that he had an older brother named Asle.

When Asle heard nothing from his brother for two weeks, he sent a pointed letter of inquiry to Mrs Gunness. The widow replied that her Andy had mysteriously disappeared and begged Asle to come to La Porte and join her in the quest, bringing with him all the money he could raise. But the man who arrived was not Asle at all, it was the sheriff of La Porte county, tipped off by the suspicious brother. The widow pleaded for time. She had just heard from Andy, she told the sheriff, and would be able to produce the missing man if he came again the following day.

But the sheriff had to return to the murder farm before the end of the day. He was greeted by a curtain of red flame against the sky. It was the Gunness farmhouse, its old timbers reduced to charcoal in a matter of minutes.

Under freshly turned earth at the back of the barn, the sheriff found six corpses. The first was that of Andrew Helgelien. In the ashes of the house were four more bodies – three of them small, one large. Belle and her children?

The authorities wanted to believe so, but there was macabre evidence which meant they could never close the file on Belle Gunness. A witness said that an hour before the fire he had seen the widow drive past his farm with a wagon and a team of horses. And in one of the local cemeteries next day, there were reports of mysterious vandalism – the gravestones of an adult and three children had been dislodged.

Unrelenting to the end of his life, Asle Helgelien went on looking for the widow. He never found her.

The Wreck of the Chantiloupe

When winter storms lash the sea to boiling and great waves pound across the bay, villagers snug in their cottages shudder at the memory of a hideous crime that taints them still. There are those who swear that, above the roar of the wind and breakers crashing on the shore, they have heard the screams of men and women who perished in a shipwreck more than 200 years ago.

But not all those who died were victims of the cruel elements. At least one, a wealthy woman passenger, was killed for her jewellery by heartless looters. Their names have remained a shameful secret ever since.

In summer, Thurlestone Sands, in south Devon, ring with the happy laughter of romping children, and the sun-bathers soak up the warmth. But in winter, long after the last holidaymaker has gone home, as the gales howl in from the Atlantic, it is easy to picture the last moments of the Plymouth-bound brig *Chantiloupe* in 1772.

It had been a smooth voyage from the West Indies but,

as she neared port, a south-westerly gale blew up so suddenly that there was no time to turn into it. The captain's only choice was to run before it, past Plymouth and up the Channel. Soon, with massive cliffs looming ahead, he was forced to strike sail and drop all anchors. But nothing could hold the *Chantiloupe* against the raging wind and sea, and the captain decided on a desperate gamble to save his passengers and crew.

Ordering full sail, he altered course by a few degrees and headed directly for the smooth, golden carpet of Thurlestone Sands. He told passengers and crew that he aimed to run his ship high up on the beach, so they could all jump to safety.

The passengers hurried to their cabins to collect what valuables they could. One of them, Mrs James Burke, whose nephew was the famous Whig politician Edmund Burke, came on deck in her finest gown wearing all her jewels.

The small ship raced for the shore as though on wings, carried on the shoulders of mighty waves, and it seemed the captain's daring bid would succeed. But one wave, higher than the rest, suddenly hoisted the stern. The keel beneath the bows struck bottom and the *Chantiloupe* swung broadside, almost capsizing under the next wave.

All on board were hurled into the raging sea, and most died within minutes. But Mrs Burke struck out the shore and, miraculously, reached it alive. Gratefully she let strong hands grasp her and pull her from the water.

But these three men were not rescuers . . . they were thieves and killers. Barely had her last scream been carried away by the wind before they were fighting over her jewels.

They ripped off her earrings and, finding her rings too tight to remove, hacked off her fingers. Then they buried her in the sand, and soon the raging sea had washed away any traces of the killing.

Perhaps it would never have come to light, if a man had

not happened to walk his dog past the burial spot two weeks later. He was Daniel Whiddon, later to be immortalized in the folk song 'Uncle Tom Cobleigh'. His dog began scrabbling in the sand and unearthed Mrs Burke's body.

The secret was out, and the local paper reported the crime in these words:

'The savage people from the adjacent villages, who were anxiously waiting for the wreck, seized and stript her of her clothes, even cutting off some of her fingers and mangling her ears in their impatience to secure the jewels and left her miserable to perish.'

There was an autopsy, which showed that Mrs Burke was alive when she reached the shore. An inquest, before the jury of local men, returned the verdict: 'Murder by person or persons unknown.'

There can be no doubt that some people in the nearby villages of Thurlestone Sands, Galmpton, Hope and Bolberry, knew the identity of the killers. But lips were sealed. Edmund Burke himself visited the area to seek the truth, and learned nothing.

More than 100 years later, the Rev Frank Coope, Rector of Thurlestone from 1897 to 1921, probed the mystery. He wrote: 'It was well known in the neighbourhood who did it, and their surnames are remembered to this day. The three men who were "in it" all came, it is said, to a bad end within the year. One hanged himself in an outhouse, another went mad, ran into the sea and was drowned, and the third was killed in an accident.'

Was this the truth – or a tale to put the rector off the scent?

Today the neatly thatched villages around Thurlestone Sands are picturesque and welcoming. But behind the whitewashed walls and stout oak doors, there may still be families who know the names of the those long-ago killers.

Vanishing
Tricks

The Disappearing Parachutist

The skyjacker who commandeered the Northwest Airlines Boeing 727 flight from Portland, Oregon, to Seattle, Washington, was cold, calculating and ruthless. He terrified the cabin staff when he opened the canvas bag he was carrying in his lap and showed them a home-made bomb – tightly wrapped sticks of dynamite packed round a detonator.

As the jet cruised at 6,000 m (20,000 ft) above the Cascade Mountains, he threatened to blow apart the aircraft, killing himself and the 35 other passengers on board.

But the man who cruelly bargained with the lives of the passengers and the crew pulled off such a daring and lucrative coup he is now fondly remembered as a folk hero, a swashbuckling pirate of the jet age. Songs have been written in his honour, fan clubs have been formed to cherish his memory and thousands of his admirers wear T-shirts emblazoned with his name. The souvenir industry and the posters in praise of D. B. Cooper would undoubtedly carry his photograph and glowing testimonials about his personal history – if anyone knew what he looked like or who he really was.

But the true identity of the man who literally vanished into thin air with his $200,000 booty still remains a mystery. No-one knows who he was, where he came from or where he went.

D. B. Cooper may be a frozen corpse, a broken body lying in a mouldering heap of banknotes in an impenetrable forest in the mountains of the northwestern United States. Or he may be sunning himself on a beach in Mexico and gloating over his perfect crime.

The last confirmed sighting of D. B. Cooper came from the pilot of the Boeing air liner from which the skyjacker leaped clutching a white cloth bag containing ten

115

thousand $20 bank notes. Cooper vanished into thin air at 2,000 m (7,000 ft) as the air whistled past in a 90 metre per second (200 mph) slipstream at a temperature of –23°C (–10°F).

That was the last time 'D. B. Cooper' was seen. The first time was in the departure lounge at Portland Airport, Oregon, when he bought his one-way ticket for the 400-mile journey to Seattle, Washington. It was 24 November 1971 – Thanksgiving Day – and the other travellers were all anxious to get home to their families for the annual holiday celebration.

The quiet middle-aged man with the canvas carrier bag and dark, tinted glasses paid cash for his ticket and gave his name as 'D. B. Cooper'. After a 45-minute wait in the lounge, where no one looked at him twice, he filed aboard when the flight was called and the jet roared off into the darkening skies.

Halfway through the one-hour flight, Cooper pushed the button in the overhead panel to summon one of his cabin crew to his seat. Stewardess Tina Mucklow approached with a tray, ready to take his order for a drink.

Cooper simply thrust a crumpled note into her hand and then reached under his seat to pull his canvas bag on to his lap. He waited a few seconds for the stewardess to read the note. It warned: 'I have a bomb with me. If I don't get $200,000 I will blow us all to bits.'

As the terrified stewardess tried to control her panic, Cooper calmly opened the bag to let her glimpse the dynamite and detonator inside. While the girl walked slowly up to the flight deck, Cooper settled back in his seat and peered out at the storm clouds below.

Within seconds a special transmitter on the flight deck of the Boeing was 'squawking' its coded electronic message over the radio frequencies . . . 'Hijack . . . Hijack . . . Hijack'

At Seattle Airport a team of FBI agents, local police

sharpshooters, hostage negotiation experts and airline officials were hastily gathered as the plane prepared to land. The passengers were still unaware of the drama when the jet came in for a perfect touchdown and rolled gently to a halt at the end of the runway.

There was a groan of annoyance from the impatient travellers when the captain made the terse announcement: 'Ladies and gentlemen, there will be a slight delay in disembarking. Please remain in your seats until we are ready to taxi to the terminal building.'

Only one passenger ignored the announcement. Cooper unbuckled his seat belt and, clutching his bag, walked swiftly up to the flight deck and positioned himself behind the crew. 'Now gentlemen,' he said softly, 'don't bother to look round.'

In 20 minutes of unyielding demands over the ground control radio from the flight deck of the airliner, Cooper stuck to his original threat and no one dared to call his bluff.

As the passengers began to grow more and more restless, there was a hiss of pneumatic power and the forward door of the Boeing slid open. The flight engineers in overalls – undercover armed FBI men – came aboard with a trolley of 'catering equipment'. They clearly saw the figure of the man with the canvas bag watching them from the flight deck door, then, under instructions by two-way radio from their superiors, they withdrew and the door slid closed and locked again.

The trolley was wheeled up to the flight deck by a stewardess and Cooper studied its contents. It contained a tough white sack with $200,000 and two backpack and two chestpack parachutes.

Cooper complained that he wanted the money in a rucksack which he could have strapped to his body. But he quickly relented and told the pilot: 'You can let the passengers go now.'

Loudly complaining, the unsuspecting travellers filed off the aircraft to a waiting bus and Seattle ground control breathed a sigh of relief. But they were still left with the problem of Cooper in charge of the aircraft and its three-man crew as the jet was refuelled to maximum capacity by two giant tankers.

Minutes before the Boeing took off again, three military pursuit fighters and a small fleet of helicopters were scrambled from Seattle Airport and a nearby US Air Force base with orders to try to keep the jet in sight.

'We are heading for Mexico now,' Cooper told the pilot, Captain W. Bill Scott. But 10 minutes after take-off he issued new instructions.

As the aircraft climbed away from Seattle and headed south, Cooper insisted with calm precision: 'Fly with the flaps lowered 15 per cent and the landing gear down, keeping the speed below 90 metres per second (2000 mph), don't climb above 2,000 m (7,000 ft) and open the rear door.'

'We'll burn up too much fuel,' Captain Scott protested. 'We'll have to put down for some more fuel if we fly like that.'

'OK,' Cooper snapped. 'Stop for refuelling in Reno, Nevada. I'll give you further orders there. Now just fly south and keep the door locked behind you.'

The hijacker paused only briefly on the flight deck to retrieve his ransom note from the captain's tunic pocket. He was determined not to leave any clues behind, not even a sample of his handwriting.

The whole aircraft filled with a deafening roar as the pilot throttled back and lowered the rear door ramp into the slipstream.

When the flight recorder 'black box' was checked later, the sensitive instrument measured a tiny change in the aircraft's altitude, equivalent to the loss of a weight of 73 kg (160 lb) in the tail section. The time was 20.13 hours, 32 minutes after leaving Seattle. That's when D. B. Cooper leaped out.

Four hours later, as the Boeing lost height and glided gently towards the twinkling lights of the airport at Reno in the Nevada Desert, the co-pilot unlocked the flight deck door to warn Cooper that the tail ramp would have to be closed for landing.

The cabin was deserted. Cooper and the money had gone.

Two parachutes had been left behind. A backpack chute was intact but a chestpack was ripped to shreds. Cooper had probably torn it apart to make a harness to strap his sack of money to his body.

The danger of mid-air death and destruction had passed. And the hunt to find D. B. Cooper was on. FBI and Federal Aviation Agency officials who plotted the flight path of the hijacked Boeing quickly realized that Cooper had bailed out over some of the most densely wooded, inhospitable mountains in the American West, where the chances of survival for an inexperienced woodsman were pretty slim. He had plummeted to earth clad only in a lightweight lounge suit, a raincoat and with a pair of flimsy moccasin shoes on his feet. In the thin atmosphere of the high altitude, the parachute would only have slowed him to a bone-crushing 18 metres per second (40 mph) before he hit the mountain peaks which tower up to the same height as the Boeing had flown.

Only a super-fit expert could have hoped to escape alive. Police began detailed and intensive scrutiny of the only group of men who would have the nerve or experience to attempt that kind of death-defying descent – the 'smoke jumpers' of the Forestry Service fire-fighting teams. But they drew a blank. Cooper was not a 'smoke jumper' and the professional experts who are trained to parachute into the high forests with full radio communication and ground support facilities agreed to a man that Cooper's leap from a speeding jet in a rain storm was suicidal.

Aerial searches covering thousands of square miles of the states of Oregon, Washington and Nevada failed to show any trace of a parachute canopy.

Then, three weeks after the hijack, came the first enigmatic clue. A typewritten note, posted in Seattle and signed by D. B. Cooper, arrived at a Los Angeles newspaper. The writer revealed:

'I am no modern-day Robin Hood, unfortunately I have only 14 months to live. The hijacking was the fastest and most profitable way to gain a few last grains of peace of mind. I didn't rob Northwest because I thought it would be romantic or heroic or any of the other euphemisms that seem to attach themselves to situations of high risk.

I don't blame people for hating me for what I've done nor do I blame anyone for wanting me caught or punished – though this can never happen. I knew from the start I would not be caught. I've come and gone on several airline flights since and I'm not holed up in some obscure backwoods town. Neither am I a psychopath, I've never even received a speeding ticket.'

The note sparked off a new hunt for Cooper and as the list of potential suspects dwindled, hundreds of troops from the Fort Lewis Army base in Portland, Oregon, were ordered to comb the mountains searching for clues. They were backed up by spotter planes and even satellite surveillance photographs from orbiting spacecraft.

There was still no sign of Cooper.

But FBI agents were confident that if Cooper had survived the jump, he would be nailed as soon as he tried to spend a penny of the ransom money. The serial numbers of every one of the bank notes in his haul had been noted and all US banks and major money clearing houses abroad had been alerted to raise the alarm as soon as they began to trickle into circulation.

In the meantime the airlines took the costly precaution of ensuring that no one would imitate Cooper's hijack and high level parachute escape ever again. All Boeing 727s were recalled to the manufacturers and their tail door ramps sealed so they could never be opened in flight.

And as the widely publicised FBI manhunt began to lose steam, the mystery hijacker began to gather a cult following from a fascinated public. Graffiti slogans appeared on public buildings and airline advertising hoardings over the Pacific north west – 'D. B. Cooper, where are you?' Disc jockeys dedicated records to Cooper.

A year after the hijack, when FBI officials adopted the official attitude that D. B. Cooper must have died in the parachute fall, they had to admit that there was no sign of the hijack money and that the $200,000 was probably still hidden with his body in the wooded mountains. Then the first group of enthusiastic amateur explorers, calling themselves the 'Ransom Rangers', began scouring the woods in Oregon and Washington, searching for the ransom treasure.

Finally on 24 November 1976, the FBI officially closed the file on D. B. Cooper. Five years had elapsed since the crime, so under the Statute of Limitations if D. B. Cooper was alive, he was now a free man.

And not a single dollar of the ransom money had ever turned up. If Cooper was a corpse in the mountains, the money was there with him, just waiting to be found.

Most of the population of Portland and Seattle seemed to catch 'Cooper fever' and the hills were alive with the sound of marching feet. But they scoured the mountains in vain.

The fever subsided until 1979 when a solitary deer hunter in the dense forest above the village of Kelso, Washington, stumbled across a man-made intrusion in the virgin forest. It was a thick plastic warning sign from the tail door hatch of a Boeing 727. Its futile message read:

'This hatch must remain firmly locked in flight.'

Overnight the village became a boom town as thousands of amateur sleuths stormed the peaks trying to find Cooper's treasure one step ahead of the FBI teams who descended by helicopter. Astrologers, mapmakers and local tourist guides made almost as much money as Cooper's missing loot from the hopeful punters.

'The mountains were almost trampled flat by the crowds,' admitted State Police Inspector Walter Wagner. 'But none of us found a thing.'

Had Cooper got clean away with all the cash?

That riddle was partially solved seven and a half years after the hijacking.

Industrial painter Harold Ingram and his son Brian, eight, were wading along the sandy shore of the Columbia River just outside the Washington state border when they stirred up a bundle of weathered banknotes from the river bank.

The money amounted to about $3,000 of Cooper's cash, according to one of the 30 FBI men who cordoned off the Ingrams' family picnic site and fought off the new wave of treasure seekers.

Scientific tests on the bank notes and the mud caked around them showed that the money had probably been washed downstream six years before from an area 80 km (50 miles) upstream – on any one of hundreds of tributaries higher up the mountain range.

The hunters vanished over the rocky skyline, sawing and digging their way through the forests once more.

'That's the closest we ever came to him,' Special Agent John Pringle of the FBI reported. 'But we are still looking for an invisible needle in a mountain range of haystacks.'

If D. B. Cooper is still alive, he can freely identify himself to the FBI now. The legal time limit on his crime means he will never face a criminal prosecution for the Thanksgiving Day hijacking. But there is probably one big obstacle which could prevent the world's only successful skyjacker from coming forward . . .

The FBI may have given up, but at the offices of the Internal Revenue in the nation's capital in Washington DC on the file on D. B. Cooper remains open forever.

The skyjacker faces a bill for $300,000 – more than his ransom haul – and a 10-year jail sentence for failing to file income tax returns.

The taxman explained:

'We tax illegal money just as we tax legal money; it's all income as far as we are concerned.

D. B. Cooper became $200,000 dollars richer after the hijack and he never paid his tax on that money. Now he owes us interest on that sum and penalty payments. We have assessed his tax liability as a bachelor with no dependants and no additional source of income. If he wants to arrange an appointment with our auditors to claim some allowances and expenses we will be happy to meet him.

Until then we are still looking for Mr D. B. Cooper, and his assets. There is no Statute of Limitations for tax dodgers.'

The Canine Sherlock Holmes

It stands, just over 0.3 m (1 ft) high, as the ultimate, golden goal of some of the world's greatest sporting stars. Whether held high in triumph or simply coveted from afar, the Jules Rimet Trophy is the prize of prizes in the field of professional soccer.

It has embraced the dreams of hundreds of nations, of legendary players such as the great Pele and of literally millions of waving, cheering fanatics from all corners of the globe.

It is more commonly known as the World Cup – a once-in-a-lifetime reward every four years to one country and its eleven most gifted, idolized footballers.

Such is the occasion of its presentation that it is passed into the hands of the football players only from those of kings and queens, presidents and prime ministers.

When it was brought to England a few weeks before the start of the 1966 World Cup tournament it was promptly stolen. The cup over which rival countries had, through the years, fought so bitterly – even off the playing field and in the political arena – was pilfered from a stamp exhibition at London's Central Hall, Westminster, where it had been on display. It was considered an international scandal.

Scotland Yard was summoned immediately. Questions were asked in parliaments around the world. Huge rewards from all sorts of organizations were offered for the cup's safe return. Outside England the mood was hostile and angry, especially in those nations where soccer seems almost to vie with religion for the hearts and souls of the people. No cost or effort was to be spared to restore not only a football trophy, but also national pride, to its rightful place.

The police who had been ordered in hot pursuit of the World Cup thief or thieves found themselves on a cold trail. The trophy had, apparently, vanished into thin air and the hunt for clues or suspects was a bitterly frustrating one. It was unlikely that anyone would have stolen the cup simply to melt it down. The actual gold content was then worth only about £2,000 despite the fact that it was insured for £30,000. The real value, however, was priceless.

Private collectors, undaunted by dealing on the black market to procure their secret hoards of treasure, would have paid a fortune to have the legendary cup in a hidden vault. This was the only theory on which the beleaguered police could pin any hope.

For a fortnight in early March 1966, the world held its

breath as the desperate search for the stolen cup continued in vain. It was a tragedy of enormous proportions to dedicated followers of football. But, more than that, it was an almighty embarrassment to England, which was playing host to the prestigious tournament for the first time in its sporting history.

It was vital that the cup was found immediately.

Screaming newspaper headlines posed all sorts of questions, some of them unthinkable to the hierarchy of FIFA, soccer's world governing body . . . Was it in the hands of an unscrupulous millionaire? Was it stolen and then simply thrown away to be lost forever when the thief realized the enormity of his crime? Was it being held by a syndicate of villains, waiting to sell it off to the highest bidder?

Had it been melted down or destroyed? The possibilities were endless.

The answer came in the most unexpected – and rather unglamorous – way on the night of 19 March.

David Corbett, a 26-year-old Thames lighterman, was taking a family dog, Pickles, for a walk near his home in Beulah Hill, Norwood, South London, when, out of the corner of his eye, he spotted a glint, a reflection that lasted for jut a split second.

It had come from what had appeared to be a bundle of dirty old newspapers under a laurel bush that Pickles, a cross-bred collie, had been sniffing and pawing at with great interest. Mr Corbett called to his dog. But Pickles would not come.

As David Corbett recalled later:
'I bent under the bush, lifted the top layer of news-papers, and there it was. I knew what it was at once. It was the World Cup.

I think that the first thing I actually saw was an inscription on the cup. The words 'Brazil 1962' were written near the base. I'm a keen football fan and I had been following all the reports in the newspapers. You can imagine how absolutely taken aback I was.

I took it back to our flat to show my wife Jeannie and then we phoned the police, who were as astounded as we were. Yet the truth is that I would not have given the old bundle of newspapers it was wrapped in a sideways glance or a second thought if it hadn't been for Pickles. He was the real hero of the hour.'

Indeed he was. Animal lovers from all over the world began to shower gifts on the canine sleuth. England's National Canine Defence League bestowed on him its highest honour: a silver medal inscribed with the words 'To Pickles, for his part in the recovery of the World Cup, 1966.' At the ceremony at which it was presented, the league's secretary enthused: 'Pickles, by his action, has given prominence to the canine world and so helped us in our task.'

At the same ceremony – and there were many others for the 'furry Sherlock Holmes' as he was dubbed – a hotel pageboy stepped up with a silver salver of further gifts. There was a rubber bone, £53, collected among the hotel's staff – and the best steak for him to eat.

Pickles, oblivious to the importance of the occasion, simply lay down and yawned.

But the still unanswered question was: who actually stole the World Cup? It was a question, despite a number of suspicions, that the police were never to answer.

Yet, as in all unsolved crimes, when the finger of suspicion is pointed, however wrongly, there are people who are bound to suffer. That, amazingly, was the sad plight of none other than Pickles' owner, Mr Corbett. Less than two months after his alertness helped recover the prized trophy, Mr Corbett told a newspaper:

'I wish I'd never seen the damn thing. I was quite excited about it at the time but I seem to have had nothing but trouble since.

When I gave it to the police, they appeared at first not to believe my story about Pickles finding it under a laurel bush. They grilled me. They asked me where I was on the day the cup was stolen, whether I collected stamps, if I had ever been to Central Hall, Westminster, and so on.

Eventually, they believed me. But the trouble didn't end with the police. Ordinary people have been suspecting me of having had something to do with the theft of the cup. My wife and I were in Trafalgar Square and a group of boys saw us. They shouted at me: "He's the one who stole it. Let's drown the dog in the fountain." It was terrible.'

In the end, of course, Mr Corbett was completely vindicated – and received rewards totalling more than £6,000. He did not watch the World Cup itself, but he did join in the spirit of Pickles's success when he allowed the dog to be taken to meet each member of the West German final team – all of whom touched him for luck, hoping they would find the cup theirs at the end of the football match.

But it was not to be. England took the trophy and, thanks to Pickles, who sadly died only four years later, erased memories of the most embarrassing episode in soccer history.

The Missing Murderers

It is more than half a century since Adolf Hitler brought the Nazis to power in Germany. Just 12 years later they were vanquished, leaving behind the evidence of what has been called the greatest crime in history: the annihilation of Europe's Jews.

The Nazis also left behind a maze of mysteries – a criminal enigma of as great a magnitude as the crime itself. For the full story of the massacre of millions of Jews can never be told until all the missing culprits are brought to account. Only then will the question marks that still hang over history's most shameful act ever be removed.

Many of the mysteries surrounding Hitler's attempted genocide were answered when his death-camp supremo, Adolf Eichmann, was captured by the world's chief Nazi hunter Simon Wiesenthal. But Eichmann's trial and execution did nothing to stop the heated debate that continues to this day about how many of those in German government, judiciary, armed forces and civil service knew and condoned the dreadful pogrom.

In 1983 a few more pieces were fitted into the jigsaw after Klaus Barbie, the wartime Gestapo chief in Lyons, was extradited from Bolivia to face trial in France. It was the excuse for Dr Wiesenthal to update his list of the most wanted Nazis still at large.

Asked why, at the age of 76, he still pursued them from his Jewish Documentation centre in Vienna, Wiesenthal said:

'When history looks back on this century I want people to know that the Nazis were not able to kill 11 million people and get away with it. Mine is the last organization in the world still hunting the Nazis. If I stopped, the Nazis and history would say, "The Jews gave up".'

Wiesenthal's list at that time named the ten most wanted Nazis, whom he placed in order of responsibility for crime as well as actual criminal activity. He said: 'I have a compact with the dead. If I could get all ten it would be an achievement. Sometimes I think if I could just get Josef Mengele my soul would finally be at peace.'

At that time, Wiesenthal believed he had located Dr Mengele, No. 3 on his list and known as the 'Angel of Death' of Auschwitz. But Mengele, said to be living in a remote Mennonite religious community on the border of

Bolivia and Paraguay, was thought to be impossible to extradite. He was reported to be a registered refugee and a Paraguayan citizen.

The escaped Nazi leaders have now grown old, however, and despite Dr Wiesenthal's patient efforts, death rather than justice is more likely to catch up with these ten killers in hiding . . .

1. Heinrich Mueller: Chief of the Gestapo.

Mueller was known as the killer with the fountain pen. He would never kill anyone himself. He only wrote out the orders. He very seldom visited a concentration camp or a gas chamber or an execution.

A World War I Army officer, he joined the Bavarian police and only in 1939 the Nazi party – out of necessity rather than belief. Hard-working, he always sheltered under the orders of others, beginning his instructions 'the Reichsführer has ordered' this or that. His industrious, low-profile, comradely but never friendly character led to his appointment as Gestapo general.

Although he himself never killed anybody, he was responsible for the deaths of millions of Jews, prisoners and hostages. He knew every detail about the concentration camps, could quote statistics about inmates and even the death rate at notorious camps like Auschwitz. The bureaucratic killer, who vanished at the end of World War 2, was thought to have died in the Berlin street fighting. But when his grave was opened three skulls were found. Not one of them was Mueller's.

Since then, the Nazi hunters have followed leads that he went over to the Russians, then moved on to Albania. Others tracked him to Spain, then Suez and in 1963 he was confidently identified as a resident in Cairo, safe from the Israelis. Israeli agents were arrested in Frau Mueller's home in Munich but they found no lead to his whereabouts.

His aliases include Jan Belinski, Pole; Amin Abdel Megid and Alfred Mardes, Arab. Officially, his fate and whereabouts are unknown.

2. Richard Gluecks: Inspector-general of all concentration camps.

Less is known about Gluecks than about most Nazi war criminals, except that he was a Gruppenführer, head of the administration bureau of the RHSA, the Reich Security Head Office in overall control of concentration camps.

In 1938, 20,000 Jews were sent to 'protective custody' in these camps. By 1939 six major camps had been established, including the notorious Dachau, Buchenwald and Ravensbrück. Eight others were to follow in the next three years including the most notorious, Auschwitz, where more than a million people died. Gluecks, who ordered deportations and managed the network of camps, vanished without trace. His fate and whereabouts are unknown.

3. Dr Josef Mengele: Chief Medical Officer, Auschwitz concentration camp.

Mengele was accused of being directly responsible for the deaths of 400,000 people. A medical graduate of both Frankfurt and Munich universities – both of which have cancelled his academic qualifications – he was known as 'The Angel of Death' to Auschwitz concentration camp.

As the prisoners filed through the main gate, beneath the sign 'Work Makes Men Free', Mengele would prod them with his stick and order them to be worked to death, to undergo hideous experiments or to be taken directly to the gas chambers. All the time, a band played on.

One of his experiments, aimed at proving Hitler's theory that Germans were a super-race, was to alter the hair and eyes of victims by genetic manipulation. Many who did not die were blinded.

He escaped from West Germany after the war, travelled to Italy and then Argentina, before settling in Paraguay where he became a naturalized citizen in 1973. He took out citizenship papers largely because West Germany, and the Nazi hunters, had located him and were offering vast sums of money in reward for his return.

Mengele had to remain constantly on the move, unable to sleep in the same bed for more than two weeks at a time.

At the end of 1978 and early 1979 his fellow Nazis put about the story that Mengele was dead in order to protect the strong war criminal colony in Paraguay. They even circulated pictures of Mengele on the mortuary slab showing the scar on his right arm where his tattooed SS number had been removed. It was, in fact, the body of SS Captain Eduardo Roschmann who sent 80,000 Jews to their deaths at the concentration camp at Riga, Latvia.

As a Paraguayan citizen, Mengele continued to live in that country under government protection.

4. Walter Rauff: Commander of a unit which provided gas trucks for concentration camps.

Rauff is accused of being responsible, directly and indirectly, for the deaths of 250,000 people – despite the fact that there is little evidence of direct contact between Rauff and his victims.

He was 'the ambulance chief'. His transports looked like ordinary Red Cross ambulances into which Jews and others regarded as racially undesirable were herded. But they were not taken to hospital, as their guards promised. Once inside the 'ambulances', the doors were locked and the guards opened the valves on cylinders attached to the vehicles. The passengers were gassed to death.

According to Weisenthal in 1983, Rauff is alive and well in Chile where he openly ran a meat freezing factory. He was even known to answer letters addressed to him in Punta Arenas, but government protection ensured he was not molested.

At one time Dr Wiesenthal pleaded with Dr Henry Kissinger, then American's roving ambassador, to help secure Rauff's extradition. Dr Kissinger, himself a Jew and of German origin, declined because he could not interfere without compromising himself and his country diplomatically.

Rauff, like Mengele, has been used in a number of works of fiction including Frederick Forsyth's famous novel, *The Odessa File*. But his real post-war existence in South America has been stranger than fiction. Both Mengele and Rauff have been suspected of drug racketeering. The Chileans have had to deny a number of stories about Rauff, notably that the Chilean government was employing him as an anti-Communist agent.

The government at one time denied that Rauff was living in Chile . . . but the former SS colonel's own letters were ample proof to the contrary.

5. Anton Burger: Field officer and assistant to Adolf Eichmann, head of the Gestapo's Department of Jewish Affairs.

Burger was deputy commander of Theresienstadt concentration camp, on the Czech-German border. The 'model' camp was used to dispel stories of Nazi atrocities. It was even opened to neutral visitors to show that stories about the concentration camps were simply Allied propaganda. But behind the scenes, the inmates of Theresienstadt were subject to 'experiments'. Some were to be poisoned. Women were forced to undergo abortions to prevent the increase of the Jewish race. Others were sterilized.

In the hunt for Nazi war criminals Anton Burger was often mistaken for Wilhelm Burger, chief administrator at Auschwitz.

In 1948 Anton Burger escaped from the prison where he was awaiting trial. In the search which ensued the authorities eventually arrested Wilhelm Burger, accused for his part in ordering lorry loads of gas with which to murder Jews to Auschwitz.

Wilhelm was jailed for eight years – but because he had spent eight years in a Polish prison he was freed. Anton vanished and his whereabouts are unknown.

6. Rolf Guenther: Deputy to Adolf Eichmann.

Rolf and his brother, Hans, were both SS majors but it was Rolf, the quiet one, who was entrusted with carrying out Hitler's programme for exterminating the Jews.

When Eichmann was kidnapped in Argentina and returned to Israel to be tried, he accused Guenther of taking a personal initiative in the death camps and of carrying out some orders behind his back. He insisted that Guenther must have had and acted on special orders direct from Mueller, by-passing Eichmann.

The truth was that Guenther had been chosen as Eichmann's second in command because he would willingly carry out the 'final solution' to the Jewish problem. He was sent to remove all Jews from Denmark. He visited Greece, Hungary and other countries as an expert on 'the Jewish problem'.

Ample documentation proves that Guenther had a confidential instruction to arrange sterilization, medical experiments and the gassing of inmates.

Guenther disappeared at the end of the war. His whereabouts are unknown.

7. Alois Brunner: Another of Eichmann's assistants.

According to Wiesenthal's files, Brunner is specially responsible for the deaths of thousands of Jews in Czechoslovakia and Greece.

Like Guenther, he worked for Eichmann in the 'Jewish Museum', a propaganda section at the head office of the Nazi Party. He then moved to the Jewish section of the Gestapo and early in the war was appointed field officer in France.

There he arranged the deportation of, at first, stateless Jews, then foreign Jews and finally French Jews. They were taken to local concentration camps and then mostly to Auschwitz.

As in the case of Guenther, Eichmann tried to maintain that once Brunner had left him to visit some other country he was out of Eichmann's jurisdiction. But Eichmann, who was not believed, and was hanged for his war crimes, left behind considerable evidence, which helps condemn Brunner.

Yet, according to Wiesenthal, in 1983 Brunner was living under Arab protection in Damascus, Syria, under the name of Dr Fisher.

8. Joseph Schwamberger: Another of Eichmann's assistants, former commander of the Jewish ghetto at Prezemysl, Poland.

Before the war about 500,000 Jews lived in Galicia, Poland. Then the Germans came and herded them into ghettos. Schwamberger is thought to have been responsible for the deaths of 15,000 of them. The Warsaw ghetto, where there was bloody revolt, uprising and suppression, was the most infamous. But there were many others.

After the war, Schwamberger, a member of the so-called Odessa escape group, fled to Italy and then to Argentina, where Nazis still received asylum. Despite denials as to his presence, Argentinian police arrested him in 1973 after requests by West Germany that he be extradited.

The powerful group of Nazis resident there intervened. The request was refused – and he was released.

9. Dr Aribert Heim: Director of the concentration camp at Mauthausen, Austria.

In February 1941, the Germans made their first mass arrests in Holland by rounding up 400 Jews in Amsterdam and sending them first to Buchenwald and then to Mauthausen. The Red Cross revealed that only one survived.

The camp's 'death book', found by the Allies, revealed 35,318 deaths, a total which compared with camps like Dachau and Buchenwald.

The inmates had a saying that if you reached Mauthausen, Dr Heim would 'look after you'. The grim truth was that many were taken from the notorious Auschwitz on a death march to Mauthausen. Some survived that march – only to be sent on another to Zeltenlager.

One witness who survived both marches said they were so hungry that when the Allies bombed the area he 'saw people eating human flesh, the flesh of victims of the air raid'.

After the war Dr Heim vanished. His whereabouts are unknown.

10. Friedrich Wartzog: Commander of the Lemberg-Janowska concentration camp, Russia, formerly Poland.

Wartzog is accused of ordering the killing of 40,000 people. Some of the worst evidence against him was given on oath by Eichmann at his trial, when he talked of 'a spring of blood gushing from the earth' where executed Jews had been buried at Lemberg-Janowska.

Prisoners were kept without food for three days, existed on grass and then if found unfit were shot. One hobby of the guards was shooting at the prisoners as they went to work – at their ears, noses, fingers. If they were badly injured an executioner would finish them off.

Wartzog, who presided, escaped. His whereabouts are unknown.

France's Uncrowned King

Before the revolutions of peasants and elected parliaments began to sweep through Europe in the 18th and 19th centuries, the royal dynasties of kings and princes jealously guarded their awesome power with strict codes of bloodline and heritage and succession.

The rulers who claimed a God-given right to govern millions of subjects, built their fabulous fortunes on elaborate rules of royal lineage. Loyal courtiers were always on hand to advise on the interpretation of the laws of succession in the tangled web of regal inter-marriage, first-born sons, feuding cousins and charlatan pretenders to great thrones and titles.

Often when powerful monarchs passed from the gilded stage and their relatives fell to squabbling among themselves, the line of succession could pass the mantle of power to tiny babies, first-born crown princes not old enough to walk or talk.

Jealous royal power brokers would often cast an envious eye on the cradle of some child-king, knowing that in many cases a quirk of fate, like a bout of fatal chicken pox, could swing an empire into the hands of a rival relative. Sometimes they were not slow to realize the advantages of giving fate a helping hand. Snatching a kingdom from a child, taking the royal candy from a baby, was fair game, even if the infant was a close blood relative.

When little Charles Louis was born into the royal family of Bourbon in 1785, he seemed set for a life of luxury. He was the younger of two royal children, but as the male heir, the Dauphin, he took priority over his older sister Marie Thérèse. His destiny was to rule France as the inheritor of its palaces and grand estates. But the over-burdened French peasants had other ideas. Louis was only four years old when the Revolution burst on to the streets of Paris and the mobs began to howl for an end to monarchy.

The little Dauphin's parents, Louis XVI and Marie Antoinette, whose free spending lifestyle had so outraged their poverty stricken subjects, were soon prisoners of the Revolution. For two years Louis and Marie and their children were kept under house arrest as French democracy went through its own turbulent infancy, ruling the country in a confusion of committees and assemblies.

Luck ran out for King Louis and his Queen in 1793 during the session of the newly appointed Convention which unleashed the infamous Reign of Terror. Louis and Marie became just two of the stream of doomed French nobility whose lives were ended by the guillotine.

While the members of the Convention transferred the little Dauphin and his sister to the Temple Prison in Paris, the exiled royalists who had fled abroad immediately proclaimed the seven-year-old boy their new King, Louis XVII.

There is little doubt that many of the fiery members of the new Republic's National Assembly would happily have guillotined the boy king and his sister. But they could not overlook his potential as a pawn in the bargaining game they had to play with their hostile neighbours of Austria, Prussia and Spain, where the ruling royal families, fought frequent invasion skirmishes with the French to try to restore the monarchy. As long as the Dauphin and his sister remained prisoners in the Temple, their continued safe-keeping had some value if the National Assembly used them as hostages to buy off the pressure from threatening outsiders.

In the meantime, the royalists in exile and their sympathizers inside Paris, began a whole series of plots to free the bewildered little Dauphin by bribery or subterfuge.

Even some National Assembly members, worried that the Revolution might be short-lived, considered smuggling the Dauphin to their own secret hideaways to bargain for their own lives if the royalists ever regained the upper hand. Soon all Paris was abuzz with rumours that the Dauphin had been spirited out of the temple to become a youthful figurehead for a Royalist revival.

To quell the speculation, the National Assembly appointed a team of guardians and commissioners to make regular visits to the Temple to check the well-being of the Dauphin and his sister, and to report back to them.

A puzzling report was recorded after a visit on 19 December 1794, when National Assembly member Harmand inspected the nine-year-old boy in his cell at the Temple. He noted he met a child in poor health, suffering from a disabling swelling on his arms and legs. The most bizarre aspect was the boy's responses to Harmand's inquiries about his treatment. The boy showed no signs of hearing his questions and never uttered a sound in reply. He was totally deaf and dumb. Harmand's report was quickly hushed up.

In may 1795, the boy in the Temple became seriously ill and doctors were ordered to attend him. The health of the boy, apparently still a deaf mute, deteriorated still further until the night of 8 June when he died.

Four doctors authorized by the Committee of Public Safety carried out a quick autopsy on the dead boy, removing his heart and dissecting his head. They diagnosed the cause of death as scrofula, tuberculosis of the glands of the neck.

But they never carried out a formal identification of him by his sister, Marie Thérèse, who had been kept prisoner for two years in another cell on the other side of the Temple. The body, the head swathed in bandages, was placed in a coffin and hustled off for burial in a common grave in the churchyard of Sainte Marguérite.

The next day, amid continuing rumours that another child had been switched for the Dauphin in the Temple, the Convention announced his death without making any further comment.

And so the royal house of Bourbon seemed doomed to wither as the French Republic embarked on a new era of its history under the leadership of a dynamic young Army officer from Corsica, Napoleon Bonaparte.

Napoleon took less than a decade of glorious military conquest before he tried to found his own royal dynasty, crowning himself Emperor and handing out royal titles to his own children, brothers and friends.

But after his defeat at Waterloo in 1815, the victorious allies decided it was time for real royalty to regain the throne of France. Their choice was the brother of the guillotined Louis XVI, the uncle of the Dauphin. The new monarch, next in line after the boy-king who had never ruled, became Louis XVIII. It was the sign for resurrected Dauphins to pop up all over Europe.

Dozens of 'dauphins', all about the right age of 30 and all well versed in the folklore of the alleged switch in the Temple, put forward their claims and were exposed as blatant frauds.

The most curious claim came 15 years later from a Prussian watchmaker living in London. In 1830, when another Revolution, less bloody and violent, had swept the royal family of Bourbon off the French throne of France yet again watchmaker Karl Wilhelm Naundorff came forward. He insisted he did not want to try to rule France, only to prove himself to be the missing Dauphin and to try to benefit from what little privilege was still attached to the title.

Naundorff gave a long, detailed account of how he recalled 35 years earlier being carried out of the Temple on 8 June, 1795, after being drugged with opium, and spending the next 14 years being passed from 'safe house' to 'safe house' in France, England and Germany. In 1800, he claimed, the King of Prussia had organized false identity papers for him in the name of Karl Naundorff. He then married and settled down, after serving a short prison term for counterfeiting coins.

In 1833 in France, Naundorff organized a meeting with Madame Rambaud, the dead Dauphin's former nanny, and Vicomte de la Rochefoucauld, an emissary from the Dauphin's sister, then Duchess of Angoulême. The nanny was convinced about his identity and the Vicomte reported that he was very impressed with Naundorff's claims and the watchmaker's striking physical resemblance to his 'father', the dead King Louis XVI.

But the Duchess, the Dauphin's sister, took no notice until 1836 when Naundorff tried to force her into a civil court case to prove his claim. He was arrested by French authorities and deported back to England. At home in London he set about pressing his claim, in an exhaustively researched book published later that year.

All copies of the book sent to France were seized by French customs officials at Calais. Naundorff continued to bombard the French authorities and the Duchess with petitions, undeterred by an attempt on his life at his home in Clarence Place, London. He was shot, literally with his pants down, in the outdoor toilet in his garden. He survived the wound and a Frenchman was later arrested and charged with the attack.

Two other attempts were made on his life in 1841 as Naundorff struggled to earn a living as an inventor of artillery weapons. He was badly burned in a deliberate explosion in his workshop and another arson attack on his home later that year.

With his business burned out, Karl Naundorff was bankrupt and spent four years in the grim Newgate debtor's prison in London.

Released in 1845, he travelled to Holland to try to interest the Dutch government in his designs for a new field gun. Before negotiations were complete, Naundorff died on 10 August.

The official Dutch death certificate identified him as Charles Louis de Bourbon, Duke of Normandy, Louis XVII, aged 60, son of Louis XVI and Marie Antoinette. The Dutch doctor who performed the routine autopsy noted his body bore certain marks – a mole on the thigh, triangular vaccination marks on his arm and a scar on his upper lip. The marks correspond exactly to the descriptions given by Madame Rambaud, the governess to the Dauphin Louis from his birth until 1792, the year before he was locked away in the Temple.

If Karl Naundorff was indeed the young Dauphin, the leaders of the French Revolution who locked him away as a child, without trial or charge, denied him his heritage and his chance to change the course of history.

But if his story was true, which cruel and heartless conspirators, royalists or double-crossing revolutionaries, snatched him from the Temple and left a terrified deaf mute boy to die of disease and maltreatment in solitary confinement in his place?

The Sinking of the *Salem*

The 96,000 ton supertanker *Salem* was a floating time bomb, in danger of erupting into a massive fire-ball at any moment. But her captain, officers and 18 crewmen were calm, apparently refusing to panic, waiting quietly on deck and scanning the horizon for passing ships.

On 17 January 1979, the Greek captain of the *Salem* noted in his log that the ship had been rocked by a series of explosions which had left it floating helpless and without engines in the Atlantic Ocean 160 km (100 miles) off the African coast of Senegal.

The ship's log also noted with relief that the mysterious explosions and small fires had failed to ignite any of the brimming cargo of 200,000 tons of volatile Kuwaiti crude oil which packed the tanker's holds.

The *Salem* remained afloat for another 30 hours. Almost inevitably in the busy shipping lanes, she was spotted by the tanker *British Trident*, outward bound from England and headed for the same Persian Gulf terminal the *Salem* had left more than a month before. Twenty minutes after the *British Trident* first sighted the *Salem*, the British ship recorded the first and only distress radio call from the stricken ship.

As *British Trident* turned to answer the SOS call a bright cloud of orange smoke billowed up from the *Salem*. But there was no need for the rescuers to approach too close. Within 30 minutes the *Salem*'s powerful lifeboats had met them halfway. The British sailors could only marvel at the *Salem*'s crew, unhurried and magnificently composed in the face of awesome danger, as they filed abroad the *British Trident* in an orderly queue, with their suitcases neatly packed.

The ship had survived a day and a night still afloat although listing slightly. With reasonable luck it could be presumed that the *Salem* might survive a lot longer, even long enough to put a damage repair and salvage crew aboard.

But within ten minutes of her crew being rescued, the *Salem*'s bows dipped below the swell and she sank out of sight.

The crew of the *British Trident* were relieved when the potential fire-bomb slipped below the waves. Now they put their own tanker's engines full ahead to get well clear of the catastrophic fountain of oil which would gush to the surface from the *Salem*'s hold. They knew that the *Salem*'s massive cargo, valued at £25 million, was likely to produce one of the worst oil slicks the world had ever known.

Almost as a warning of the impending pollution disaster, one gigantic oil bubble broke the surface of the ocean. And then it stopped.

The *Salem* slipped further and further downward into the Atlantic, in water too deep for any diver to reach her. She was gone and lost for good, of that there was no doubt.

The following day the crew of the *Salem* were put ashore in Dakar, the capital of Senegal. The captain dismissed his grateful crew and prepared himself for questioning at a routine inquiry into the loss of his ship. He notified the owners of the *Salem*, a newly formed shipping company sharing the same accommodation address in Monrovia, Liberia, as 200 other shipping owners, that their vessel had foundered. He informed the owners of the oil, Shell International Trading in London, that their valuable cargo had been lost and compensation would have to come from the insurers.

The skipper carefully filed his own insurance claim, £12 million for the cost of the *Salem*, less than half the value of its cargo. Then, as soon as the Senegal authorities agreed to release him, he flew home to Athens.

As insurance investigators began to unravel some of the unexplained causes of the sinking of the *Salem*, one of the tanker's crew added a new twist to the riddle.

The crewman, a Tunisian, turned up in Paris, spending money like water. He claimed that the money he flung so recklessly around the nightclubs came from a bonus of thousands of Swiss francs paid by the owners of the *Salem*.

And that bonus, he claimed, was paid to all the crewmen who entered into a conspiracy of silence a few days after the *Salem* left the Kuwaiti oil loading terminal at Mena Al Ahmdi and cleared the Persian Gulf. The high living crewmen boasted that the shadowy businessmen who owned the *Salem* had bluffed their way into a fortune by offering their services to carry the cargo of oil from Kuwait to England.

The Kuwaiti oil would have been worth double its value to one group of customers 3,220 km (2,000 miles) away, the industries of South Africa. Most Arab oil exporters maintain a united anti-apartheid policy against the South African regime and refuse to sell them any of their output. South Africa buys its oil wherever and whenever it can – and pays top price.

The crewman insisted that this ship made a secret rendezvous with a South African tanker off the Cape of Good Hope, transferred its precious cargo and then partially flooded its tanks to prevent it riding suspiciously high in the water. Then it continued its journey as part of an elaborate charade. It sank conveniently off Senegal, its nearest point to land after leaving South African waters.

In Athens the skipper of the *Salem* dismissed his crewman's uncorroborated allegations as a sailor's yarn, meant to add spice and intrigue to a sad but perfectly plausible explanation for the loss of the tanker. The South African government maintained a discreet silence.

But insurance investigators were already suspicious that the *Salem* had taken more than a month to reach the Senegal coast after leaving Kuwait. It should have made that part of its journey in only three weeks. The time gap, many of them claim, can only be explained by an unscheduled detour somewhere along the route.

It is unlikely that anyone will ever be able to solve the riddle of the ship which seemed to sink on cue. The wreck of the *Salem* lies deep beneath the stormy waters of the Atlantic Ocean. Are its cargo tanks filled with £25 million worth of oil, seeping away quietly and unnoticed? Or are they filled with nothing more than sea water?

A Peer's Great Gamble

When Veronica, Lady Lucan, ran hysterical and bloodstained from her home in Lower Belgrave Street, Belgravia, London, on the night of 7 November 1974, her frantic cries for help sparked off one of the most baffling unsolved murder mysteries of the age.

Lying behind her in the elegant town house, just a stone's throw from Buckingham Palace, was the body of her children's nanny Sandra Rivett, aged 29, brutally battered to death, her body thrust into a canvas sack.

Lady Lucan reached the door of the crowded saloon bar of the nearby pub, The Plumbers Arms, and sobbed: 'Help me. Help me, I've just escaped from a murderer.'

And the tale she told from her hospital bed to detectives a few hours later set them on the fruitless search to find her husband, John Bingham, the 7th Earl of Lucan. With bruising on her face and severe lacerations to her scalp,

Lady Lucan, 26, told how she had tackled a tall, powerful maniac bent on murder.

She recalled how she had been spending a quiet evening at home with her two children – with the unexpected company of nanny Sandra who had originally been given the evening off to spend with her boyfriend. Sandra, who doted on Lady Lucan's children, had decided instead to stay in the house, in her own quarters.

Around 21.00 Sandra had popped her head round the door of Lady Lucan's lounge and offered to make a cup of tea for the family. Half an hour later when the nanny had not re-appeared, Lady Lucan walked down two floors to the kitchen, puzzled by the delay.

There she saw the shadowy figure of a man, crouched over the dead body of the nanny, bundling her lifeless form into a canvas sack.

As soon as Lady Lucan screamed, the man attacked her, beating her badly. She could not recognize the figure in the darkness, but as she struggled free and ran upstairs, she heard what she said was the unmistakable voice of her estranged husband call out after her.

Moments later, as she lay trembling on her bed, her husband was at her side, trying to comfort her. And when Lady Lucan ran from the house for help, her husband slipped away into the night.

A massive hunt immediately began for Lord Lucan. Police first checked his rented flat only a few streets away, where he had moved the previous year when he had separated from Lady Lucan and started divorce proceedings. But by that time, barely two hours after the murder, Lord Lucan had already turned up at a friend's house 72 km (45 miles) from the scene of the crime, driving a borrowed car.

There the socialite peer, a man-about-town and professional gambler, told one of his closest family friends his own version of the horror of the nanny's murder. He claimed he had been walking past his wife's home on his way to his own flat to change for dinner at one of his fashionable gambling clubs and saw through the venetian blinds of the basement kitchen what looked like a man attacking Lady Lucan.

'I let myself in with my own key and rushed down to protect her,' Lucan told his friend. 'I slipped on a pool of blood and the attacker ran off. My wife was hysterical and accusing me of being her attacker.'

Despite his denial, Lord Lucan never stayed around to confirm his version of events to the police – or to anyone else. The day after the murder, his car, which carried a portion of the same lead pipe which had been used to kill Sandra Rivett, was found abandoned at Newhaven, Sussex, a port with a regular ferry service to France.

Police began a thorough check of Lucan's aristocratic friends in England, suspecting that wealthy socialites might be shielding him. But all lines of inquiry petered out.

A year later the coroner's inquest into the death of the nanny weighed up all the evidence and took the unusual step of officially recording her death as murder – and naming Lord Lucan as the man who had committed the murder. English law was changed shortly after that judgement to ensure that never again could anyone be named as a murderer until they were found, charged, tried and found guilty under normal criminal procedure.

Seven years after the murder, when Lucan had vanished without touching any of his bank accounts, without surrendering himself, and still undiscovered by any of the police searches which spread from Africa to America, the fugitive peer was declared legally dead.

The two policemen who led the search have both retired from Scotland Yard, still arguing about the unsolved crime. Superintendent Roy Ransom, who studied every single statement and grilled scores of witnesses, maintained: 'He killed the nanny by mistake, thinking he could dispose of his wife and get custody of the children he loved. When he realized the error, he killed himself in some remote spot, like a lord and a gentleman.'

But Superintendent Dave Gerring, who supervised the same murder hunt, concluded: 'Lucan is still in hiding somewhere and he is the only man who knows the full story. He is a lord and a gentleman, but he is still a gambler. And he is still gambling on the odds that no one will ever find him.'

Suspect Deceased

The finger of suspicion pointed unwaveringly at Graham Sturley. He was the classic murder suspect. The 37-year-old former private detective had certainly studied case histories of people who had vanished and never been seen alive again. And when Linda, his own wife, went missing, Sturley had the know-how, the motive and the opportunity to have murdered her.

The detectives who first called at his home in Biggin Hill, Kent, were quickly convinced that Sturley, earning a living as a property developer, had killed his petite, unfaithful 29-year-old wife. He openly admitted to them his hatred for her flaunted love affairs with other men.

But the police began their investigation with one great disadvantage. Linda Sturley had been missing for 12 months by the time her worried mother, Mrs Ada Webb, walked into her local police station and reported her daughter's disappearance. She had been stalled long enough by assurances from son-in-law Sturley that, although Linda had left home, she had been in touch with him by telephone.

When the police arrived on the doorstep of Sturley's neat suburban bungalow he told them frankly: 'Yes, she's gone and I don't expect to see her again. I don't know where she is and I'm glad to get rid of her.'

Then the detectives began to piece together the facts.

Linda Sturley had last been seen at her home in July 1981, when her sister visited her. Tearfully Linda, who was six months pregnant, confessed that her husband had beaten her and punched her in the stomach during a violent argument the night before, when he raged that one of her lovers was the father of the child she was expecting.

The next day Linda, a pretty and vivacious sales representative for the Avon cosmetics company, vanished.

With an air of finality, Sturley had told his two children, a six-year-old girl and a four-year-old boy, that their mother would never be returning. Neighbours noticed that Sturley had a garden bonfire, burning a complete wardrobe of his wife's clothes. And for the next year, until July 1982, Sturley lived as if Linda had simply gone away.

He even telephoned his wife's family to reassure them that Linda was still well, at the same time as someone with a detailed knowledge of the missing woman's bank passbooks had forged her signature to take everything out of her savings accounts and cash cheques for her maternity benefit payments.

Linda Sturley's family doctor revealed that the missing woman would need to give birth to her baby by Caesarean operation. Government health officials checked the records of every maternity hospital and clinic in Britain and no patient answering her description had been admitted.

And the police discovered that her jealous husband had even used the techniques of his former detective agency to tap his own telephone and record conversations between Linda and her lovers.

'We know your wife had a string of lovers and she was a bad wife,' one policeman told Sturley sympathetically. 'And we understand that sometimes pressure like that can drive a man to murder.'

But Sturley, who had a history of poor health and heart

ailments, never faltered once during long sessions of police interrogation. 'You think I have buried her in the garden,' he accused bitterly. 'Well I wouldn't have been so silly, that would have poisoned the flowers.'

It was only a matter of time, police thought, before they would find Linda Sturley's body and break through her husband's brooding, angry defiance to gain a confession.

Sturley, unshakably refusing to admit any part of his wife's disappearance, told them: 'She had walked out on me so many times in the past I didn't bother to report her as a missing person. I'm glad she's gone, I never want to see her again.'

When intense publicity in national newspapers and on TV and radio failed to bring any response from the missing woman, the search began in earnest for Linda Sturley's body.

The floorboards were ripped up in the living room of Sturley's house and the brickwork of walls probed for hidden cavities. Infra-red and heat-seeking detection equipment was used to scan the gardens around the house and tracker teams with dogs combed the surrounding woodland and parks. Police divers plunged into lakes, streams and ponds and forensic experts were sent to examine the bones of a woman's body unearthed in a forest 48 km (30 miles) away. But there was still no sign of Linda Sturley, dead or alive.

In a series of thorough interrogations Graham Sturley taunted the police, mocking their failure at every attempt to discover the fate of his wife. Detectives, aware of his history of heart trouble, handled him with kid gloves, probing and questioning as toughly as they dared.

After three months of intensive investigation, the head of the murder inquiry squad, Detective Chief Inspector George Cressy, examined all the circumstantial evidence and decided he had enough to recommend arresting Graham Sturley and charging him with the murder of his wife.

As police legal experts began preparing the case for his arrest, confident of their prosecution and eventual conviction, Graham Sturley died of a heart attack. The murder inquiry on Linda Sturley was closed, the case file marked 'Suspect deceased'.

Graham Sturley's lawyer revealed later: 'A will was left by Mr Sturley disposing of his assets, but there was nothing dramatic in it one way or another, no confessions, no admissions.'

The Kent detectives saw no useful purpose to be served by their presence a week later at Sturley's cremation after a ceremony in the quiet chapel in Honor Oak, London.

They never saw the strange final tribute that was laid on his coffin – a wreath with the message: 'Well you got that out of the way, Sturley. All my love . . .'

The Disappearance of Goodtime Joe

With a leggy showgirl on his arm, Judge Joseph Crater stepped out of a plush nightclub on New York's 45th Street and hailed a taxi. He gave his companion an affectionate squeeze and a kiss on the cheek. 'See you tomorrow, Ruby,' said the judge, whose unorthodox social life had earned him the nickname Goodtime Joe. But he didn't. A litter later, he was seen buying a theatre ticket for the Broadway hit, *Dancing Partners*.

From that moment, on 6 August 1930, Judge Joseph Crater vanished, and it happened so mysteriously and in such politically-scandalous circumstances that in America 'pulling a Crater' is still used to describe a baffling disappearance. In New York, he is still officially listed as missing, although he would now be 93 years old, and the police department still checks regular reports of sightings.

Judge Crater was a sentimental family man – and a womanizer on a grand scale. He was a pillar of society, yet he enjoyed the company of rogues. He believed fervently in the sanctity of the law but became part of the most corrupt administration in New York's history. He had been a brilliant professor of law at New York University, but he wanted to be rich. As a lawyer with an obvious interest in making money, he was welcomed by the city's then-shady administration. In the summer of 1929 he acted as a receiver when the bankrupt Libby Hotel was sold to a finance company for $75,000. Six weeks later, the hotel was resold to the city of New York to be demolished in a road widening scheme. The price: $2,800,000. Many members of the administration, including Crater, made a lot of money from the deal.

By 1930, he had the life-style of a very rich man. More good fortune came his way when Franklin D. Roosevelt, then Governor of New York State, made him a justice of the city's Supreme Court. Crater had finally made it. He was rich and powerful. Then, on the evening of 2 August, something happened to threaten his cosy world.

He was on holiday with his wife at their summer cottage in Maine when he received a mysterious phone call. It was enough to send the judge hurrying back to New York. 'I've got to straighten some fellows out,' was all he told his wife, promising to return for her birthday a week later. She never saw him again.

In New York on 6 August he wrote two cheques for a total of $4,100 and sent his assistant, Joe Mara, to the bank to cash them. When Mara returned, Crater had stuffed papers from his office files into four large portfolios and two briefcases. He told Mara he was going 'up Westchester way for a few days'.

That evening, however, he turned up at his favourite nightclub on 45th Street, but after a few drinks with show-girl Ruby Ritz he left, saying he was going to the theatre.

Amazingly, it was four weeks and a day before the disappearance of one of the city's top judges finally leaked out. Friends and enemies alike, terrified at the idea of a scandal which might implicate them, were desperate to hush up the affair. Manhattan District Attorney, Thomas Crain, was anxious to question Mrs Crater. She refused to talk and the judge's politically-powerful friends kept Crain at bay.

Soon, reports of alleged sightings were coming in from around the world.

In 1955 a photograph of Crater was shown to the Dutch clairvoyant Gerard Croiset. He claimed that the judge had been murdered on the first floor of a farmhouse near the Bronx, New York, and his body buried in the garden.

Remarkably, there was just such a house in the area, which in Crater's day had been used by city officials for secret meetings with their girlfriends. Investigators discovered that the late owner, Henry Krauss, had once claimed that on the morning of 10 August 1930, he had found the kitchen covered with blood . . . But of a body there was no sign.

Death at the Opera House

Snow swirled silently through the deserted streets and only the footprints of an occasional policeman or passer-by marred its crisp whiteness. It was Christmas in Toronto. But while most people were surrounded by joy, and laughter and goodwill, one woman remained alone, surrounded by silence and suspicion. Three weeks before Christmas Day 1919, Theresa Small's husband had mysteriously disappeared – and there were rumours of murder.

In a few years Ambrose Small, ruthless and mean, had made a fortune out of property. His most important possession was Toronto Grand Opera House. He had started there as an usher. Then he became treasurer. In the end he owned it. He was a millionaire before he was 40 and owned theatres throughout Canada.

At 56 he decided to sell his theatrical empire. A deal was fixed with a financier from Montreal and on 2 December 1919, Small and his wife met him at his lawyers in Toronto. The financier gave Small a cheque for $1,000,000 as down-payment and Small gave the cheque to his wife, who deposited it in his account. The Smalls then went to lunch with their solicitor.

Afterwards Mrs Small went home alone in her chauffeur-driven car while her husband went back to the opera house. He had arranged to meet his solicitor there at 16.00. He was seen entering the theatre. But nobody saw him leave.

His solicitor said later he had stayed with Small and his secretary, John Doughty, for an hour and a half. Small, he said, was still at the opera house when he left at 17.30.

Doughty left the theatre to have supper with his sister. Later he said he had to go to Montreal and was driven to the station by his sister's husband. On the way they stopped at the opera house, where Doughty collected a small brown paper parcel. He gave this to a second sister in the car and asked her to look after it. Doughty caught the Montreal train – and it was to be two years before he would be back in Toronto.

Small failed to come home that night, so Theresa assumed he had gone to Montreal with Doughty. She waited and waited. But there was no sign of her husband.

It was the opera house manager who raised the alarm. Police issued Small's description – and at once there was a sensational development. Found pinned to the door of a Toronto church was a card which read: 'Prayers for the soul of Ambrose Small.'

The search for a missing man had now become a hunt

for a possible murderer. Suspicion fell first on Theresa Small. She was of German extraction, and Germans were far from popular just after World War I.

Doughty, too, fell under suspicion. But where was he? The police announced rewards of $50,000 for the discovery of Small dead or alive and $15,000 for Doughty.

In the summer of 1920 police obtained a court order to open the strongbox at Small's bank. From their inquiries they expected to find a fortune inside. But bonds worth $105,000 were missing – and the last recorded visitor to Small's safety vaults had been John Doughty. Police investigations intensified. A boilerman at the opera house said that there had been a fight between Small and Doughty on the night Small was last seen alive. Officers raked out the boilers at the opera house looking for human remains.

Then a year later Doughty was discovered working in a lumber camp in Oregon. He was taken back to Toronto and the missing bonds were found in the attic of his sister's house. The police, convinced that they had a murder charge on their hands, confronted Doughty with the alleged fight in the opera house. He vehemently denied it and he was eventually charged with theft.

Doughty said he had taken the bonds from the bank on 2 December to use as a lever against Small who had promised him a share in the theatre deal. But he said he had panicked and fled across the border when he heard of Small's disappearance. Doughty was found guilty of theft and jailed for five years in March 1921.

Yet still there was no sign of Small. Police dug up the floors of his wife's house, but found nothing. Rumours persisted that he had been murdered by racketeers but again widespread searches revealed nothing.

Small was officially declared dead in 1924. Twenty years later the opera house was demolished and detectives made one last effort to solve the case. Again nothing.

To this day what happened to Ambrose Small remains as much a mystery as it was when he vanished off the face of the earth in 1919.

The Impossible *is* Possible

Neither the woman nor her 13-year-old daughter heard the alarm clock ring at 04.00 in the adjoining bedroom. Nor did they hear the soft 'phut' of the silenced gun. If they had, one of America's most baffling murder mysteries might have yielded a clue, however tiny.

Respectable family man Roy Orsini was dead, face-down in his pyjamas, shot in the back of the head by a .38 bullet fired at close range.

On the morning of 12 March 1981, veteran homicide detective Sergeant Tom Farley realized he had the 'impossible' crime on his hands. Orsini had been shot in his bedroom, with the door and windows locked from the inside. He could not possibly have committed suicide.

Orsini, a 38-year-old heating engineer, was a model husband and father. He lived with his wife, Lee, and schoolgirl daughter, Tiffany, in a pleasant suburb at North Little Rock, Arkansas. As far as anyone knew, he hadn't an enemy in the world.

Orsini went to bed early on 11 March to prepare for an early appointment with a client 96 km (60 miles) out of town. He set the alarm for 04.00 to beat the morning traffic jams.

Orsini always slept alone on such nights so that his early rising would not wake the household. The family would sleep in Tiffany's room, next to his own. Soon after 21.00 he kissed them both goodnight and went upstairs to the main bedroom. It was the last time they saw him alive.

Next morning Mrs Orsini rose at 07.00. She and Tiffany had breakfast and walked to the daughter's school nearby.

Back home, she began her housework. When her down-stairs work finished, she went upstairs to do the bed-rooms, starting with her husband's. It was closed, not like Roy at all, she thought. Normally, when he was making an early start, he left the door wide open, and left the room in a bit of a mess.

She tried the handle. The door was locked from the inside. That door had never been locked since they moved in before Tiffany was born 13 years ago. Had he somehow slept in? Had he been taken ill? Again and again, she twisted the handle of the door, knocked and called: 'Roy, Roy, are you all right?'

There was no reply. Lee Orsini, by this time thoroughly alarmed, dashed out of the house and frantically called on next door neighbour Mrs Glenda Bell. Together the two women managed to prise open the bedroom door. Lee Orsini uttered a piercing scream. Her husband still in his striped pyjamas, lay on the bed.

Sergeant Farley and his squad were on the scene within minutes of receiving Mrs Bell's telephone call. They quickly established that, like many Americans, Roy Orsini had a gun. But it was in a closed drawer several feet from the bed and, although it was a .38, the same calibre as the weapon which had been used to kill him, it was a Smith and Wesson. The fatal bullet had been fired from a Colt. It would anyway have been impossible for Orsini to shoot himself in the back of the head, replace the gun in the drawer and then go back to the bed.

Then there was the problem of the door and windows, all of which had been securely locked from the inside. The alarm clock had been set for 04.00 and had run down. Had the death shot been fired before or after this? There was no means of knowing.

Neither Mrs Orsini nor Tiffany had heard the shot, so the .38 must have been fitted with a silencer.

Farley ordered detailed inquiries into every known

relative or business contact of Orsini. A similar discreet check was made on his wife. Both had led totally blameless lives and had been devoted to each other and their daughter. There was nobody who could have had a motive for murder.

Farley said: 'I've been involved with many homicides, but never anything like this. Any way you look at it, it belongs in a book, not in real life.'

A Riddle in Life and a Riddle in Death

One sweltering lunchtime in July, Jimmy Hoffa kissed his wife Josephine, promised to be home by four, and drove away in a bullet-proof limousine.

He was on his way to a lunch date. But how far he got towards keeping his appointment no one knows. For after leaving his luxury home on the outskirts of Detroit at 12.30 on 30 July 1975, Jimmy Hoffa, America's most notorious union boss, was never seen again.

A few hours later an anonymous gravel-voiced caller told the police where they could find Hoffa's abandoned car. It sounded more like an epitaph than a tip-off. They found it shining in the sun, with no sign of a struggle and no body. Just a pair of white gloves neatly folded on the back seat.

There were three main theories about the disappearance of James – middle name Riddle – Hoffa, former president of the Teamsters Union.

The first suggestion was that he was eliminated by the Mafia who feared he would expose illegal 'loans' made by the Teamsters to underworld figures. The second theory was that he died because of a battle for power within the union. The third – and most intriguing – theory was that, knowing there was a contract on his life, he chose to disappear of his own free will. Just two days earlier he had withdrawn more than a million dollars from union funds. Like Hoffa, the money never came back to its rightful home.

His distraught family offered a $200,000 reward for information which might lead to the finding of his body, dead or alive. But there were no takers.

If there were violent and sinister overtones to the disappearance, no one should have been surprised. For this had been the pattern of Hoffa's life almost from the very beginning. As a teenager, he got a job loading trucks and, at 17, he organized his first strike. As a union leader, he favoured lieutenants who had criminal records. Many were chosen for their expertise in terror and extortion. Nevertheless, Hoffa became a hero to many of the Teamsters who had seen their wages virtually doubled in the space of a decade. He also poured millions of dollars into his own pockets and then bought a Miami bank to look after his wealth.

When the crusading Robert Kennedy was made chairman of the Senate Rackets Committee, Hoffa became his prime and very personal target. He described Hoffa's leadership of the Teamsters as a 'conspiracy of evil'. As a result of this probe initiated by Kennedy, Hoffa eventually jailed in 1967, sentenced to serve 13 years for jury tampering and defrauding the union's pension fund to the tune of almost two million dollars.

Hoffa decreed that Frank Fitzsimmons, a long-time ally, should take his place as president on the strict understanding that he was simply holding down the job until Hoffa regained his freedom.

In 1971, Hoffa was pardoned by President Nixon on condition that he should hold no union office until 1980. But he still had a taste for power, and so began a campaign to persuade the appeal court to lift Nixon's ban.

Fitzsimmons, however, had no intention of relinquishing the reins. Detroit became a battleground as the Fitzsimmons and Hoffa factions fought for supremacy.

This, then, was the background against which Jimmy Hoffa disappeared. It seems probable that the lunch meeting never actually took place. A Hoffa aide received a phone call, supposedly from Hoffa, saying that his companions had not turned up.

But had someone set up the lunch with the intention of luring Hoffa into a trap and then abducting him at gunpoint? This was the theory the FBI favoured.

The FBI also investigated the story of Charles Allen, a former crook turned informer, who became friendly with Hoffa when they were in prison together. Allen claimed that Hoffa was beaten to death by a contract killer known as 'Monster Man' who was 2 m (6 ft 4 in) and weighed 108 kg (17 stone). The body, said Allen, was then taken to New Jersey, cut into small pieces, hidden in two oildrums, and flown to Florida.

The police, unable to verify the story, replaced the Hoffa file in the 'unsolved' category. James Riddle Hoffa was well named.

The Mysterious Mummy

A 'wax' mummy hung in an old amusement park funhouse for 50 years until a strange event revealed its horrible secret – that underneath the ghastly bandages was the embalmed body of an outlaw killed in a turn-of-the-century shootout.

The grim reality surfaced in December 1976, when a television production crew visited the old house to shoot an episode of the TV series *The Six-Million Dollar Man*. Filming was under way when one of the crew gave out a shrill scream . . . One of the mummy's stick-like arms had snapped off and fallen. Where it had shattered were leathery shreds of skin and horrible clumps of human tissue clinging to the human bone.

The mummy was rushed to an autopsy room in the Los Angeles county morgue and history's strangest manhunt began. Under the many layers of wax, Los Angeles coroner Dr Thomas Noguchi found the withered body of a man. He had died long ago in his early 30s from a gunshot wound. The corpse had then been carefully embalmed with such heavy concentrations of arsenic that it had turned into a virtual mummy.

The thing had been on display in the Long Beach, California, funhouse since the 1920s, when it was brought from a bankrupt carnival operator. The time lapse meant that the police had little chance of solving the mystery. They feared that the mummy was the victim of a crime. But the only theory that anyone could come up with was stranger even than that. For it was suggested the mummy might have been a criminal himself!

The incredible story put forward by a former employee of the funhouse was that underneath the wax coating was the corpse of an Oklahoma outlaw named Elmer McCurdy.

Oklahoma authorities confirmed that there had been an Elmer McCurdy operating in the wild Oklahoma Territory in the early 1900s. He specialized in robbing trains and banks. After a Jesse James-type robbery in October 1911, McCurdy escaped to an outlaw hangout on the Big Caney River. When a posse from Pawhuska tracked him down, he died in the shootout.

But who would pick up the bill for embalming a foot-loose outlaw? The undertaker saw only one way to get his money: An embalmed Elmer stood in the corner of the funeral parlour where visitors could gape at him for a nickel apiece. He then fell into the hands of the travelling carnival man who sold him to the amusement park.

Fact or fiction? No one can be sure. The only question

worrying Los Angeles county was what to do with the body. The answer was supplied by the Oklahoma Territorial Museum in Guthrie. The outlaw was returned to Oklahoma on 14 April 1977, and in an elegant old hearse pulled by a team of horses, Elmer was buried in the town's Boot Hill cemetery.

The Prairie's Murder Inn

One of the most notorious women in frontier America, bloody Kate Bender, operated a 'murder inn' on the Kansas prairie. Travellers who stopped there for the night were never seen again. For the few dollars in their carpetbags, Kate hid behind a curtain and split the lodger's skulls with a hatchet while they were enjoying one of her home-cooked meals.

Suspicious authorities finally raided the inn, but by that time Kate herself had grown wary. Officials found no trace of the woman, though evidence of her handiwork was plentiful. Digging behind the inn, they unearthed a human boneyard. Few of her victims were identified and the number of dead remains unknown. Even more grisly was the suspicion that Kate had fed some of her victims the flesh of earlier ones.

The riddle of Kate Bender's eerie disappearance intrigued mystery-lovers everywhere. In the hectic little mining camp of Silver City, Idaho, old-timers in the mercantile store pondered it as they sat around the pot-bellied stove.

When Joe Monahan came in for his weekly supplies, they tested their theories on him. Not much of a talker, the young man was always a good listener. When they suggested Kate might have entered a convent or might even be running another murder inn, he simply nodded and went on his way.

To the rest of Silver City, Joe himself was a riddle. A frail little man, he shunned the camp's roaring saloons and girls of the line. Joe's home was a dugout cut into a cliff on Succor Creek near Silver City. To raise the few dollars he spent in the store he kept chickens, pigs and six scrawny cows.

In December 1903, Joe drove his cattle to winter pasture on the Boise River. But the hardships of the trail were too much. Soon after his return to Succor Creek he fell ill and died. When his body was prepared for burial, the barber-mortician ran out of the back room, stunned and sick . . .

Unbelievably, little Joe Monahan had been a woman.

The dugout was ransacked for any clues to her identity. All they found was a yellowed clipping from the *Kansas City Star* about the unsuccessful hunt for Kate Bender. Inevitably, the camp drew its own conclusions: in spite of 'Little Joe's' mild personality, had she been the ruthless killer?

To the day of the funeral there were rumours that a group of 'public minded citizens' meant to dig up the body and send it to Kansas for identification. The minister had heard the rumours too. On that windswept afternoon, he murmured a brief prayer for the unknown woman, then raised his eyes to the graveyard which was jammed with miners. 'I don't believe that this poor woman was a killer,' the minister said. 'Whatever her secret may have been, she died trying to protect it – and, in simple mercy, I ask that you let it die with her.'

The miners drifted away. There was a public subscription that evening in Silver City saloons to cover the burial costs. No one disturbed the unmarked grave. So the mystery lived on.

Who Did She Bury?

In the little coal mining town of McVey, Washington State, Nels Stenstrom and his wife Anna were among the most industrious merchants. Working side by side, they spent twelve hours of almost every day of the week in the McVey Mercantile Store – 'Where Everybody Finds Everything.'

Then a mysterious tragedy entered their lives. On 5 June 1895, Nels Stenstrom vanished without a trace. There were those who said the big man had a roving eye and might possibly have left with a woman. But no one wanted to carry that rumour to the steely-eyed Anna, who was devoted to her husband.

But Anna kept on running the store as if Nels were at her side, and it expanded and grew more prosperous.

In the summer of 1902, Stenstrom was declared legally dead. And that same day Anna made the strange announcement that was to reach newspapers throughout the US: Although he might be legally dead, she said, he would have a proper grave.

With or without a body, she wanted a casket, a burial plot and fitting church services for her husband.

It was an idea so unusual that crowds of reporters and curious spectators poured into the little town. There was standing room only in the church when the funeral began at 14.30 on 1 July 1902. Nels had been a war veteran, and the vacant coffin was prominently displayed under a US flag. After a few words from the minister, old friends appeared at the lectern to eulogize the departed.

Anna was the last to speak. But she had scarcely started when there was sudden confusion in the crowd. A grizzled derelict in shreds of clothing staggered into an aisle whimpering and clutching his breast. Some said he looked imploringly into Anna's face before he collapsed, unconscious, to the floor.

She was the first to reach him and grope for a pulse. The tears were running down her cheeks when she raised her eyes. All she could say was 'It's Nels.'

The town's one doctor signed the death certificate, marvelling that this alcoholic wreck could be the once powerful Nels. Hundreds watched as the remains of the vagrant were borne to the Stenstrom burial plot.

But the story had an incredible sequel.

While the nearby towns of Roslyn and Cle Elum prospered, the veins of coal ran thin in McVey. It became a shabby ghost town. After Anna died and was buried with her husband, a contractor bought the store for its old lumber.

When he was bulldozing the building down, shallow graves were found beneath the floorboards. Two skeletons lay side by side. Between them was the axe that had split their skulls.

One was the skeleton of a woman destined to remain as nameless as the vagrant buried with Anna. The man's body was equally unidentifiable . . . Could it have been the body of the real Nels Stenstrom?

Acrobats of Death

Ugo Pavesi stepped out onto the third-storey balcony of his home. An extortionist and general hoodlum, he liked to spend his evenings there while he plotted further criminal enterprises.

Usually, he would have been accompanied by his girl-friend but on this occasion 17-year-old Lorna Perricone was in hospital. As a disciplinary measure, he had put her there himself with a dozen savage blows to the face and stomach.

In the street below Pavesi's home, there were three witnesses who later reported seeing an impossible sight.

They claimed to have seen a black giant 5.4 m (18 ft) tall emerge from the shadows and make his way towards the man on the balcony. The giant lifted him casually from the deck chair and let his squat body plunge to the pavement. Pavesi's severed head fell beside it, wrung from the body in an incredible display of strength.

In the deep, soft soil of the shrubbery surrounding Pavesi's home, police found the footprints of the killer. Displacement of the soil indicated that he had weighed no less than 410 kg (900 lb). But he had vanished completely in the confusion that followed the murder at Van Nuys, California, on the night of 13 November 1941, and no one knew where he would strike again.

A shrewd policeman who had been only a few blocks from the area was put on the case. Sergeant Lou Grandin toured the run-down area. One of his calls was on a psychic who called herself Madame Olga.

His visit was interrupted by the entrance of the old lady's three boarders, the powerful Perricone brothers Mario, Tony and Giorgio. Big, balding men with no-nonsense eyes, their timing and precision as an acrobatic team had won them high praise.

Mario, the spokesman, told Grandin that in 50 years of theatrical experience he had never known a giant like the alleged Van Nuys killer. Then he shocked the policeman by telling him: 'The girl Pavesi put in hospital was our sister, sergeant. And I'm using the past tense because she died a few minutes ago.'

'I'm sorry,' Grandin said humbly. 'I ask only that you stay in San Francisco until we get this thing cleaned up.'

But it was a warning that went unheeded. The date was 7 December, 1941 and something was to happen that day that changed the history of the world. The Perricone brothers were among the first to enlist after Pearl Harbor. So, too, was Sergeant Lou Grandin.

The case of the vanishing giant preyed on Grandin's

mind throughout the war. On his return to the United States, he decided to pay one last visit to Madame Olga. The aged psychic was still alive but frail.

She told the ex-cop that the Perricone brothers had all died in the war – which was why she felt free to suggest a possible explanation for the death of Ugo Pavesi.

She drew out a yellowed vaudeville poster. There were the three Perricone brothers in the centre of the stage, Mario with Tony standing proudly on his shoulders. And on Tony's shoulders stood Giorgio, ripping a thick telephone directory to shreds in his big hands. The three would have made an impressive giant: Mario the planner, Tony the middleman, and Giorgio – with the huge, powerful hands.

The Oldest Kidnap Victim?

Excited scientists named him Peking Man. He was a collection of bones about 500,000 years old, unearthed near Peking in the 1920s and a vital missing link in man's knowledge of evolution. Then, in 1941, with the Japanese advancing on the city it was decided to ship the bones to America – they still have not arrived.

Dr Harry L Shapiro, former Professor of Anthropology at Columbia University, has been searching for them ever since. His theory is that they were purloined by a Marine officer who took Peking man back to America.

The story was given credence when a Chicago businessman offered $5,000 to anybody with information. A mysterious woman met the businessman on the 102nd floor of the Empire State Building in New York. She said that her husband had returned from China with fossils of some prehistoric man. She produced a photograph of the remains but before a deal could be made the woman disappeared without trace.

The FBI have followed reports of GIs returning home

from Asia with strange-looking skulls, as souvenirs – without success.

A Sydney businessman maintained he had acquired the bones and buried them in a forest in Tasmania. He would reveal the spot at a price.

It is possible that Peking Man is now in both America and Australia or even in Britain. The mystery of this strange kidnap remains unsolved.

Suzy Lamplugh

On Monday 28 July 1986, Suzy Lamplugh made an entry in her business diary. It read: '12.45. Mr Kipper, 37 Shorrolds Road, O/S.'

For 25-year-old Suzy, the summons to get out of doors and meet a perfect stranger must have been a welcome opportunity to have a break from her busy office routine at Sturgis Estate Agents in Fulham Road, west London, where she had worked for 16 months.

The diary note was a simple shorthand reminder to herself. Suzy, a young, ambitious and hard-working estate agent negotiator, was due to meet a client outside that address at the appointed time. The property – a furnished three-storey terraced house – had come on to the books a few days before. The asking price was £128,000 and a successful sale would have meant a tidy commission bonus for the eager young estate agent.

Suzy had spent a wasteful and frustrating morning taking phone calls from potential clients who just wanted to compare house prices with those of rival estate agents, making her own calls to friends, trying to locate her pocket diary and a postcard she had lost before the previous weekend, and notifying her bank manager about her cheque book which had been misplaced at the same time.

But nothing distracted her from her meeting with Mr

Kipper. That appointment seemed like a real sales prospect. Mr Kipper could be a serious potential purchaser.

Just before her lunch break she strode over to the desk of Mark Gurdon, the office manager, and collected the keys to the house in Shorrolds Road. The Ford Fiesta car supplied by her employers was parked just outside the office. It would take only three or four minutes for Suzy to drive to her appointment. The office manager expected Suzy would be gone just along enough to show her potential client around the property before heading back to the office. She would probably bring back a sandwich to eat at her desk, because she was always keen to be there, ready to answer any calls that might lead to more sales and more commission bonuses.

Suzy took only her purse with her, leaving her handbag behind. Then she left the office and drove away to become the subject of the biggest and most puzzling missing persons mystery which has ever baffled the experts at New Scotland Yard.

It was only a few hours before her friends and colleagues at the estate agent's began to become concerned about Suzy's absence. At first Mark Gurdon was simply irritated that Suzy seemed to be taking too much time over her visit to the terraced house. He assumed there might be unforeseen complications with the client, possibly caused by lengthy on-the-spot negotiating over the price for the property. But if that had been the case, she should have returned immediately to the office, where she could have taken advice and hammered out any financial details.

He strolled over to Suzy's desk and checked her diary entry. By late afternoon he had become worried. It was unlike Suzy to take long, unauthorized lunch breaks. He decided to check for himself. With another of Suzy's colleagues he drove round to the vacant property. There was no sign of Suzy or her car. But as the two estate agents prepared to leave Shorrolds Road, next door neighbour

58-year-old unemployed bachelor Harry Riglin asked them: 'Are you looking for the young couple?'

Riglin confirmed that Suzy had indeed been at the house with a young man. He had thought they looked like a nice, prosperous young couple as they stood outside and looked up admiringly at the house. The kind of people he would have liked as neighbours.

Mark Gurdon returned to his office. He checked his file of clients. They had never done business before with a 'Mr Kipper'. The mystery client may have only phoned that morning and by sheer chance Suzy had taken the call; or he may have stepped into the office at any time in the past few days after seeing a property in the window display which had caught his eye.

Gurdon's next call was to Suzy's mother, 54-year-old swimming teacher and slimming counsellor Diana Lamplugh, at her home in East Sheen, a few miles away. Gurdon asked if Suzy had skipped work to have lunch with her mother, but Mrs Lamplugh had not seen her daughter since she had paid a visit to her family the day before.

Increasingly worried, Gurdon then began to phone the casualty departments of local hospitals. He went to Fulham police station to report his young sales agent's disappearance, but couldn't afford the time to wait in the lengthy queue at the desk. He hurried off to an appointment with a client, checked Shorrolds Road again, and returned to his office.

Six hours after Suzy had last been seen, Gurdon phoned Fulham police station and spoke to PC Duncan Parker. Immediately, Missing Person Report FF584/1/54 was filed. Next, an urgent call was made to the home of Detective Inspector Peter Johnstone, the officer on call for emergencies, instructing him to take charge of the investigation.

Detective Inspector Johnstone was, at the time, heading

the hunt for the murderer of an elderly London woman who had been raped and strangled the week before. When he heard the first details of Suzy's disappearance, he feared he had another murder case on this hands.

Missing persons reports at London police stations fall into two categories: 'active' and 'inactive'. Inactive files cover those whose overwhelming family, career or financial problems seem to give them some melancholy but logical reason for dropping out of sight, cutting off all contact with those closest to them.

But the case of Suzy Lamplugh definitely fell into the 'active' category. For this was a well-adjusted, normal, happy young woman. She had gone for a lunchtime appointment leaving her handbag behind at her office, obviously expecting to return. There was no apparent reason for Suzy Lamplugh to vanish, unless she had been the victim of foul play.

Johnstone quickly ordered local police officers to go to Suzy's own home – a two-bedroomed flat in Putney – and smash their way in if need be. He wanted to make sure that Suzy had not become unwell that day and had simply gone home to sleep off a sudden bout of illness; or that the missing estate agent had not suddenly lost her heart in a mad moment of passion with the mysterious Mr Kipper and had taken him home with her.

At Suzy's flat there was no sign of her or her flatmate, 25-year-old advertising executive Nick Bryant. He was still at work, unaware of Suzy's disappearance.

In Suzy's neat and orderly bedroom lay the material for a dress; there was a partially completed sleeve beside the sewing machine her mother had lent her. There were no signs of a struggle; nor of any visitors; nor of any empty wardrobes, which might have hinted at Suzy running away.

At the same time, two detectives forced their way into the unoccupied 'House for Sale' in Shorrolds Road. There were no clues there either.

Throughout London, a general alert was flashed to all mobile patrols and beat bobbies to locate Suzy's Ford Fiesta, registration number B396 GAN. A 'grid search' was organized, marking off the immediate vicinity of Shorrolds Road into squares, so that every road and side-street could be checked out for signs of Suzy or her car.

Detectives began to build up a picture of Suzy, her friends, her contacts, her boyfriends, her business associates. They found nothing sinister whatsoever. In fact, the picture they had was of a wholesome, beautiful girl-next-door type, who could have been anyone's daughter, sister or friend.

Suzy was a go-ahead, strong-willed girl, the second oldest child of the Lamplugh family, with an older brother and two younger sisters. She had overcome the handicap dyslexia, the inability to read letters and numbers properly, which also afflicted her mother and her brother and sisters. Sufferers from dyslexia see script and text only as a confusing jumble of letters. With the patient help and support of her father, 55-year-old solicitor Paul Lamplugh, Suzy had learned to read and had successfully passed her exams.

After leaving school, Suzy had trained and qualified as a beautician, and went to work in the floating beauty salon of the *Queen Elizabeth II* luxury cruise ship. On board the liner she was known to her shipmates as 'H', because she insisted on being called by her full name and was constantly telling the crew and passengers that her name was 'Susannah – with an H!'

She had cruised the world and dreamed of settling down in South Africa with a boyfriend she had met on board, but back on dry land, practical and ambitious Suzy had buckled down to hard work as an estate agent, eventually buying her own £70,000 flat in Putney, just south of the river Thames and near to her parents' home.

Although she had lived independently away from

home for six years, she visited her parents regularly. In fact, she had been to see her parents the night before she went missing. Just before she kissed them goodbye, Suzy had summed up her own easy-going vitality. 'Life is for living,' she told them.

Mr Riglin, the neighbour who had seen the young couple viewing the house at Shorrolds Road, was able to give police an accurate description of Suzy as she was last seen: 5ft 6 in tall, pretty, medium-built with blonde streaked hair, wearing a peach blouse, black jacket and grey skirt with high-heeled shoes.

The detectives grilled Riglin at length about Suzy's companion, the man known to everyone on the case as 'Mr Kipper'. He was a couple of inches taller than Suzy, aged between 25 and 30. He was handsome, slimly built, clean shaven and looked prosperous and wealthy in his neatly tailored dark business suit.

At home in East Sheen, Suzy's parents were frantic with worry. Her father, Paul, travelled to Fulham, anxious to witness for himself the massive police effort now being mounted to locate his daughter. Meanwhile, Diana Lamplugh waited at home by the telephone, hoping against hope that Suzy would call her. Even a message from a kidnapper demanding a ransom would have been welcome.

Offering what little help he could, Paul Lamplugh joined two detectives in their patrol car and toured the streets of west London, hoping to spot his daughter among the happy crowds of young people sipping drinks in wine bars or queueing for cinema seats. He had only been in the patrol car a few minutes when he heard the radio message announcing the first clue to Suzy's disappearance. The Ford Fiesta car she had driven that day had been found in Stevenage Road, a quiet residential street. It was a little over a mile from the vacant property where Suzy had met Mr Kipper and in the opposite direction from the route she would have taken to return to the office.

By now, it was 10 p.m., and Detective Inspector Johnstone decided that a full forensic examination would have to wait until daylight. In the meantime, careful not to accidentally wipe out any fingerprints or disturb any microscopic hairs or fibres invisible to the naked eye, the police inspected the abandoned car as closely as they dared.

The Ford Fiesta had been parked at a slight angle to the kerb and the rear end of the car was partially blocking the entrance to a garage. It had been dumped there by someone in a hurry; the handbrake had been left in the off position.

The driver's door was unlocked, but the passenger door was firmly secure, suggesting that only one person had been in the car. On the back shelf they could clearly see Suzy's straw hat.

The police meticulously opened the driver's door and prised up the back shelf to check the boot of the car. It was empty. But in the rack of the door, they found a purse.

Then they found the most intriguing clue of all: the driver's seat, which would normally have been moved forward in the position closest to the steering wheel for a girl like Suzy, had been pushed back several notches. It seemed likely that the car had been driven to its final parking place by someone several inches taller than Suzy; possibly a man; probably Mr Kipper.

There the clues stopped.

Since the disappearance of Suzy Lamplugh there have been reports of her being seen alive in many different locations, from London nightspots to the sun-soaked beaches of Spanish and Greek holiday resorts. The release of a photo-fit impression of the shadowy figure of Mr Kipper produced a flood of calls to the police, but no solid leads.

In the search for Suzy, the biggest ever mounted by New Scotland Yard, more than 26,000 separate index cards were filed on computer, detailing every aspect of Suzy's life and those of her friends, family and almost everyone who had come in contact with her.

In the busy sales offices of estate agents throughout London, worried staff began to change their carefree office routines. Before any male customers were fixed up with appointments with young female negotiators with a prospect of buying property, they were asked to call in at the office where colleagues could discreetly make a note of their description and the number of the vehicle they drove.

Potential buyers making telephone appointments were asked for contact numbers and business addresses, where their identities could be verified before any female negotiator was despatched to meet them.

Nine months after Susannah Jane Lamplugh disappeared with the mysterious Mr Kipper, a remembrance service was held at her family's local church, All Saints, East Sheen. Everyone who attended wore bright clothes and buttonhole flowers, like at a wedding. It was a celebration of the life of the young estate agent, they were told. They heard of the launch of the Suzy Lamplugh Trust, a charity dedicated to making life safer and less fearful for young career girls.

And they heard Paul Lamplugh say of his daughter: 'While we do not believe that Suzy is alive, we do not believe she is dead. That is the paradox.'

Oscar Mike

When Aer Lingus Flight 712 departed from Cork in Ireland for London's Heathrow Airport on Sunday 24 March 1968, it should have been a routine journey lasting little more than an hour and 20 minutes.

On board the Viscount turbo-prop airliner were four crew members and 57 passengers. At the controls was 35-year-old Captain Bernard O'Beirne, one of the airline's most senior pilots, with over 6,600 hours of flying to his credit. More than 1,600 of the hours listed in his pilot's log book had been spent flying Viscounts, considered to be one of the world's safest and most carefully engineered aircraft. O'Beirne's co-pilot, 22-year-old First Officer Paul Heffernan, had 900 hours flying experience on the same type of tried and tested four-engined airliner.

The weather was cloudless and Captain O'Beirne assured his passengers they should enjoy a pleasant, smooth flight. But, half an hour later, the Viscount, code-named Echo India Alpha Oscar Mike, was a tangled mass of wreckage sinking under the waves in the Irish Sea, and Flight 712 entered the history books as one of the most baffling aviation mysteries ever.

Despite a detailed technical examination of the crumpled remains of the airliner, dredged from the bottom of the sea, and the painstaking analysis of the last frantic and garbled messages from Captain O'Beirne, no real answer has ever been found to the riddle of the disaster which left Oscar Mike spinning helplessly to its doom. There was no evidence of a structural or mechanical defect which could have led to the crash; there were no signs of a fire or explosion and no indication of metal fatigue; the weather in the area at the time was good; there were no other aircraft in the vicinity, and the possibility of a collision with a flock of birds was ruled out because Oscar Mike had been flying so high. The only spine-chilling theory, supported by the accounts of eye witnesses, is that Oscar Mike was blown from the sky by a glowing red, supersonic, unidentified flying object.

Within five minutes of take-off from Cork Airport in south-west Ireland, at 11.32 a.m. on a perfect spring morning, the Viscount was climbing up smoothly through the

7,000 feet level. Local Air Traffic Controllers gave Captain O'Beirne clearance to continue his ascent to 17,000 feet and advised him of his course for Tuskar Rock, the craggy prominence with its flashing lighthouse off the Irish coast in the Saint George's Channel, separating Ireland from Wales. The cabin crew prepared to serve a light snack to the passengers, who included more than a score of enthusiastic Swedish anglers happily swapping tales of the salmon they had caught during their week-long expedition in the lakes and rivers of Killarney. The anglers were due to catch a connecting flight at London to take them on the last leg of their journey. With the sight of Tuskar Rock slipping smoothly beneath him, the Captain steered Oscar Mike along the air corridor towards his next landfall, barely 50 miles away, at Strumble Head on the rocky Welsh coast. Twenty-five minutes into the flight, Oscar Mike's radio make a routine check call, reporting that the aircraft was expected to cross over the Welsh mainland within the next six minutes. Everything was going perfectly to schedule.

Two minutes later the master Air Traffic Control for Irish flights, at Shannon on the west coast, radioed the Viscount and instructed Captain O'Beirne to switch his frequency to London Air Traffic Control at Heathrow to be picked up and guided by his new controller.

Captain O'Beirne was calm and unruffled. He acknowledged the message by repeating, confidently, '131.2' – the frequency for the control tower operators who were awaiting his arrival in London just 50 minutes later.

Then disaster, unexpected and violent, shook Oscar Mike from its flight deck to its tailplane. The Shannon Air Traffic Controller no longer had responsibility for monitoring Flight 712 and he turned his attention to other flights inside Irish airspace. Meanwhile, at the radio and radar centre in London, the controllers were busy plotting the paths of dozens of flights heading for Heathrow that day.

The crew of one transatlantic flight were already report-ing their position to the control room and Captain O'Beirne should have followed procedure by waiting for that con-versation to end before he came on the air to announce his own presence entering the London air traffic zone. Instead, he broke into the other radio transmission. His message to London simply said: 'Echo India Alpha Oscar Mike, with you.' There was no sound of urgency or distress, but his call irritated the controllers because it partially blotted out the other aircraft already reporting their positions. They waited for Oscar Mike to repeat his check call when the airwaves were clear.

Only eight seconds later the next report came. This time it was frantic and desperate, distorted by a roaring and screaming noise in the background. Captain O'Beirne was gasping as he wrestled with the controls and yelled into his radio: 'Twelve thousand feet, descending, spinning rapidly.'

The controllers could hardly believe their ears. Two other listeners heard the heart-rending distress call from Oscar Mike: the pilot of the transatlantic flight, nearing the English coast, and the flight crew of Aer Lingus 362, Oscar Mike's sister aircraft. Both pilots acted independently, checking with London Traffic Control to make sure that the emergency message had been received clearly. The London controller made repeated attempts to contact the stricken aircraft. There was no reply.

But Oscar Mike was still airborne. Captain O'Beirne, struggling with the controls, had turned his aircraft away from the forbidding mountains around the Welsh coast and he was already retracing his flight path back across the Irish Sea. Perhaps he thought he had a slim chance of bringing the Viscount safely down on the smooth, sandy beaches near Rosslare, back on the Irish coast, just over the horizon.

The anxious listeners got no clue. There was only baffling and ominous radio silence from Oscar Mike.

With fear mounting, the pilot of the other Aer Lingus flight, bound from Dublin to Bristol, aborted his approach to his destination and sped north towards Strumble Head, Oscar Mike's last reported position, to begin an immediate search. Unbeknownst to him, however, the final moments of the fatal drama were being played out 30 miles to the west of him.

At 12.10 p.m., a deckhand on board the German cargo ship *Metric*, steaming southbound through St George's Channel, ten miles off Rosslare, thought he saw a large bird close by suddenly whirl from the sky and plunge into the sea. He thought no more about it. At the same time another witness, walking along the shore near Greenore Point, heard a roaring splash, and saw a column of water rising from the sea just off the Tuskar lighthouse.

The routine flight of Oscar Mike had ended in tragedy, less than an hour after it had begun.

Within a few minute of the time Flight 712 had been due to land at Heathrow Airport with its crew and passengers, a major search and rescue operation had been mounted across the width of the Irish Sea, with aircraft, helicopters and high speed launches hunting for a clue to the disappearance of Oscar Mike. By nightfall, when the search was called off without success, the news of the disaster was broadcast. At home, watching television reports of the missing Viscount, the lunchtime beachcomber remembered the giant water splash he had seen off Tuskar Rock and phoned his local police station.

As a general appeal for all shipping to watch out for wreckage or survivors was broadcast on the marine shipping frequencies, the deckhand on the cargo ship *Metric* thought of the silver bird he had seen splashing into the sea. Could it have been an aircraft, its size distorted by distance? Thinking the worst, he radioed search headquarters.

The following day, using the approximate bearings supplied by the two witnesses, the search was resumed. Within a few hours a floating wreckage had been sighted, having drifted less than six miles from Tuskar Rock. Over the course of the next few days, 14 bodies and more cabin wreckage was found. There were no survivors.

It took two more months for the bulk of the wreckage of Oscar Mike to be located, lying in 39 fathoms of water. The job of recovering the sunken aircraft and beginning an exhaustive examination of the mass of twisted metal began immediately. Accident investigators began to piece together a grim jigsaw puzzle of the remains of Oscar Mike in a deserted hangar at the headquarters of the Irish Air Force at Casement Aerodrome, Baldonnel.

Most of the twisted fuselage, wings and engines of the Viscount were recovered, but the tail plane sections and elevators were missing. One small section of elevator spring tab, a small control needed to trim the aircraft in flight, was found six months after the crash, entangled in seaweed on the coast of Rosslare, seven miles from the scene of the crash. The small metal flap couldn't have floated. Had it fallen off from the wrecked tail section as Captain O'Beirne tried to make a landing on the beach?

In the meantime, other eye witnesses had come forward with evidence, turning the disaster from an unexplained accident into a mystery of deadly intrigue. During the late morning on the day of the Viscount crash, hundreds of devout Roman Catholics in the small seaside parishes around Rosslare had been going to and from the celebration of Mass in their local churches. The first Mass, which had begun at 10 a.m. had finished and now the church bells were calling the faithful to 11 o'clock Mass. The precise timings of the church services and the ringing of the chapel bells had etched the events into the memories of the witnesses with reliable accuracy.

In the official accident investigation report published

two years after the crash, the identity of these witnesses is masked by code numbers which refer to their sworn affidavits of evidence. None of the witnesses had noticed the uneventful flight of Oscar Mike as it passed overhead. But they all heard and saw strange sounds and sights in the sky a few minutes later.

Shortly after the Viscount flew over Tuskar Rock, bound for the Welsh coast, ten witnesses near the village of Broadway, three miles inland, heard loud cracking noises and rolling explosions in the air, like peals of thunder. Four witnesses saw a high-speed object in the air, its wings bright red and its tail glowing 'as if on fire' as it streaked out to sea towards Wales. Another witness saw it turn sharply in mid-air 'as if fired out of the clouds'. A witness ten miles away from Broadway, across the sweeping Ballyteige Bay, saw the same object 'enveloped in a small dark cloud which travelled along with the aeroplane, swirling'. This was followed by a bang, which died away 'like thunder'.

The evidence of the witnesses is all technically consistent with a supersonic flying machine, trailing clouds of turbulent air from its wings and leaving a wake of booming shock waves as it streaks through the sound barrier.

The investigators turned immediately to the possibility that Oscar Mike had been struck by an air-to-air missile or had collided with a military jet fighter, but checks with Britain's Royal Air Force, the only operator of supersonic aircraft over the Irish Sea, only deepened the mystery. No RAF jets were in the area at the time and none had been reported missing. The only missile firing range near the flight path of Oscar Mike, the Ministry of Defence rocket range at Aberporth in Wales, had been closed that Sunday.

Government officials in Dublin made approaches to the NATO military powers to check the flights of supersonic aircraft. The answer came back that no jets had been operational anywhere near Oscar Mike. They even asked the

Soviet Navy if any of their aircraft carriers had been prowling undetected around the southern stretches of the Atlantic where it reaches into the Irish Sea. They drew a blank.

In the final dossier, which drew a veil of mystery over the fate of Oscar Mike, the Irish government's official accident investigator, R W O'Sullivan, confirmed: There is not enough evidence available on which to reach a conclusion of reasonable probability as to the initial cause of this accident.' But he did reveal that only one theory, even though 'improbable', covers all the bizarre unexplained elements in the accounts of the Viscount crash.

In his report, R W O'Sullivan admitted the possibility that: 'While Viscount EI-AOM was in normal cruising flight at 17,000 feet, and within six minutes of reaching Strumble Head, another aircraft, which could have been a manned or unmanned aeroplane or missile, passed in close proximity, possibly even colliding with the tail of the Viscount, causing an upset before control was finally lost.'

Amelia Earhart

When aviation pioneer Amelia Earhart roared off into the skies on 1 June 1937, she may have carried a guilty secret with her. The darling girl of the air, who had become the first woman to fly solo across the Atlantic and the first pilot ever to fly solo from Hawaii to California, was determined to add one more flying record to her list of achievements.

Amelia was willing to risk her life to make the first flight around the world by the longest possible route – the closest course to the equator, a distance of 27,000 miles. She was confident that she had the flying skill to make the gruelling journey and that her twin-engined Lockheed Electra 10-E aircraft was mechanically tough and reliable enough to carry her through the worst of the weather the

Earth's tropics would throw at her.

But determined and self-sufficient though she was, Amelia Earhart could not hope to smash the world record again on initiative and guts alone. She needed help from friends in high places to make her record attempt possible.

There were certainly many powerful and important people who saw that cooperation with Amelia Earhart could pay dividends to suit all parties. Earhart would have to enlist the aid of the best technical experts at the Lockheed aircraft builders and the vast resources of the United States navy for her enterprise. Without them, the project was doomed to failure.

Normally, the American aircraft builders would have been only too willing to promote and sponsor any move by Earhart to get herself in the record books once more. Her exploits of daring marathon flights had captured the headlines and the country's imagination, and had helped to convince a hesitant public that travel by commercial airline was becoming a safe and commonplace event. They helped to sell hundreds of small airliners to more and more new operators each years.

But in 1937, the planemakers had different priorities. Their production lines were producing fewer civilian aircraft and were being increasingly committed to turning out combat planes for the US Army Air Corps and the US Navy. Washington was nervously eyeing the expansion of Japanese military ambitions in the Pacific and they had themselves begun a growing programme of rearming and updating the squadrons of America's own flying forces.

During the First World War, Japan had occupied the Marshall, Caroline and Mariana Islands and had managed to retain these under a League of Nations mandate. In 1934, the Japanese began isolating the islands from their Pacific neighbours. Both America and Japan had agreed, at the Naval Treaty Conference in Washington in 1923, that military construction of the Pacific islands occupied by either side should be strictly banned. Now American strategists believed the Japanese were secretly preparing their captive islands as giant munitions dumps, communications bases and airfields for an attack on the US controlled Pacific islands – or even the American mainland – in defiance of all the guarantees they had given the League of Nations.

The Americans themselves had launched a defensive military build-up in the Pacific, aimed mainly at developing radio facilities to control a series of direction-finding stations strung out across the ocean to detect any large movements of aircraft. The War Department had entered into a secret partnership with Pan American Airways to build a series of direction-finding bases on Midway and Wake Island, under the guise of providing navigation facilities for the airline's trans-oceanic flights across the Pacific.

The years of hidden preparation by the Japanese were to climax in 1941, with their surprise attack on Pearl Harbour. Even by 1937, the troubled skies over the Pacific were no place for amateur pilots to tax strained diplomatic relations by making trail-blazing publicity stunts in their aircraft. Amelia Earhart, however, was no unknown amateur. She had served as a lecturer and counsellor at the Purdue Research Foundation at Purdue University in Lafayette, Indiana; and the Foundation openly admitted its aims were to conduct aviation research 'with particular reference to National Defence'. The research unit was also in receipt of government grants backed by the US War Department, and the Foundation openly admitted it was providing the money to buy the Lockheed Electra for Earhart, for the scientific purpose of testing and improving radio direction-finding equipment.

In her eagerness to claim the glory for new achievements in flying history, Amelia had originally wanted to go one step further. She planned to fly the Pacific from east to west and carry out the first mid-air refuelling, using specially adapted US Navy planes. But the War Department ruled out her plan as too risky. Instead, they proposed an alternative, which would provide them with a strategic military bonus.

Amelia, they suggested, should be provided with a safe landing and refuelling stop in the middle of the vast ocean. The place they chose was remote Howland Island, only a few degrees north of the Equator and less than 600 miles from the Japanese-controlled Marshall Islands. Work began immediately on the construction of an airstrip and fuel dump, while suspicious Japanese warships patrolled around Howland on spying missions. Any muted protests from the Japanese were countered with outraged indignation on the part of the Americans, who explained that the airbase on the tiny speck of land, only three-quarters of a mile long and half a mile wide, was essential for the safety of the daring woman air pioneer.

In the meantime, Amelia continued with the preparations for her record-breaking flight and her aircraft was flown to Lockheed's private factory for special modifications. Amelia's technical supervisor, Paul Mantz, tried to monitor all the changes, but even he was unaware that Lockheed's chief specialist in its latest top-secret radio gear, Joseph Gurr, was detailed to fit experimental direction-finding equipment inside the plane.

On 17 March, Amelia set out on the first leg of the trip. But this proved only to be a disastrous false start after the first 2,410 miles, from San Francisco to Honolulu, had been covered. On take-off from Honolulu, overburdened with the weight of 1,100 US gallons of fuel and two navigators, the Electra crashed and its undercarriage collapsed.

Amelia sat down to an urgent conference with her technical advisors and her husband, George Palmer Putnam, and changed her plans completely. The flight would not circumnavigate the globe from west to east. With the help of prevailing winds on the new route, she would be able to dispense with the weight of one navigator and give herself some margin of safety. (The delay in her plans also gave the US Navy and the Army Air Corps a valuable breathing space in which to install more and more secret defence equipment on Howland Island.)

On 1 June, Earhart started again from scratch. By this time her aircraft was bristling with a bewildering array of low and high frequency radio equipment and direction-finders.

There can be little doubt that, as she took off, Amelia may have realized that she had already become a pawn in the deadly mock war games the US military chiefs were planning in the Pacific. But for Amelia, her one goal was the successful achievement of her round-the-world trip. If her plane was being used as some kind of military flying test bed, it was a small price to pay for the chance to circle the globe. The flight was publicized every step of the way, with cheering crowds to greet her as she touched down, rested, refuelled and took off again from the various airfields in South America, Africa, Asia and Australia.

A month after her voyage had begun, her navigator, Captain Frederick Noonan, strapped himself into the cockpit behind her and the pair prepared to take-off from Lae, in New Guinea, for the riskiest part of the flight. Their course was to go over a stretch of the Pacific never crossed by an aircraft before – the 2,556 miles from the coast of New Guinea to Howland Island. It was the major leg of the flight across open water. The next stop should have been Honolulu, then Oakland in San Francisco Bay and finally home in triumph to Lafayette, Indiana.

The flight plan between Lae and Howland island was also the most crucial part of the journey for the US Navy's warship *Ontario* and the Coastguard cutter USS *Itasca*, supposedly acting as safety and rescue standby vessels, but secretly using Earhart's Electra as a 'target' plane to check and test their direction-finding equipment. As Amelia took off, the American radio operator in Lae, Harry Balfour, received a weather forecast on his radio and teleprinter from the US Navy Fleet base at Pearl Harbour. Although he called the information through to Earhart and her navigator several times, he received no reply.

Just five hours after his transmission, at 3 p.m., Balfour picked up Amelia's voice, clear and unflustered. All seemed to be going well. Two hours later the pilot radioed again, this time reporting that adverse weather conditions were forcing her to lose height and speed. But she was still unconcerned.

In mid-ocean, on board the warship *Ontario*, navigation officer Lieutenant Horace Blakeslee, who had estimated the plane should be overhead at 10 p.m., failed to make radio contact, although one of his deck officers thought he heard the sound of an aircraft overhead. The *Ontario*'s searchlights were switched on full, but heavy rain clouds had blotted out the sky. The warship, low on fuel supplies, was soon forced to return to base on a nearby island, and to leave the task of locating Amelia and her plane to the Coast Guard vessel *Itasca* almost 1,000 miles further along the course, off Howland Island. As the *Ontario* turned away, a land-based radio operator on Nauru island to the north picked up a broadcast from her, reporting the words: 'A ship in sight ahead.'

In the early hours of the morning, at 2.45 a.m., the radio room of the *Itasca* heard Amelia's voice on the radio again. The only part of the message they could understand was: 'Cloudy weather . . . cloudy'. On the island itself, a top-secret frequency radio direction-finder failed to track the location of the transmissions.

An hour later Amelia broadcast again, forlornly reporting overcast weather and asking the Coastguard ship to contact her on a new radio frequency. Again, they failed to locate her or raise her on the radio. Throughout the night they heard sporadic plaintive calls from Amelia Earhart, fragments of weary speech, but despite all their high-powered equipment they still could not reach her.

After 8.43 a.m. came Amelia's final message, frantic and desperate. She gave a confusing, wide-ranging compass position, which could have put her anywhere on a line stretching hundreds of miles both north or south of Howland Island. Then, all contact was lost for good, and soon the massive, but fruitless search began.

President Franklyn Roosevelt personally ordered the battleship USS *Colorado* from Hawaii to steam full-speed to the search area with its three catapult-launched spotter aircraft. The following day he instructed the aircraft carrier USS *Lexington* and three destroyers to set off on a ten-day voyage from the west coast of America to join the search.

Nervous US Navy senior brass, who had secretly organized the seemingly innocent Earhart flight as an experimental trial, now began to complain they were 'spending millions of dollars and disrupting Navy training schedules to search for a couple of stunt fliers'.

There were a spate of heartless and cruel hoax calls from American radio hams, claiming that they had picked up distress messages from Amelia. Some claimed she was 'injured but alive' and quoted her call sign – KHAQQ.

On 5 July newspaper stories reported that a radio message had been picked up from Amelia by the Pan American Airways bases on Midway and Wake Island. The message indicated that Amelia had been forced down several miles south-east of Howland, near the Phoenix Islands. War Department chiefs rushed to deny the reports, afraid that the Japanese might learn of the existence and power of these covert radio installations. For two weeks, an entire task force of US warships and planes scoured more than 150,000 square miles of the Pacific, skirting the

Japanese-held islands to the north.

Then, speculation erupted among the more sceptical and scandal-hungry Americans that Amelia Earhart had been on a mission for the Government and had landed safely on Howland Island, in order to give the War Department an excuse to send warships and aircraft to spy on the Japanese war preparations in the Pacific. There were reports that US pilots, supposedly engaged in the search for their public heroine, had returned to base with aerial photographs of Japanese bases.

The rumours persisted for almost a year. One newspaper in Oakland, California, began a series of articles about Earhart's disappearance. Their first issue claimed that the woman pilot had been lost because the direction-finding equipment on Howland had been supplied with the wrong kind of batteries and had failed the moment it was switched on. But Washington soon put a stop to this, and no further articles were published.

Amelia Earhart and Captain Noonan were never seen again. Three years later, after the attack on Pearl Harbour and the overwhelming carnage of the war in the Pacific, the fate of the two fliers paled into insignificance until, as America fought back against the Japanese and began to drive them westward across the ocean, the mystery of Amelia Earhart slowly began to unravel.

Then it suddenly deepened again. In 1944, the victorious US forces captured the Marshall Islands from the Japanese. During routine interrogation, Vice Admiral Edgar Cruise was told by a native interpreter that two American fliers, a man and a woman, had been brought to the islands by Japanese captors in 1937. The couple had been transferred to the grim Garapon Prison at Japanese military head-quarters in Saipan in the Mariana Islands. The woman was dispirited and broken. After only a few months in the hellish conditions of the military torture centre, she died of dysentery. Her male companion, of no further use to his interrogators, was executed.

Twenty years later, in 1964, two former US Marines, who had served in the Pacific, announced publicly that they had recovered the remains of Amelia Earhart and Frederick Noonan from unmarked graves on Saipan in July 1944 and had transferred them back to the United States for burial. But the US Marine Corps still refuses to confirm or deny their stories.

And so, the mystery remains. Was Amelia Earhart an intrepid espionage agent who gave her life to help her country develop its air defences? Did she die an unsung heroine with her brave navigator in the squalor of a Japanese prison camp? Is she buried in a secret grave back in her American homeland with the location of her final resting place known only to a handful of military intelligence officials? Or was she simply an enthusiastic amateur glory-seeker who didn't care who organized and subsidized her daring exploits, just as long as she made the headlines?

The unemotional answer may lie in a report in a small Australian newspaper, published a year after her disappearance. The Sydney newspaper claimed that the United States had secretly informed the Australian Government, their Pacific ally, of their plans to monitor Amelia's last flight as cover for its preparations for war. The US War Department, which made great propaganda of the treachery of the Japanese sneak attack on Pearl Harbour, had refused to admit that it had duped her into a peacetime spying mission. The newspaper claimed the last distress signal had, in fact, come from the location of the Phoenix Islands, but the search squadrons used it as an excuse to turn north and spy on the potential enemy.

The paper concluded: 'Sentiment comes second to Secret Service.'

Murder
Most Foul

House of Horror

John Reginald Christie got his kicks by murdering women and sexually abusing their corpses. He went about his grisly business in his shabby house in Notting Hill Gate, London, whose address – 10 Rillington Place – has since become infamous.

Christie was born on 8 April 1898 in Halifax, Yorkshire. His father, Ernest, a designer for Crossley Carpets, was a pillar of local society, being a leader of the Primrose League (an organisation intended to promote morality among the working classes) and a founder member of the Halifax Conservative Party. He was also a stern disciplinarian and his son was terrified of him. 'We almost had to ask if we could speak to him', he later wrote. Christie also had other problems within his family: one of seven children, he was completely dominated by his older sisters.

Christie did well at school and sang in the choir. He was first a boy scout and then assistant scout master. But there were other, deeper, tides flowing within Christie. When he was eight, for example, his grandfather died and Christie reported having felt a trembling sensation of both fascination and pleasure on seeing the body.

After leaving school Christie started work at the Gem Cinema in Halifax. One day he was part of a gang of boys and girls who went down to the Monkey Run, as the local lovers' lane was known. They paired off and Christie found himself with a girl who was much more sexually experienced than he was. Intimidated, he could not rise to the occasion and when word of it got around his friends started taunting him, calling him 'Reggie-no-dick' and 'Can't-do-it-Reggie'.

At the age of 17 Christie was caught stealing at work and sacked, whereupon his father kicked him out of the house; he had to sleep on the family's allotment and his mother took him food. He then drifted from job to job until he was called up to serve as a soldier during World War I. He was gassed in France before being sent home and discharged from the army with a disability pension.

On 20 May 1920 Christie married the long-suffering Ethel Waddington. He got a job as a postman, but was caught stealing money from letters. In 1921 he was jailed for nine months. Two years later he was bound over for posing as a former officer. Following a violent incident he was put on probation, and when he was sent down for another nine months for theft Ethel left him. In 1929 he was sentenced to six months' hard labour for assaulting a prostitute. A Roman Catholic priest befriended him, but Christie stole his car, which earned him another spell in prison.

On his release Christie wrote to Ethel asking her to come back to him and she foolishly did so. They moved to London, and on a visit to Ethel's family in Leeds Christie boasted of his 'big house in London' and his servants. In fact, he and Ethel lived in a shabby little flat in North Kensington, with no servants. He never earned over £8 a week, which was the going rate for a junior clerk.

On the outbreak of World War II in 1939 Christie became a special constable in the War Reserve Police. No checks were carried out to see if he had a criminal record, but in any case he seemed to be a reformed character. He was never much liked, however, because of his petty-mindedness – indeed, Christie and another special constable were known as the 'rat and the weasel'   .

Although he was balding, Christie still regarded himself as a charmer. Deep down, however, he feared and hated women. 'Women who give you the come-on wouldn't look nearly so saucy if they were helpless and dead', he thought. He took pride in hiding his violent intentions from the women whom he took back to 10

Rillington Place, and by the time that they arrived there it was too late for them to save themselves.

His first victim was an Austrian refugee, the 17-year-old Ruth Fuerst. Ruth worked in a munitions factory, but because the pay was poor she supplemented her income with the proceeds of a little prostitution. Christie had met her while he was trying to trace a man who was wanted for theft; she had asked him to lend her ten shillings and Christie had invited her home. On one hot, August afternoon in 1943, while Ethel was in Sheffield, she called again at 10 Rillington Place. At first Christie refused to engage in sexual intercourse, but Ruth encouraged him. Once the sex was over he strangled her. Christie said that he had felt a great sense of peace after he had killed Ruth. He had been fascinated by the beauty of her corpse and had wanted to keep it, but his wife had returned home unexpectedly that night and he had had to bury Ruth's body in the garden. He compared his debut in murder to an artist's first painting. 'It was thrilling because I had embarked on the career I had chosen for myself, the career of murder. But it was only the beginning', he later said.

Christie left the police force at the end of 1943 and went to work at the Ultra Radio Works in west London, where he met an attractive, 31-year-old woman, Muriel Eady. Muriel suffered from catarrh and Christie claimed that he had a remedy for it. On one afternoon in October 1944 she therefore went to see him at 10 Rillington Place and he showed her what he claimed was his patent inhaler. In fact, it was nothing more than a jar containing perfumed water that had two holes in its lid with rubber tubes leading from them. Christie then persuaded Muriel to inhale his remedy through one of them; unbeknownst to her the other tube was connected to the gas pipe. The perfume in the jar concealed the smell of gas and when Muriel lapsed into unconsciousness Christie had sex with her and then strangled her. He was thrilled by the notion that his second murder was much cleverer than the first.

In 1948 Timothy Evans, a lorry driver, and his wife, Beryl, moved into the top-floor flat at 10 Rillington Place. Born in Merthyr Vale on 20 November 1924, Evans was educationally challenged and also had a speech impediment (when he was a child he could not even pronounce his own name). His schooling had been held back further by a foot injury which caused him to spend long spells in hospital. Evans' father had walked out on his mother before Timothy was born (his mother subsequently procured a certificate saying he was presumed dead). She later remarried and the family moved to Notting Hill Gate, where Timothy married a local girl, Beryl Thorley, in 1947.

Evans was 24 when he saw the 'To Let' sign outside 10 Rillington Place. He and the pregnant Beryl were still living with his mother and stepfather and because the young couple desperately needed a place of their own they took the cramped attic flat. Charles Kitchener, a railway worker with failing eyesight, lived on the floor below. He kept himself to himself and was often in hospital. The ground floor was occupied by John and Ethel Christie. Shortly after the Evanses moved in Beryl gave birth to a baby daughter, whom they named Geraldine. The Evanses and Christies were soon getting on well and Ethel, who was fond of the baby, looked after Geraldine when Beryl was working part-time.

In the summer of 1949 Beryl became pregnant again. There was little money coming in and the Evanses were behind on their hire-purchase payments. Beryl, who was still 19, wanted an abortion, but Timothy, a Roman Catholic, forbade it. The adamant Beryl then discovered that there was a back-street abortionist on the Edgware Road who could help her out by performing the abortion himself. She in turn told Timothy of Christie's offer, who said that he had not realised that Christie knew anything about medical procedures. In order to reassure him Christie showed him the St John's Ambulance Brigade's first-aid manual; Evans, who was illiterate, knew no better.

On 8 November 1949 Evans came home to find Christie waiting for him with bad news: the operation had not been a success, Christie explained, and Beryl had died. Christie begged Evans not to go to the police, saying that he would charged with manslaughter because Beryl had died during an illegal abortion. Evans' first concern was who would look after Geraldine and therefore suggested his mother, but Christie said that he would find someone else to care for the baby. When Evans returned from work on 10 November Christie said that he had delivered the child to a couple in East Acton, and that evening Evans assisted Christie in disposing of Beryl's body down the outside drain.

Christie helped Evans to sell off his furniture and Evans then returned to Wales with £40 in his pocket. He was plagued by guilt, however, believing that as Catholic he should have stopped Beryl from having the abortion; if he had done so, he reasoned, she would still have been alive. So he walked into Merthyr Vale's police station and confessed. Evans thought that he could take the blame for Beryl's death without implicating Christie, whom he considered to be his friend. He therefore told the police that he had obtained a bottle that contained something that would make his wife miscarry from a man whom he had met in a transport café. He had not intended to give it to his wife, he said, but explained that she must have found it while he was out at work. When he returned he had found her dead and had opened a drain outside the front door into which he had dropped her body.

The Merthyr Vale police contacted their counterparts at Notting Hill Gate, who sent police officers to 10 Rillington Place. It took three of them to lift the manhole cover the drain, only to find that it was empty. Back in Merthyr Vale the police then challenged Evans' statement: he could not possibly have lifted the manhole cover himself, they said. Unable to continue the pretence, Evans made a second statement, this time telling the truth: Christie, he said, had performed an illegal abortion on his wife, who had consequently died; together he and Christie had disposed of the body.

The police had searched 10 Rillington Place, but not very thoroughly – they did not even notice Muriel Eady's thighbone, which was propped up against the garden fence. Christie made a statement saying that he had overheard the Evanses quarrelling; Beryl had complained that her husband had grabbed her by the throat, he elaborted. The police believed Christie – after all, the man had been policeman.

The house was searched again and this time Beryl's corpse was found. It had been wrapped in a green tablecloth and hidden behind a stack of wood in a downstairs washroom. Beside it was the body of the 14-month-old Geraldine. Both had been strangled. An autopsy revealed that there was bruising in Beryl's vagina and that her right eye and upper lip were swollen. In the police view this evidence confirmed their belief that Beryl's murder had been a simple 'domestic'.

Evans' trial took place at the Old Bailey in the January of 1950. Standing in the witness box, Christie apologised to the judge for speaking softly, explaining that this was the result of having been gassed during World War I. The court was also told of his service as a special constable. His long record of petty crime was not mentioned and the impression was given that he was a solid citizen whose word was not to be doubted. When he was asked if he had performed an illegal abortion on Beryl Evans he denied it, saying that he had been lying ill in bed on the day of Beryl's death.

Evans cut a much shabbier figure. He was out of his

depth in the courtroom and gave his evidence poorly. His allegation that his wife had died during an illegal abortion performed by Christie held no water with the court as the evidence proved that she had been strangled. Furthermore, he could not explain the death of the baby. The jury deliberated for just 40 minutes before returning a verdict of guilty. The sentence imposed by the judge was death by hanging.

Evans maintained to the end that Christie had killed his wife and daughter. There was some public disquiet about the verdict and a petition bearing nearly 2,000 signatures was presented to the home secretary appealing against the verdict. It did no good and Evans was hanged on 9 March 1950.

Christie later said that on 14 December 1952 he had been woken when his wife, Ethel, went into convulsions. She seemed to have overdosed on phenobarbital and Christie decided that it was too late to get help. It would be kindest to put her out of her misery, he reasoned, so he put a stocking around his wife's neck and strangled her. Unsure of what to do with it, he then left his wife's body in the bed for two days before pulling up the floor-boards in the front room and burying her under them. The couple had been married for 32 years.

Over the next four months Christie sold his furniture to fund a sex-and-murder spree. The 25-year-old prostitute Rita Nelson had just discovered that she was pregnant when, on 12 January 1953, she visited 10 Rillington Place, where Christie strangled her, subsequently shoving her body into an alcove in the kitchen. The 26-year-old Kathleen Maloney was lured into his flat to pose nude while he photographed her. Instead she was gassed and sexually abused, her body then also being placed in the alcove.

Christie had more trouble with his final victim, Hectorina MacLennan. He had met her in the café in which he picked up prostitutes and had offered her somewhere to stay. She had turned up at 10 Rillington Place with her boyfriend, however. After they had been there for three nights Christie at last found her alone on 6 March 1953. He gave her a drink and offered her a whiff of his inhaler, which she did not enjoy. Following a struggle Christie strangled her and had sex with her corpse. He then bundled her body into the alcove, joining those of Rita Nelson and Kathleen Maloney, propping her up into a sitting position, with her bra hooked to Maloney's leg.

After that Christie built a false wall in front of the alcove and papered over it. He sub-let the flat to a couple called Reilly, took his dog to the vet to be put to sleep and moved out. The landlord subsequently evicted the Reillys and gave Beresford Brown, who was living in the flat that had previously been occupied by the Evanses, permission to use the kitchen in the ground-floor flat provided that he cleared it out.

After Brown removed the clothes, rubbish and filth that Christie had left behind him, he started to redecorate the kitchen. He had wanted to put up some brackets on the rear wall, but when he tapped it he found that it was hollow. Pulling away some of the wallpaper, he saw a papered-over, wooden door. On opening it he discerned a partially clothed woman's body sitting on a pile of rubbish. Brown promptly called the police.

The police soon discovered that there was more than one body at 10 Rillington Place. A thorough search of the alcove revealed a second, wrapped in a blanket, and then a third, whose ankles had been tied together with plastic flex. All three had been strangled. Next, the corpse of Ethel Christie was found under the floorboards in the front room.

The police quickly realised that John Reginald Christie was the man for whom they should be searching and issued his description to the press. His picture appeared in every national newspaper and appeals for information regarding his whereabouts were made over the loudspeaker systems at football matches. Soon the whole country was looking for a slight, balding, middle-aged multiple murder. There were numerous reported sightings of Christie, but few were genuine.

Meanwhile, in the tiny garden of 10 Rillington Place, the police had unearthed the skeletons of two more women, which, they estimated, had lain buried for about ten years. Both women had been strangled and the skull of one was missing.

On the day that he left 10 Rillington Place Christie had moved into a hotel in King's Cross Road. He had soon moved on, however, tramping back and forth across London homeless and alone. At around 11pm on the night of 19 March 1953, at the height of the biggest manhunt that the country had ever known, Norman Rae, the chief crime reporter of the Sunday newspaper, the *News of the World*, received a phone call. 'Do you recognise my voice?' the caller asked. Rae did: he had met Christie during the trial of Timothy Evans. 'I can't stand it any more', said Christie. 'They're hunting me like a dog.' In return for a meal, some cigarettes and a warm place in which to sit, Christie promised that he would give the *News of the World* an exclusive. They arranged to meet at 11.30am, outside Wood Green's town hall, and as Rae parked outside it two policemen walked by. It was pure chance, but Christie ran off, thinking that he had been double-crossed.

Two days later PC Thomas Ledger stopped a man near Putney Bridge, who, in response to the constable's questioning, said that he was John Waddington, of 35 Westbourne Grove. The young policeman then asked him to turn out his pockets, one of which proved to contain a newspaper cutting from 1950 concerning Timothy Evans' murder trial. The hunt for Christie was over.

Christie made a detailed confession, providing a separate – and self-serving – explanation for each killing. The prostitutes had forced themselves upon him, he said, and things had got out of hand. His wife had had to be put out of her misery. The murders of Muriel Eady and Beryl Evans had been mercy killings, too.

At his trial Christie pleaded insanity, but could not disguise the fact that he had carefully planned the killings (which he described with a chilling lack of contrition as 'those regrettable happenings'). He had even constructed a special apparatus with which to gas four of his victims. Christie was found guilty and sentenced to death. There was no appeal and he was hanged at Pentonville at 9am on 15 July 1953.

There remained a legal problem, however, in that Timothy Evans had been convicted of the murder of his wife, Beryl, and their daughter, Geraldine – murders to which Christie had subsequently confessed. A formal inquiry was therefore set up, which concluded that two murderers had been operating at 10 Rillington Place; Christie had told the truth at Evans' trial, it reasoned, but had lied at his own.

In 1966 a judicial review of the case under Mr Justice Brabin concluded it more probable that Evans murdered his own wife but not his baby daughter. No one knows for sure who killed Beryl Evans. Her husband Timothy and Reginald Christie both took their terrible secrets to the gallows with them. Only one of the two men knew the complete certainty whether or not the other one was lying.

Poetry, Passion and Prison

Adelaide Bartlett was boyishly attractive, with bobbed hair, full lips and flashing eyes. She had few friends outside her husband's immediate family, and even they were often at loggerheads with the wilful young foreigner who had come into their midst.

Adelaide was born in Orléans, France, in 1856 to an English father and a wealthy, but unmarried, French mother. At the age of 17 she came to England to complete her education, staying in London at the home of her guardian. A regular visitor to the house was her guardian's brother, Edwin Bartlett, who speedily wooed, won and wed her.

Edwin, who at 29 was 10 years older than Adelaide, was a hard working and prosperous family grocer, a kindly man – but one whose life-style was not to his young bride's taste.

Adelaide fell out with Edwin's family – all except his younger brother, Frederick, with whom she had an affair. While Edwin devoted himself ever more diligently to his business, the bored wife remained at home sewing and organizing the household chores – and waiting for Frederick's illicit visits.

She made so little secret of her attraction to Frederick that the brothers' father intervened. After one acrimonious row, during which Adelaide learned that the older Mr Bartlett was planning to move in to the family home at her husband's invitation, she stormed from the house and was not seen again for some days. Since Frederick was also absent for this period, tongues began to wag . . . so much so that when Adelaide's anger cooled and she returned home, she forced her father-in-law to write a letter of apology to her.

In 1885 the Bartletts moved to a grander home in Pimlico. There they were visited regularly by a young Wesleyan minister with a penchant for poetry, the Rev. George Dyson.

Edwin considered Dyson to be an improving influence on his wife and encouraged their friendship. What he may not have realized was that the minister's flowery poetry was often directed at Adelaide. He wrote to her:

> Who is it that hath burst the door,
> Unclosed the heart that shut before
> And set her queen-like on its throne
> And made its homage all her own?
> My Birdie!

The Rev. Dyson did not confine his expressions of love to the written word. And his love affair with Adelaide was aided by her husband's strange reaction to the couple's growing closeness. Bartlett not only condoned his wife's friendship, he actively encouraged it. He even made a will leaving everything to his wife and naming Dyson as the executor.

Then, in December 1885, Edwin Bartlett fell ill. He had always prided himself on being particularly fit but this illness, diagnosed by the family doctor as acute gastritis, took its toll on him and he sank fast. Edwin died on New Year's Day 1886.

The doctor was sufficiently suspicious to press for a post-mortem examination, which revealed large quantities of liquid chloroform in his stomach. Everything pointed to poisoning. Yet there was one inexplicable fact . . . there were no traces of the burning chloroform in Edwin's mouth or throat.

Both lovers were charged with murder, although the case against Dyson was later dropped for lack of evidence despite his admission that he had bought quantities of chloroform at various chemists' shops.

At her trial, the attractive Adelaide played brilliantly on the emotions and Victorian prejudices to the jury. She admitted dosing her husband with chloroform. But she claimed pathetically that she had first used the drug to curb his sexual demands, then later to help Edwin sleep during his illness.

The jury were sympathetic. They were also baffled by the means by which the chloroform was administered without causing burning of the throat. They acquitted Adelaide Bartlett, who disappeared without trace after her trial. It was reported that she had emigrated to America.

A famous surgeon, Sir James Paget of London's St Bartholomew's Hospital, commented: 'Now that it is all over, she should tell us in the interests of science how she did it.'

The Vicar and the Choirmistress

Even today the headlines would cause a sensation . . . 'Vicar And Choirmistress Murdered In Lovers' Lane'. The congregation were both scandalized to learn of the love affair between their clergyman and a married woman and horrified by the killing. Yet no one was ever convicted of the double murder, and the mystery remains to this day.

A courting couple discovered the bodies of the Rev. Edward Wheeler Hall and Mrs Eleanor Mills, choir leader at his church, on 16 September 1922. The spot, by an abandoned farm near New Brunswick, New Jersey, was a favourite with lovers seeking solitude.

Hall, minister of St John the Evangelist Church, in New Brunswick, and his mistress had both been shot through the head. But more sinister . . . the choir leader's vocal cords had been cut in an act of savage hate. The pair's passionate letters to each other were stewn contemptuously around the bodies.

Hall's wife Frances was questioned, as was Mrs Mills' husband James, but no charges were brought. Mrs Hall was a popular figure among the church-going community. There were stories of detectives ignoring clues, of vital evidence going missing, and of a prosecutor unwilling to take action. There was neither a post-mortem nor an inquest.

There the case might have been conveniently closed, but for a news-hungry editor convinced there had been a cover-up.

Philip Payne of the *New York Mirror*, sent his own sleuths to the scene to piece together the evidence. They managed to get hold of Hall's calling card, which police had found propped against his body, and Payne claimed it carried the fingerprints of Mrs Hall's brother Willie.

Faced with this and other evidence, police brought murder charges against Mrs Hall, her cousin Henry Carpender, a brother Henry Stevens and Willie.

Willie, the strangest defendant, was an eccentric who liked to dress up in fireman's uniform and put out fires in his own backyard.

They were finally brought to trial four years after the killings, in November 1926. After so long, memories were failing. The wealthy Mrs Hall's high-powered lawyers made mincemeat of the prosecution witnesses' shaky testimony.

Soon it became clear that the prosecution's case rested on one alleged eye-witness – Jane Gibson, a pig farmer. Dying of cancer, she was wheeled into court in a hospital bed and whispered her vital evidence.

Four years earlier, then a fit and vigorous country-woman, she said she had been exercising her mule Jennie on the night of the murders. She identified the four defendants and said she had seen them in the lane where the bodies were later found.

With them were the Rev. Hall and Mrs Mills. Voices were raised in anger, she said and there was mention of love letters. Mrs Gibson rode away, wanting no part of a family quarrel.

Her testimony, delivered firmly despite her pain, obviously impressed the jury. But then a relative gave evidence denying that Mrs Gibson had been out of the house that night.

Moments later the courtroom was rocked by the news that a prisoner in jail in New York had confessed to the killings. But he was exposed as a sensation-seeker who was nowhere near New Brunswick when the murders were committed.

Witnesses gave the Stevens brothers and cousin Henry watertight alibis, and the defence then suggested that Mrs Gibson had shot the couple, thinking they were thieves after her corn.

But the most telling witness of all was the incredibly calm Mrs Hall. She had loved her husband dearly, she said, and had never suspected an infidelity. Least of all with Eleanor Mills, whom she had always regarded as her dearest friend.

Mrs Hall said she could not account for Jane Gibson's testimony, but would forgive her because of her suffering. The jury believed the wronged wife, and all four defendants were acquitted.

It was a subdued crowd who left the courtroom, knowing that somewhere in their midst a killer was still at large.

And some strange events followed.

Mrs Hall sued the *New York Mirror* for two million dollars.

Philip Payne, desperate to rebuild his reputation, set out to make a record transatlantic flight to Rome. His plane vanished.

Officials who had been accused of concealing evidence lived under a cloud. And those involved in the prosecution were eased from office.

Witnesses for both sides were struck by a succession of tragedies. Soon after Mrs Gibson's death, Mrs Hall also died of cancer. And so, one by one, did the other defendants.

The case remains unsolved.

Death in Happy Valley

When 57-year-old Sir Henry 'Jock' Delves Broughton married a young blonde with a passion for clothes and jewels in 1940, he told her: 'If you ever fall in love with someone else and want a divorce, I won't stand in your way.'

The old Etonian baronet also promised his beautiful bride Diana, 30 years his junior, an income of £5,000 a year for seven years should she ever leave him for another man.

Just three months after the marriage, Diana did exactly that. She fell in love with another Old Etonian, Josslyn Hay, the 39-year-old Earl of Erroll.

The brevity of the marriage would seem extraordinary even in more modern, permissive times. But in the strange, close circle in which Hay and the Broughton's lived, it was not too unorthodox. Their home was an area of colonial Kenya known as Happy Valley, where wild drinking, cocaine-snorting and wife-swapping were prevalent in 1940.

Josslyn Hay himself was a dedicated philanderer whose favourite saying was 'to hell with husbands'. But his amoral attitude appeared not to worry Sir Henry, the cuckolded husband. At a dinner party he threw at the local country club, he toasted his wife and her lover: 'I wish them every happiness and may their union be blessed with an heir. To Diana and Joss.'

Broughton returned home visibly drunk, leaving Erroll

and Diana to dance. Erroll then drove off alone, remarking as he left: 'The old boy's so nice, it smells bad.'

Two hours later Erroll was found on the floor of his Buick, a bullet through his head. But the murder weapon was not to be seen.

Though Broughton seemed the obvious suspect, such was the cuckolded baronet's calm and masterful conduct in the witness box that he was found 'not guilty'.

After the acquittal Broughton and Diana soon split up. He committed suicide the following year, still protesting his innocence.

Lizzie and the Axe

According to the immortal rhyme, Lizzie Borden took an axe and gave her mother forty whacks; when she saw what she had done she gave her father forty one. But according to American justice; the 32-year-old spinster was not responsible for the bloody slaughter of Andrew J. Borden and his wife Abby. She was acquitted after a ten-day trial, and the courtroom rang with applause at the verdict. Ever since, the world has wondered why.

The Borden household at 92 Second Street in the Massachussettes cotton spinning town of Fall River had never been a happy one. Andrew was a crusty, puritanical character whose one aim in life was making money, and holding on to it. He had amassed half a million dollars from shrewd business dealings, first as an undertaker, then as a property speculator and banker. His first wife, Sarah Morse Borden, died in 1862, two years after giving birth to his second daughter, christened Lizzie Andrew because Borden wanted a boy. Borden married again two years later, but it was no love match. Abby Durfee Gray was a plain, plump woman of 37, more of a housekeeper than a wife. And there was no love lost between her and Borden's two girls. The elder sister Emma called her Abby. Lizzie called her Mrs Borden, refused to eat at the same table as her, and spoke with her only when it was essential.

Despite Borden's wealth, the family lived in conditions worse than many of the town's humble millworkers. The unsanitary whitewood house had staircases at the front and back, which was as well, because the friction in the family meant that bedroom doors upstairs were kept locked at all times, the parents reaching their room via the rear stairs, the girls using the front ones.

Lizzie's resentment of her stepmother, and the way they lived, boiled over when her father, whom she loved dearly, put up the money for Abby's sister, Mrs Whitehead, to buy the house from which she faced eviction. Borden presented the title deeds to his wife, and when Lizzie found out, she regarded it as further proof that Mrs Borden was only after her father's riches. Shortly afterwards, Mr Borden arrived home from business to be told by Lizzie that his wife's bedroom had been ransacked by a burglar. He reported the incident to police, but soon cut short their inquiries when it became clear that Lizzie herself had done the damage during 'one of her funny turns'.

Lizzie was plain, introspective and repressed with genteel pretensions. The curly-haired redhead had a small circle of very close friends. Though she belonged to the Women's Christian Temperance Union, was treasurer and secretary of the local Christian Endeavour Society, and taught a Sunday School of Chinese men at the local Congregational church, she spent most of her time in more solitary pursuits – fishing, or merely brooding at her bedroom window. There was plenty for her to brood about.

In the summer of 1892 Fall River sweltered in a heatwave. In May the tedium of the Bordens' lifestyle was interrupted when intruders twice broke into outhouses at the bottom of their garden. Mr Borden's reaction was somewhat bizzare. Sure that the intruders were after Lizzie's pet pigeons, he took an axe to the birds and decapitated them.

By August the heat had become so bad that Emma left to stay with friends in the country at Fairhaven, 20 miles away. Lizzie stayed at home for a special meeting of the Christian Endeavour Society. The weather made no difference to Mr Borden's plans for running an economical household. The family sat down to a monstrous joint of mutton, cooked by their only servant, an Irish girl called Bridget, and served up in various guises at every meal. Everyone except Lizzie was violently ill.

Although 4 August dawned as the hottest day of the year, the family routine went on just the same. After breakfast Mr Borden set out to check on his businesses; John Morse, brother of his first wife, who was staying for a few days, left to visit other relatives; Mrs Borden began dusting the rooms, and Bridget, still queasy from food poisoning, washed the windows. Lizzie came down later than the rest, and was soon seen ironing some clothes in the kitchen.

Shortly after 09.30, Mrs Borden, on her knees dusting in the spare bedroom upstairs at the front of the house, was struck from behind with a hatchet. It was a crushing blow to the head, and killed her instantly. But 18 more blows were inflicted before she was left in a room awash with blood.

Just before 11.00, Mr Borden arrived home to find the front door locked and bolted. Bridget the maid, by now cleaning the windows inside the house, went to let him in, and expressed surprise that the door was double locked. She heard a laugh behind her, and turned to see Lizzie coming down the front staircase, smiling.

Mr Borden was nearly 70, and walking in the morning heat had clearly tired him. Lizzie fussed round him, told him his wife had gone out after receiving a note about a sick friend, and settled him on the living room settee where he began to doze, his head resting on a cushion. Lizzie went back to the kitchen, and chatted to Bridget about some cheap dress material on sale in town. But Bridget was still feeling unwell, and decided to retire to her attic bedroom for a while. She heard the clock strike 11.00 as she went up the back stairs.

Ten minutes later she dashed downstairs again. She heard Lizzie shouting: 'Come down quick. Father's dead. Someone came in and killed him.' Lizzie would not let the maid into the living room – she sent her across the road to fetch the local doctor, a man called Bowen. He was out on a call. Lizzie then sent Bridget to fetch Alice Russell, one of her closest friends. By this time, the maid's rushing about had attracted the attention of neighbours. Mrs Adelaide Churchill, who lived next door, spotted Lizzie looking distressed, and asked what was wrong. She was told: 'Someone has killed father.'

Mr Borden had been hacked to death in exactly the same way as his wife, though his head had been shattered with only ten blows. The hatchet had landed from behind as he slept, a tricky task as the settee was against a wall. Blood had splashed everything – wall, settee, floral carpet. Dr Bowen arrived and examined the body. The blows seemed directed at the eyes, ears and nose. He was completely satisfied the first blow had killed the old man. He placed a sheet over the body.

Mrs Russell and Mrs Churchill did their best to comfort the bereaved Lizzie, fanning her, dabbing her face with cold cloths, rubbing her hands. But both noticed that she did not really need comforting. She was not crying or hysterical, and she assured them she did not feel faint. She was still strangely calm when the police arrived, declining their offer of delaying the necessary interview until she had had a chance to rest.

At first suspicion fell on John Morse, who behaved

strangely when he returned to the house. Though a large and excited crowd had gathered in front of the building, he was seen to slow down as he approached. Then, instead of going inside, he wandered round to the back garden, picked some fruit off one of the trees, and started munching it. Inside the house, his alibi came so glibly, in the most minute detail, that it almost seemed too perfect. But when tested it was found to be true.

Attention then turned to Lizzie, whose behaviour had been equally strange, and whose statements were not only curious but contradictory. When Bridget had asked her where she was when her father was killed, she replied: 'I was out in the yard and heard a groan.' When Mrs Churchill asked the same question, she said: 'I went out to the barn to get a piece of iron.' She told the same story to the police, saying she had eaten three pears while searching in the attic of the barn. But a policeman who checked the attic found no cores, only undisturbed dust.

Mrs Churchill also recalled the extraordinary reply Lizzie had given when she first arrived, and asked where her mother was. Lizzie said: 'I'm sure I don't know, for she had a note from someone to go and see somebody who is sick. But I don't know perhaps that she isn't killed also, for I thought I heard her coming in.' It was some minutes before Mrs Churchill and Bridget began to search for Mrs Borden. They knew she was not in her own room, for the sheet that covered her husband came from there. So they started climbing the front staircase. Halfway up, Mrs Churchill glanced through the open door of the spare bedroom, and saw the body lying on the floor beyond the bed. Why had Lizzie not seen it there when she came down the stairs to welcome her father home? Why had she been trying to buy prussic acid, a lethal poison, only the day before from shops in town? And why, the previous evening, had she visited her friend Mrs Russell, told her of the food poisoning episode, and complained about her father's brusque way with people, saying she was afraid one of his enemies would take revenge on him soon?

Those were the questions police asked themselves as they pieced together the clues, and studied Lizzie's statements. They were sure that the murders had been committed by someone in the household. Though neighbours had noticed a young man outside the Borden home at 09.30, looking agitated, they had not seen him go in. And police thought it unlikely that a killer could hide in the house for 90 minutes between the murders while Bridget and Lizzie were going about their chores. Bridget was considered as a suspect and dismissed. Neighbours had seen her cleaning the windows. Some had even seen her vomiting because of the food poisoning. And she had no known reason for killing her employers. But Lizzie had motives in plenty. The tension in the family, the quarrels about money, the hatred of the stepmother, were all well known in the area. She was warned that she was under suspicion and told not to leave the house. She accepted the conditions, in the arrogant, off-hand way that she had death with all the police's questions.

The police obtained a warrant for her arrest, but did not serve it until after the inquest. Though they had found an axe-head that had recently been cleaned in the cellar of the Borden house, they had no proof that it was the murder weapon, or that Lizzie was the murderer. Once she was arrested, she could use her legal right to silence. It was important to hear her evidence at the inquest.

More than 4,000 attended the funeral of Mr and Mrs Borden. The two heads were cut off before burial, and the battered skulls sent for forensic examination. A few days later, the inquest opened. It was held in secret, conducted by the public prosecutor, who gave Lizzie a tough time in cross-questioning. And once again she started contradicting herself.

She claimed now the she had not been on the stairs when her father arrived home shortly before 11.00, but was downstairs in the kitchen. Asked why she had changed her story, she explained: 'I thought I was on the stairs, but now I know I was in the kitchen.' She also denied saying she heard her stepmother returning to the house. The public prosecutor was certain she was guilty of the killings. So were the newspapers, which daily poured out torrents of emotional calumny on Lizzie, adding smears and lies to the known facts. But it was one thing to obtain a conviction in print, quite another to win one in a court of law. And the public prosecutor confided in a letter to the Attorney General that he was not confident.

His fears were well founded. The tide of anti-Lizzie propaganda in the press turned public feeling in her favour. How could such a God-fearing, quiet, respectable girl do such horrible and bloody deeds? Flowers and good luck messages began pouring into Fall River for her from all over the country. Suddenly the state was the villain of the piece for persecuting her.

Lizzie had something else on her side also. She hired the best lawyer in Massachussetts, George Robinson, a former governor of the state. One of the three trial judges was a man Robinson had elevated to the bench while governor. He owed the defence lawyer a favour – and he delivered. The judges refused to allow evidence of Lizzie's attempts to buy prussic acid, saying it was irrelevant to the case, and they ruled that transcripts of her questioning at the inquest were inadmissible.

Lizzie's friends also rallied round. Both Emma and Bridget gave favourable evidence, playing down Lizzie's enmity for her stepmother. Mrs Russell admitted that Lizzie had burnt one of her dresses the day after her parents' funeral, but insisted there were no blood stains on it. Lizzie, too, played her part perfectly in court. When she fainted halfway through the hearing, there was an outcry at the way she was being tortured. And as she stood in the dock, modest, refined, neatly dressed, it was easy for George Robinson to say to the jury; 'To find her guilty, you must believe she is a fiend. Gentlemen, does she look it?'

The jury agreed she did not. After a ten-day trial her ordeal was over, and she was whisked off for a lavish celebration party, laughing at newspaper clippings of the hearing that friends gave her. She was not very rich, able to inherit her murdered father's wealth, but surprisingly she chose to stay on in Fall River, buying a larger house in the better part of town. Bridget, whom many suspected of helping Lizzie to dispose of clues to the killing, returned to Ireland, allegedly with a lot of money from the Borden bank account. She later returned to America and died in Montana in 1947, aged 82.

For a while Emma shared the new home with Lizzie, but the sisters quarrelled, and Emma moved out. Lizzie became something of a recluse, living alone, unloved and whispered about, until she died in 1927, aged 67. Emma, nine years older, died a few days later. They were both buried in the family plot, alongside their real mother, their stepmother, their father and their sister, Alice, who had died as a child.

Can Lizzie rest in peace beside the victims of that hot morning in August, 1892? No-one else was ever arrested for the murders. No-one else was even seriously suspected. The case has become one of the most intriguing unresolved mysteries in the annals of crime. Five stage plays, a ballet, and countless books have been written about it. Opinions range from those who say she was a cunning, calculating killer who twice stripped naked to ensure her butchery left no blood-stained clothes, to the Society of Friends of Lizzie Borden, which still exists today to persuade us she was innocent.

Perhaps, in a way, she was. In her book *A Private Disgrace*, American authoress Victoria Lincoln argues convincingly that Lizzie committed the murders while having attacks of temporarily epilepsy, the 'funny turns' her family were accustomed to. Lizzie suffered attacks four times a year, usually during menstruation. Miss Lincoln says: 'During a seizure, there are periods of automatic action which the patient in some cases forgets completely and in others remembers only dimly.' That could explain Lizzie's confusing statements and her coolness when accused of the killings.

Miss Lincoln even suggests the trigger to Lizzie's attacks. A note was delivered to 92 Second Street on the morning of 4 August, but it was not from a sick friend. It was to do with the transfer of a property to Mrs Borden's name. The first such transaction had driven to vandalism. Did the second drive her to murder?

The Harry Oakes Affair

The sub-tropical paradise of the Bahamas boasts 700 islands and rocky islets or cays, most of them uninhabited, surrounded by the sparkling blue-green waters of the Gulf Stream. Only 80 km (50 miles) away across the horizon is the millionaire's paradise of Miami and all the brash excitement of Florida, Land of the Stars and Stripes.

The Union Jack flies in Nassau, capital of the Bahamas, testimony to its position as an outpost of British civilization and administration, a veneer of respectability over its fabled history as a haven for buccaneers and rum runners, adventurers and soldiers of fortune.

But to Edward Albert Patrick David, Duke of Windsor, former monarch of the British Empire, life in the Bahamas had held all the appeal of exile in an Arctic waste. His appointment as Governor General in August 1940 was seen as a deliberate punishment by the wartime cabinet of Winston Churchill.

For four years, since his abdication as King Edward VIII, the headstrong and impetuous duke had been a grave embarrassment to his government and loyal subjects. He had provoked a constitutional crisis and world-wide scandal when he abdicated his throne to marry the woman he loved, American divorcee Wallis Simpson. A year after their marriage the duke and his restless American duchess had even visited Nazi Chancellor Adolf Hitler in Germany while he was arming his nation for war against Britain. The duke quickly became a propaganda pawn for the Nazis.

The duke had only set foot on English soil since his marriage before being caught up in the roaring tide of war as the Germans invaded France and sped towards the Windsors' new adopted home in Paris.

The former king and his wife fled south to neutral Spain and sought safety in Madrid. Fearful that the duke might be the victim of a kidnap and used as a hostage, Churchill asked him to return home by flying boat to Britain.

But the Duke of Windsor, resentful that his wife would not be accorded any privilege or status as a member of the royal family, refused. He chose the only alternative Churchill gave him, the post of Governor General of the Bahamas, thousands of miles across the Atlantic where he could be safely isolated from the intrigues of wartime Europe.

Lonely and ostracized, the Windsors arrived in Nassau to be greeted by the Bahamas' most prominent citizen, Sir Harry Oakes. Sir Harry's title was no genteel hereditary honour from a long line of ennobled forefathers. He was reputedly one of the richest men in the Empire, newly created baronet, a self-made multi-millionaire. He was a ruthless businessman who had battled and bullied his way to the top from a hell-raising existence as a Yukon and Alaskan gold prospector. This hardened man of the world swiftly became the Duke of Windsor's close friend.

Their social and personal lives became entwined and Oakes even turned over his palatial home in Nassau to the Windsors while the Governor General's mansion was refurbished. The two men were constant drinking and dining companions on their frequent trips to the American mainland where Oakes introduced the duke to his social and business acquaintances.

The duke's lifetime of royal grooming as a man born to handle the gravest of personal and national crises helped him maintain his composure on the morning of 8 July 1943 when his equerry roused him from sleep and told him that Oakes was dead. He had been savagely beaten and stabbed, his skull had been fractured and an attempt had been made to burn his bloodstained body beyond recognition.

The former king quickly invoked his authority under the Emergency War Powers Act, using his powers of censorship to insist that news of Sir Harry's murder should be hushed up. A few hours later he belatedly put the wheels of legal investigation into motion – by calling in a personal contact in the Miami police.

The duke made the baffling request to Miami Police Department: 'I think one of our leading citizens has committed suicide. Can you come and confirm this?' In fact Sir Harry Oakes 'suicide' had all the hallmarks of a Mafia gangland contract killing.

Harry Oakes had not been born a British subject. The son of a schoolteacher in Sangerville, Maine, he was a daydreamer who spent his college days boasting of the great fortune he planned to amass. After two years as a student doctor at Syracuse he gave up college. Harry told his fellow students, all dedicated young medical men: 'You can make a good living, but you'll never get filthy rich as a doctor. I want to be filthy rich.'

Harry put his medical training to use as a hospital orderly in the prospecting camps of the Canadian north, treating frostbite and gangrene and malnutrition, while he gleaned every scrap of information he could from experienced old panhandlers.

For 14 years he followed the restless waves of prospectors chasing every elusive strike from California to Yukon, Australia and the Congo. His dogged persistence paid off in 1910 when, with a partner, he finally struck gold at Kirkland Lake in northern Ontario. It was the second largest gold find in North America and over the next 12 years he connived and wheedled and spent part of his growing fortune to buy out his partner's interests and gain sole control.

Oakes was a crude and ruthless tycoon by 1923 when, at the age of 48, he married Australian bank typist Eunice MacIntyre who he met on a cruise liner. To strengthen his links with the country which provided his massive wealth, Oakes renounced his American citizenship and became a naturalized Canadian.

But Harry Oakes became disenchanted with his adopted country as his tax bill climbed higher and higher and he found himself paying 85 per cent of his income to the taxman.

On holiday with his wife and five children at one of his homes in Palm Beach, he met real estate promoter Harold Christie who boasted of the tax advantages of the Bahamas, where the British administration charged no income tax or death duties. It did not take Oakes long to decide to protect his fortune by moving to Nassau and he became a grateful benefactor. He poured millions of pounds into the islands, buying hotels and landscaping golf courses, funding charities to provide milk for children and hospitals for the poor.

His generosity soon spilled over into Britain itself where he bestowed £250,000 on one hospital. A grateful King George VI, the Duke of Windsor's younger brother who had succeeded the throne after the Abdication, conferred a baronetcy on him in 1939.

The colourful and brash businessman who greeted the Windsors on their arrival set about making himself the power behind the Duke of Windsor's new 'throne'. All major legislation required the consent of the Governor General – the duke – and Sir Harry had him eating out of his hand.

This was the cosy relationship that real estate developer Harold Christie had to explain to his business associate when they met in Palm Beach, Florida, to discuss the prospect of opening a casino in the Bahamas.

He had already ingratiated himself with the duke and had his tacit endorsement. But Sir Harry was blowing hot and cold about the plan. Harold Christie may have wanted to apply some more gentle persuasion to the cantankerous old tycoon when he met him on the night of 7 July 1943 at Sir Harry's palatial home 'Westbourne' in Nassau.

Sir Harry was due to leave in two days time to join his family at yet another holiday home, in Maine, and Christie could not afford to miss the opportunity for some business talk. Sir Harry had guests to a small dinner party that night but they left at 23.00.

Then, according to Harold Christie, he went to bed and Christie retired to another bedroom further down the corridor. Neither man left the house again that night, Christie claimed, and although wakened during the night by the thunder of a tropical storm, he heard no sound from Sir Harry's bedroom.

When he rose for breakfast at 07.00 he strolled along the balcony to the screen door leading to the master bedroom and called out for Sir Harry. There was no reply, so he waited a few seconds and stepped inside.

Christie chilled at the sight that greeted him. The room was filled with smoke, but there was no fire. Sir Harry Oakes lay on his back on the bed, his face caked with blood, his skull fractured with four puncture marks, his flimsy pyjamas burned off and sticking to the open blisters on his charred skin.

Christie's calls of alarm alerted a housekeeper and within minutes he made the first of his frantic telephone calls to the Island Police Commissioner and to the Governor General, the Duke of Windsor.

The Bahamas police were no experts in matters of sudden, violent death and it was not entirely without relief that the commissioner received the news that the duke had asked for help from the Miami Police Department to confirm Sir Harry's 'suicide'.

The duke had spoken to Captain Edward Melchen, chief of the homicide bureau, a policeman who was also a personal friend, having acted as a bodyguard for the duke on his frequent visits to Miami. Within hours, Melchen arrived in Nassau accompanied by another trusted detective, Captain James Barker. The two men made one cursory inspection of the blistered body on the smoke-blackened bed.

'Face up to it,' Melchen told the Duke. 'This is no suicide.'

Throughout the following day, while the two Americans set up a temporary headquarters at 'Westbourne' interviewing members of the staff and the dead baronet's family, Christie and the Duke of Windsor kept in constant touch with each other by telephone. That afternoon the duke visited the murder house himself to see the scene of the gruesome crime and he spent some twenty minutes alone with Captain James Barker.

Two hours later, a suspect for the murder of Sir Harry Oakes was arrested.

Alfred de Marigny was a lean, lanky 36-year-old with a dark complexion, a native of the Indian Ocean island of Mauritius. He was also Sir Harry Oakes's son-in-law.

De Marigny had been married and divorced twice before he began his courtship of 17-year-old Nancy, Sir Harry's eldest daughter. He had been living in the

Bahamas squandering the divorce settlement from his wealthy second wife when he set his sights on Nancy, and the locals all agreed he was a shiftless gigolo.

His relationship with her mercurial father-in-law had been stormy ever since de Marigny's marriage to Nancy in New York two days after her 18th birthday . . . two days after becoming old enough to marry without her parents' consent.

At the time of her father's death, Nancy de Marigny had been in Florida for medical treatment and Alfred had thrown a dinner party with his houseguest and 'hanger-on', fellow Mauritian playboy George de Videlou.

Alfred left the house at 01.00 to drive two of his guests home. His route could have taken him past 'Westbourne' in the middle of the night, the prosecution insisted at his trial.

And there was evidence to link him with the murder, prosecuting attorney Eric Hallinan claimed. Whoever killed Sir Harry tried to spread flames around the room to burn evidence of the crime. And when de Marigny was examined by police, it was found the hairs on his right arm had been singed and burned.

More importantly, according to the prosecution de Marigny's fingerprint was found on an ornamental Chinese screen in the murder bedroom.

The importance of the singed hairs on de Marigny's arm was quickly squashed by defence counsel Godfrey Higgs who extracted testimony from a witness, one of de Marigny's dinner guests, that Sir Harry's son-in-law had scorched his arm trying to light a candle inside a lantern on the dinner table.

The evidence of the fingerprint became the crucial turning point in the case and highlighted some inexplicably inept investigation. Miami cop Captain James Barker testified that he had 'lifted' a fingerprint of Alfred de Marigny from the Chinese screen. He had used a gummed strip of runner to obtain the imprint of the moist finger-mark – at the same time destroying any permanent evidence that the print had been on the surface of the screen.

The space where de Marigny's print was alleged to have been was blank. Captain Barker, whose evidence became more hesitant, admitted he had not brought his own camera with him from Miami to photograph fingerprint evidence 'in situ'. He told the court, quite reasonably: 'I thought I was coming to confirm a suicide. The fingerprint camera didn't seem important.'

Barker's credibility was finally demolished by the defence's own expert, Maurice O'Neil of the New Orleans Police Department, a past president of the International Association of Identification. He examined a photograph of the sharp contours of de Marigny's fingerprint and declared it could not have been lifted off the screen with-out being superimposed on the pattern of intricate etchings which also covered the screen.

De Marigny's fingerprint, he deduced, had been lifted from a smooth surface, possibly a tumbler or a cigarette packet the accused man had handled in Sir Harry's bed-room long after the murder when he was invited to the house by the American detectives.

Defence attorney Higgs never made any suggestion why he thought Captain Barker should give such blatantly phoney evidence. And there was little explanation for another crucial piece of cross examination . . .

Harold Christie, the property developer who slept in the murder house, swore on oath that neither he nor Sir Harry had left 'Westbourne' after 23.00 that night. Then Higgs called to the witness stand Captain Edward Sears, a reliable Bahamian policeman, assistant superintendent in charge or traffic.

Sears, who had known Christie since their schooldays together, confidently testified that he had seen him in George Street, Nassau, at 01.00 on the night of the murder.

Christie had been a passenger in a station wagon speeding away from the direction of Nassau harbour. Sears could not identify the other man in the car, the driver. He only knew he was a white man, a stranger to the islands.

The jury retired for two hours to consider their verdict. They found Alfred de Marigny not guilty of the murder of his father-in-law.

No one else was ever charged with the murder of Sir Harry Oakes.

One blood-spattered clue to the identity of the man who may have murdered Sir Harry was uncovered nearly ten years later in Miami, on 26 December 1952, when Captain James Barker was killed by a .38 bullet from his own revolver.

The trigger was pulled by his son who tearfully told Dade County Court that Captain Barker had become a violent drug addict, corrupt and depraved. The policeman's slaying at the hands of his son was ruled 'justifiable homicide'.

It came as no surprise to his colleagues who had known for years that Barker was on the payroll of Meyer Lansky, the tough and ruthless gangster who ran the Mafia crime syndicate in Florida and Cuba.

At the time of Sir Harry's death, Lansky desperately wanted official approval to open a lucrative gambling casino in Nassau. He pulled every trick he knew and used the services of any influential people in the Bahamas he thought could be won over to his cause.

Lansky told his henchmen that one obstinate man was standing in his path and would have to be taught a lesson.

To this day people in the Bahamas still talk about the powerful motor cruisers which used to slip in and out of Nassau harbour any time they pleased, without bothering with customs and immigration formalities. They were the ships of Lansky's fleet, crewed by gun-toting skippers who knew the waters between Miami and Nassau from the days of Prohibition, when they ran illicit booze from the liquor warehouses of the British Bahamas to the speak-easies of Florida.

If Harold Christie was seen sitting as a terrified passenger in a car speeding from the docks the night Sir Harry Oakes was murdered, had he been to a meeting aboard one of those boats? Had Sir Harry been with him?

Was Sir Harry's bleeding body hunched in the back of the station wagon, fatally beaten after telling Lansky's emissaries that nobody pushed Harry Oakes around, not even the Mob?

The unidentified white man seen by police Superintendent Sears . . . was the man Meyer Lansky sent to Nassau to teach Sir Harry Oakes a lesson?

Did Captain James Barker, the Miami policeman on Lansky's payroll, have orders to find a scapegoat? Did he try to frame the hapless de Marigny to shift suspicion from a contract killer?

As soon as decently possible after the end of World War 2 the Duke of Windsor left the Bahamas, hurrying back to a civilized European exile in Paris. He never discussed the Oakes murder.

Harold Christie was later knighted for his services to the Government of the Bahamas. He died in September 1973 while travelling in Germany.

Killings in the Congo

Assassination is the murder which touches the lives of millions and changes the course of history. The life of a national hero is ended by a bullet from a telescopic rifle, or a tyrant and his entourage are swept away in one blast from a hidden bomb.

The motives of a single assassin can be complex, from a madman harbouring a murderous grudge for some imagined injustice, to a lone patriot willing to sacrifice his own life to end the rule of a dictator. Often assassination is murder by committee, by a political group who want to wrest power from their opponents by destroying their figurehead.

Almost always assassination is an open outrage. The murder of a public figure usually has to be carried out in a public place, a factor dictated by the need to catch the victim when he is most exposed and vulnerable – and often a grisly ploy by the assassins to demonstrate their power and determination before a stunned audience. Assassins plot murder in secret and kill in public. And they are not slow to accept the responsibility for their crime. The lone madman is rewarded with the public platform he seeks, the political committee want to announce their success widely and clearly.

But the deaths of two prominent political figures within nine months of each other in 1961 may have provided rare case histories of assassinations unadmitted and undeclared.

Both deaths are linked together in the turbulent world of African politics. One was explained away as an unplanned, unfortunate killing. The other was neatly catalogued as a fatal flying accident, the understandable failure of man and machine on a tricky night flight. Doubts still linger about the real causes of the deaths of firebrand African revolutionary Patrice Lumumba and international statesman Dag Hammarskjoeld, the peacemaking Secretary General of the United Nations.

Patrice Emergy Lumumba was a fiery, erratic orator, a 35-year-old inexperienced politician with a driving, ruthless ambition. His lust for power and his ability to whip up an emotional crowd made him a force to be reckoned with in 1960 when the colonial rulers of the vast tract of the Belgian Congo felt the wind of change sweeping through Africa.

Foreseeing the explosive force of rising African nationalism, the Belgians had no great wish to pay the heavy price for hanging on to their African colony. But neither could they see any prospect for a smooth transition to independence as they began to hand over power to the people of the Congo in the elections of 1960. They were dismayed by the growing support for rebel leader Moise Tshombe who was leading the movement to wrench his own rich Katanga Province from the new independent Congo into a separate nation. But they watched most closely two political rivals who both swore to force Katanga to stay within the new Congo and who would hold the balance of power between them.

The Belgians were quietly satisfied when the election returned the quiet, educated civil servant Joseph Kasavubu to the post of President. They saw danger signs in the wave of popular support which swept Patrice Lumumba, a rebellious postmaster, into power as Prime Minister. Lumumba, they knew, had courted the promise of military backing from the Soviet Union to help him win office.

The new Prime Minister, expelled from a Roman Catholic mission school as a teenager for sexual promiscuity and later jailed for two years for embezzlement, confirmed their worst fears. Within weeks the enthusiastic and naive Lumumba found he had unleashed forces he could not control. The political theorists and policy managers of Moscow supervized his every move as the Congolese began to feel they were being freed from one foreign colonial ruler just in time to inherit another. Lumumba's reaction was to begin a bloody purge against dissident tribesmen using the resources of the teams of Russian technicians and military advisers pouring into the country.

Lumumba personally directed his troops to carry out the massacre of 3,000 Baluba tribesmen, flying his army to the scene in 19 Ilyushin jet transports provided by the Russians.

Some international observers condoned his ruthlessness as the brute force needed to weld the newly born country together. Others saw him provoking an increasingly bitter civil war.

Under pressure from the Belgians, President Kasavubu had Lumumba arrested and removed from office. There followed a cat and mouse game in which Lumumba escaped from house arrest and, according to his supporters, was greeted by cheering crowds in every village he visited.

The departing Belgians, who wanted to have a stable ally in the new Congo Republic to promote their commercial interests, were angered by Lumumba's freedom, although they seemed to regard him more as a nuisance than a serious menace, a naive troublemaker who would soon outlive his usefulness to his political controllers.

Lumumba was re-arrested in January 1961 and sent to an area where he could not expect any cheering crowds or villagers, the rebellious province of Katanga. Within a week he was dead, together with his two trusted followers Joseph Okito and Mauruce Mpolo.

But that was not the way the story was told . . . Initially, Patrice Lumumba was reported to have escaped from custody yet again. A poker-faced Katanga Minister of the Interior Paul Munungo held a brief press conference to show newsmen the hole in the wall where he claimed Lumumba and his accomplices had tunnelled their way to freedom from their villa in Elisabethville, under the noses of their guards. 'We are offering a reward for their capture,' he explained.

His next press conference, three days later, was equally brief and subdued. Lumumba, according to the minister, had escaped from Elisabethville by car, travelling more than 321 km (200 miles) through unfriendly country, and stopped at a remote settlement in the bush outside the town of Kolwezi. There the villagers, anxious to claim the

£3,000 reward, had promptly hacked him and his companions to death. A Katangese official had visited the site and confirmed the three men were buried in an unmarked grave.

All pressure from the journalists for further details was brushed aside.

'We forgot to specify on the reward posters that we wanted Lumumba captured alive,' the Minister apologized. 'So the villagers are not to blame for his death. Besides he was a criminal so there's no harm done.'

And the location of the un-named village? It had to be kept secret, was the reply, to prevent any potentially ill-advized pilgrimages by Lumumba supporters. Lumumba's untimely death was doubtless a relief to the harassed Belgians. But the Russians who had been seen to be powerless to protect their protégé, were furious.

'Assassination' they cried and grandly set about planning a university for African revolutionaries in Moscow, to be named as a memorial to Patrice Lumumba. In the meantime they demanded the resignation of the Secretary General of the United Nations, the international body which was overseeing the Congo's transition to independence.

Being the target of scathing abuse and demands that he quit his job were nothing new for Dag Hammarskjoeld. The Scandinavian elder statesman suffered the violent criticism of Western leaders who claimed he was not making enough use of the multinational UN armed forces at his command to speed up the creation of the new Congo state. Eastern leaders complained bitterly that he interfered too much.

When Gurkha troops provided by India for the UN peace-keeping operation beat and killed hundreds of Katangan rebels, Hammarskjoeld shouldered the responsibility, burdened by the sharp condemnation of world leaders who were appalled by his mishandling of the delicate situation. Russian premier Nikita Krushchev branded the UN official: 'A bloody handed lackey of the colonial powers'.

Hammarskjoeld simply went about his job as he saw it, impartially trying to be a peaceful midwife in the bloody and painful birth of the new Congo.

He seems not to have hesitated when he received the invitation from the Katangan rebel leader, Moise Tschombe, to meet him for talks on a possible peace initiative in the battle between the breakaway province and the rest of the Congo. The talks were to be held in neutral territory, in Ndola in Rhodesia, the neighbouring country to Katanga.

From the outset, the flight was surrounded in furtive secrecy and disastrous planning. Hammarskjoeld planned to fly from Leopoldville in a DC4 Skymaster plane, specially prepared at the airport for him. At the last minute, to avoid the waiting packs of journalists, he switched to another aircraft, a DC6 airliner.

The DC6 was certainly better equipped. It was the personal plane of General Sean McKeown, commander of the UN forces in the Congo. With its four powerful engines it had a comfortable cruising range of more than 4,000 km (2,500 miles).

But 24 hours before, the DC6 had come under attack as Congolese soldiers had blasted one of its engines with anti-aircraft fire. The DC6 had been hastily repaired and left unguarded in a dispersal bay at Leopoldville Airport.

The pilot, Per-Erik Hallonquist, added to the confusion, designed to throw journalists off the track, by filing a flight plan for a journey to a small airport in Kisai Province, about halfway along his secret route to the Rhodesian border town of Ndola.

He took off in mid-afternoon, with 15 other people on board, including a radio operator with no flying experience. Only minutes before becoming airborne did he realize that the page of maps and instructions giving details of his approach to Ndola, was missing from his flight briefing book.

The flight, however, seems to have begun uneventfully. After four hours flying, around his expected time of arrival, Hallonquist contacted Ndola air traffic control, asking about weather and runway conditions and reporting his intention to descend from high altitude to 9,700 km (6,000 ft), obviously preparing to begin his approach to the airport.

The control tower responded and waited. And waited and waited . . .

Two and a half hours later, the controllers were startled to see the DC6 approach the airfield from the south-west, flying from deep inside Rhodesian territory as if it had overshot its destination by 160 km (100 miles) and was retracing its route. There had been consternation over the non-arrival of the DC6 but no panic. The aircraft still had enough fuel to stay aloft for another seven hours.

Hallonquist radioed again, with matter-of-fact calmness. 'I have your runway lights in sight . . . Overhead Ndola . . . Now descending.' Without the benefit of radar coverage, the air traffic control staff peered into the night, beyond the runway, waiting for a glimpse of the DC6. They saw only a sudden brilliant flash of flame. Then darkness. The DC6, turning on its final approach, had struck a tree with its wingtip and plunged burning into a forest close to the airport.

In the confusion, darkness and thick jungle, it took almost two hours for the first rescue team to locate the aircraft. They found bodies scattered all round the strewn wreckage. And they found the macabre clues which seemed to show that the final fatal plunge of the DC6 might not have been a simple misjudgement by its pilot.

The fuselage, near the flight deck, was peppered with bullet holes. The body of Dag Hammarskjoeld lay sprawled in the aisle between the twisted seats. A few feet away was a revolver. And tucked into the lapel of his jacket was a playing card, the Ace of Spades.

Only one man was found alive that night, security officer Harry Jullian, an American. He was unconscious, suffering broken limbs and burns to 50 per cent of his body.

The next day the investigators began to piece together the evidence. Hammarskjoeld had not died instantly of his injuries and he had not been shot. But the long delay in reaching the crash site meant that he died without being able to tell anything about the final few minutes of the flight.

Smashed bottles of whisky and brandy had been found in the wreckage, adding weight to reports that many of the flight crew and security escort had boarded the plane weary and staggering after an all-night binge in a Leopoldville drinking club.

Technical experts found that the plane's altimeter had an inexplicable mechanical error of 37 m (1,200 ft), giving the pilot a deceptively safe reading of his height above the ground.

And one witness had reported hearing the whistle of jets above the airport only minutes before the DC6 crashed. The only jets within flying distance were the fighter aircraft of the rebel Katangese, 160 km (100 miles) away in Elisabethville.

Later that day Sergeant Jullian recovered consciousness. The investigators sat by his bedside.

'Where had you been during the missing two hours?' they asked. 'Why didn't you arrive when you were expected?'

'Mr Hammarskjoeld told us to turn back, he didn't say why,' was all the injured man could reply. He died two days later without speaking again.

A Rhodesian inquiry firmly blamed the crash on pilot error. Later a five-man UN Commission sifted through the evidence, considering sabotage and gunfire, and concluded that the cause of the crash still remained unexplained.

The Katangese, who had bitter memories of their treatment at the hands of the UN's Gurkha troops, refused to take part in any investigation.

If Dag Hammarskjoeld's plane was brought down by a time delay bomb or a gunfight in the cabin or an attack by jet fighters, no one gloated openly or took the blame for killing him.

But who put the mark of death, the Ace of Spades, across the chest of the dying statesman? Could it have been someone who shared that last flight with him?

Jack the Ripper

Jack the Ripper was the first serial killer to come to public attention. Although he killed only five women for certain – a pitifully low body count compared to those who came after him – he must count as one of the world's greatest serial killers because today, over a century since his savage murder spree ended, his name still chills the blood. In the East End of London, where he went about his gruesome business, tours of his murder site are conducted. Experts still speculate about his identity. Each new serial killer that hits the headlines is compared to him. This is fame – or notoriety – indeed.

Jack the Ripper qualifies as the first true serial killer because his ten-week campaign of murder was a media event. Indeed, he courted the press, writing to the news papers and giving them his sobriquet. He even sent them body parts of his victims that had been excised during his bizarre mutilation of their corpses. The Ripper's murderous activities gripped the public's imagination like no single individual's crimes before them and London was paralysed by fear. Again thanks to the mass media, Jack the Ripper was soon as famous in New York, San

Francisco, Paris, Sydney and Berlin as he was in London. In Arles, the painter Vincent Van Gogh had been avidly following the accounts of his deeds in the French newspapers before he sliced off part of his ear (some biographers have concluded that he was influenced by the Ripper's method of dissection).

Whitechapel was the Ripper's stamping ground. In 1888, when the killings started, there were 62 brothels in the London district, along with 233 boarding houses that catered for prostitutes and their clients. On top of that there was also an army of older, pox-ridden, middle-aged alcoholics who offered their sexual favours in alleys and door ways for the price of a slug of gin.

On the night of 3 April 1888 the 45-year-old Emma Elizabeth Smith solicited a well-dressed gentleman. Later that night she collapsed in the arms of a police constable, saying that she had been attacked by four men. A foreign object had been shoved up her vagina and she died a few hours later. What connected her death to the Ripper's subsequent murders was the fact that her ear had been cut off. Then, on the night of 7 August 1888, Martha Tabram was stabbed to death. There were 39 wounds on her corpse, mainly around her breasts and vagina – the areas of the body that the Ripper liked to mutilate when he had the time. Both Martha Tabram and Emma Elizabeth Smith had been attacked from behind. The police assumed that (like the Ripper's later victims) the women had turned their backs on their client and had hoisted up their skirts of rear-entry sex when they were attacked. It is not known for certain that these two women were killed by Jack the Ripper, but their killer was never caught and their murders shared many similarities with the Ripper's slayings.

The first woman definitely to have been killed by Jack the Ripper was the 42-year-old Polly Nichols, whose body was found in Buck's Row, Whitechapel, at 3.15am on 31

August 1888. Although she had fought her attacker she had not cried out, for her murder had taken place under the window of a sleeping woman who had not been woken by the struggle. She also appeared to have turned her back on her attacker, who slashed her throat twice, so savagely that he almost decapitated her. There were deep wounds around her sexual organs, too, although no body parts had been removed. The doctor who examined the corpse speculated that the attacker had some medical knowledge and was possibly a doctor himself.

The police concluded that Polly had turned away from her killer during the assignation (a common practice among London street prostitutes of the time). She had therefore had her back to her killer when he pulled his knife, which was why she had not cried out. He had then put the knife to her throat and had pushed her forward on to it, which explained the depth of the wound. It also meant that the blood from the arteries and veins in her neck would have spurted forward, away from the killer, enabling him to escape from the scene unsullied.

With the murder of Polly Nichols the police realised that they had a maniac on their hands who seemed to be motivated by a hatred of prostitutes. Detectives were accordingly sent into the East End to search for men who mistreated prostitutes. The name 'Leather Apron' came up several times during the investigation and a shoemaker called Pizer was arrested. Although he used a leather apron and sharp knives in hist trade, his family swore that he had been at home on the three occasions on which women hand been attacked in this manner.

On 8 September 1888, in various pubs in Whitechapel, the 47-year-old Annie Chapman bragged that the killer would meet his match if he ever came near her. She was wrong, however. She was subsequently seen talking to a 'gentleman' in the street; having apparently struck a bargain they went off arm in arm. Half an hour later she was found lying dead in an alleyway. Her head was connected to her body by only a strand of flesh. Her intestines had been thrown over her right shoulder and the flesh from her lower abdomen over her left. Her kidneys and ovaries had been removed.

The killer had left a blood-soaked envelope bearing the crest of the Sussex Regiment. It had been reported that Martha Tabram had been seen in the company of a soldier shortly before her death and the newspapers now speculated that her wounds could have been caused by a bayonet or army knife.

Three weeks after the death of Annie Chapman the Central News Agency received a letter that gloated about both the murder and the tantalising clues that had been left. The author expressed his regret that the letter had not been written in the victim's blood, which had gone 'thick like glue', and promised to send the ear of his next victims. The letter was signed 'Jack the Ripper'. At last the murderer had a name. On 30 September 1888 the Central News Agency received another letter from the Ripper, apologising for not having enclosed an ear, as promised. But he nevertheless had exciting news for the papers, he wrote: he was going to commit a 'double' – two murders in one night.

At 1am on the night on which the letter had been received the 45-year-old 'Long Liz' Stride, a Swedish prostitute whose real name was Elizabeth Gustaafsdotter, was found lying in a pool of blood; her throat had been slashed. The delivery man who discovered her body heard her attacker escaping over the cobblestones. At around the same time 43-year-old prostitute Catherine Eddowes was being thrown out of Bishopsgate Police Station, where she had been held for being drunk and disorderly. As she walked to wards Houndsditch she met Jack the Ripper, who cut her throat, slashed her face and cut her ear, thought not severing it completely. He also opened up her stomach, pulled out her intestines and threw them over her shoulder. Her left kidney was found to be missing altogether.

The murder of two women in one night – so soon after a letter from the Ripper promising just that – sent London into a panic. Queen Victoria demanded action, but the police had no idea where to begin. (The public did not even have that great fictional detective Sherlock Holmes to turn to, for he did not make his debut in Strand magazine for another three years.)

In a blaze of publicity, East End resident George Lusk set up the Whitechapel Vigilance Committee with which to patrol the streets. For his pains, two weeks later Mr Lusk received a small package through the post. It was from Jack the Ripper and contained half of Catherine Eddowes' kidney; the other half, an accompanying note explained, had been fried and eaten. On hearing this Queen Victoria concluded that the Ripper must be a foreigner: no Englishman would behave in such a beastly way, she asserted. A Cabinet meeting was called to discuss the matter and the government consequently ordered checks on all of the ships that were tied up in London docks. This action proved merely to be a huge waste of police manpower and in the meantime the Ripper continued on his grisly business.

On the night of 9 November 1888 Mary Kelly was seen soliciting a 'well-dressed gentleman' on the streets. Mary was unlike the Ripper's previous victims, being attractive and young – just 24. She was not a full-time prostitute, only going on to the street occasionally, when she needed to pay the rent. She was furthermore killed indoors and was also the only one of the Ripper's victims to cry out. Despite her screams, the Ripper was not disturbed and spent more than an hour going about his dreadful task.

Mary Kelly's clothes were found folded neatly on a chair, from which it was assumed that she had brought her 'gentleman' back to her room and had taken off her clothes in readiness for sex. The theory was that it was then that he had pulled a knife. Unlike the Ripper's other victims, Mary had been facing her killer and had cried out on seeing the knife. Some time between 3.30 and 4am a woman who had been sleeping in the room above had heard Mary scream 'Oh, murder' before going back to sleep.

The Ripper slashed Mary's throat, almost decapitating her. As she was facing him, some of her blood must have splashed onto his clothes, which were found burnt in the stove. Then the Ripper set about his dissection work. He cut off both of her breasts and put them on the table, placing her severed nose and flesh from her thighs and legs along side. Her forehead and legs were stripped of flesh and her abdomen was slashed open. Her liver and intestines were removed and her hand shoved into the gaping hole in her belly. (Mary was three months pregnant when she died.) There was blood around the window from which the Ripper was thought to have escaped. He would have been naked, except for a long cloak and boots.

The next day the rent man called and discovered Mary's mutilated corpse. He called the police, who were horrified and, once again, baffled.

Mary Kelly was last woman whom we know to have been a victim of the Ripper. Other murders followed that may have been his handiwork or the work of a copycat killer. In June 1889, for example the headless corpse of Elizabeth Jackson, a prostitute who worked in the Chelsea area, was found floating in the Thames. The following month the body of Alice McKenzie, a prostitute working in Whitechapel, was found; her throat had been cut from ear to ear and her sexual organs cut out. Frances Cole, a streetwalker known as 'Carroty Nell' because of her flamming-red hair, was also found dead in Whitechapel with her throat cut and slashes around her abdomen. Her assailant may have been planning a more thorough mutilation, but had been disturbed by a policeman, who reported having seen a man stooping over the body who had run away before the constable could get a good look at him.

The newspapers had already produced an image of the Ripper that had seized the public's imagination. It was based on a description given by the friend of Mary Kelly who had seen her with a client on the night of her death. She said that he was 5 feet 6 inches (1.65 metres) tall, about 35 and well dressed, and that he had had a gold watch chain dangling from his waistcoat pocket.

Mary had been heard in conversation with the man. 'Will you be alright for what I have told you?' he had asked. 'All right, me dear', she had replied, taking him by the arm. 'Come along, you will be comfortable.' A few hours later a roast-chestnut vendor had seen a man matching the same description, wearing a long cloak and silk hat, with a thin moustache that turned up at the ends. Ominously, he was carrying a black bag, which could have contained surgical instruments. 'Have you heard that there has been another murder?' the man had asked. 'I have', the chestnut vendor had replied. 'I know more of it than you do', the man had said as he walked away.

The Ripper was never caught, and over the past century an enormous number of theories have been put forward regarding who he was. The police alone came up with 176 suspects, of whom perhaps the most likely was Russian physician, Dr Alexander Pedachenko, who had worked under an assumed name at a Camberwell clinic that catered to prostitutes, including four of the victims. He had died in an asylum in St Petersburg after killing a woman in the Russian town. A document naming him as the Ripper was said to have been found in the basement of Rasputin's home in St Petersburg after the monk's murder in 1916; sceptics, however, have pointed out the house did not have a basement.

Another popular suspect was a Dr Stanley, a Harley Street physician who had contracted syphilis form a prostitute called Kelly in Whitechapel. It was said that he had gone about killing prostitutes out of vengeance until he hit upon the right one. Stanley subsequently fled to Buenos Aires, in Argentina, where he died in 1929 after supposedly confessing all to a student.

At the time of the murders Jewish immigrants to the East End were blamed for having perpetrated them. It was said that they represented ritual Jewish slaughters and had been performed by a *shochet*, a butcher who kills animals according to Talmudic law. The *shochet* theory was given some credence by a strange message that was found scrawled on a wall in Whitechapel after the murder of Catherine Eddowes, which said 'The juwes are not the men that will be blamed for nothing'. It was also noted that 'juwes' was a Masonic spelling of 'Jews', which gave rise to the theory that the murders had been part of a Masonic rite. The police commissioner, Sir Charles Warren, himself a leading Mason, had the graffiti removed in order to prevent the inflammation of anti-Jewish sentiments. He resigned from the police force after the murder of Mary Kelly, admitting his utter failure to solve the case.

A Polish Jew named V Kosminski, who lived in Whitechapel and had further more threatened to slice up prostitutes, was a suspect, but later became insane and died in an asylum. Another Polish immigrant, Severin Klosowich – alias George Chapman – was also under suspicion. A barber and surgeon in Whitechapel, he kept sharp knives for bloodletting and the removal of warts and moles. He also poisoned three of his mistresses and went to gallows in 1903. A further suspect was Thomas Cutbush, who was arrested after the murder of Frances

Cole for stabbing women in the buttocks; he died in an mental institution, too.

A newspaper reporter named Roslyn D'Onston wrote to the police in 1888 accusing Dr Morgan Davies, a surgeon at the London Hospital in Whitechapel, of being Jack the Ripper. Yet D'Onston was himself a suspect; a failed doctor and a drug addict, he was said by some to have killed the women in order to give his career a fillip. It was claimed that the stories that he published in the newspapers contained details about the murders that were never released by the police. D'Onston subsequently became a Satanist; his fellow devil-worshipper, Aleister Crowley, claimed that he had ritually murdered killed the women in an attempt to become invisible.

The insomniac G Wentworth Bell Smith, who lived at 27 Sun Street, off Finsbury Square, became a suspect because he railed against prostitutes, saying that they should all be drowned. For his part, Frederick Bailey Deeming confessed to the Ripper's murders. Deeming had murdered his wife and children in England and had then fled to Australia, where he had killed a second wife; he had been about to murder a third when he was arrested in Melbourne. It is thought that his confession was an attempt to postpone, if not evade, his trip to gallows. Another popular suspect was the 'Lambeth Poisoner', Dr Thomas Neil Cream, who poisoned a number of prostitutes during the 1890s. Before he was hanged he told his executioner 'I am Jack the ...', just as the trap opened.

The police's prime suspect was Montague John Druitt, an Oxford graduate and scion of a once wealthy family. After failing as a barrister, Druitt became a school teacher. Unable to keep his homosexual urges under control, he was dismissed for molesting a boy. He then moved to Whitechapel, where he was seen walking the streets. In December 1888 his body was fished out of the Thames; there were stones in his pocket and he appeared to have drowned himself.

Somewhat surprisingly, the secretary of William Booth (the latter the founder of the Salvation Army), also found himself on the list of suspects – apparently he had said 'Carroty Nell will be the next to go' a few days before the slaying of Frances Cole. Another man, the alcoholic railway worker Thomas Salder, was arrested after the murder of alice McKenzie; he also knew Frances Cole, but was released due to lack of evidence.

Although Sherlock Holmes was not around to solve the case, his creator, Sir Arthur Conan Doyle, was, and used all of his considerable powers of reasoning to deduce that the Ripper was a woman. According to his theory, 'Jill the Ripper' was a midwife who had gone mad after having been sent to prison for performing illegal abortions.

The spiritualist William Lees staged a seance for Queen Victoria in an attempt to discover who the Ripper was, but the results frightened him so much that he fled to the Continent. The Ripper, he believed, was none other than the queen's physician, Sir William Gull. The theory that was later developed was that Prince Eddy, the Duke of Clarence – Victoria's grandson and heir to the throne – had secretly married a shop girl called Crook, who had borne him a child which was placed in the care of one Mary Kelly. Gull and some of his Masonic cronies, it was said, went about killing prostitutes until they got to Kelly and retrieved the child. Gull's papers were examined by Dr Thomas Stowell and were discovered to name Prince Eddy, who died of syphilis before he could ascend the throne, as Jack the Ripper. Another suspect was James Kenneth Stephen, the prince's tutor and possibly also his lover; the pair frequented homosexual clubs in Whitechapel together.

The painter Frank Miles, an intimate of Oscar Wilde, was named as the Ripper, too, but the truth is that the identity of Jack the Ripper will probably never be known.

Jack the Stripper

The file on Jack the Ripper has never been closed. Neither has the file on Jack the Stripper – even though Scotland Yard is sure that it knows who killed six women in 1964 and early 1965 and left their naked bodies lying along the bank of the river Thames.

The police found the first body under a pontoon at Hammersmith on 2 February 1964. The victim had been strangled and the remnants of her underwear had been shoved down her throat; she was small, at 5 foot 2 inches (1.60 metres) tall, and was naked, apart from her stockings.

The body was identified as being that of Hannah Tailford, who was 30 years old and lived with her boyfriend in the West Norwood district of London. She had a three-year-old daughter and an eighteen-month-old son and was pregnant again. She was employed as a waitress and a cleaner and supplemented her meagre wages by working as a prostitute on the streets of Bayswater (her record showed four convictions for soliciting). She had disappeared from her flat ten days before her body was found, although a couple had seen her on Charing Cross Road only two days before that. She had appeared depressed and suicidal and they had tried to cheer her up, they said.

Forensic experts concluded that she had been dead for just 24 hours when her corpse was found and believed that she may have been drowned in a bath or pond before she was dumped in the river. Tide tables showed that she must have been dropped in the Thames at Duke's Meadow, in Chiswick, a popular spot with prostitutes and their clients. The police discovered that Hannah had been a star turn at sex parties and that she had often attended kinky orgies in Mayfair and Kensington. A foreign diplomat known for his perverted tastes had been one of her clients, but he had been out of the country at the time of her disappearance.

This gave the police little to go on. Although they believed that Hannah had been attacked and sexually assaulted (her knickers having been shoved into her mouth to stop her from screaming as she was killed) they could not even prove that she had been murdered. The inquest into her death recorded an open verdict.

On 8 April 1964 the naked body of the 26-year-old Irene Lockwood was found among the tangled weeds and branches on the river bank at Duke's Meadow. Irene was a pretty, young redhead who, like Hannah, had also worked on the streets of Bayswater and Notting Hill and had attended kinky parties, too (she had furthermore performed in blue movies). Both girls had solicited cab drives late at night and both had been pregnant when they died.

It was impossible to determine how either Hannah or Irene had died, although marks on the back of Irene's head indicated that she could have been attacked from behind. Like Hannah, the police believed that Irene had been killed elsewhere and then brought to Duke's Meadow. The police also suspected that both girls had been mixed up in a blackmail racket. They had found an address book and photographic equipment in Hannah's flat, while Irene's flatmate, Vicki Pender (who had been found battered to death a year earlier), had once been beaten up after trying to blackmail a client who had been photographed with her without his knowledge. The most striking similarity between the two killings, however, was that the victims were found naked; there was no sign of their clothes, which were never discovered.

On 24 April 1964 another naked female corpse was found, this time in an alleyway off Swyncombe Avenue in nearby Brentford, Middlesex. The victim, the 22-year-old

Helen Barthelemy, had been strangled, probably from behind. Strangely enough, three of her front teeth had been extracted after her death. It was also established that she had been stripped of her clothes post mortem; fresh tyre marks in the alley furthermore indicated that she had been killed elsewhere and then dumped there.

Helen was also a prostitute. Educated in a convent, she had later become a stripper in Blackpool. She had served a prison sentence in Liverpool for luring a man into a trap, after which he had been robbed. She had then come to London, where she had gone on the game. She was known to cater for any sort of perversion, but would often entertain local black men for free because they were more sympathetic to her than her kinky clientele. One Jamaican man admitted having been with her on the night of her disappearance, but because he had a strong alibi he was quickly ruled out as a suspect.

The newspapers soon picked up on the story of the three similar killings, and because the victims' nudity was the most sensational aspect the tabloids dubbed their murderer 'Jack the Stripper'.

On reviewing its records Scotland Yard identified another case that matched Jack the Stripper's *modus operandi*. On 8 November 1963, three months before Hannah's murder, the body of the 22-year-old Gwynneth Rees had been found buried in a shallow grave in an ash tip near Chiswick Bridge. She was naked, except for one stocking, and had been sexually assaulted. The body had lain there since May or June of 1963 and it was thought that she may have been sunbathing when she was attacked. The police concluded that she had been another victim of Jack the Stripper.

Kenneth Archibald, a 24-year-old caretaker, then walked into Notting Hill's police station and confessed to the murder of Irene Lockwood. (He was already a suspect because his card had been discovered in Irene's flat.) He

246

said that he had met her in a pub on the night of the murder, after which they had quarrelled over money on some open land near Barnes Bridge. He has lost his temper, he said, and after placing his hands around her throat to stop her from screaming he had accidentally strangled her. When she was dead he had taken off her clothing and had rolled her into the river. Then he had taken her clothes home and had burned them.

Archibald said that he knew nothing about the murders of Hannah Tailford, Helen Barthelemy or Gwynneth Rees, however. Although he was charged with the murder of Irene Lockwood, when he appeared in the Old Bailey he retracted his confession, and as there was no other evidence against him the jury acquitted him.

The forensic scientists paid special attention to Helen Barthelemy's body, which had not been buried, like that of Gwynneth Rees, and had not come into contact with water. It was, however, filthy, as if it had been stored somewhere dirty before being dumped. A minute examination of the corpse's skin showed that it was covered from head to toe in tiny flecks of paint and it was therefore concluded that Helen's naked body had been kept near a spray-painting shop.

It was clear that the man who had killed Helen Barthelemy and the others sought the company of prostitutes in the Bayswater area. The police next organised an amnesty for women working on the streets in that area and appealed to any who had made them strip naked – to come forward. The women's response was overwhelming. Policemen posing as prostitutes were also sent out on to the streets.

On 14 July 1964 another body was found. At around 5.30am a man who was driving to work down Acton Lane had to brake hard in order to miss a van that was speeding out of a cul-de-sac. He subsequently called the police and at the end of the cul-de-sac, outside a garage, they found the naked body of Mary Flemming.

The murdered girl had again been a prostitute who had worked in the Bayswater area. As with Helen Barthelemy, her clothes had been removed after her death and there were tiny flecks of paint all over her body, It furthermore appeared that before being dumped her body had been kept for approximately three days after her killing. Mary had been warned of the dangers of continuing to work the streets which Jack the Stripper was prowling and had taken to carrying a knife in her handbag. It had done her no good, however, for she had been attacked from behind, like the stripper's other victims. No trace of her handbag, knife or clothes were ever found.

By this time Scotland Yard had interviewed 8,000 people and taken 4,000 statements, but it was still no nearer to finding the culprit. Plainclothes policemen now blanketed the area in which the murdered girls had worked, but despite their presence the body of the 21-year-old Margaret McGowan was found lying on some rough ground in Kensington on 25 November 1964. Margaret had been a prostitute and an associate of the society pimp Dr Stephen Ward (who stood trial during the Profumo scandal). Her naked body had lain on the open ground for at least a week when it was found, but before that the forensic scientists believed that it had been stored somewhere else. She had been strangled and her skin was also covered in tiny flecks of paint. The hallmarks of Jack the Stripper were unmistakable.

On the evening on which she had gone missing Margaret and a friend had been in the Warwick Castle, a pub on the Portobello Road, where they had talked about the murders. Margaret had then met a client and she and her friend had gone their separate ways. Her friend gave a good enough description of Margaret's client for the police to issue an Identikit picture of the man, but no one answering the description was ever identified. The police also noticed that Margaret's jewellery was missing, but a check on all the local pawn shops drew a blank.

Although Christmas and New Year passed uneventfully, on 16 February 1965 the naked body of the 28-year-old Bridie O'Hara was found lying in the bracken behind a depot in Acton. In common with the Stripper's previous victims she was short – 5 feet 2 inches (1.60 metres) tall – and worked as a prostitute. Along with her engagement and wedding rings her clothes were nowhere to be found (and never were). The corpse was furthermore covered with minute flecks of paint. This time, however, there was a new clue: one of her hands was mummified, which meant that it had been kept near a source of heat, which had dried out the flesh.

Scotland Yard now threw all of its resources into the case and ordered every business premises within an area of 24 square miles (62 square kilometres) to be searched for samples of paint that matched the flecks on the victims' bodies. The police also worked out that all of the Stripper's victims had been picked up between 11pm and 1am, their bodies being disposed of between 5 and 6am. They concluded that the murderer was therefore a night worker, probably a night watchman who guarded premises near a spray-painting shop. In addition, they speculated that he was a man of about 40 who had a highly charged libido and curious sexual tastes.

The police now dismissed a theory that had been put forward earlier, which held that the culprit was on a crusade against prostitution. They instead believed that because he could not satisfy his bizarre sexual requirements at home he turned to the prostitutes who would do anything for money. The detectives felt sure that the man went into a frenzy during orgasm, which resulted in the women's deaths. He could not help himself, they guessed, and had thus learned to accept that murder was the price that he had to pay for his sexual satisfaction.

This was not much to go on, but the police nevertheless held regular press conferences at which they stated that a list of suspects had been drawn up which they were working their way through. The killer would soon be behind bars, they promised. In fact, although the police had no such list and were not nearly as confident as they pretend, they felt that this strategy was the best way in which to keep putting pressure on the culprit.

This murder coincided with a ten-week cycle, and the police were determined to prevent the next one. They therefore threw a cordon around a 2 square-mile (52-square-kilometre) area of central London and recorded every vehicle that entered or left it at night. Anyone who was found to have moved in or out of the zone on more than three occasions was traced, the police then visiting their home under the pretext of investigating a traffic accident (in order to avoid embarrassing those who had been where they were not supposed to have been). The suspect was then interviewed out of his family's earshot.

Weeks of searching at last paid off when a perfect match was made between the paint flecks on the victims' bodies and paint found under a covered transformer at the rear of a spray-painting shop in the Heron Factory Estate in Acton. (The transformer itself also generated enough heat to mummify any flesh that was left near it.) Every car entering or leaving the estate was then logged and all 7,000 people living in the vicinity were interviewed. At specially convened press conferences the police announced that the number of their suspects was being whittled down to three, then two, and finally one. Once again, these statements were not true, but it is likely that the strategy behind the press conferences worked.

In March 1965 a quiet, family man who lived in south London killed himself, leaving a suicide note that said that he could not 'stand the strain any longer'. At the time the police took little notice of the man's death. By June 1965, however, they had concluded that Jack the Stripper had not struck again – the ten-week cycle had been broken – and because they wanted to know why he had stopped killing they began investigating the suicides that had occurred since the murder of Bridie O'Hara in January 1965. They discovered that this particular suicide victim had worked at a security firm at night. Despite an intensive search of his house and extensive interviews with members of his family no evidence linking him directly to the murders was ever found. Nevertheless, the killings seemed to have stopped and from the circumstantial evidence alone the police were convinced that the man had been Jack the Stripper.

By July 1965 the murder inquiry had been scaled down, to be wound up in the following year. In 1970 Scotland Yard announced that the south London suicide had been Jack the Stripper. It never named him, however, and, indeed, the file on the Jack-the-Stripper case remains officially open. Was he really Jack the Stripper? Probably no one will ever know.

Death in the Churchyard

Nurse Olive Bennett was leading a double life . . . and it was to bring her a violent death. For most of her adult life, 45-year-old Olive had lived in the prim, starchy style expected of a midwife and spinster. But since joining the staff of a maternity home at Tiddington, Warwickshire, she had begun to kick over the traces.

She had taken up smoking, and was making large withdrawals from her Post Office savings account. On her evenings off she would spend an hour or two dressing and making-up, and usually take the bus to nearby Stratford-on-Avon.

She became a familiar figure in the town's old-world

pubs, chain-smoking and drinking large sherries. She would often arrive back to the nurses' home by taxi in the early hours of the morning. Once she told a colleague she had been with her boyfriend.

So nothing seemed amiss when she was still not back by midnight on 23 April 1954.

It was Shakespeare's 390th birthday, and all Stratford was celebrating. The Memorial Theatre was staging *A Midsummer Night's Dream* and restaurants and pubs were packed.

That night Olive caught the 20.15 bus to Stratford. Her first call was probably the Red Horse Hotel, where she was seen drinking until 21.00. She was seen later in other pubs. In one she said to a man: 'I've had five schooners of sherry already. Aren't I a naughty girl?' The night porter at the Red Horse Hotel recalled seeing her again at 23.45 standing outside the hotel. He was the last man to see Olive alive.

Next morning the gardener at Holy Trinity Church beside the river noticed a headstone was missing. Nearby were a pair of spectacles a woman's brown shoe and a set of lower dentures.

Within hours police had found Olive's body in the river, weighted down with the missing headstone. She had been strangled.

Her diary contained the names of several men friends. All were questioned and eliminated from police enquiries. Every soldier at the nearby Long Marston camp was interviewed.

Scotland Yard was called in, and the legendary Detective Superintendent Jack Capstick – famed for his motto 'Softly, softly, catchee monkey' – arrived to head the case. Hundreds more people were questioned, but still the police drew a blank. Reluctantly, Capstick returned to the Yard leaving the case wide open.

Not until eight years later did two sisters come forward

with a story that could be linked with the murder. The girls, both bus conductresses, from Leamington Spa, said they had been in Stratford on the night of the murder and had been picked up by two soldiers. At 23.00 the four of them had gone for a walk in Holy Trinity churchyard.

The older girl said: 'We were standing by some graves when my soldier began getting fresh. I told him to stop it.' The soldier said, apparently as a joke, that he would push her in the river, with a headstone to weigh her down.

The girls had kept quiet at the time because one was married, and the other did not want her mother to know. Perhaps if they had spoken up at the time Olive's murderer would have been found and brought to justice. The time lapse made that impossible.

Painstakingly the police traced and re-interviewed soldiers who had been at Long Marston camp at the time of the murder. Again, they drew a blank, and today it seems unlikely that the mystery of who killed Olive Bennett will ever be solved.

Murder on the Opening Night

It wasn't a very good show. Some of the biggest names in New York high society had turned up to see the new musical comedy opening on the roof garden of Madison Square Garden. *Mam'zelle Champagne* the entertainment was billed as, but its bubbles were flat and the fashionable socialites were yawning when the male lead got up to sing about love.

Then there was a gunshot; and another two shots. The orchestra stopped playing. And nobody yawned any more.

Harry Kendall Thaw, 34-year-old son of a Pittsburgh railroad magnate, was standing among the cafe-concert tables with a pistol smoking in his hand. Before him,

Stanford White, the nation's most celebrated architect, was crumpled in his chair. Slowly he slid to the floor, blood spilling in crimson cataracts over his expensive shirt front. There were two bullet holes in his body. The third shot was lodged in his brain.

All around, people screamed and stampeded for the exits; vainly the manager called for the show to go on. The date was 25 June 1906, and the roof garden murder was to keep America reeling for months to come.

The public learned quickly that it was a love triangle killing. Thaw had publicly gunned down the seducer of his wife. 'I am glad I killed him. He ruined my wife', he had called on the fateful evening. But in this particular triangle were caught lurid shapes – of lust, sadism and madness – all refracted in the prism of big money.

The woman in the case was Evelyn Nesbit Thaw, the beautiful wife of the arrested gunman. Standards of prettiness change with the decades, but her beauty stands somehow outside time. The photographs show a pale, oval face, dark eyes, sensual mouth and lustrous curls. Frail and voluptuous, her features might have embodied the feminine mystique in a painting of any era.

In fact, Evelyn Nesbit had started out as an artist's model. But she soon moved on into the show world. At the age of 15 she was already appearing as a chorus girl in *Floradora,* a smash musical of the period. From the show one song is still well remembered: *Tell Me Pretty Maiden (Are There Any More at Home Like You?)* And from the high-kicking chorus line came another pretty maiden who appears in the pages of this book: Nan Patterson.

Evelyn Nesbit had known the murdered architect long before she had known her husband. Stanford White was internationally respected for his building designs which included, ironically, Madison Square Garden itself. He was a large man with a florid complexion, moustachioed face and roué's lifestyle. On his first meeting with Evelyn he took her and another girl upstairs to a luxurious room in his apartment. It was equipped with a red velvet swing, and he gave the girls turns on it, pushing them right up to the ceiling where their feet reached a Japanese umbrella. But beyond his exotic décor and his playful games, White exhibited deeper passions. In his studio at the apartment, he soon had Evelyn posing for photographs in a silken kimono. On a later occasion, having dizzied her with champagne, he took her to a room whose walls and ceiling were covered with mirrors. There he seduced her while she was sleeping. She was still only 16 years old.

Evelyn went on to become one among several mistresses kept by the architect. He paid her weekly sums of money, brought her out into society and showed her off. Being married, to a very long-suffering wife, White could not offer the girl his hand. And that was one advantage which Harry K. Thaw had over the middle-aged architect.

Thaw met Evelyn Nesbit while she was going around with her seducer. And in the murder trial which was to come, his lawyers did what they could to suggest that Thaw had chivalrously redeemed the fallen showgirl. Certainly, Thaw was outraged by the story of the girl's initial seduction. He hated the architect always referring to him as 'The Beast' and 'The Bastard'. But Thaw himself was no noble knight errant. Actually, he was a monster.

The spoiled playboy son of a millionaire family, Harry Thaw promised to marry Evelyn if she would run away with him to Europe. She accepted the offer, little knowing her admirer's sexual tastes. It was in the Tyrolean castle of Schloss Katzenstein that they were first revealed. One morning at breakfast in the rented castle, he stripped her of her bathrobe and left her naked except for her slippers. Producing a cowhide whip, he threw her onto the bed. 'I was powerless and attempted to scream,' the girl was to testify, 'but Thaw placed his fingers in my mouth and tried to choke me. He then, without any provocation, and without the slightest reason, began to inflict on me several severe and violent blows with the cowhide whip.'

She was in bed for three weeks afterwards, and other similar episodes were to occur before the marriage. It was one of Thaw's kinks, like the cocaine habit he had acquired. Other girls had received the same treatment at his hand.

Why did the chorus girl marry a man with such malevolent passions? Part of the answer must lie in the lure of the Thaw millions, amassed in railroads, coal and coke. There is evidence that some pressure was applied on Evelyn by her own family, and it is not hard to imagine their promptings: darling, your good looks won't last forever ...

Stanford White could scarcely offer protection. In fact, he seems to have collaborated with her family in pressing for the marriage to go ahead. Whatever the reason, Evelyn Nesbit married Harry Thaw on 4 April 1905. It was a big society wedding in which the bride wore white despite the fact that the pair were known to have cohabited in New York already. The couple set up home in the Thaws' Pittsburgh mansion, and if the playboy's own family were none too happy about the marriage they made the best of it that they could.

It was Harry Thaw who became more and more unbalanced. He bought a pistol and was seen posing with it like a duellist in his bedroom. On 25 June, 1906, just over a year after his wedding, he took Evelyn to New York where they dined together at the Café Martin before going with friends to Madison Square Garden for the opening of *Mam'zelle Champagne*. Stanford White arrived later, and took a table on his own. The lacklustre performance had been going on for some time before Evelyn decided it was too dull to endure. The party rose, heading for the elevator. Evelyn in fact reached the lobby before noticing that her husband was not with the party.

Disarmed in the elevator moments after the shooting. Thaw was to explain to the District Attorney: 'I saw him sitting there, big, fat and healthy, and there Evelyn was, poor delicate little thing, all trembling and nervous.'

So spoke the sadist. The Thaw family was to spend hundreds of thousands of dollars not only on their son's legal defence, but on press campaigns to smear his victim. White, of course, presented an easy target for slander considering his roué's lifestyle. But Harry Thaw made no promising defendant either. His first trial for murder opened in January 1907 and did not end until some four months later. The jury eventually arrived at a split verdict. Seven declared Thaw guilty of first degree murder, but five held out for not guilty – by reason of insanity.

A year later, at a second trial, more was made of the issue of madness. Cases of mental disorders in the Thaw family were discussed; a brothel keeper described savage whippings that the defendant had administered to young girls. The jury on this occasion achieved a unanimous verdict. After 72 hours they voted Harry Thaw to be not guilty by reason of insanity.

Thaw was committed to the New York State Asylum for the Criminally Insane. And the story might have ended there but for the wealth and energy of his family who pressed continually for his release. Thaw did in fact taste freedom in 1913 – but not through any court decision. One morning in August he escaped the asylum, climbed into a waiting car and fled for sanctuary to Canada.

Much diplomatic pressure was exerted by the United States Government, and the fugitive was forced to return after only a month. He was jailed at Concord, New Hampshire, and eventually sent back to New York. Tirelessly, the Thaw family campaigned through their lawyers for his release. And in the end they won. In July 1915, as a result of yet another trial, Harry K. Thaw was declared both sane, and innocent of charges against him.

It was an extraordinary decision. Evelyn immediately divorced him and went off to live her own life. A free man, Harry Thaw responded to his good fortune only a few months later by kidnapping and cruelly horsewhipping a Kansas City youth who had incurred his displeasure. Again declared insane, he was again committed to an asylum. Again a court found him to be sane after all – and again, in 1924, he was released from custody.

Harry Thaw died of a coronary in Florida in February 1947. His case had made New York a Babel of gossip, loud rumour and frank accusation. But you do not have to be especially cynical to believe that, in the end, the most persuasive voice of all was the voice of money.

The Black Perambulator

The woman was found in a Hampstead street, lying on a heap of builders' rubbish. Moonlight played softly on the black jacket with its trimming of imitation Astrakhan. Her skull was crushed, and the head itself had almost been severed from the body – it remained attached by only a sliver of skin and muscle.

The date was 24 October 1890, and rumours soon started to circulate. It was whispered that the murder was the work of Jack the Ripper, the phantasmal figure who had stalked the East End only two years earlier. Had the Ripper now returned to claim victims in North London?

A mile or so away was an abandoned perambulator whose cushions were soaked with blood. And the following day, detectives made another grim discovery. The corpse of an 18-month-old baby was recovered from waste ground in Finchley. It was not very long before the three gruesome finds were connected.

The murdered woman was found to have the initials

P.H. embroidered on her underlothes. The fact was reported in the morning newspaper which caught the attention of a certain Clara Hogg, who lived in Kentish Town. She knew that her sister-in-law, Mrs Phoebe Hogg, had gone out on the afternoon of 24 October with her baby. She had not come back that night. The initials fitted the missing woman, and Clara went with a friend to the mortuary where the body had been taken. There, choking back her nausea, Clara recognised her sister-in-law as the grisly figure on the slab.

What puzzled the police was the behaviour of Clara's friend, a tall redheaded woman named Mary Pearcey. She insisted that the corpse was not Phoebe Hogg's; she became hysterical and tried to drag Clara away. It was, in fact, to visit Mary Pearcey that Phoebe Hogg had set out on the fateful afternoon. Yet the russet-haired Mary first denied the fact; then admitted that the visit had taken place.

Clearly, Mary Pearcey's role in the affair needed some investigation. And it did not take much probing for detectives to discover a familiar geometry in the mystery – the geometry of a love triangle.

Frank Hogg, husband of the murdered Phoebe, turned out to be a man with an eye for the ladies. A bearded and jovial furniture remover, he had lived with his wife at Prince of Wales Road, Kentish Town. But Frank also possessed the latchkey to Mary's home at Priory Road nearby. He was regular visitor there, and had been since before his marriage.

Probing deeper, the police discovered that the marriage itself was a forced affair. While he was still a bachelor in 1888, Frank had been seeing both women. His true affection was for the strong-willed and vivacious Mary Pearcey. It was, however, the meeker Phoebe Styles who became pregnant by him. Although leading a double love-life, Frank was a regular church-goer who knew which course he ought to pursue. He wrestled for some time with his conscience, at one point proposing to abandon the whole mess by making a new life abroad. It was Mary Pearcey who told him not to emigrate, but to marry the pregnant Phoebe. The redhead wrote him passionate letters which expressed little jealousy of her rival: 'Oh, Frank! I should not like to think I was the cause of all your troubles, and yet you make me think so. What can I do? I love you with all my heart, and I will love her because she will belong to you.'

Again: 'Do not think of going away, for my heart will break if you do; don't go dear. I won't ask too much, only to see you for five minutes when you can get away; but if you go quite away, how do you think I can live? I would see you get married 50 times over – yes, I could bear that far better than parting with you for ever . . . you must not go away. My heart throbs with pain only to think about it.'

Mixed in these protestations of love were phrases culled from the romantic loveletters which Mary read avidly. One has an especially ironic ring in retrospect: 'In this false world we do not always know who are our friends and who our enemies, and all need friends...'

In the end, Frank did marry Phoebe Styles, settling down with her, his mother and sister Clara at Prince of Wales Road. Phoebe seems to have known all about her husband's liaison with Mary, but raised no strong objections to it. Curiously, the two women were friends, and when Phoebe's second child miscarried, Mary even nursed her rival through the pain and trauma. As for the first baby, Mary doted on it, almost as if she shared in the motherhood of the infant in every way.

To this day, what triggered the bloody climax remains a mystery. The police did determine, though, that on the day before the fateful visit, Mary sent Phoebe a note: 'Dearest: come round this afternoon and bring our little darling, don't fail.' On that occasion, the blinds at Mary's house were seen to be drawn down as if in preparation. As it happened, Phoebe Hogg was unable to go round that day, but after receiving a second note she went to the house the following day.

Mary did admit to police that Phoebe arrived with the baby in the pram, but claimed it was only to borrow some money. Asked why she had first denied the visit, she replied improbably: 'I did not tell you before because Phoebe asked me not to let anybody know that she had been here.' Later, to a police matron, she was to hint that there had been an argument: 'As we were having tea Mrs Hogg made some remark which I did not like – one word brought up another. Perhaps I had better not say any more.'

The neighbours had heard screaming in Mary Pearcey's house at 16.00 – screaming, and the smashing of crockery.

The police produced a search warrant and examined the premises. They found that they had been recently cleaned, but not very thoroughly. Spatters of blood could be seen on the walls and ceiling; the poker had blood and hairs on it. In a dresser drawer was a carving knife, also stained with blood. A skirt, an apron, curtains, a rug – all bore tell-tale stains.

Mary Pearcey sat at a piano during the search, and tinkled out nursery rhymes. When asked why so many bloodstains were to be found about the place she continued to play at the keyboard, eerily chanting, 'Killing mice, killing mice, killing mice!'

Later, the police discovered that Mary was wearing two wedding rings; no ring had been found on the body of Phoebe Hogg.

Arrested and charged with murder, 24-year-old Mary Pearcey was tried at the Old Bailey in December 1890. Throughout the proceedings, the accused woman protested her innocence, but the circumstantial evidence against her was overwhelming. Some two hours after the cries were heard at her home, a neighbour had seen Mary Pearcey pushing the perambulator, draped with a black shawl, along Priory Road. Night had now fallen, and she was hunched over the vehicle as if hoping not be recognised. The pram itself appeared heavily laden, with something strangely bulky crammed up towards the hood ...

The extraordinary journey which followed covered a circuit of some six miles. The murdered woman was found at Crossfield Road, Hampstead, and the baby was abandoned off Finchley Road. There was no evidence of violence being done to the infant, but its clothing was stained with blood. The impression was that it may have been suffocated by the weight of the corpse above it. As for the perambulator, it was found abandoned in Hamilton Terrace, St John's Wood, its grim freight shed at last.

Frank Hogg admitted to the police that he had gone round to Priory Road late that night, and let himself in with his latchkey. When he found the place empty, he pencilled a brief note: 'Twenty past ten. Cannot stay.' Had he lingered, he might have encountered Mary Pearcey returning from her macabre excursion.

The jury took only an hour to consider its verdict and found Mary Eleanor Pearcey guilty of murder. Asked if she had anything to say why sentence of death should not be passed, she swiftly answered: 'Only that I am innocent of the charge.'

Now wretched and reviled, Frank Hogg refused to see his mistress in the condemned cell, a rebuff which Mary lamented: 'He might have made death easier to bear.' On 23 December 1890 she was led to the scaffold and she faced her end with great calm and composure. To the prison chaplain accompanying her, she observed enigmatically: 'The sentence is just, the evidence was false.'

A puzzling remark. And it is just one of the untidy strands left in the Pearcey case. Some have doubted whether Mary could have accomplished the crime alone: Phoebe had been clubbed senseless and had her head severed by a knife drawn across the throat several times. It was done with such force that it cut clean through the vertebrae. Then there was the business of cramming the corpse into the pram. This was a formidable task even granted the point made by F. Tennyson Jesse in her *Murder and Its Motives:* 'the matter was made easier by the fact that there was nothing to prevent the head being doubled right back.'

What provoked the maniacal assault? Was it premeditated, or sparked by that 'remark which I did not like'? And if the evidence was false, who had falsified it?

London in the 1890s was the city of yellow fog and gaslit streets known to readers of Sherlock Holmes stories. And for afficionados of great unsolved murder mysteries there is one tantalizing postscript piece which in no way fits the jigsaw.

It emerged at the trial that Mary Pearcey's true name was Mary Eleanor Wheeler. She had taken her surname from that of a carpenter, John Charles Pearcey, with whom she had once cohabited. He stated at the trial that they were never formally married, and that he had left Mary because of her roving eye. But some mysterious figure seems to have occupied a special place in her affections. For on the day of her execution, Mary instructed her solicitor to place the following advertisement in the Madrid newspapers: 'M.E.C.P. Last wish of M.E.W. Have not betrayed.'

There is little doubt that Mary Pearcey lured Phoebe Hogg to Priory Road and there killed the unfortunate woman. The motive seems clearly to have been rooted in jealous love. Who then was M.E.C.P? And what was the secret they shared? The puzzle has prompted one fantastic solution: that Mary was a member of a nefarious secret society, and liquidated Phoebe when she found out about it. More prosaically, it has been suggested that Mary was secretly married as a teenager to a man whose name she did not want sullied at the trial. Finally, it is possible that the novelette-reading Mary simply invented a little enigma to lend romance to her appalling crime.

We simply do not know. But reading and re-reading the last cryptic message you cannot help believing that a fascinating dimension to the case of Mary Pearcey may have dropped into the void when the hangman's fatal trap was sprung.

The Arm in the Shark Case

The story hit the headlines on Anzac Day – 25 April 1935. It was labelled in shrieking type across the front pages as 'The Arm In The Shark Case'. To incredulous newspaper readers that day, to police and forensic experts, it was one of the most bizarre mysteries ever.

The mystery began in the Sydney seaside suburb of Coogee. Fisherman Bert Hodson had set out in his small boat to examine lines he had baited with mackerel about 1.5 km off shore. He was after shark. Hodson was in luck: he found not one but two of the dread killers. One small shark was already firmly hooked to one of his lines. Another, a 4.2 m (14 ft) tiger shark, was in the process of devouring the smaller one. The fisherman hauled in the line and found the tiger shark was not firmly ensnared. Turning his boat for the shored, he headed home with the creature in tow.

Hodson would normally have killed the shark and hung it on the boathouse scales. But the fisherman's brother, Charles, ran an aquarium at Coogee and Bert knew that the prize tiger shark would provide an excellent attraction for the paying customers who crowded down from the city.

And so it proved. The shark circled menacingly round the aquarium to the delight of the trippers for a few days. Then, on 25 April the fascination on the faces of the visitors turned to horror as they witnessed the most astonishing spectacle. The tiger shark went into convulsions. It surged around the water, disgorging the contents of its stomach: rats, birds, parts of the smaller shark – and a human arm.

Charles Hodson acted swiftly. He fished out the arm and telephoned the police. They found the grisly specimen to be the left arm of a man, with a tattoo of two boxers slugging it out. Attached was a length of rope.

At first, police put the case down as a shark attack on a lone swimmer or yachtsman until, over the days, their suspicions became aroused. No one had been reported missing off a Sydney beach. And a police surgeon who examined the arm claimed that it had not been bitten off by a shark but cleanly amputated with a sharp knife.

Fingerprints were taken of the hand and, although they were blurred, experts were able to match the prints of the thumb and ring finger with those of a man in police files. They belonged to James Smith, who ran a billiard room grandly titled the Rozelle Sports Club, and who had once been arrested for illegal bookmaking. Smith had been missing from his home for 28 days. His brother, Edward, positively identified the arm but was unable to give any hint as to Smith's movements. And all that the victim's wife, Gladys, knew was that her husband had left home saying that he was taking a party on a paid fishing trip.

The police sought out Smith's friends. One of them John Brady, was not easy to find for he was wanted by Tasmanian police on a forgery charge. But he was eventually run to ground on 17 May, living with his wife in a small flat in north Sydney. Under interrogation, Brady admitted having stayed with Smith in a cottage at Cronulla, on the same stretch of coastline as the shark had been caught, but denied knowing anything about the crime.

Over the next few months, divers and chartered aircraft searched the waters of Cunnamatta Bay, near Cronulla, hoping to find further clues.

The police had a theory, however. They believed that Smith went to stay with Brady at Cronulla to plan their next fraud, but that the two men fell out over the sharing of the loot. Brady, they believed, killed his accomplice and hacked up the body. He placed the remains in a metal trunk – but could not fit in the arm. So he roped it to the outside of the trunk and dumped the terrible evidence into the sea. A small shark, attracted by the blood, attacked the trunk, severing the rope with its razor-sharp teeth. As the arm floated free, the shark swallowed it whole.

The shark's next meal was the mackerel on Bert Hodson's line. And that was when the shark became a meal for the larger tiger shark.

The police theory sounded far-fetched. But the 'Arm In The Shark Case' was soon to prove that fact can be even stranger than fiction.

The crime that detectives believed Smith and Brady had been plotting was an insurance fraud over a yacht that had apparently disappeared. Police interviewed the yacht's former owner, whom they regarded as a key witness. But the day before an inquest was due to be held into Smith's death, the witness was found shot in his car beneath the approaches to Sydney's famous Harbour Bridge.

The following day, detectives received another blow. The coroner who was to have held the inquest ruled that he could not do so without a complete body. Nevertheless, Brady was charged with murder and sent for trial.

The trial lasted only two days. The judge refused to admit as evidence signed statements that had been taken from the witness before he was found shot dead. Without this evidence, the jury was directed to acquit Brady. Two men were charged with murdering the witness, but they too were acquitted.

Brady continued his career of crime. In all, he spent more than 20 years of his life in jail. During all that time, the only person who knew the full facts of the 'Arm In The Shark Case' never once hinted at what the truth might be.

And the full story never will be known. John Brady suffered a heart attack at the age of 71 in a prison repatriation hostel. His secret died with him.

The Motorway Monster

The brutal killing of an attractive woman hitchhiker led to Britain's biggest-ever motorway murder hunt. In all, 1,500 police officers quizzed more than 125,000 people and took nearly 50,000 statements in their fruitless bid to track down the killer of schoolteacher Barbara Mayo.

Tall, dark-haired Barbara set off from her flat in Hammersmith, London, in October 1970 to hitchhike to Catterick, Yorkshire, to pick up her boyfriend's car which had broken down there. Her own car had been giving her trouble and she did not want to risk a breakdown in it. Two days after she had left London, her boyfriend physics graduate David Pollard, reported her missing.

Four days later a miner rambling with his family in a wood just off the M1 at Ault Hucknall, near Chesterfield, Derbyshire, stumbled on her partly clothed body under a pile of leaves. Barbara, aged 24, had been raped and strangled.

Police knew it would be a tough case to crack. For the most baffling murder cases are those in which an element of association between victim and killer is missing. In the case of Barbara Mayo, there were no locals with helpful information; she was found 321 km (200 miles) from her home and there was nothing to connect her murderer with her or the area where she was found. The killer could have

been a commercial traveller, a commuter or a driver looking for casual sex with hitchhikers.

The police investigators – headed by Detective Chief
Superintendent Charles Palmer of Scotland Yard – followed
up every lead. They spent months checking thousands of
Morris 1000 Travellers after a witness said he had seen
Barbara, or a girl fitting her description, in a white Morris
Traveller at Kimberley, Nottinghamshire. At that time
more than 100,000 of this type of car were still on the road.
Each owner had to be traced and eliminated.

The murder hunt also revealed something of the murky
world of the motorway hitchhiker. In tests along the M1,
police discovered that a man might have to wait between
30 and two hours for a lift. But an attractive girl would be
picked up in minutes. It seemed to indicate that there were
men who drove on motorways simply to pick up girl
hikers – and one of them might have picked up Barbara.

But the most worrying aspect was that girls, knowing
the dangers they faced, still hitchhiked alone – often
wearing provocative clothing to catch the eye of the drivers.

Police set up checkpoints along 320 km (200 miles) of
the M1 between London and Leeds and asked motorists:
'Were you on this motorway 14 days ago? Did you see this
girl?'

Each driver was shown a picture of Barbara with this
description: 'Barbara Janet Mayo, aged 24 years, 1.7 m
(5 ft 9 in), slim build, high cheekbones, brown eyes, light
tanned complexion, good teeth . . . wearing navy-blue coat
with eight silver buttons, gold and tan brocade slacks,
hipster style, lilac jersey, blue socks, corduroy lace-up
shoes.' But nothing led the police any closer to 'The
Monster of the Motorway', as the newspapers dubbed the
ruthless killer.

Next, police plastered posters with Barbara's picture
and a detailed description all over Britain. Chief Superintendent Palmer said: 'I let it be known that if any

motorist who had given a girl a lift on the M1 on 12 October came forward, I would meet him anywhere – and his wife would not be told.' But nobody came forward.

A London policewoman impersonating Barbara went from Barbara's flat by tube to Hendon, where the M1 then began. She stood at the roadside, thumbing lifts.

A butcher at Kimberley, Nottinghamshire, who saw the reconstruction on television told police: 'I'm sure she came into my shop and asked for two freshly cooked faggots.' She had then crossed the road and walked down a hill towards the main road.

Was it Barbara Mayo? Or just another girl who looked like her? The question remains unanswered.

Charles Palmer said:

'I still hope that somebody, somewhere will come forward with vital information. And though there are people who can live with murder on their conscience, I still don't rule out the possibility that the person or persons responsible for Barbara's death will confess.'

There is one person, however, who believed that the police were largely wasting their time in the nationwide hunt for Barbara's killer. That person is her mother, widow Mrs Marjorie Mayo. She said:

'I have never believed Barbara was hitchhiking. I believe her murder took place in London and was carried out by somebody in a bad crowd Barbara had got in with. Her body was probably taken in her own car and left by the M1 to put the police off the trail. She came to see me the day before she disappeared. She said: 'Mummy I'm so frightened.' But before she could explain, some people called at the house and the conversation was lost.

Barbara is never far from my thoughts – she is still very real to me. And I don't believe her murder will ever be solved.'

Death of the Black Dahlia

The corpse found on an undeveloped building site in a Los Angeles suburb on 15 January 1947 had been savagely mutilated. It was the body of a young woman, cut in half at the waist and with the initials 'B. D.' carved into her thigh.

It was the use of those initials that gave the case its notoriety. They stood for 'Black Dahlia', the nickname given to a pretty 22-year-old small-time movie actress, Elizabeth Short. She was known simply as Betty or Beth to her friends. But she also revelled in the nickname of Black Dahlia because of her liking for jet-black clothes. And, from fingerprints, the body was identified as being hers.

Elizabeth Short's brief life was not a happy one. She had been a juvenile delinquent but found love and a chance for a fresh start when she met a young serviceman. He proposed, they became engaged, then parted when he was posted overseas in World War 2.

He never came home – and his death sent Elizabeth on a downhill path. She turned to drink and tried her luck as a bit-part actress in Hollywood. But jobs were hard to come by and she began working as a waitress by day and haunting sleazy bars and pick-up joints by night. The inevitable happened. Elizabeth started to accept money for her favours. She soon became known for her black apparel – including her black silk underwear.

The Black Dahlia had one further chance of rescue when a second lover proposed to her. Cruelly, he too died . . . and Elizabeth's fate was sealed.

When the discovery of the poor girl's butchered body was reported in the Los Angeles newspapers, a strange reaction set in. Perhaps it was the photographs of the beautiful young victim – before and after death – that incited an astonishing spate of false reports and confessions.

The first came from a waitress who said she had heard two killers discussing the crime at a table. She gave the police a description – and inquiries revealed that the 'killers' were a couple of detectives having an off-duty coffee. Another tip came from a blonde dancer who told police: 'I'm meeting a man at First and Temple Streets at nine o'clock and I have reason to believe he's the Black Dahlia killer.' Detectives arrested the pair and took them in for questioning. The man turned out to be an innocent executive who had once spent a night with the blonde, following which she had been trying to blackmail him, without success. The 'tip off' to the police was just her way of applying extra pressure.

One piece of evidence the police took much more seriously was a package sent to a Los Angeles newspaper enclosing a message cut from press headlines. It said: 'Here are Dahlia's belongings. Letter to follow.' The package also contained Elizabeth's social security card, her birth certificate and an address book – with one page torn out. Police said they believed that these articles had been removed from the body – no clothing was found at the scene – and that the missing page in the address book would have revealed the name of the killer. Fingerprints were taken from the social security card but they matched none in police files.

Later, a small-time underworld figure gave himself up to police, saying 'I killed the Black Dahlia'. This time detectives thought they had solved the case, because in Elizabeth's address book had been the name of a firm the suspect had once worked for. But a lie-detector test showed he was just another crank.

Years later, a 29-year-old army corporal was held on suspicion after volunteering the information: 'When I get drunk I get rough with women.' He knew many details of the killing. But again, he was finally dismissed as being mentally unbalanced.

In all, around 50 men have claimed they committed the murder – but the case of the Black Dahlia remains unsolved.

The Torso in the Trunk

Barely glancing up, the left-luggage clerk handed the man a ticket and heaved his heavy trunk into a corner of the office. 6 June, 1934 – Derby Day – was a busy day at Brighton railway station, with racegoers bound for Epsom and early holidaymakers swelling the usual commuting crowd.

The trunk was the seventieth to be deposited in a few hours and stuffing ticket CT1945 in his pocket, the man vanished in the crowd. He probably caught the next train to London.

It was not until 17 June that a clerk at Brighton station, noticing an unpleasant smell, opened the trunk and recoiled in horror at the terrible sight that met his eyes. Inside was the torso of a woman, wrapped in brown paper and tied around with a venetian blind cord.

An immediate search of other railway left-luggage offices led to the discovery of a suitcase containing the murder victim's severed legs at London's King's Cross station. It had been deposited there on 7 June.

What had happened to the head and arms? No one can be sure. But on 10 June a couple walking on the beach found a female human head in a pool.

Incredibly, they left it there and reported it to no one. When police heard of their find a month later and questioned them, they said they assumed someone had committed suicide by jumping off a cliff, and that the police had swept the remains they did not need into the sea.

Pathologist Sir Bernard Spilsbury said the murder had taken place on about 30 or 31 May, and that the victim had been a healthy young woman aged 21 to 28. She was about 1.7 m (5 ft 2 in) tall, weighed 54 kg (8 st 7 lb) and was pregnant. And there was no other means of identification.

Police came to the conclusion that the killer was probably a married man of some social standing who had an affair with the woman. She became pregnant, and when her condition became noticeable she asked him for help. He refused, and she threatened to tell his wife about their affair. They had a row, which became violent, and in the heat of the moment she was killed by a blow to the head.

On one of the pieces of brown paper detectives found the final part of a word written in blue pencil. The syllable FORD was easily recognizable, and the previous letter could have been a D or an L.

A woman working in a London warehouse came forward to identify the writing as her own. She regularly returned defective consignments to a confectionery firm at Bedford.

Police identified the brown paper she used as the type wrapped around the woman's remains. And they established that when such sheets arrived at the Bedford factory, they were re-used to dispatch goods to all parts of the country.

They followed every possible lead, but the trail went cold.

Chief Inspector Robert Donaldson from Scotland Yard took charge of the case. In an attempt to identify the victim, he launched a massive round-up of missing girls. In all, 732 who had left home were traced. He had detectives check every hospital, nursing home and doctor's surgery for details of women who had sought pre-natal advice. One London hospital alone produced 5,000 names.

Other detectives checked makers and retailers of trunks, and made discreet enquiries into thousands of purchases. But again they drew a blank.

Of all the thousands of clues that led nowhere, one statement seems to point to the killer. Porter Todd, at

London Bridge Station, recalled helping a man with a heavy trunk on the 15.00 train for Brighton on 6 June. He had bought his cheap-day third-class ticket at Dartford, and was noticed by a girl on the same train. Only five cheap-day tickets to Brighton had been sold at Dartford that day. Four of the travellers were traced by the police . . . but the fifth was never found.

A Question of Murder

'A dingo has got my baby!'

Shortly before nightfall on the evening of 17 August 1980, a group of campers were enjoying a barbecue near Ayers Rock in the Australian outback. Suddenly there was a shout.

'A dingo has got my baby!' called Mrs Lindy Chamberlain. In horror, her husband and other campers ran back to the Chamberlains' tent to find the baby girl's basket empty. 'All I could see was a horrible, lonely whiteness in that basket,' the father told police some time later. But other witnesses remembered traces of blood around the tent. And about a week later, the child's torn and bloodstained jumpsuit, singlet and nappy were found near the base of Ayers Rock. Of nine-week-old Azaria Chamberlain, however, there was no trace. She had vanished, never to be seen again.

It seemed a horrific tragedy, made all the nightmarish by the looming presence of Ayers Rock – one of the weirdest things on planet earth. The vast red platform rises abruptly to more than 1,000 feet above the outback of the Northern Territory, forming the largest monolith in the world. Chameleon-like, its colour changes according to atmospheric conditions and the sun's position. The Aborigines have always regarded it as a magical place and the site of many strange happenings.

The baby's mysterious disappearance prompted a flood of gossip and speculation. Lindy and Michael Chamberlain, both in their thirties, were members of the Seventh Day Adventist Church, he being a minister. It was rumoured that the baby's name, Azaria, meant 'sacrifice in the wilderness'; had the little girl really been taken by a wild dog? How was it that the clothing had been found, while the baby's body had completely vanished? Many people came to regard the circumstances as suspicious, and the case won nationwide attention.

In February 1981 the coroner at Alice Springs delivered his verdict on the missing child. Taking the unprecedented step of reading his finding (a 13-page document) before television cameras, he informed an estimated viewing audience of two million people that the parents were entirely blameless. Azaria Chantal Loren Chamberlain had met her death while being attacked by a wild dingo; in trying to make off with the baby, 'the dingo would have caused severe crushing to the base of the skull and neck and lacerations to the throat and neck'. The body had been disposed of by a person or persons unknown, and neither the parents nor their sons Aidan (7) and Reagan (4), who had been camping with them at the time, were in any degree responsible. Moreover, 'I find that the name Azaria does not mean and never has meant "sacrifice in the wilderness".'

The coroner expressed sympathy for the bereaved parents: 'You have not only suffered the loss of your beloved child in the most tragic circumstances, but you have all been subjected to months of innuendoes, suspicion and probably the most malicious gossip ever witnessed in this country.' He declared that he had permitted TV coverage to stop the rumours in the most direct way possible.

It was a very emphatic performance – but the case simply would not die. A year later, in February 1982, a second inquest was called on the basis of new forensic evidence. On this occasion a forensic expert testified that traces of blood had been found on the clasp of a camera bag belonging to the parents. It was foetal blood – that is, the blood of a baby less than six months old – and with it was found baby hair. Blood had also been cleaned from conspicuous areas in the couple's car, but it had not been eradicated completely: there were traces in all sorts of nooks and crannies such as the door handles, the door hinge and places under the dashboard. The evidence was

278

consistent with what was to become the prosecution's extraordinary allegation – that Mrs Chamberlain had taken the baby from the tent to the front seat of the car and there cut her throat. Afterwards, it was alleged, the body had been buried at the camp site, but dug up again. Azaria's clothing had been removed and placed at the spot where it was found several days later.

The coroner decided that there was a case for Mrs Chamberlain being sent to trial for murder, and her husband as an accessory in seeking to cover the act up. The accused parents were clearly stunned by the finding, and Michael Chamberlain remained for some time with his head buried in his hands, visibly distressed.

The 'Dingo Case' had now acquired a worldwide audience, and Lindy Chamberlain went into hiding before the trial. When proceedings opened on Monday 13 September, the world learned of a new twist in the drama. Mrs Chamberlain, 34, was seven months' pregnant – she might well give birth to another child during the trial.

The Supreme Court at Darwin was packed. So great was foreign interest that a separate room had to be set aside for the news media, with its own closed-circuit TV system linking up with proceedings in the court. The judge warned the jury not to allow anything they might have read to prejudice their verdict, while acknowledging that the publicity was 'without precedent in our lifetime'.

Mr Ian Barker QC, opening for the prosecution, said the foetal blood found in the car exploded the dingo story, which was no more than a 'fanciful lie to conceal the truth'. The prosecution would not try to establish Mrs Chamberlain's motive. But the evidence, he said, pointed conclusively to the fact that she had murdered her baby, entering the tent afterwards to leave the smears of blood that were found there later. The body was probably placed in the camera bag in the car prior to its eventual disposal.

In the weeks that followed, powerful evidence was

marshalled to support the case. For example, Professor Malcolm Chaikin, head of textile technology at New South Wales University, declared that the baby's clothing had not been torn by a dingo's teeth but cut with some fairly sharp scissors; moreover, he claimed to have found some fragments of the material in Mrs Chamberlain's camera bag. James Malcolm Cameron, professor of forensic medicine, was flown in from the London Hospital medical college and also denied the likelihood of a wild dog's involvement. Asked what the clothing evidence pointed to, he said, 'It suggests that there was an incised wound of the neck. In other words, a cut throat.' The wound was caused by 'a cutting instrument across or around the neck held by a human element.'

The human story which emerged from campsite witnesses was, however, generally favourable to the defence. A Mrs Lowe was asked if anything in Lindy's behaviour prior to the disappearance had suggested that murder was on her mind. 'No, exactly the opposite,' replied the woman. 'She had a "new mum" glow about her.'

There was sobbing from the parents in the dock when another witness described how Lindy Chamberlain told her she had called her baby Azaria because it meant 'Blessed of God'.

Mrs Alice Amy Whittaker said she had seen a dingo emerging from the bush while she was washing up at the camp site. It was skirting the lighted area and seemed to be moving towards the Chamberlains' tent. This was only 20 minutes before Michael Chamberlain rushed up to her and begged her and her husband to pray for Azaria because she had been taken by a dingo. Later that night Mrs Whittaker had comforted Lindy Chamberlain by saying that what had happened was God's will. Lindy tried to resign herself: 'It says, doesn't it, that at the Second Coming babies will be restored back to their mothers' arms?' But she was distressed and seemed particularly agitated by the idea that the searchers might be looking in the wrong place: 'I will have to live with this for the rest of my life. I don't want to have to if my baby simply died because I did not look in the right place.'

Some controversy surrounded the issue of dingoes' general habits. Was such an attack – with the removal of the prey – consistent with the wild dogs' known behaviour? Mr Leslie Harris, president of the Dingo Foundation, testified for the defence, asserting that a dingo might well regard a sleeping baby as prey and would be capable of carrying one off. A dingo, he said, might close its jaws over the entire head and make off with it so as not to lose its meal to other dingoes.

Several other witnesses testified to dingo attacks in the Ayers Rock area. One man described how his four-year-old son had been attacked by a wild dog at the same camp site only a month before Azaria's disappearance.

What of the bloodstains in the car? In June 1979 – a year before the event – the Chamberlains had picked up a man injured in a road accident. The victim testified in court that he had been bleeding profusely from the head. Of course, his was not the foetal blood, but the damning evidence of this issue was challenged by the defence's own forensic witness, who claimed that the foetal blood test results were not reliable.

At one stage, the whole court travelled 800 miles to study the scene of the disappearance. Lindy Chamberlain was permitted to stay in Darwin, for she was by now eight months' pregnant. But she did give evidence when the court returned, in the fifth week of the trial.

Her version of events was already embodied in a statement made to police. She claimed that she had put Azaria to bed while her husband was at the barbecue, and afterwards came back to the cooking place to prepare a meal for her oldest son, Aidan. A baby's cry was heard from somewhere near the tent, and Lindy went back to check that all was well. As she walked towards the tent she saw a youngish dingo coming out of it; she yelled and briefly gave chase. Then, thinking only that her baby might have been bitten, she hurried into the tent.

In the box, Lindy Chamberlain was often emotional. She broke down in tears when asked to examine her baby's bloodstained clothing. When the judge asked if she was all right she said that she was – but two of the three women on the jury began crying and the trial had to be temporarily adjourned.

Lindy Chamberlain wept again that day when the prosecution's allegations were repeated; 'It's not true,' she declared through stifled sobs. The next day she broke down again, complaining to the prosecutor that 'you are talking about my baby, not some object'. And when it was alleged that she deliberately smeared the family tent with blood, she replied fiercely, 'No, that's pure fabrication'.

Summing up for the defence, her counsel asserted that there was no conceivable motive for the killing. Ten independent witnesses had been brought forward to testify that Lindy was a loving and caring mother to Azaria. The prosecution's whole story would be 'laughable if it was not such a horribly serious matter'.

What was the jury to make of it all? From the press reports, the forensic evidence did not appear conclusive either way, while the problem of motive was tormenting. Why should Lindy Chamberlain murder her baby? Was there anything in the rumour of a sacrifice? Or had she suffered from post-natal depression? Then again, if she was innocent, what on earth had happened to the body? Why were no bones or other human relics found? The fact of the matter was that, to many outsiders, the dingo and murder stories seemed improbable.

The jury of nine men and three women had, however, observed all the long and complex proceedings. And on Friday, 29 October, after deliberating for six hours, they returned unanimous verdicts of guilty: Lindy Chamberlain of murdering her baby and Michael Chamberlain of being an accessory after the fact. The trial judge, Mr Justice James Muirhead, passed the mandatory sentence of life imprisonment with hard labour on the convicted woman.

She received the sentence impassively, but was tear-stained when driven from the court to Berrimah Prison on the outskirts of Darwin. Her husband, subsequently given an 18-month suspended sentence, was released on a promise of good behaviour, and immediately attended a church service with his sons.

A verdict had been reached on the missing baby – but what of the one to be born? On 17 November, under guard at a Darwin hospital, Lindy Chamberlain gave birth to a second girl. But she was not permitted to keep the child in prison, and Kahlia, as the baby was called, was taken from her mother only hours after the delivery. Australian justice was so cruel, though, as to enforce a permanent separation. Two days later, Lindy Chamberlain was freed on bail pending an appeal; out of concern for the baby's welfare the mother was permitted to retire to an Adventist Church college with her family while awaiting the Appeal Court's ruling.

The judgement came in April 1983, when the Chamberlains' joint appeals were dismissed by the Federal Court in Sydney. The judges referred to the importance of seeing and hearing scientific witnesses in order to evaluate their testimony. As for the couple's credibility: 'If the jury disbelieved them, as they must have done, we are quite unable to say that they were wrong.'

Lindy Chamberlain was returned to jail, and all attempts to obtain her release failed until sensational new forensic evidence, including a baby's jacket, was found at Ayers Rock in January 1986. Yet another inquiry was ordered: Lindy Chamberlain was freed pending its outcome – and officials declared that whatever the result she would not be sent back to jail.

The Mad Major – a True Story

Five blows with a rolling pin ended the life of 25-year-old prostitute Olive Young. She was bludgeoned to death in her basement flat in Fulham by a man who called himself Major True, and to make sure, the murderer thrust a towel down her throat and strangled her with the girdle of her dressing gown. Then True dragged the corpse into the bathroom and left it lying on the floor. He took his time, arranging a couple of pillows in the bed to make it look as though someone was asleep. Methodically, he went through the woman's possessions, taking £8 along with the best of her jewellery. And he was still there when the prostitute's cleaning lady arrived. He told her not to wake her mistress, and tipped her half a crown before leaving the flat.

The events had unfolded on the morning of 6 March 1922, and later that day True bought a new suit to replace the one bloodstained in the assault. He also pawned some of the stolen jewellery. All were acts of a cold and calculating murderer, you might think, of a man sufficiently in control of himself to both cover up and to profit from his crime. But the 'Major' had been recognized by the cleaning lady from an earlier visit, and was tracked down that night at the Hammersmith Palace of Varieties. Though he denied all knowledge of the murder, he was arrested and taken to Brixton Prison. He was not held there in the ordinary cells, however, but taken to the prison hospital. For the police and everyone else concerned with the case could see that True was stark, staring mad.

He really was mad: when the case came to trial at the Old Bailey the prosecution scarcely bothered to deny it, for the medical evidence was overwhelming and conclusive. But that did not mean that the defence could automatically expect an acquittal on grounds of insanity. It was to be a classic test for the rules governing crime and madness under the law of the land.

From his childhood, Ronald True had always been thought odd, and when he grew to manhood he became addicted to morphine, which cannot have helped his mental balance. But his strangeness worsened dramatically after accidents sustained as a trainee pilot in World War I. True never flew in combat for the Royal Flying Corps: he suffered a bad crash at Farnborough which resulted in concussion and left him unconscious for two days. After a second, less serious, accident at Gosport he was invalided out of the Corps.

From 1916 onwards, Ronald True lived his life in and out of nursing homes, where he alternated between fits of speechless gloom, of violence, and of wild exultation when he might, for example, speed around in his bath chair clutching a hooter and a doll. Around 1920 he also started to develop a persistent and sinister delusion. At a nursing home run by a Dr Parham, True used to place bets on horse races, receiving results by telegram. He was happy enough when he picked a winner, but when he lost he would complain that the result was not for him – it was for 'the other Ronald True'.

As time passed, 'the other Ronald True' came to take the blame for everything awkward and unpleasant such as unpaid bills and cheques that bounced. There would come a day of reckoning, True warned, if he ever caught up with his villainous double. There would be a fine 'how d'ye do'.

Outside the nursing homes, True was capable of seeming sane and agreeable – even rather good company – to passing acquaintances. The war had, after all, left a lot of decent young men prone to the horrors; to bouts of over-animated conversation and to sudden silences, and you could not blame True for such eccentricities as going about hatless, claiming that hats 'hurt his head'. He spoke of his wartime injuries. He posed as a 'Major' and fantasized about his exploits as a fighter ace in France. He claimed to be living a life of danger now, too, flying on secret and mysterious missions. To casual clubland friends all these things were acceptable as tallish stories. It was only on closer acquaintance that his lunacy became evident; his eyes, especially, were said to be terrifying.

Women in particular seem to have shunned him. For some time he pursued a Mrs Wilson, offering to act as her protector and scaring her out of her wits by threatening violence if she danced with other men. She showed Mrs Wilson his gun, too. Scotland Yard, he said, had given him permission to carry the revolver, loaded with dum-dum bullets, in case he should meet 'the other Ronald True' – a dangerous criminal who was going around the West End passing cheques which he, 'the real Ronald True', had to keep paying. Mrs Wilson tried her best to escape the lunatic's attentions, and finally freed herself from him in February 1922.

That was when Ronald True started pursuing the ill-fated prostitute Olive Young, alias Gertrude Yates. After an early and sinister encounter, she, like Mrs Wilson, perceived his derangement and tried to have nothing to do with him. But he was relentless in pursuit, phoning incessantly and trying to arrange meetings. True was also falling into debt, and signals seem to have got crossed in his brain. His shadow self and the woman who shunned him seem to have fused into one. For two weeks before the night of the murder, True was telling his acquaintances that he would shortly be going to a basement flat in Fulham to shoot a man who owed him money.

Late on the night of 5 March 1922, he was waiting on Olive Young's doorstep. Exhausted no doubt by his persecutions, and anxious to avoid a scene, she finally let the murderer in. . . .

When his case came to trial, the defence had no trouble in producing evidence of True's insanity. Even in prison he had exhibited his crazy cunning, managing to escape from his own cell and attain that of another killer with the declared intention of forming a Murderers' Club. But the prosecution looked coldly at the case in relation to the law. Here was a man in debt, who murdered a prostitute for her money and took some trouble to conceal the event afterwards. Mad or not, he *knew* what he was doing. And under the M'Naghten Rules, that prohibited a plea of insanity.

The judge summed up in favour of the prosecution on the point of law: 'You will probably feel that the prisoner *did* know at the time the physical nature and quality of the acts he had perpetrated.' On 5 May 1922, Ronald True was found guilty of murder and sentenced to death.

Inevitably, there was an appeal – but the Appeal Court found no reason to disagree with the jury's verdict, and responsibility for his case rested finally with the Home Secretary, who ordered a commission to examine True's mental condition. Three doctors unanimously agreed that the prisoner was insane.

It was the doctors' decision at this stage which saved True's life. For it was a paradox of English law at the time of capital punishment that you could not hang a lunatic – you might sentence him or her to death, but the idea of executing mad creatures had been considered an abomination since Tudor times and before. For one thing the insane were not in a position to raise valid legal objections; for another, they could not make their peace with the Almighty.

And so Ronald True was reprieved and committed to Broadmoor. He died there in 1951, at the age of 60.

The Arsenic-eater's Wife

In 1884 an extraordinary murder case was reported from Liverpool. Two women, Mrs Flanagan and Mrs Higgins, confessed to killing Mr Higgins by poison which they had obtained by soaking arsenic out of flypapers. Since the women came from the working class, the case never quite became a classic. But only five years later another flypaper poison drama hit the headlines in Liverpool, and this one unfolded in a comfortable middle-class setting. Moreover, it featured a delicious cocktail of arsenic mixed with adultery – and culminated in one of the most controversial trial verdicts ever reached in an English court. The Maybrick Mystery was one of the grand Victorian crime block-busters, and more than 30 years after the trial the name of the leading lady was still well remembered. When James Joyce wrote his novel *Ulysses* (1922) he had Molly solilo-quize at length about the case in a passage beginning: take that Mrs Maybrick that poisoned her husband . . . white Arsenic she put in his tea off flypaper . . .' but did she?

Born Florence Elizabeth Chandler, the future Mrs Maybrick was a Southern belle from Mobile, Alabama, who was educated partly in Europe. In 1881, at the age of only 18, she married James Maybrick, a wealthy English cotton broker of 42. Three years later the couple settled down at Battlecrease House in Liverpool, where Mrs Maybrick bore her husband two children, a boy and a girl. And their family life seems to have been happy enough until, in 1887, Florence discovered that her husband had a mistress in Liverpool. James had sired no fewer than five children by the woman – two of them since his wedding.

It is clear that, afterwards, something froze between Mr and Mrs Maybrick. While keeping up outward appear-ances, they stopped sleeping together as man and wife.

288

Increasingly, Florence looked for pleasure in the company of Alfred Brierley, a handsome young friend of her husband, while James continued to visit his mistress and indulge his favourite pastime – of eating arsenic.

It may sound incredible, but the people of Styria and the Tyrol had long practised arsenic-eating for therapeutic purposes; James Maybrick was a hypochondriac who took the substance both as a tonic and as an aphrodisiac. The Victorians were more cavalier with their medicines than we are today, and Maybrick also took a host of other potentially lethal preparations, including strychnine. But arsenic seems to have been his favourite. 'It is meat and liquor to me,' he once told a friend. 'I don't tell everybody. I take it when I can get it, but the doctors won't put any into my medicine except now and then. That only tantalizes me.' To another acquaintance he confided as he added some grey powder to a dish of food, 'You would be horrified, I dare say, if you knew what this is – it is arsenic. We all take some poison more or less. For instance, I am now taking arsenic enough to kill you.'

Mrs Maybrick knew something of her husband's addiction to medicines, and in March of 1889 she mentioned to the family doctor that James sometimes took a white powder which she though might be strychnine. What was the likely result? The doctor replied that her husband ought to take care, because he could die. Then he joked, 'Well, if he should ever die suddenly, call me, and I can say you have had some conversation with me about it.'

Not long after this exchange, Mrs Maybrick for the first time spent an illicit weekend in London with Brierley. Her husband grew suspicious and on 29 March the Maybricks were seen quarrelling openly at the Grand National. There was a furious row at home, too, that evening, in which Maybrick beat his wife and dragged her around the bedroom. The following day, when the doctor treated her black eye, Mrs Maybrick told him that she intended to seek a separation.

Mrs Maybrick did not, in fact, open legal proceedings But the row simmered on through April, and it was at the end of the month that Florence made a soon-to-be-notorious trip to a local chemist, where she bought a dozen arsenic-coated flypapers. Soon afterwards, the papers were seen by servants to be soaking in a washstand in Mrs Maybrick's bedroom.

On 25 April, James Maybrick drew up a new will leaving almost everything in trust for his children – and almost nothing to Florence.

On 28 April, James Maybrick was taken violently sick after eating a lunch that his wife had prepared for him. It was not the first time he had felt unwell – he had long suffered from dyspepsia, and complained of headaches and stiffness of the limbs. But that night he was dazed, vomiting, and practically numb in the legs. He recovered somewhat the next day, but in the week that followed he relapsed repeatedly. During this period Mrs Maybrick visited another local chemist – and bought another two dozen flypapers.

On 7 May, Maybrick collapsed, vomiting so severely that he could keep practically no food down. His tongue was badly furred and he experienced the tormenting and persistent sensation that he had a hair in his throat. The servants had never much liked Florence, and neither had Maybrick's family; nor had the flypaper poisonings of Mrs Flanagan and Mrs Higgins been forgotten in Liverpool. It was Alice Yapp, the children's nurse, who first voiced her suspicions, declaring to a family friend, 'Thank God, Mrs Briggs, you have come, for the mistress is poisoning the master.'

Was she? None of the doctors concerned with the case had suspected poisoning before; but now nurses, family and servants all started watching Mrs Maybrick with keen interest. And one evening, Florence was seen furtively removing a bottle of meat juice from the sick man's bedroom table; equally furtively, she brought it back two minutes later. Had she tampered with the contents? The bottle was quietly removed by a doctor, pending chemical analysis.

On other occasions, curious fragments of conversation were overheard from the sick room. Once, for example, Mrs Maybrick tried to get her husband to take some medicine. Maybrick flatly refused and said, 'Don't give me the wrong medicine again.'

'What are you talking about?' Mrs Maybrick replied. 'You never had the wrong medicine.'

James Maybrick died at 8.40 pm on the evening of Saturday, 11 May. And almost immediately his brothers Edwin and Michael locked Florence up while a search of the house was made. Hidden in a trunk in a linen cupboard was a packet labelled 'Arsenic – Poison for Cats'. Analysis confirmed that the bottle of meat juice, handled by Florence, had contained arsenic. And when arsenic was found in the dead man's stomach, Mrs Maybrick was formally arrested.

The trial opened on Wednesday, 31 July 1889 amid the most intense public interest. The press had got hold of all the key details and had effectively found the prisoner guilty already, so that the black van which conducted her to the Liverpool courthouse was booed and jeered by a vast crowd. Nevertheless, Mrs Maybrick – who bore black crêpe in the dock – replied with a clear 'Not guilty' when charged with murder, and the trial did not go entirely as the papers had anticipated.

The prosecutor's case was straightforward. He described the adulterous meeting with Brierley in London; the subsequent quarrel; the buying of flypapers and the sudden onset of the dead man's illness. There was the bottle of meat juice treated with arsenic, the packet of 'Arsenic – Poison for Cats'; a handkerchief had also been found soaked in arsenic, and arsenic was even found soaked into the pocket of a dressing gown worn by Mrs Maybrick. To cap it all, nurse Yapp had intercepted a letter written by Mrs Maybrick to Brierley, and this was read out at the trial. It had been composed during the early stages of Maybrick's illness, and to the Victorian court it was a thoroughly shocking document. While writing of her husband being 'sick unto death', Florence had seemed chiefly concerned to reassure her lover ('my own darling') that the details of their liaison were safe. Moreover, the doctors at that stage did not suspect that Maybrick's illness might be fatal – how did Florence know that he was 'sick unto death'?

But Mrs Maybrick was powerfully represented by a brilliant defence counsel in Sir Charles Russell, who had an answer for every suspicious circumstance. Take the famous flypapers, for example: Mrs Maybrick had from the moment of her arrest maintained that she bought and soaked these in order to prepare an arsenical face-wash to treat her complexion. Arsenic was in fact widely used in cosmetics at the time, and as Sir Charles pointed out, Mrs Maybrick bought the papers quite openly at shops where she was well known. Would she do so if she had any malign purpose? The papers, were, moreover, left soaking all day for the servants to see.

The cosmetic face-wash explained the stained handkerchief and dressing-gown pocket. But what of the poisoned meat juice? Again, Mrs Maybrick had kept nothing back. She had candidly stated on arrest that throughout that particular evening her husband had been nagging her to give him one of the powders which he habitually took. She at first refused, but he begged her so piteously to put some in his food that in the end she agreed. But she had no idea that the substance concerned was arsenic – it was just one of James's 'powders'. As for the expression 'sick unto death' which had been used apparently prematurely, it was merely a Southern figure of speech meaning gravely – not necessarily fatally – ill.

Ultimately, the strength of the defence case lay in the medical evidence. Only a small quantity of arsenic was found in James Maybrick's stomach at the post mortem; there were traces of strychnine, hyoscine and morphine too. The hypochondriac had badly abused his stomach and had died from an acute inflammation which, the defence alleged, might have been provoked by almost anything. The distinguished Dr Tidy, one of the nation's leading forensic experts, testified for the defence and was quite unshakeable in his refusal to diagnose arsenic poisoning – or poisoning of any kind.

Prosecutor: He died from gastro-enteritis caused by an irritant?

Dr Tidy: Yes.

Prosecutor: It was some strong irritant, probably poison?

Dr Tidy: Some substance which to him acted as an irritant.

Prosecutor: Which was poisonous enough to kill him?

Dr Tidy: Which to him acted as an irritant.

Prosecutor: Can you suggest to us what it was?

Dr Tidy: No, I cannot.

This exchange continued for some time before the prosecutor retired defeated. The climax of the trial came when Mrs Maybrick herself was permitted, by the judge, to make a brief statement. (Under the law of the time, she was not allowed to give evidence and submit to questioning. Although this was changed in 1898 with the introduction of the Criminal Evidence Act.) Halting and tearful, she described how she prepared her arsenical face-wash; how she had mixed the powder into her husband's meat juice; and how, on the day before he died, she had fully confessed her adultery and received 'his entire forgiveness for the fearful wrong I had done him'.

Mrs Maybrick collapsed after speaking, and had to be

revived with smelling salts. By now the court, the press and the public were all firmly on her side and an acquittal seemed almost certain. After all, it had not been conclusively proved that Maybrick died from arsenic at all – let alone that the prisoner had poisoned him. And if he *did* die of arsenic, it might well have been self-administered.

However, throughout the trial the judge, Mr Justice Stephen, had shown a certain lack of grip on the proceedings. He had recently suffered a stroke (and was soon to be admitted to an asylum) and in summing up he repeatedly blundered over the facts in a way detrimental to Mrs Maybrick's cause. To everyone's astonishment the jury found the prisoner guilty of murder, and while she sobbed and protested in the dock, sentence of death was passed upon her.

There was an immediate public outcry. The prosecution's witnesses were hissed and jostled as they left the court; nationwide petitions were raised; questions were asked in Parliament while, at the gaol where Mrs Maybrick was being held, flowers arrived by the cartload. In fact, Mrs Maybrick received several offers of marriage as the day of her execution drew nearer. Then, at the last minute, with her scaffold already built, the Home Secretary bowed to public pressure and commuted the sentence to life imprisonment.

Florence Maybrick served 15 years as a model prisoner before, in 1904, she was released. She went back to the United States, where she lectured for some time on the need for penal reform, always including her declaration, 'I swear to you I am innocent'. Eventually she disappeared from the public eye to live out her life as a recluse dependent chiefly on the charity of friends. She died in South Kent, Connecticut, in 1941 at the age of 76.

Did she do it? All who have studied the case agree that she should never have been convicted on the evidence. 'The element of doubt existed and it should have been resolved in her favour, because that is the law. . . . She was entitled to an acquittal,' wrote thriller-writer Raymond Chandler, a keen student of the case. He was fascinated not only by the mystery but by the coincidence that Mrs Maybrick's maiden name, Florence Chandler, was the same as his mother's. In fact, Chandler at one time planned a history of the affair, and took the trouble to itemize all the points for and against Mrs Maybrick's case.

What did the creator of private eye Philip Marlowe make of it all? 'I am pretty well convinced the dame was guilty,' Chandler wrote to a friend. But that was only one man's verdict – the fact is, nobody knows.

'This huge mass of flesh . . .'

He is the most notorious domestic murderer in the annals of crime. Born in Michigan, Dr Hawley Harvey Crippen came to England in 1900. With him came his wife Cora, a failed opera singer and would-be music-hall artist who used the stage name of Belle Elmore. They were an outwardly respectable couple, though almost comically ill-matched: she was loud, ample-bosomed and domineering; he was small, balding and mild-mannered. Eventually the pair set up home at 39 Hilldrop Crescent, a semi-detached house in north London. And there, early in 1910, he murdered her.

Was there ever any doubt about it? Crippen's name has for so long been reviled that it is hard to imagine the time when his guilt was at all in question. But the case against him did not prove itself; some brilliant police and forensic work was required to prepare the evidence for a conviction. Spilsbury, who became an eminent forensic expert, contributed important evidence to this, his first famous case.

The last that any outsider saw of Belle Elmore was at a

dinner party held by the Crippens on 31 January 1910. Afterwards, the little doctor informed his wife's friends that Belle had gone to America and died of a sudden illness there. He issued some suitably black-edged letters to that effect, and also moved his secretary and mistress, Ethel Le Neve, into Hilldrop Crescent, decking her out in Belle's jewellery and furs.

When the police asked questions about Belle's disappearance, Crippen changed his story and confided to them that his wife had really run away with another man. Since a search of the house revealed nothing, the case might have rested there. But the police inquiries seem to have broken Crippen's nerve, for he fled to Antwerp with Ethel Le Neve and there, using assumed names, the couple boarded the SS *Montrose* for Quebec. Crippen posed as a 'Mr John Robinson', while Ethel – her hair cropped and wearing boy's clothing – was 'Master Robinson', his son.

When Crippen fled the country, the police searched Hilldrop Crescent again, and this time Chief Inspector Walter Dew discovered human remains buried under the cellar floor. Warrants were quickly issued for the fugitives' arrest, and police bills were posted at the ports. The SS *Montrose* was only two hours out of Antwerp before the captain began to suspect the 'Robinsons', father and son; they were squeezing one another's hand in a manner 'unnatural for two males'.

Later identifying the couple as Crippen and Le Neve, the captain radioed reports back to London. It was the first time that wireless telegraphy was used in a murder hunt, and it lent a sensational dimension to what was already a case packed with drama. Even as Inspector Dew hastened after the *Montrose* in a faster vessel, the captain's reports about the fugitives were being printed in the *Daily Mail* for the benefit of an enthralled public. Readers learned, for example, that Le Neve's disguise was flawed, her trousers being 'very tight about the hips, and are split a bit down the back and secured with large safety pins'. They discovered too that the unsuspecting Crippen 'is now reading *The Four Just Men*, which is all about murder in London and £1,000 reward'.

Overtaken by Inspector Dew, Crippen was arrested on board the *Montrose* on 31 July 1910. As he was taken into custody, he said, 'I am not sorry; the anxiety has been too much.' In his pocket was found what appeared to be a suicide note addressed to his mistress:

'I cannot stand the horrors I go through every night any longer and as I see nothing bright ahead and money has come to an end I have made up my mind to jump overboard tonight. I know I have spoilt your life but I hope someday you can learn to forgive me. With last words of love. Your H.'

It has often been said that Crippen's trial, which opened on 18 October 1910, at the Old Bailey, was a mere formality. But Crippen pleaded not guilty, and throughout the proceedings remained calm, polite and quietly firm in protesting his innocence.

Briefly, his defence was that his wife had always been 'rather hasty in her temper', but that from around 1904 things got worse. Belle was always finding fault and picking quarrels, and this, he discovered, was because she had struck up a liaison with an American music-hall artist named Bruce Miller. Depressed at first, Crippen had later pursued an affair with his secretary, Ethel Le Neve, and had found in her all the love and companionship he needed. What motive could he have for suddenly murdering his wife?

Crippen said that after the dinner party on 31 January, Belle had worked herself up into one of her rages, informed him that she was leaving him the next day, and told him to 'cover up the scandal in the best way you can'. And that is precisely what he did. He went to work the following morning and never saw Belle again, so to 'cover up the scandal' he invented the story about her going to America and dying there of sudden pneumonia. He then moved his mistress in with him quite openly. Only when the police called did it occur to him that Belle's disappearance might be construed in a sinister way. And since he had lied about her death he foolishly decided to flee. The rest just followed naturally: expecting to be arrested on arrival in Canada, he had faked the suicide note to enable him to jump ship and disappear for a while until everything had blown over.

The story was not entirely implausible. But it ignored the gruesome remains found in the cellar at Hilldrop Crescent. Whose were they if not Belle Elmore's? And who could have buried them there if not Crippen himself?

The result of the trial really would have been a foregone conclusion had the remains comprised the recognizable corpse of Crippen's wife. But they did not. What Inspector Dew discovered under the cellar at Hilldrop Crescent was a makeshift grave where, buried in lime, was a mass of boneless flesh:

'The remains were what might be called close packed, heavily packed, with clay above them to a depth of 5 inches.'

'They were rammed in?' asked the prosecuting counsel.

'Yes, rammed in,' replied the inspector.

'Mixed up and folded over in parts, jumbled up all together?'

'All together; this huge mass of flesh was all together.'

The head, skeleton and limbs of Mrs Crippen were never found. A human heart, liver, lungs and kidneys were all present – but not the genitals, so that it was impossible to determine the sex of the victim. Crippen's counsel produced an expert to testify that flesh and organs can survive in an excellent state of preservation when buried in clay and quicklime. In short, the thrust of the defence was that the remains, 'whosesoever they were and whoever had buried them', could have been there for years; been buried therefore the Crippens moved into the house in 1905.

And that was where the Crippen's case collapsed. The prosecution showed that on 17 January Crippen bought from a chemist five grains of the potentially lethal drug hyoscine; chemical analysis demonstrated that a fatal dose of hyoscine was present in the remains. A piece of abdominal scar tissue was recovered and identified as the mark of an operation sustained by Mrs Crippen some years before. Also found was a woman's hair curler with a lock of dyed blonde hair in it – and Mrs Crippen dyed her hair blonde.

But the clinching detail was a piece of a man's pyjama jacket in which remains had been wrapped; this, it was shown, had been bought by Crippen from Jones Brothers of Holloway as recently as January 1909.

Crippen's case sank under the weight of that 'huge mass of flesh' and what could be deduced from it. And it provided a macabre counterpoint to the romantic comedy of his flight in disguise with Le Neve. You had to picture the quiet, rather kindly little man poisoning his wife, then patiently dissecting the corpse; disposing of such durable items as head, hands and feet; burying the flesh; and tidying up before inviting his mistress, the shy typist Ethel Le Neve, to come and live on those same premises.

In a separate trial, Ethel Le Neve was acquitted of being an accessory. But Dr Hawley Harvey Crippen was found guilty of murder, and on 23 November 1910 was hanged at Pentonville.

'The last moment belongs to us . . .'

On 15 April 1920, a paymaster and guard were killed during a payroll hold-up outside a shoe factory near Boston, Massachussetts. The bandits escaped, but three weeks later a pair of Italian immigrants were arrested on firearms charges and subsequently charged with the payroll murders. They were Nicola Sacco, a shoemaker, and Bartolomeo Vanzetti, a fish peddler – and their names were to echo through the decades to the shame of American justice.

The events occurred during one of America's periodic 'Red scares'. Sacco and Vanzetti held anarchist views, and their trial in May 1921 proved a grotesque travesty. The mere facts that the accused were immigrants and anarchists were practically enough to convict them, and their fates were sealed when the prosecution tried to prove by dubious means that Sacco's .32 Colt was the murder weapon. The prejudicial atmosphere of the court was barely credibly: the accused were freely referred to as 'wops', 'dagos', and 'sons of bitches', and Judge Webster Thayer, in summing up, disclosed an open detestation of foreigners ('Did you see what I did to those anarchistic bastards?' he asked after the proceedings).

Sacco and Vanzetti were found guilty of first degree murder, but the courtroom charade had not passed unnoticed among American liberals. The immigrants' case became a *cause célèbre*, and through the next six years a campaign for retrial gathered ground on both sides of the Atlantic. Worldwide protests and mass fund-raising meetings contributed to various appeals, and the whole affair was complicated in 1925 when a convicted gangster, Celestino Madeiros, confessed to the payroll robbery and stated that Sacco and Vanzetti played no part in it. Since Madeiros himself was awaiting execution, however, his testimony was of limited value.

In July 1927, a three-man committee was appointed to re-examine the evidence. Authoritative new testimony for the prosecution came from Major Calvin Goddard, a pioneer of forensic ballistics. Using the recent invention of the comparison microscope, he showed conclusively that the fatal bullets *had* allegedly been fired by Sacco's gun (but had the bullets been planted on him? So much was at stake by now in the case that both defence and prosecution were fighting dirty).

On 3 August the state Governor refused a retrial. Sacco and Vanzetti must die, and following the final denial of clemency, riot squads were called out in several US cities, while bombs went off in New York and Philadelphia and there were strikes and riots in Europe and South America. It was all to no avail. Sacco and Vanzetti went to the electric chair in Boston's Charlestown Prison on 23 August 1927. Both men maintained their innocence to the end, and their deaths inspired a wealth of poems, novels and plays. If historians still raise some question marks over their innocence, it is certain that they should never have been convicted on the evidence: in 1977, a special proclamation by the Governor of Massachussetts officially cleared their names.

The most moving tribute to their memory, though, was penned by Vanzetti himself. In a statement written before his death he willingly accepted his martyrdom. He wrote of his pride that the pair of them – a shoemaker and a poor fish peddler – should have contributed by chance to such an upheaval in public conscience: 'Never in our full life could we hope to do such work for tolerance, for justice, for man's understanding of men as now we do by accident. . . . The last moment belongs to us – that agony is our triumph.'

Murder for Kicks

Richard Loeb and Nathan Leopold were members of wealthy Chicago families: 18-year-old Loeb was the son of the Vice President of Sears, Roebuck and Company, giants in the field of mail-order merchandise, while Leopold, 19, came from a similarly prosperous background. Both were intelligent; neither needed the money. Yet on 21 May 1924 they committed a stupid and brutal murder. The ostensible motive was $10,000 ransom – the truth was they did it for kicks.

The two youths enjoyed a weird relationship. Both were admirers of Nietzche's philosophy, which taught that some people are supermen, not to be shackled by conventional morality. The suave Richard Loeb considered himself one of this elect, and the shorter, weak-sighted Nathan Leopold was happy to describe himself as his friend's slave.

It was Loeb who conceived the idea of the murder: 'a perfect crime' without motive, committed for the thrill of breaking the ultimate taboo. The ransom arrangements would all be invented to throw the authorities off the scent.

Fourteen-year-old Bobby Franks, son of a millionaire Chicago businessman, became their victim. The killers invited him into a car, which Leopold drove while Loeb clubbed the boy to death. The naked body was subsequently hidden in a culvert on some waste ground near a railway line, and acid was poured over the face to make it unidentifiable.

Afterwards, the killers telephoned the boy's mother, posing as kidnappers, and sent a typewritten ransom note signed 'GEORGE JOHNSON', giving instructions on how the money should be paid.

It turned out to be a far from perfect crime. The body was quickly discovered and identified without trouble, despite the disfiguring acid. Spectacles found near the scene were traced through oculists' records to Leopold, who offered a very weak story for their presence there. Then he was asked about his typewriter. The ransom note had been tapped out on an Underwood portable, and Leopold denied possessing such a machine. But it was soon discovered that he had loaned his typewriter to some fellow students. When located, it was identified as the machine which had typed the ransom note.

Meanwhile Loeb had made himself conspicuous during routine inquiries among wealthy Chicago families, by being over-talkative and 'helpful' about the murder inquiry. He was known to be a close friend of Leopold, and under persistent questioning, the superman broke down and fully confessed.

What more callous murder could possibly be committed? The case outraged public opinion in the United States, and there were loud calls for the death penalty to be applied. Indeed, it was executed that the two youths would be expected, until Clarence Darrow took on the case for the defence. A humanitarian and social reformer, the great Clarence Seward Darrow was passionately opposed to capital punishment. He was also a brilliant lawyer – so brilliant that during his entire career only one out of the 50-odd people he defended on charges of first degree murder was ever executed.

Darrow was basically a pessimist. 'We all know life is futile,' he once wrote. 'A man who considers that his life is of very wonderful importance is awfully close to a padded cell.' But out of that pessimism he drew strength: life might be futile, but people could through hope and reason invent a kind of sense for it.

The trial took place in July 1924. Darrow asked for mitigation on grounds of reduced responsibility and mental illness. How, he asked, could an act so bad *not* be mad? By what standards could the crime of Leopold and

Loeb be described as the work of sane young men?

It is a paradox that has often been raised since in the cases of infamous murderers. But it carried no great legal weight; more to their advantage was the sheer youth of Darrow's clients. Teenage violence and juvenile delinquency were not yet familiar concepts, capable of hardening adult attitudes. Leopold and Loeb seemed so very young, with so much of their lives before them. In an impassioned speech which spanned two days, Darrow quoted freely from literature on the horror of youth meeting death on the scaffold. He quoted from Omar Khayyám and from A. E. Housman (or rather, in Housman's case he *mis*quoted, as the poet himself testily complained). And at the end of the sensational murder trial, his pleas saved two young men. The judge passed sentences of life imprisonment for murder, with 99 years on the kidnapping charge.

Richard Loeb was killed in 1936, during a prison brawl. Nathan Leopold served 33 years of his sentence before, amid some controversy, he was paroled in 1958. He married and lived in Puerto Rico, dying in 1971, having written a book about his experiences.

Death of a Playboy Prince

The public in the 1920s was fascinated by the mysterious East: it was the decade when Valentino was *The Sheik* and Fairbanks was *The Thief of Baghdad*; when Tutankhamun's tomb was opened and when, throughout the Western world, crop-haired jazz girls daubed their eyelids with Egyptian kohl. And in 1923 there occurred a sensational murder trial to match the taste of the period. In a sumptuous suite at the Savoy Hotel, Madame Marie-Marguérite Fahmy shot dead her Egyptian playboy husband, Prince Ali Kamel Fahmy Bey. He had treated her, it seemed, like an Oriental beast. To the case's exotic mixture of sex, luxury and blood were added the talents of Sir Edward Marshall Hall, the most flamboyant defence counsel of the age. Small wonder that the Savoy Shooting stole the front-page headlines.

Madame Fahmy, the accused, was a glamorous Parisian brunette aged 32 at the time of the trial. The Prince, ten years younger, was a wealthy Egyptian and attaché at the French Legation in Cairo. The couple had met in Paris during May of 1922, at which time she was a divorcee. And she progressed quickly from becoming the Prince's mistress to becoming his wife; the pair were married in December of that year. Madame Fahmy accepted the Muslim faith for the purpose of the wedding, but insisted on her right to wear Western clothes. She also stipulated that she retain the right of divorce, but this was not acknowledged by her husband. Prince Fahmy considered his wife bound to him under Muslim law: he possessed the sole right of divorce (as well as the right to take three more wives should he wish to do so).

The marriage was disastrous. Whatever infatuation was present at the outset, the couple quarrelled wherever they lived as man and wife: in Paris, Cairo and in London, to which they came in July of 1923. Often Prince Fahmy beat his wife, once so severely that her jaw was dislocated. On another occasion he kept her locked up for three days on his yacht; on yet another he swore an oath on the Koran that one day he would kill her. This was done with such solemnity that the frightened woman wrote formally to her lawyer accusing her husband if she should ever disappear: 'Yesterday, January 21, 1923, at three o'clock in the afternoon, he took his Bible or Koran – I do not know how it is called – kissed it, put his hand on it, and swore to avenge himself upon me tomorrow, in eight days, a month, three months, but I must disappear in his hands. This oath was taken without any reason, neither jealousy, nor a scene on my part.' As for the Prince, he really does seem to have regarded his wife as a creature to be mastered by force. 'Just now I am engaged in training her,' he once wrote. 'With women one must be severe – no bad habits.'

They had been at the Savoy for barely a week when the fatal row broke out. On the evening of 9 July, the couple quarrelled violently in the hotel restaurant, and Madame Fahmy, it was to be said at the trial, shouted in French, 'You shut up. I will smash this bottle over your head.' Asked by the band leader if she wanted anything special played, she answered, 'I don't want any music – my husband has threatened to kill me tonight.' Upstairs, at about 1.30 am, the quarrel was still going on. A porter saw Prince Fahmy burst from his room in his pyjamas, a flushed mark on his cheek. 'Look at my face!' he fumed. 'Look what she has done!' Then Madame Fahmy came out too, still in her white, beaded evening dress, and shouted furiously in French.

The porter ushered them back into their suite, and walked on down the corridor. Moments later, three shots detonated. Rushing back to the suite, the porter saw Madame Fahmy toss down a .32 Browning automatic. The Prince lay bleeding from headwounds, and died not long after in hospital.

Charged with murder, Madame Fahmy was brought to trial at the Old Bailey in September 1923. Her cause inevitably stirred up a lot of public sympathy, but sympathy alone does not win court cases. Madame Fahmy had manifestly shot her husband dead at point-blank range in the heat of a domestic quarrel. And it would need all the talents of her defence counsel, Marshall Hall, to get her off the hook.

He gave the case everything he had got. Handsome, and flamboyant in style, the advocate was famed for theatrical effects which have disappeared from the modern lawyer's repertoire. But they still swayed juries in the 1920s, and Marshall Hall was their leading exponent.

Of course, he dwelled on Prince Fahmy's cruelty, cataloguing the beatings and humiliations endured by his wife. But there was more to be said against the dead man. Marshall Hall suggested that he was a homosexual who enjoyed a compromising relationship with his male secretary. Madame Fahmy, it was alleged, had been made to submit to a nameless but nauseating sexual indignity (presumably anal intercourse), and suffered painful illness in consequence. In fact, that illness was what provoked the quarrel on the fateful night. She had asked for money to pay for an operation in Paris, and he told her that she could only have it if she agreed to indulge his whim. 'I will if you do something for me,' he had said, before starting to tear off her dress.

When Madame Fahmy refused, he half strangled her. 'He seized me suddenly and brutally by the throat with his left hand,' she testified in French. (All of her statements were made in her native tongue and delivered to the court through an interpreter.) 'His thumb was on my windpipe and his fingers were pressing on my neck. I pushed him away but he crouched to spring on me, and said "I will kill you!"'

'I lifted my arm in front of me and without looking pulled the trigger. The next moment I saw him on the ground before me. I do not know how many times the revolver went off.' She had thought that the gun was empty of cartridges. 'I thought the sight of the pistol might frighten him,' she sobbed under cross-examination.

Marshall Hall's final speech to the jury was regarded as the most dramatic of his brilliant career. Having cast the Prince as an Oriental monster of depravity, he impersonated him, stalking across the court in emulation of his advance on his wife. Then, pistol in hand, the advocate took the part of his client: 'As he crouched for the last time, crouched like an animal, retired for the last time to get a bound forward – she turned the pistol and put it to his face.'

Suddenly, Marshall Hall levelled the gun at the foreman of the jury. He paused for a moment. 'And to her horror the thing went off!'

All eyes were fixed on the tableau. The court was in total silence. And then Marshall Hunt released the gun, which clattered to the floor – exactly as Madame Fahmy had dropped it.

It was a spellbinding moment, and the advocate had further touches of courtroom magic in store. Concluding his address, he referred to the Oriental darkness into which the prisoner had been plunged by her marriage. 'I ask you to open the gate and let this Western woman go back into the light of God's great Western sun,' he ended, extending a prophetic arm high up on the Old Bailey skylight. A shaft of sun came through – right on cue.

In no time at all, the jury had found Madame Fahmy not guilty of murder; not guilty of manslaughter either. Such volcanic cheers erupted with the verdict that the judge ordered the public benches to be cleared and it was in an emptied court that Madame Fahmy sobbed her gratitude as she was released from custody, a free woman.

The whole case had become a triumph for 'Western light' over 'Oriental darkness' in an almost offensive manner. In fact, Marshall Hall received a formal complaint from the leader of the Egyptian Bar, accusing him of castigating all Egypt and indeed the entire East in order to save his client. The truth is that the fictional ideal of *The Sheik* had met a horribly flawed counterpart in Prince Fahmy. Marshall Hall had merely toyed with the conventions of his day, reversing the romantic image to make the dead playboy an archetype of evil.

Judgement on the Ripper

A notice, handwritten by Bradford lorry-driver Peter Sutcliffe, was displayed in the cab of his vehicle. It read:

IN THIS TRUCK IS A MAN WHOSE LATENT GENIUS
IF UNLEASHED WOULD ROCK THE NATION,
WHOSE DYNAMIC ENERGY WOULD
OVERPOWER THOSE AROUND HIM.
BETTER LET HIM SLEEP?

The humour sours when you remember that Sutcliffe turned out to be the Yorkshire Ripper – a man who killed and horribly mutilated 13 women in his five-year reign of terror.

The murders began in October 1975 with the killing of Wilma McCann, a 28-year-old prostitute whose corpse, battered by hammer-blows to the skull and pierced by screwdriver stab-wounds, was discovered on a Leeds playing field. The Ripper's next three victims had all plied the same trade in the red light districts of Leeds and Bradford. But the pattern of murder changed in June 1977 when a perfectly respectable 16-year-old girl fell victim to the killer's brutal impulse. Other non-prostitutes were to succumb later; the case brought stark terror to the women of West Yorkshire, and indeed all over Britain.

It also prompted the biggest murder hunt of the century. But in January 1981, when the Ripper was finally caught, it happened almost by chance. The bearded Sutcliffe was discovered by Sheffield police in his Rover V8 with a coloured prostitute named Ava Reivers. The car carried false number plates, and contained the grim tools of the Ripper's trade: a hammer, garotte and sharpened Philips type screwdriver. Ava Reivers could count herself the luckiest woman in Britain that night – she would have been the next victim.

Back at the police station, the police knew that they had found the Ripper at last. He turned out to be a married man, born in 1946 at Bingley near Bradford and now living in a respectable middle-class district of that city. In his time he had held down a variety of jobs – including that of gravedigger at Bingley Cemetery. Ironically, he had been interviewed routinely no fewer than nine times before in the police trawl for the mystery killer.

What had motivated him? In August 1974, Sutcliffe had married a demure schoolteacher named Sonia Szurma; the murders started little more than a year later and many people speculated that, in killing his victims, Sutcliffe was really trying to destroy his wife.

Though the couple seemed loving and were well liked, there were known to be rows. It was Sonia who did the shouting; the slightly built Sutcliffe would meekly ask only that she keep her voice down so as not to disturb the neighbours. Sonia had, moreover, suffered a period of mental illness in which she believed, among other things, that she was the Second Coming of Christ. In short, there were tensions in the household – tensions which hardly explain the Ripper's acts, but help to fill in their background.

The three-week trial took place at the Old Bailey in May 1981. Fascination with the case was international, and illegally taken photographs of Sutcliffe in the dock were published in foreign magazines. The trial also raised important questions about the way in which the Ripper case had been handled by police: the £4 million manhunt had been badly misled by a hoax tape sent by a man with a Geordie accent who had posed as the Ripper. But the overriding issue, on which Sutcliffe's fate depended, was whether he was mad or not.

Peter William Sutcliffe was charged with the murder of 13 women and attempts to kill another seven. He denied the murder charges – but admitted manslaughter on the grounds of diminished responsibility.

Under the 1957 Homicide Act, a prisoner may plead for a reduced charge of manslaughter on the grounds that he or she suffered some 'abnormality of mind' which impaired his or her mental responsibility. In the Ripper case, the Attorney General was prepared to accept such a plea. But the judge was unhappy that the murder charges should be so easily disposed of; he insisted that the case go before a jury. And so it was left to twelve ordinary people – six men, six women – to judge the killer's state of mind.

From a certain point of view, anyone who did what Sutcliffe did must be mad. But the law cannot accept such a proposition, for it would result in a legal absurdity. Every crime is an abnormal act, so anyone who committed one might claim 'abnormality of mind' in expectation of lenient treatment. Sutcliffe's defence was more specific: he alleged that he had heard voices ordering him to kill prostitutes; his had been a 'divine mission'. In prison, he had been examined by three psychiatrists who unanimously declared him to be a paranoid schizophrenic.

Impassive in the dock, Sutcliffe gave no clue as to his mental condition. But against the experts' testimony was the possibility that the prisoner had simply faked his symptoms. For example, he had not mentioned hearing voices until several interviews after his capture. In custody he was alleged to have remarked that if found to be 'loony' he would serve only 10 years instead of 30. From Sonia's bout of mental disturbance he could have recalled convincing symptoms such as tactile hallucinations (he claimed that he had experienced a hand tightening around his heart).

But perhaps the most damning flaw in his story was the simple fact that many of his victims were not prostitutes at all. There was teenage Jayne Macdonald, Josephine

Whitaker, clerk in a building society, Barbara Leach and Jacqueline Hill, students, Margo Walls, a 47-year-old civil servant.

On 22 May 1981, the jury retired, deliberating for 5 hours and 55 minutes. On return, they found Peter William Sutcliffe guilty of murder. He was sentenced to life imprisonment, the judge recommending that a minimum of 30 years be served. In the streets outside the Old Bailey, when news of the verdict arrived, a large crowd gave three cheers for the jury. It was reported that even in the psychiatric community, relief was immense that the experts' testimony had been rejected.

Mystery, though, still surrounds the Ripper's mind. In prison at Parkhurst he continued to claim hearing voices, and in March 1984 the Home Secretary ordered his removal to Broadmoor. Peter Sutcliffe, he disclosed, was in a condition of grave mental illness, doctors both at Parkhurst and Broadmoor diagnosing paranoid schizophrenia. His state of mind had seriously deteriorated since admission to prison, and he could now be a threat to prison staff and others.

Was he mad all along? Or did he go mad faking madness?

Helen Smith

As a former detective with the Leeds police force in Yorkshire, Ron Smith was no stranger to seeing the bodies of victims of violent death. But he had to steel his courage to near breaking point on the night of Saturday 26 May 1979, when he was led into the mortuary of the Baksh Hospital in Jeddah, Saudi Arabia. The body he had come to view was not that of some faceless stranger – it was the body of his own daughter, Helen.

Ron Smith had been living with the grief of his

daughter's death since he had received a phonecall a week earlier telling him that 23-year-old Helen had died tragically in an accident in Jeddah, falling from a balcony of a block of flats where she had gone to a party.

Choking back his emotions, the ex-policeman, now a successful businessman, had flown to the Middle East, where Helen had been working as a nurse since the Baksh Hospital had opened 15 months earlier. He simply wanted to bring her body home for burial.

Sympathetic Foreign Office officials who met him in the Saudi capital could offer him little comfort. In an attempt to explain the circumstances surrounding Helen's death, they escorted him to the local prison to meet Richard Arnot, the English senior surgeon at Baksh Hospital.

Arnot was awaiting trial for breaching the strict Saudi Muslim law banning alcohol. He had hosted the drinks party at which Helen had died.

Arnot could only outline briefly that Helen had died as a result of a fall from the balcony of his sixth-floor flat in the hospital complex. There had been a lot of heavy, illegal drinking at the party and another party guest, a 31-year-old Dutchman, Johannes Otten, had also been killed in a 70-foot tumble from the same balcony. Arnot claimed he had slept through the fatal drama, and knew none of the details.

The distressed father brushed aside diplomatic objections and demanded to see the body of his dead daughter. When mortuary attendant Subi Bakir drew back the shroud over Helen's body, Ron Smith began to have doubts about the authorities' simple explanation for her death. Helen's body showed some signs of internal bleeding but, apart from this, there was no evidence of the massive injuries one would normally expect to see in someone who had crashed from a great height on to the solid concrete forecourt outside the block of flats.

Ron Smith was soon convinced that his daughter's

death was not a simple accident, but a bizarre murder mystery. He set out on a dogged crusade of investigation and inquiry which was still unresolved a decade later. In fact, the mystery of his daughter's death may *never* be explained.

The official Saudi police report accepted Helen Smith's death as a tragic accident. But when Ron Smith gave them the results of his own detective work – five days spent interviewing hospital staff who knew the background to the events leading up to Doctor Arnot's wild drinks party – they began to change their minds.

On 2 June, Saudi government pathologist Dr Ali Kheir carried out a detailed post mortem examination on the body. He found no evidence of fractures of the neck, shoulder blades or spine. As Ron Smith prepared to fly home to England, he was assured that police were now treating his daughter's death as a murder enquiry.

A year later, when he had only received evasive answers from the Saudi Government and British Foreign Office diplomats about the progress of the murder investigation, Ron Smith was informed that heavy punishments for the hosts of the party and some of their guests had been ordered by the Serious Crimes Court: three German guests at the party suffered no further penalties; two other Germans were sentenced to 30 lashes each; Richard Arnot was sentenced to a year in prison and 80 lashes for consuming alcohol and allowing his wife Penny to commit adultery with a party guest, New Zealand-born deep sea diver Tim Hayter. Mrs Arnot and Hayter were also sentenced to 80 lashes, to be administered in front of a crowd. But there were no charges against anyone in relation to Helen Smith's death.

After five months in prison, the Arnots and their party friends were all released on bail.

In June 1980, Ron Smith decided his only hope of unravelling the mystery of the fatal drinks party lay in uncovering the facts before a British court. He flew to Jeddah, collected his daughter's body and returned to Leeds. There he petitioned acting coroner Mr Miles Coverdale for an inquest.

Coroners can, if they wish, conduct inquests into the death of any British subject anywhere in the world, but Mr Coverdale ruled that the death had taken place outside his jurisdiction and would, therefore, not conduct an inquest. He did, however, agree to carry out his legal obligation to commission an official autopsy, which was carried out by Home Office pathologist Dr Michael Green, at Leeds University. The coroner later announced that the autopsy report confirmed that Helen had suffered injuries consistent with a fall from a height, and an inquest would not be necessary.

But Ron Smith claimed the autopsy report was full of inaccuracies. He found, for instance, references to 'bruises to the face that were consistent with slaps and punches'. He saw this as proof that Helen had been severely beaten, and possibly even murdered, before her body was thrown over the balcony, or placed there by her murderer to make it look as if she and the Dutch guest, Johannes Otten, had both fallen to their deaths.

A month after his report, Dr Green, the pathologist, admitted in a newspaper interview: 'If I was to say Helen Smith's death was an accident, I would be a liar. My conscience would not allow me to say so.'

The interview led to a storm of publicity about the mystery death, and public interest was suddenly aroused. Ron Smith, who had already travelled to Holland to consult the family of Johannes Otten, then hired one of Europe's most respected pathologists to carry out another post mortem.

In December 1980, Danish Professor Jorgen Dalgaard conducted his own autopsy, with Dr Green also present. Professor Dalgaard's report, submitted three months later, uncovered an injury unnoticed until then: a wound covering the whole of the left side of the scalp. He concluded that the wound could have caused bleeding inside the brain leading to Helen falling unconscious or possibly even dying before she sustained any of the other injuries.

It wasn't until March 1982, after a long and bitter legal battle, that two High Court judges ruled that an inquest should be held into Helen's death. The inquest finally opened before a jury in Leeds in November 1982.

It was to be a costly hearing, with witnesses flown in from around the world. Dr Richard Arnot, now divorced, had to travel from Australia. His ex-wife, the party hostess Penelope Arnot, announced her marriage to an American journalist and was no longer subject to a subpoena from a British court. And Tim Hayter – another vital witness – did not attend the inquest either.

The evidence of the witnesses at the inquest was a tale of drunkenness and confusion. The party had been organized as a farewell gesture for New Zealander Hayter, who had become a friend of the Arnots' when he had offered to teach the doctor and his wife scuba diving.

At the party there had been five German salvage experts working on a Saudi contract. One German witness said that their hosts, the Arnots, had provided liberal supplies of whisky for the party and had invited Helen because she worked at the hospital with Dr Arnot and often acted as a babysitter for their children. Salvage worker Martin Fleischer testified that they had all helped themselves to large quantities of drink, risking harsh penalties under Saudi law, which strictly prohibits alcohol even for foreign residents and guest workers.

Some time after the party was already under way, Helen arrived and chatted and mingled with the guests. Later still, Doctor Arnot turned up, although his wife had already been acting as a general hostess.

Dr Arnot went to bed around 2 a.m. leaving his guests

to continue the party. Fleischer added that he and his German friends had drifted away shortly afterwards and returned to their digs on board a floating accommodation barge in Jeddah Harbour. When he and his workmates left, Helen and Johannes, Tim Hayter and Mrs Arnot, and a French guest, Jacques Texier, a marine biologist, were still drinking and enjoying the party.

Fleischer had only been in bed for a couple of hours when he was shaken awake by a terrified and trembling Tim Hayter, who told him that there had been a tragedy at the party. Hayter claimed that Helen and Johannes had fallen to their deaths from the balcony while having sex.

Dr Arnot told the court that he had only spent three hours at the party before leaving for a tour of the hospital to check on patients who had undergone surgery earlier that day. When he returned, around 2 a.m., tired and weary, he had gone to bed. He had slept soundly until his wife woke him around 5.30 a.m. to tell him, 'something terrible has happened. Helen and Johannes have fallen from the balcony.'

He had gone down to the forecourt and saw Helen's body crumpled at the foot of the building. But he didn't see any signs of violence on her body. Johannes Otten's body was a few feet away. He was not lying on the forecourt, but was slumped across a set of low pointed railings, his legs gruesomely impaled by the sharp spikes. His trousers were missing and he was wearing only a pair of underpants.

In the street, Arnot found Otten's passport and some private papers. Otten's trousers were never found. There was no sign of them inside the Arnots' flat, and the doctor said he presumed that some passing heartless thief had stolen the trousers from the corpse and thrown away the passport.

Dr Arnot admitted that his next concern, as a matter of urgency, was to get back inside his flat and try to hide all evidence of illicit alcohol.

Frenchman Jacques Texier was able to add more detail. He said he had seen Helen and Otten out on the balcony when he had gone into the kitchen to make himself a sandwich. When it was pointed out to him that the kitchen window looked out on to a different balcony, he changed his evidence, saying he had seen them from another window.

At about 3 a.m. he had asked Mrs Arnot if he could stay the night at the flat, because he did not want to wake up the official at the French Embassy who had offered him a bed for the night. Penelope Arnot agreed, and after the German guests had left Texier stretched out on a sofa. He did not notice where Helen Smith and Johannes Otten had gone, but he was wakened from his sleep around 5 a.m. by the unmistakeable sound of Mrs Arnot and Tim Hayter making passionate love in the room beside him. Later, all three of them had gone into the kitchen to make coffee. When they strolled unsuspectingly out on to the balcony, they were startled to see the two bodies beneath them.

The inquest also heard from witness Dr Hag Abdel Rachman, a gynaecologist who lived in the same block of flats. He had been wakened by the building's night porter and told there were two bodies outside the block. Dr Rachman said: 'I went to investigate and saw the man hanging upside down on an iron bar. The girl was on the ground, wearing a blue dress and no underwear, there was no blood or indications of violence.'

Dr Rachman gave one vital piece of evidence which left all the other witnesses puzzled. He testified he had knocked on Doctor Arnot's door after the discovery, and the surgeon opened it quickly, saying: 'If you mean that event down the building, I know about that, leave it to me and I will deal with it.' There was a lot of noise coming from the flat and, behind Dr Arnot, the gynaecologist saw a mystery man – a white, short man with a beard – who was never identified by any of the party guests.

The inquest jury retired for eight hours to consider the evidence. After their deliberations they still could not say that Helen's death was an accident, nor could they decide if she had been murdered. Eventually, they returned an open verdict.

Ron Smith remained convinced that all the medical evidence pointed to his daughter having been beaten unconscious, possibly resisting rape, and being placed under the balcony to make it look as if she had fallen to her death. There was evidence that her sternum, or chest bone, had been fractured, perhaps by violent chest massage in an attempt to revive her. Johannes Otten may have been thrown to his death on the railings to silence him.

Helen smith took her camera to the party. She carried her camera everywhere and was constantly taking photographs. Yet, when the Saudi police recovered it from the death flat, they told Ron Smith there was no film in it. Helen, they said, had taken her camera to the party but hadn't bothered to load it. Another camera in the flat that fateful night belonged to Martin Fleischer; but when he developed the film he found that all the frames were double-exposed.

No evidence remains of the mystery guest at the party, the white, short, bearded man.

A decade after her death, Helen Smith's body was still in the mortuary in Leeds. Her father's struggle to find out how his daughter died continues undiminished and relentless.

After the inquest, which still proclaimed his Helen's death a mystery, Ron Smith said: 'Honesty and justice will prevail. Everything will be resolved in God's good time.'

Death and the Diet Doctor

His book was a bestseller. When the case came to court it was found that eight out of the twelve women vetted for the jury had followed the Scarsdale Diet. A feeble joke went the rounds when the murder suspect was named: it was said that Mrs Harris had killed Dr Tarnower because she failed to lose weight as promised. And at the autopsy, a fascinating statistic was revealed. Dr Tarnower, 69, 'a moderately well-developed and well-nourished white male,' measured 70 inches tall and weighed 175 lbs. By his own diet plan, the millionaire physician was 15 lbs over-weight!

Dr Herman Tarnower ('Hi' to his friends) lived in a fashionable section of New York's Westchester suburb. He helped to found a flourishing clinic at Scarsdale, and there used to recommend a diet programme for his overweight patients. Originally, the plan was no more than two pages long, but in 1979 the doctor published a greatly expanded version under the title of *The Complete Scarsdale Medical Diet*. 'Lose 20 lbs in 14 days', was the book's boast. Besides the initial Basic Plan there were Gourmet, International, Vegetarian and Money-saving variations. Millions followed the diet, and the doctor became world-famous.

Physically fit and active for his age, Tarnower had a taste for the good life. He enjoyed golf, fishing, travel to exotic places – and good eating, too, at the intimate dinner parties he gave at his Westchester home. A bachelor of long standing, Dr Tarnower also enjoyed women.

He had many casual affairs. But for some 14 years, the doctor had pursued a steady liaison with Mrs Jean Harris, headmistress of the highly respectable Madeira Girls' School in Virginia. It was a very 'adult relationship'. Mrs Harris was a divorcee whose own husband had died. She expressed no special jealousy about his philanderings.

Nor did she ask for marriage; yet she was hostess at his dinners, the couple shared foreign holidays, and Mrs Harris helped to edit the famous book.

This civilized arrangement was jeopardized, however, when Lynne Tryforos entered the scene. She was the doctor's nurse-secretary at the clinic, an attractive young woman with whom Tarnower began to spend more and more time. In the year before the fatal event, for example, Dr Tarnower took two winter holidays: the first at Palm Beach with the headmistress; the second in Jamaica with the nurse.

In March 1980, the time of the shooting, Mrs Harris was 56 and Lynne Tryforos only 37. The 'Swinging Diet Doc' as the press was to call him, was trying to jilt his long-standing mistress in favour of a replacement some 20 years younger. Nothing that emerged in the coming case could mask the essential callousness of the doctor's action. It was almost as if he were trading a life rather as he might have traded an old car – for a new model. Public sympathy was heavily in favour of Mrs Harris at the outset of the trial. And for feminists especially, she seemed to embody the whole plight of exploited womanhood.

The trial was one of the longest ever held in the history of New York State. And amid all the courtroom wranglings, some facts were beyond dispute. On Monday 10 March 1980, Mrs Harris drove the 500 miles from Virginia to New York in a blue Chrysler which belonged to the school. She arrived at around 23.00 on a stormy night and let herself into the house. With her she took a .32 calibre Harrington and Richardson revolver, bought some 18 months earlier. Five of its six chambers were loaded – five more rounds were on her person. She entered the doctor's bedroom while he slept, and in the period which followed several shots were fired. The doctor received four bullet wounds from which he died within the hour.

During the fracas, Tarnower's cook heard the buzzer

from the bedroom sounding in the kitchen. She rushed and picked up the receiver, heard a shot and much shouting and screaming. The cook woke her husband and called the police as Mrs Harris left the house. A police officer in the neighbourhood drove to the scene and saw the blue Chrysler ahead. Mrs Harris did a U-turn in the road and went back to the house with the police car following behind.

'Hurry up, hurry up! He's been shot,' she said to the officer. Tarnower was crumpled on the bedroom floor when they arrived, his pyjamas drenched in blood. He died in hospital.

The statements Mrs Harris made on the fateful night included: 'I've been through so much hell with him, I loved him very much, he slept with every woman he could find, and I had it.' She said she had come to the house with the intention of committing suicide. There had been a struggle with the gun, which went off several times. Asked who had control of the weapon and who did the shooting, she said: 'I don't know . . . I remember holding the gun and shooting him in the hand.'

Mrs Harris was brought to trial on a murder charge. The hearings began in October 1980, by which time the case was already a *cause célèbre*. And it was five weeks before the trial proper began with a full complement of jurors (8 women, 4 men) agreed on by both sides.

Mrs Harris pleaded not guilty, her counsel claiming, 'We don't want special sympathy because she is a woman, because of her age, because she is frail . . .' The defence asked for no mitigation on grounds of temporary insanity or diminished responsibility. Its case rested squarely on the contention that the defendant went to Westchester to take her own life, and the doctor died in a 'tragic accident'.

Formidable obstacles were ranged against this version of event. For example, if suicide were her intention, why did Mrs Harris take a loaded revolver – *and* carry spare rounds on her person? In fact, by a legal nicety, the prosecution was forbidden to mention that she had much more ammunition in the car.

Then there was the struggle itself. How come the doctor sustained four bullet wounds, and Mrs Harris none at all?

The defence marshalled plenty of evidence to show that Mrs Harris had been feeling suicidal. She had been taking drugs (prescribed by Dr Tarnower) to combat depression. She had recently been facing problems at her school. And she had left several farewell notes to friends and colleagues before the fateful night. One said: 'I wish to be immediately cremated and thrown away'. Another included the sad reflection, 'I was a person and no one ever knew'.

Briefly, her own account of events was that she arrived and found Tarnower in bed. 'Jesus,' he had said, 'it's the middle of the night,' and he told her to go away. She asked for a chance to talk for a little while, and he refused. Wandering into the bathroom, Mrs Harris saw a greenish-blue satin négligée (belonging to her rival). She went back into the bedroom and threw it to the floor. Returning to the bathroom she picked up a box of curlers and hurled them at the window. Tarnower came then to the bathroom and hit her across the face; her mouth was bruised when the police found her. She threw another box, and Tarnower hit her again.

Back in the bedroom she sat on the bed, saying 'Hit me again, Hi. Make it hard enough to kill'. Then, unzipping her bag, she took out the gun. 'Never mind,' she said, 'I'll do it myself.'

By her account, Mrs Harris raised the gun to her head, and as she squeezed the trigger he pushed it away. The shot exploded, Tarnower withdrew his hand and it was covered with blood. 'Jesus Christ,' he said. 'Look what you did.'

In a struggle that followed, Tarnower prised the gun off her, pressing the buzzer with his left hand. The gun lay briefly on the bed, Mrs Harris lunged for it and felt what she thought was the muzzle pressing into her abdomen. Again she pulled the trigger; there was a second explosion – and Tarnower fell back.

Now she held the gun to her head and pulled the trigger, but it only clicked. She tried again and a wild shot ricocheted somewhere. She put the gun to her head 'and I shot and I shot and I shot' but the gun just went on clicking. Back in the bathroom she banged the weapon repeatedly against the tub, trying to empty the chambers, planning to reload. In the end the gun just broke.

Tarnower was still conscious and she didn't realize he was dying as she ran out to find help. She was driving to a nearby phone booth when the police car appeared with its flashing lights. Spotting it, she U-turned to lead it back to the house.

Incredibly complex ballistics evidence was heard at the trial, with abstruse talk about ricochet points, in-and-out gunshot wounds and so on. Additionally, it was shown that the police had behaved with some carelessness in handling the material evidence. Suffice to say that four bullet wounds were found in the doctor's body, and Mrs Harris could only remember three shots being fired. This tended to weight against her. But it was easy to imagine in the heat of the struggle, more shots might have been fired without murderous intent. Ultimately, the ballistics evidence was inconclusive.

It was in essence a psychological drama. Mrs Harris was something of an enigma even to partisans of her cause. Small, attractive and neatly turned out, she was very composed in the dock. She showed no apparent remorse for the death of her long-standing lover, and even handled the bloodstained sheets without visible emotion. Sometimes she was petulant with the prosecutor; constantly she could be seen forwarding notes to her own defence counsel. Hers was a sharp mind – she looked neither frail, aged nor abandoned. Nor did she look like a victim.

The defence stressed her suicidal weariness, claiming that no vengeful feelings had motivated her as she drove to Westchester that night. There was no hatred for Tarnower in her soul, only a mortal exhaustion. They had never quarrelled before, she quipped in the box, except over the correct use of the subjunctive. But one piece of evidence weighed massively against her version of events. It came to be known as the Scarsdale Letter.

This was a very long and very angry letter mailed by Mrs Harris on the very morning of the fateful day. It was sent to Tarnower by registered post and recovered from the mail. And the text was one long shriek of outrage against the wrongs she had endured.

Mrs Harris claimed in the letter that Tarnower had cut her out of his will in favour of Lynn Tryforos. She called her rival 'a vicious, adulterous psychotic', and a 'self-serving, ignorant slut'. The headmistress charged Lynne with ripping up dresses from her wardrobe at Tarnower's house. She suspected her of stealing her jewellery too, and of making anonymous phone calls.

The whole tone of the letter was ugly, betraying a violent intensity of emotions. Mrs Harris's central demand was that she be allowed to spend April 19th with Tarnower. This was an important occasion at which the doctor was to be honoured. Mrs Harris was determined to attend 'even if the slut comes – indeed, I don't care if she pops naked out of a cake with her tits frosted with chocolate!'

This from the headmistress of the Madeira Girls' School! The letter undermined all the character witnesses who had been brought from the school to the courtroom. But it did much more. It demonstrated unequivocally that jealousy and rage were burning in her soul. In the box the prosecutor had asked: 'Did you ever consider yourself publicly humiliated by the fact that Dr Tarnower was seeing Lynne Tryforos in public?' She had replied 'No'. Yet, in the letter, she had written: 'I have been publicly humiliated again and again and again . . .'

The defence had refused to plead for leniency on the grounds of diminished responsibility. They had decided to go for complete acquittal on the 'tragic accident' theory. And it now seemed with hindsight a downright mistake.

The prosecution described a phone call from the doctor on the fateful morning. 'Goddamit, Jean, stop bothering me', he had said. And this, it was alleged, was the triggering incident which caused her to take the revolver, the many rounds of ammunition, and head the blue Chrysler to Westchester. No doubt she did intend suicide. But she intended to kill the doctor first.

At the end of a trial lasting nearly a year, the jury delivered its verdict. And it agreed with the prosecution. On 24 February 1981, Mrs Harris was found guilty of the murder charge. She displayed no reaction, but two defence lawyers burst into tears when the result was announced. The verdict carried at automatic jail sentence of at least 15 years which was duly delivered by the judge. Standing upright in the dock, Mrs Harris replied with a lengthy statement beginning: 'I want to say that I did not murder Dr Herman Tarnower, that I loved him very much and I never wished him ill, and I am innocent as I stand here . . .'

She was sent to the Bedford Hills Correctional Facility in Westchester. In December 1981, *The Times* reported that Mrs Harris had abandoned the Scarsdale Diet and had gained 30 lb on prison food.

'There Has Been an Accident . . .'

They called them the Bright Young Things. In the 1920s, the gilded children of London society pursued gaiety with a special kind of frenzy. The horrors of World War One lay in the past; for the future few thoughts were spared.

Instead privileged youth grasped feverishly for the here and now: drinking heavily, driving recklessly and making promiscuous love. They danced to jazz, they held fancy dress balls – life was a funfair of glittering silliness. And inevitably it happened that, once in a while, somebody fell off a roundabout.

Elvira Dolores Barney, 27, belonged to the lost generation. The daughter of Sir John and Lady Mullens, she was a conspicuous figure in society: slender, attractive and arrogant. A brief marriage to an older man had ended in quarrels and separation. With her own inheritance and a rich allowance from her parents, the young Mrs Barney returned to the circuit, looking for a good time – and a lover.

She found him in 24-year-old Michael Scott Stephen, one-time dress designer and all-purpose man-about-town. He was something of a gambler who also sponged off rich women. And when the couple set up home at 21 Williams Mews, Knightsbridge, it was Elvira Barney who paid the bills.

The house lay off Lowndes Square, and the couple scandalized the neighbours with their noisy parties. They had equally noisy quarrels too, and it was on the night of 31 May 1932 that one of these proved fatal.

Around midnight, Mrs Barney's doctor received a telephone call. The woman's voice at the other end of the line was near hysterical: 'For God's sake, doctor, come at once. There has been a terrible accident.' Arriving at the mews cottage, the doctor found Stephen lying dead in the upstairs bedroom. He had been shot at close range through the chest. Nearby was a .32 Smith and Wesson revolver, in which two of the chambers were empty.

'He can't be dead,' Mrs Barney was moaning. 'I love him so . . . Let me die, let me die. I will kill myself.'

That, then, was the tableau: Mrs Barney, her dead lover, and the gun. When the police arrived she was still in a state of distress. A detective asked her to accompany him to the station; she struck him, calling out: 'I'll teach you to put me in a cell, you foul swine.' Alternately tearful and imperious, Mrs Barney telephoned her parents, afterwards warning: 'Now you know who my mother is, you will be more careful of what you say.' But when her parents arrived she went quietly to the station. There she made the same statement that she had made to her doctor. It was a version of events from which she never departed.

She said that she and her lover had come back to the mews cottage, half drunk, from a party at the Café de Paris. Stephen declared that he was going to leave her, and she had threatened to kill herself if he did so. She took the gun from under a cushion where it had been hidden; he leaped at her to prevent the suicide. In the struggle which followed, Stephen grabbed the revolver which went off by accident and killed him.

Since Mrs Barney's was the only evidence then available, she was released from custody. Three days later, however, she was formally arrested. The police had been making enquiries in the neighbourhood.

No one could doubt the violent nature of Elvira Barney's romance. Three weeks before Stephen's death, for example, Mrs Hall, a resident, had seen him come to the mews cottage in the early hours of the morning. He was asking for money, but was told by Mrs Barney to go away. He did so, but came back later that night. He was repulsed again, and on that occasion Mrs Barney had looked out of her window, apparently naked, and shouted down, 'Laugh, baby, laugh for the last time!'

Then she had fired a revolver.

The same witness declared that on the fateful night there had been a loud argument in which Mrs Barney had cried out, 'I will shoot you!' before the gun was fired.

Brought to trial at the Old Bailey on a murder charge, Elvira Barney found some formidable forensic experts ranged against her. Sir Bernard Spilsbury, the eminent pathologist, testified that there were no smoke or scorch marks on the dead man's clothes or body. These were generally found when a victim was shot at point blank range. In fact, the angle of the bullet wound implied that Stephen had been shot from a distance of several feet. Moreover, the gunsmith Robert Churchill noted that the Smith and Wesson had a very heavy action – its pull amounting to 14 lbs. It was hard to see how it could have been fired by accident.

Finally, a mysterious bullet hole had been found in the bedroom wall, but no bullet had been recovered from it. If *two* shots had been fired, it made the case for an accident appear doubly improbable.

Defending Elvira Barney, however, was one of the most brilliant advocates of the day. His name was Sir Patrick Hastings, and although a specialist in civil actions he brought an outstanding legal mind to bear on the criminal case. Significantly, Mrs Hall who had first claimed to hear the words, 'I'll shoot *you*,' changed the words at the trial to 'I'll shoot.' This could well carry the implication that Mrs Barney was threatening suicide, not murder. Moreover Hastings had the same witness support the case for a suicide threat. Discussing the earlier shooting incident, Mrs Hall agreed that Stephen and Mrs Barney seemed very friendly on the morning after the 'Laugh, baby, laugh' episode.

'What conversation passed between you and the young man?' asked Hastings.

'I told him to clear off, as he was a perfect nuisance in the mews.'

'What did he reply?'

'He apologized and said he didn't want to leave Mrs Barney because he was afraid that she might kill herself.'

In fact, Hastings was to contend, the shot fired by Mrs Barney three weeks before Stephen died was not aimed after him in the mews. It was the shot which accounted for the mysterious bullet hole in the bedroom wall. Mrs Barney had fired the run at random, hoping to persuade her lover that her suicide threats were genuine.

Spilsbury's apparent damning forensic evidence was dismissed as theorizing rather than hard fact. As for Robert Churchill's claim that the gun could not have gone off by accident, Hastings had a dramatic answer. Brandishing the revolver before the court, he pulled the trigger repeatedly at the ceiling. It was a gesture accomplished with the utmost panache (although Hastings is said to have later admitted that the effort made his finger sore).

Mrs Barney herself made a more than favourable impression. She spoke in low, dignified tones, her emotion evident but never overstated. She readily admitted that both her marriage and her affair had been unhappy. A tragic figure in the dock, she seemed more ill-fated than ill-intentioned. They had made love, she said, on the fateful night, but it had not been successful: 'He said that he was not pleased with the way things were going and he wanted to go away the next day and not see me at all. That made me very unhappy. He got up from the bed and dressed. I asked him not to leave me and said that if he did I should kill myself.'

'Did he say or do anything then?'

'He got up and took the revolver, saying, "Well, you don't do it with this!"'

There followed the struggle, and the shot.

In his final speech, Hastings meticulously reiterated the thrust of the defence's case. Only Mrs Barney could say what happened on the night of Stephen's death, and she had never departed from her story. In summing up, the judge paid tribute to the power of Sir Patrick's speech, but left the facts for the jury to interpret.

It was a case, *par excellence*, for a jury. The best experts available had given their testimony, the best legal minds had presided in court. But when all was said and done, the outcome had to revolve around a human assessment of the case. Did she do it, or didn't she?

After only one hour and 50 minutes, the jury declared that she didn't.

Elvira Barney's acquittal was greeted with cheers from a crowd outside the court. A free woman, she went to France to escape the burden of publicity. But it seems that she had not been greatly chastened by the long courtroom ordeal. As chance would have it, Sir Patrick Hastings also crossed the Channel after the trial, for a holiday with his family. While driving from Boulogne he narrowly escaped death when a car coming from behind overtook him on the wrong side of the road. The driver of the car was Mrs. Barney.

Socialite, beauty and subject of scandal, Elvira Barney never got a chance to outlive the label of Bright Young Thing. Four years after the trial she was found dead in a paris hotel bedroom. She was 31 years old.

A Rifle at the Party

The pre-Christmas staff party at New Zealand's Dunedin General Hospital was held on 12 December 1954. Dr John William 'Bill' Saunders, 27-year-old medical officer, took Frances Kearney, a senior student at the hospital. Also present at the party was Dr Florence Whittingham, a house surgeon who had been Saunders' fiancée. She went alone to the party – alone, that is, except for a .303 rifle.

She arrived late. While the party was getting into its swing, Florence Whittingham stayed in her own apartment, writing to a friend a letter that she never in fact posted. Its sentiments were bitter and despondent: 'I can no longer cope and Bill makes things so miserable for me there seems little left. I have so much pain . . .'

She came after midnight, nursing her pain and her rifle.

Groups of partygoers had by now crowded into the quarters of one of the hospital surgeons. Florence Whittingham found her former lover in the corridor; and suddenly, above the chatter and the chink of glasses in the living room, voices could be heard raised in anger outside. There was shouting and screaming – a shot detonated – and the guests rushed out into the corridor.

For a moment the scene was frozen, as in some nightmarish tableau. Dr Saunders was kneeling, blood-spattered, on the floor. Florence Whittingham stood before him and, as the wounded man swayed on his knees, she lent forward to embrace him. She was babbling hysterically: 'Bill, listen to me, Bill.' But the medical officer heard nothing as he slid dying from her arms. No-one called for a doctor – the apartment was crowded with medics. But all of their expertise counted for nothing in the case of Dr Saunders. He was dead before the stretcher arrived.

The case stunned New Zealand. Explosions of love and despair were not expected in the sober professional community of Dunedin, the South Island seaport founded by Scottish Presbyterians. And although clearly a crime of passion, the affair had its perplexing features too. A rifle is no natural choice of weapon for suicide. Did Dr Whittingham go to the party intending murder or, as she claimed, something else?

Dr Senga Florence Whittingham was 27; the same age as her former fiancé. And no-one could deny that she had cause for grievance in the events leading up to the tragedy. She had taken up the post of house surgeon at Dunedin early in 1953, and her duties involved working closely with Dr Saunders. Soon they formed a relationship which extended out of hours. As early as May 1953, the medical officer asked Florence to marry him and she was only too happy to accept. In June, the couple went to see Saunders' mother and announced their engagement. They hoped for an early wedding, for Florence was expecting a baby.

Mrs Saunders had her reservations. It had been a lightning romance, and both had their careers to think about. Mrs Saunders advised a period of reflection. They should not get married only for the baby's sake. If necessary, she declared, she would adopt it.

In the event, there was no quick wedding – indeed, no wedding at all. After that meeting with Mrs Saunders, the couple still went on seeing one another. But it seemed to Florence that Bill's ardour had cooled. She sensed that he no longer wanted the baby. When asked about his feelings, Bill denied that he was falling out of love, but he was evasive about the future.

That summer, Florence Whittingham procured an abortion. She knew immediately afterwards that a bond had been broken. Bill was clearly relieved, and in September, with no pressing reason for the marriage to go ahead, he broke off the engagement.

Florence was in despair. Even in the most supportive environment, an abortion may leave deep emotional scars. Had the child been truly 'unwanted' the loss might have been easier to bear. But this baby had been joyfully anticipated – by Florence, at least – as the fruit of love and in the promise of a shared future. She still loved Dr Saunders, still urgently wanted to marry him. But far from easing the relationship, her sacrifice had left her bereft of her lover too. For Dr Saunders, breaking the engagement recalled a more carefree way of living. Once again he became Dunedin's popular – and very eligible – bachelor medical officer.

It was when the bitter realization of her double-loss dawned that Florence Whittingham bought the .303 rifle. She told a friend who once noticed the gun in her rooms that it was for her brother. In fact, Dr Whittingham had no brother. But if a sudden urge to violence provoked the purchase it seems to have faded away. She took no immediate action, enduring instead long months of waiting and of faint hope. Perhaps Saunders' love would quicken again?

It never did. Through all of 1954, Florence Whittingham was prey to black depression which eroded her vitality. She became a wraith in the corridors of the General Hospital, attending as capably as ever to her patients, but inwardly broken in spirit. Her health was affected and she underwent a major operation. To combat her loss of vitality, she began taking insulin, a drug normally prescribed for diabetics. It proved no cure, though, for lovesickness.

The affair was over, and no amount of pleading could bring Dr Saunders back. Yet she still saw him practically daily in the hospital, confident, ambitious and relishing his restored bachelorhood. What provoked the climax was a trivial enough event. Florence Whittingham learned that her ex-lover would be taking Miss Kearney to the staff party at Christmas. A sense of outrage seems to have seized Florence, for she phoned her rival and in a near-shriek declared, 'This is the mother of Bill Saunders' child speaking!' No doubt a pent flood of recrimination was at her lips, but she got no chance to release it. When Miss Kearney identified the caller's voice as Dr Whittingham's she prudently hung up.

Florence Whittingham was shut out now; shut out of her lover's life and his future. And it was in a mood of total frustration and despair that she had recourse to the rifle.

In the letter she wrote to her friend before taking the gun to the party, Dr Whittingham began: 'I should like you to be of special comfort to my mother and Bill's mother.' By implication, she was considering some kind of dramatic action if 'special comfort' would be required. But the rest of the text expressed, in broken paragraphs, only misery: 'I have had a year of hell . . . I love him but my pleadings are useless.' There was no specific threat.

After the sensational shooting at the party, she was to say quietly, 'It's the first time I've been at peace for a year.' And later: 'I loved him – I couldn't stop loving him. I wanted to frighten him. That's all. Just to frighten him. I didn't mean to shoot him. Just frighten him. That's all.'

When a crime is committed in a state of high emotion, the word 'intention' becomes opaque. Dr Whittingham was brought to trial for wilful murder in February 1955, and the prosecution had a formidable case. The accused had, after all, taken a loaded rifle to the party. The letter she had written was shown in evidence. A ballistics expert, moreover, testified that the .303 could not easily be fired by chance.

In defence, Florence Whittingham's counsel contended that she had pointed the gun at Saunders only as a threatening gesture; the discharge was accidental. Obviously there was great sympathy for the accused when the story of her abortion and operation was made known. But assessing her precise intention at the moment of discharge called for careful consideration. At the end of the six-day trial, the jury deliberated over its verdict for more than seven hours. Returning to the crowded courtroom, the members found Dr Whittingham guilty of manslaughter, but added a strong recommendation to mercy on the grounds that the rifle was fired accidentally. She received a three-year sentence.

In retrospect, the case is as hard to assess as it was in the Supreme Court Building. But the verdict was a fair one. However the gun went off, its purpose at the party was not to destroy a life. It was brought to shock the victim into recognition of wronged love and misery endured. Behind the echo of gunshot, a voice was calling, 'Bill, listen to me, Bill. *Listen* to me.' It was the voice of love locked out.

'I am a Lady'

In March 1914, as war clouds gathered over Europe, a public scandal shook France to its roots. It was a shooting incident – an *affaire d'honneur* – which swept all other issues from the front pages. Even the assassination of the Archduke Franz Ferdinand at Sarajevo was given lesser prominence in the press. That obscure event in Bosnia was to usher in the holocaust of World War One but its significance was not at first grasped. France's Caillaux Affair, in contrast, was reported worldwide and followed with complete fascination.

It did not conform to the classic pattern of a crime of passion, but had all the elements associated with one. There were the tangled emotions of a love triangle, and shots fired by an outraged wife. The victim, though, was the newspaper editor who brought the affair to light.

Gaston Calmette, editor of *Le Figaro*, was the most influential journalist in France. For months he has used the power of his paper to direct a campaign against Henri Caillaux, Finance Minister. The attacks came daily in the form of lampoons as well as bitter textual denunciations. What provoked the editor's wrath was Caillaux's pacificism and – more serious – supposedly treasonable contacts with Germany.

Things came to a head when the editor resorted to personal smears. On the morning of 16 March 1914, *Le Figaro* published a compromising love letter from Caillaux on its front page. The letter was one of several written by the Minister during the period of his first marriage. They were addressed to Henriette, the society beauty who became his second wife. Caillaux's first wife had acquired some of the correspondence and had used it to obtain a hefty cash settlement after the divorce. The business was over, it was a private affair – but reflected no credit on the Minister.

It was the second Madame Caillaux who took action. When the letter was published Henriette could not find her husband, and so headed straight for a gunsmith. In the shop, having tested a Smith and Wesson, she judiciously opted for a Browning automatic. Then she went round to the offices of *Le Figaro* where she shot the editor dead with five bullets. As nervous staff sought to apprehend the killer, Madame Caillaux replied magisterially, 'Let me go. I am a lady. I am Madame Caillaux. I have my car waiting to take me to the police station.'

The Minister was forced to resign, and his wife was brought to trial at the Assize Court of the Seine in July 1914. She faced the charge of murder amid a national furore. Initially, at least, the dead man was presented as a patriot gunned down by a traitor's wife.

The courtroom turned into a political theatre of war, in which charges and counter-charges were fired like mortar shells from the entrenched ranks of the rival counsels. In the end, the Caillauxs emerged the political victors, bringing evidence to show that Calmette himself had been involved in unpatriotic propaganda.

But what of the murder charge? Incredibly, Madame Caillaux declared herself innocent of the crime, on the grounds that the gun went off by accident. After the first chance shot, she contended, the rest of the bullets simply streamed out automatically. She gave evidence in the dock with a stately calm and with every appearance of truthfulness. The jury came to the unanimous verdict that Madame Caillaux was not guilty – and she walked from the court a free woman.

Two Cab Mysteries

When one of two lovers gets shot in a sealed cab, the event may be problematic for the law. Should the victim die, the case is likely to rest on the testimony of the survivor. The two stories that follow were different in outcome, yet they shared many features in common. Both shootings, for example, tragically concluded love affairs which were supposedly over already. Both also involved ladies of the stage and took place during the champagne years before the outbreak of World War One.

The first drama was played out in New York, 1904, where Mrs 'Caesar' Young had had enough. Everyone knew about her husband's affair with Nan Patterson, 22-year-old chorus girl from the hit musical *Floradora*. Mrs Young had thwarted one attempted elopement, and now booked passages for her husband and herself on a trans-atlantic steamer. Maybe a holiday in England would provide a chance of a reconciliation, in which memories of the chorus girl would fade from his mind.

Francis 'Caesar' Young, New York gambler and promi-nent man of the turf, agreed to the vacation. The passages were booked for 4 June 1904, but on the day before the ship was due to leave, Caesar Young spent a long time with Nan Patterson. The bonds that had united them could not easily be severed: he drank, they argued, and on the morning of the sailing he was again in Nan's company. The couple shared a hansom cab which led along Broad-way to a theatreland sensation – and an amazing triple series of trials.

Exactly what happened in the cab? One shot detonated in the vehicle and a passer-by heard Nan cry out, 'Look at me, Frank. Why did you do it?' First, the chorus girl told the driver to make for a nearby drugstore, then to hurry on to a hospital. But it was too late. When the cab doors

338

were opened, Caesar Young was already dead, slumped in the lap of his mistress. His shirt was stained with blood from the bullet-wound in his chest, and the pistol was found in his coat pocket.

Nan Patterson was arrested and charged with murder. If a verdict of guilty was reached, she would go to the electric chair, a device used in New York from 1890, when it had been applied for the first time in the world.

Nan's case first came to court in November 1904, but a mistrial was announced before she could give evidence: one of the jurors had died. At trial two, held the following month, the jury could not agree on a verdict. At the third trial, held in April 1905, the jury was again unable to come to a majority decision.

Throughout her ordeal, Nan had fervently protested her innocence and public opinion was firmly on her side. Ten days after the last trial was concluded, the judge granted a motion that she be discharged. Outside the court, a delirious crowd cheered her to freedom, and in the playgrounds little children were heard to chant:

> Nan is free, Nan is free,
> She escaped the electric chair,
> Now she's out in the open air!

The second cab mystery occurred in the City of London, two years after Broadway's incident. At midnight on Saturday 28 September 1912, the driver of a taxi moving along Fenchurch Street heard three loud bangs behind him. Assuming his tyres had burst, the driver got out to examine the vehicle's wheels. A police constable on night duty also heard the reports and came up to find out what was going on. The tyres were firm and the driver opened the cab door to see if his two passengers were all right. Immediately, a woman toppled headlong out, moaning, 'Mind, cabby, he has a revolver. He has shot me. Drive me to a hospital.'

No sooner were the words uttered than two more deafening reports were heard. Inside the taxi, her companion had tried to shoot himself – blood was spattered all around. The drive rushed his cab with its freight of wounded fares to Guy's Hospital where the woman died within minutes of arrival from wounds to her head and chest. The man, though bleeding severely from head and hands, was saved from death. His name was Edward Hopwood, a failed company director. The dead woman was Florence Alice Silles, stage-name 'Flo Dudley', a music-hall comedienne.

Edward Hopwood was a short man – short of stature and short of funds. Though married with children, he lived apart from his wife and was practically bankrupt when he first met Flo Dudley. The pair quickly became lovers and must have made a slightly improbable couple for she was statuesque and ample-bosomed, with the full-blown figure so admired in the period. Despite his dire financial straits and his matrimonial state, Hopwood proposed marriage to Florence. She was a widow at 34 and, having no idea that Edward had other commitments, readily accepted. Being a strict Catholic she insisted that they see a priest, to which her lover consented. She also brought Hopwood home to Ilford to meet the sister with whom she shared a house. He was introduced as her betrothed.

Florence's intended, though, seemed curiously evasive about naming the day. He offered a registry office wedding but even the would-be bigamist clearly baulked at the idea of a formal Catholic service. In August 1912, five months after the affair began, Florence would endure no further delay and broke the relationship off. She would have no more to do with the diminutive company director.

Edward grew jealous. He knew Florence was friendly with a man living in Southampton and desiring one last rendezvous, Hopwood resorted to subterfuge. He went to Southampton and, using the other man's name, wired

Florence to meet him for dinner at the Holbourn Restaurant for dinner on the night of 28 September.

It was the night of the fatal shooting. That Saturday morning, Hopwood bought an automatic revolver. In the afternoon, he made out his will and wrote a suicide note. At night he made his surprise appearance at the Holbourn Restaurant. Shortly before midnight, the couple hired a cab to go to Fenchurch Street Station. It was during the course of this short trip that the three shots rang out.

Edward Hopwood was tried for murder in December 1912. He refused legal aid, preferring instead to present his own case before the jury. Hopwood's contention was that he pulled out the gun intending suicide, but Florence grabbed him as he produced the revolver. The gun fired accidentally in one rapid burst of three shots.

The judge was by no means unsympathetic. But the prosecution brought forward a forensic scientist who testified that Florence's head wounds could not have been caused by chance. At one point during his final address to the jury, the accused was overcome with emotion and broke into a fit of sobbing. Eventually, when prompted by the judge to continue, Hopwood wept, 'I can say no more'.

There was no triple trial for Edward Hopwood. The jury found him guilty of wilful murder, and sentence of death was passed. Late in December, only three months after doctors at Guy's Hospital had saved Hopwood's life, the hangman took it back at Pentonville.

The Lost Flyer

On Saturday 15 April 1933, *The Times* reported:
    No news has been received of Captain Lancaster, who was flying from England to the Cape, since Wednesday. Our Algiers Correspondent reports that he left Reggan, an oasis in the Sahara, at half past six on the

evening of that day for Gao, on the Niger. Sandstorms were causing bad visibility. A car was sent yesterday by the Trans-Saharan Company to search for him.

The celebrated airman had left England at 05.38 on the morning of 11 April, in an attempt to beat the record for a flight to the Cape. He had reached Oran at 21.00 that night and taken a brief rest there before setting out across the Sahara desert.

The following day he drifted off course because of heavy sandstorms. Nevertheless, he managed to reach Reggan where he rested for three hours, worn out. There was no moon, and a strong northwest wind was blowing. The local head of the Trans-Saharan Company told him it was madness to take off when he would not be able to see the day beacons on the main desert motor track. Lancaster did not even have lighting on his instrument board, for steering a compass course.

But Lancaster was determined to go. As for lighting, he said, he would manage with matches and a borrowed pocket torch. Witnesses saw him make a very bad take-off before vanishing into the evening sky. It was 18.30 on 12th April. He was not seen alive again.

Was he prompted to make the fatal flight by that reckless spirit shared by all the pioneer aviators? Or was something else on his mind, urging him to risk the treachery of the desert? Captain Lancaster had hit the headlines less than a year before, for something very different. At Miami in August 1932, he had been brought to trial on a charge of murder.

William Newton Lancaster had served in the RAF during World War One. He subsequently married and left the Air Force to make a name for himself as a long-distance flyer. The twenties was the decade of Lindbergh, Cobham and Kingsford Smith – men who opened up the world's air routes. Women, too, played their part in those pioneer years, and one of them was Australia's Mrs Keith 'Chubbie'

Miller.

In 1927, Lancaster and Mrs Miller flew as partners in a record-breaking flight which covered the 13,000 miles from London to Australia. And although both were married they continued to fly as a team, becoming lovers on the ground as well as partners in the air. After their record-breaking flight to Australia, the couple did most of their flying in the United States, and it was there that their tragedy was enacted.

While Lancaster was in Mexico for a spell, Chubbie developed a liaison with American writer Charles Haden Clarke. The pair fell in love and wrote to Lancaster of their plans for marriage. Lancaster returned to Florida with a revolver and confronted the lovers at Mrs Miller's house. There followed a quarrel which ended when the three actors in the drama retired to their respective beds.

During that night, Chubbie was awakened by Lancaster who told her that Clarke had shot himself. The writer was slumped in his room with a pistol lying on the bed. Blood seeped from the head wound from which he later died. Lying by the dying man were typed suicide notes – written on Lancaster's machine.

The death occurred on 21 April 1932. On 2 August of that year, Captain W. N. Lancaster was brought to trial for murder. Much of the 16-day courtroom case revolved around the nature of the fatal wound. Forensic experts debated the possibilities of suicide and murder, while the character of the two men was discussed. According to Chubbie, Clarke had called Lancaster 'one of the finest men he knew'. The defence intended to support the case for suicide by bringing forward a doctor who, after post mortem examination, declared the dead man to be a drug addict. The doctor was sick at the time of the trial, and a motion for adjournment was denied. Nevertheless, after deliberating for six hours, the jury found Lancaster not guilty.

Chubbie had stood by the airman at his trial, but their relationship had inevitably suffered. Though both returned to England, Lancaster's record-breaking attempt of 1933 was a solo flight, made in the 100 h.p. *Southern Cross Minor* – a single-seater plane.

When the plane went missing over the Sahara, search parties were called out. But within ten days of the disappearance, the experts were acknowledging there was very little hope indeed of ever finding the missing aviator alive. In fact, the pilot was not to be found in any condition at all – until more than 29 years later.

In February 1962, a French desert patrol came upon the wreckage of Lancaster's Avro-Avian. The remains of the missing flyer were found beside the debris. His log-book contained entries for eight days after the crash – eight days awaiting death in the desert, in which he recorded his love for Chubbie Miller. Curiously enough, the last entry was made exactly one year to the day after Charles Haden Clarke's death.

What Kind of Murder?

It happened the wrong way round. When a husband comes home to find his wife with another man, it is the husband who traditionally resorts to violence. But the case of Melvyn and Lorraine Clark was rather different . . .

Melvyn Clark was an electronics engineer who lived with his wife and three children in a suburb of Boston. And beneath the surface of domestic content, there lurked illicit passions. When Melvyn was away from home, Lorraine used to attend wife-swapping parties. The partners were selected 'blind': men threw down keys, and the women picked them up without knowing whose bedroom they would be sharing.

Melvyn knew nothing of these frolics. On 10 April 1954,

the engineer returned to his home unexpectedly to find Lorraine with another man. The interloper made his excuses and left. A quarrel broke out in the Clark household, during which Lorraine stabbed her husband with a darning needle. Then she shot him dead with two bullets from a revolver.

Afterwards, Lorraine trussed up her husband with wire and lugged his body into the car. She drove to a nearby river and, on the bridge, fixed weights to his legs and heaved him over the edge.

The body was discovered six weeks later, and during interrogation Lorraine confessed to the murder. But what kind of murder was it? Under United States law, first degree murder is deliberate and premeditated, designed to effect a death. Second degree murder is a killing in which deliberation and premeditation are missing. In Lorraine's case, the stab of the darning needle may well have been impulsive. But the two subsequent revolver shots . . . ?

In a decision which aroused controversy, her plea of guilty to second degree murder was accepted, and she received a sentence of life imprisonment.

2.

Whodunnit?

Reverend Babykins and
His Gay Gipsy

On Saturday 16 September, 1922, an adultery was exposed at a lover's lane in New Brunswick, New Jersey. The Reverend Edward Wheeler Hall, Rector of St John's Episcopal Church, was found lying under a crab apple-tree with Mrs Eleanor Mills, the sexton's wife. He was 41 and balding; she a petite 34-year-old. And the couple never got a chance to defend or explain their activities. They were found dead – murdered at their rendezvous, their bodies scattered with their torn-up love letters.

The pastor's head had been pierced by a single bullet; a bloodsoaked Panama hat lay over his face. Eleanor Mills had been shot three times; her throat, moreover had been slashed. And as for the love letters, they told in the clearest possible terms of the special relationship which had existed between the minister and the soprano who had sung in his choir.

The letters strewn all around had been written by Eleanor Mills. Scribbled in pencil, they bore witness to intense emotions: 'I know there are girls with more shapely bodies,' the sexton's wife had written, 'but I do not care what they have. I have the greatest of all blessings, the deep, true and eternal love of a noble man. My heart is his, my life is his, all I have is his, poor as my body is, scrawny as they say my skin may be, but I am his forever.'

Someone had emptied the minister's pockets, and his gold watch had been stolen. But mere theft could not have been the motive for the killing. Propped against the dead man's foot was one of his own visiting cards, as if advertising his identity. Whoever shot the lovers had arranged their bodies side by side in a grotesque embrace. Special savagery had been reserved for Eleanor Mills; not only had

349

her throat been slashed but her tongue and vocal cords had been cut out. With the confetti of love letters playing about their bodies, everything pointed to a crime of passion.

The police interviewed the dead clergyman's wife, Frances Hall. A plain, grey-haired woman nine years older than her husband, she professed complete ignorance of the liaison between her husband and his chorister. All she knew was that on the evening of Thursday 14th, her husband had received a phone call and left the house. He did not come back that night. And although it was a whole day and another night before the bodies were discovered, Mrs Hall at no stage called the police.

James Mills, husband of the dead woman, came up with a strikingly similar story. His wife had not come home on Thursday evening, but he too failed to call the police. When pressed, he said that he thought his wife might have been round at her sister's house. Like Frances Hall, he claimed to know nothing of the secret love affair.

There were many in the pastor's congregation who were not so blinkered. Rumours of the affair had been circulating in New Brunswick long before the murders took place. Perhaps one, or both, of the spouses did know of the liaison, and failed to call the police suspecting an elopement? Speculation along these lines led nowhere.

With the lack of concrete evidence, public interest in the case began to flag. But while a blameless suspect named Hayes was under investigation, a witness turned up – a colourful middle-aged Mrs Jane Gibson who came to be known as the Pig Woman.

Mrs Gibson kept pigs on a smallholding, and claimed to have seen the murder occur on the Thursday evening. Hearing noises that night, and suspecting thieves, she had mounted her mule and gone down the lane. Four figures were arguing under the crab apple-tree: two men and two women. One of these was a white-haired lady, and another a kinky-haired man. There were shouts of 'Don't, don't, don't'. Something glinted in the moonlight. Four shots rang out – and the Pig Woman fled the scene.

When questioned by the police, the Pig Woman identified Mrs Hall as the white-haired woman, and her brother Willie Stevens as the kinky-haired man.

Could the testimony be believed? The case came alive again, and the new evidence coincided with the publication of a batch of letters between Eleanor Mills and the late minister. They were all that a sensation-seeking public could have wished.

To the pastor, for example, Mrs Mills had written: 'I am on my knees, darling, looking up at my noble man, worshipping, adoring . . . I want you – your arms to hold me and hold me close if only to forget this pain for a minute. Dearest, give me some words of comfort.'

In reply, the clergyman had penned a note arranging a tryst for the following day: 'My dearest, my treasure, my anchor, my rock – oh, how I did want to fly off with you this afternoon – I wanted to get away to dreamland – heaven-land – everything seemed so sordid, earthy, commonplace . . . Dearest – love me hard, hard – harder than ever, for your Babykins is longing for his mother.'

Earthbound in New Brunswick, the clandestine lovers had allowed their fancies to roam in an illicit paradise where truth, nobility and wonder, crystal eyes and crushing embraces were all yearned for with equal intensity. Eleanor was the pastor's 'gay gipsy' and, 'when my arrow enters your haven I am transported to ecstasy,' wrote the stalwart.

And where had this new correspondence come from? The cache of letters was sold to the press for $500 by James Mills. The transaction of course cast considerable doubt on the sexton's claim to know nothing of his wife's affair.

A grand jury was convened in November to assess the case. But the inquiry led to no indictment. For four years the case was as if frozen, neither formally closed nor under active investigation. What broke the ice was a bombshell lobbed from within the late pastor's household.

Louise Geist, who had served the Halls as a maid, got involved in a lawsuit for marriage annulment. Her husband claimed that Louise had been bribed to keep silent before the grand jury: she had in fact accompanied Mrs Hall and her two brothers to the scene of the crime and been a witness to – or a participant in – the vile deeds.

Back to the front pages came the Crab Apple-tree murder. Back to the limelight came James Mills, the Pig Woman and the rest. And into the dock went the clergyman's wife, and her brothers Willie and Henry Stevens.

The trial was held at Somerville, New Jersey, in November 1926. And it seemed at last that the solution was clear. But was it? Actually, Louise Geist repudiated her husband's claims, still insisting she knew nothing of the murder. The Pig Woman was readier than ever to point the finger at Mrs Hall and her brothers, but the hog-farming witness was now dying of cancer. She had to be brought into court on a stretcher, and her aged mother confounded everyone by constantly interrupting: 'She's a liar, a liar, a liar! That's what she is, and what she's always been.'

James Mills, meanwhile, was fiercely cross-questioned and now candidly admitted that he had known all about the affair between his wife and the clergyman. He had read the love letters and, it seemed, had quarrelled bitterly with his wife about the liaison.

Maybe Mills did it? Maybe the Pig Woman did it! (This suggestion was actually made by the defence counsel.)

At the end of the long, confused trial the jury retired for five hours. When they returned, it was with a verdict of not guilty.

Mrs Hall and her brothers were discharged, the pastor's widow becoming a recluse and dying in 1942. The whole affair had scandalised America, and remains one of crime's great unsolved mysteries. One plausible theory has been put forward by William Kunstler in his *The Minister and the Choir Singer* (1964). He suggests that the Klu Klux Klan engineered the double murder as retribution for the couple's violation of Bible teaching on adultery. Certainly, the disposition of the bodies and the mutilation of the errant choir singer suggest ritual elements in the crime. But the theory remains pure conjecture. All that can be said with certainty of the affair is that the love between Edward Hall and Eleanor Mills was true love lived in a morass of deception. And that the lovers paid a terrible price for their idyll in heaven-land.

Whose Hand on the Mallet?

In a conventional whodunnit it you might expect to find a host of different suspects. But the Rattenbury case of 1935 had a very limited cast. There was Mrs Alma Rattenbury, 38, a writer of popular songs. There was her lover, George Stoner, a chauffeur-handyman barely 18 years of age. And there was 67-year-old Francis Rattenbury, the brutally murdered husband.

The distinguished architect was found battered to death in his favourite armchair. His hair was matted with blood, and there were bloodstains too on the carpet. Rattenbury had been clubbed with a mallet by three heavy blows struck from behind. The question which tormented the public concerned who had wielded the weapon.

Mrs Rattenbury? Her lover? Or had the pair connived at the murder together?

When Alma married Francis Rattenbury in 1925, some comment was made about the disparity between their ages. She was an attractive young woman of great musical talent who had been awarded the *Croix de Guerre* for her services as a nurse in World War One. He in contrast was already middle-aged, a solitary and rather morose man. Rattenbury had, however, won fame and fortune for his architectural designs (his parliament buildings at Victoria B.C. still stand). Alma had no money to speak of.

Yet for ten years their union was happy enough. Not long after the wedding, the coupled retired to the Villa Madeira, a pleasant residence in the quietness of Bournemouth. Alma had a son by a previous marriage who came to visit them at holiday time. Rattenbury too had had children by his first wife. And now Alma bore the architect a new son named John. On the whole, the Rattenbury's was an affectionate ménage, in which such tensions as existed hinted little at the coming tragedy.

'Ratz', as his wife called him, was still prone to his fits of melancholy. Sometimes in the evenings he drank rather too much whisky; sometimes he talked morbidly of suicide. But Alma usually restored his spirits, and to occupy her days she took to writing popular songs. She won considerable success in this field, under the name of 'Lozanne'. Her music was published, broadcast and recorded, the most popular of her discs being *Dark-Haired Marie*:

> Are you waiting in your garden
> By the deep wide azure sea?
> Are you waiting for your loveship,
> Dark-Haired Marie?
>
> I shall come to claim you someday,
> In my arms at last you'll be,
> I shall kiss your lips and love you,
> Dark-Haired Marie.

The lyrics, like many of Alma's, evoked a troubled and sensual yearning which is not hard to understand. After the birth of their son John, she and her husband no longer slept together: they had their own separate bedrooms. Rattenbury told her she could 'lead her own life', and perhaps there were many evenings when the Dark-Haired Marie of the Villa Madeira dreamed of the loveship that would come to claim her. It arrived in the form of George

Percy Stoner, hired as a chauffeur in September 1934.

He gave his age as 22; in reality he was not yet 18. The affable, good-looking son of a local bricklayer, Stoner was soon driving Alma to the London shops, theatres and cinemas. By the end of November, she and Stoner were lovers, and the young man had moved in to the Villa. It was not a big house. His room was just across the landing from hers.

They quarrelled sometimes. Stoner was an inexperienced young man who clearly felt the need to assert his masculinity before the woman who was old enough to be his mother. He told her to give up drinking cocktails, for example, as they were bad for her. Alma agreed. He used to carry a knife with him and on one occasion threatened to kill her; on another he expressed the urge to take his own life. Perhaps the older woman derived some dark excitement from these adolescent theatricals. But she knew her responsibilities. When he confessed his real age, Mrs Rattenbury tried unsuccessfully to break off the relationship. And when Stoner hinted to her that he was taking drugs, she became worried for her children. Alma confessed the whole affair to the family doctor, and asked him to warn the youth off drug-taking, which Dr O'Donnell duly did.

The affair continued into the spring of 1935. In March 1935, the couple took rooms at a Kensington hotel, posing as brother and sister. They went on a shopping spree in which Mrs Rattenbury bought for her lover a suit, shirts, shoes and silk pyjamas. She even bought him a ring which, humiliatingly, he then presented to her as a token of his love. It was on the day after their return to Bournemouth that the tragedy occurred.

On Sunday 24 March, 'Ratz' was in one of his moods. At teatime he read aloud passages from a novel in which the hero contemplates suicide. Alma only managed to brighten his spirits by suggesting that they take a trip to Bridport the next day, and stay there that night. Rattenbury had a friend and business colleague at Bridport, called Mr Jenks. The architect was worried at the time about raising finances for a block of flats. Jenks could help him out in this respect.

The Bridport trip was duly arranged, and the couple played cards that night. At exactly 21.30, Alma went up to bed while her husband returned to his armchair and his novel. Ironically, the book was found folded the next day at a passage where the hero meditates on the problems faced by elderly men who marry younger women . . .

Around 22.15 the home help, Irene Riggs, came back to the Villa Madeira after visiting her parents. She heard a strange, heavy breathing coming from somewhere in the house, but after a brief investigation thought no more of it. Her employer was not in his bedroom; no doubt he had dozed off downstairs. Upstairs, she met Stoner on the landing. He was wearing pyjamas and said he was checking to see that the lights were out. Irene Riggs then went to bed, and was briefly joined in her room by Mrs Rattenbury who often dropped in last thing at night to chat about the day's events. Alma seemed in good spirits, and was looking forward to the proposed trip to Bridport.

Alma then left, and Irene Riggs was just dozing off when she heard someone rushing downstairs. Alma's voice shrieked, 'Irene!' and the servant followed quickly down to the drawing room. The lights were on, and there in his chair sat her employer, his head a wreck of blood. Mrs Rattenbury was desperately trying to bring him round, cramming his false teeth into his mouth so that he could speak to them. Her first words to Irene were 'Someone has hurt Ratz! Telephone the doctor!'

In the panic which followed, Alma started drinking whisky continuously. The pair tried to bathe and bandage the victim. Mrs Rattenbury was specially worried that her little son John would come down and be frightened by the blood. The doctor arrived at 23.15 and a surgeon was called for. Later, an ambulance arrived at the Villa, but the victim was to die in the operating theatre without ever regaining consciousness.

By the time the police arrived at 02.00 Alma had consumed a lot of whisky. She was chattering, now, in a hysterical fashion: she played records and danced and even tried to kiss a policeman. Out of the wild staccato of her utterances, several key phrases were recorded: 'I know who did it! I did it with a mallet! It is hidden . . . Ratz has lived too long. No, my lover did it. I will give you £10. No, I won't bribe you.'

Informed at about 03.30 that her husband's condition was critical, she said: 'I will tell you in the morning where the mallet is. I shall make a better job of it next time. I made a proper muddle of it. I thought I was strong enough.'

The doctor gave her an injection of morphia and put her to bed. She came round at one point and said: 'I know who did it – his son . . . but he is not here.' Lastly, when she appeared much calmer, she made a written statement:

About 9 p.m. on Sunday, 24th March 1935, I was playing cards with my husband when he dared me to kill him, as he wanted to die. I picked up the mallet. He then said: 'You have not guts enough to do it.' I then hit him with the mallet. I hid the mallet outside the house. I would have shot him if I'd had a gun.

When Mrs Rattenbury was being escorted from the house the next morning, she was met by Stoner who was heard to say: 'You have got yourself into this mess by talking too much.'

Stoner himself had been questioned by police during the night and claimed that the first he knew of the murder was when he heard Mrs Rattenbury shouting for help from the drawing room. Three days later, however, he made a confession: 'Do you know Mrs Rattenbury had nothing to do with the affair? When I did the job I believed he was asleep. I hit him, and then came upstairs and told Mrs Rattenbury. She rushed down then . . .'

What were people to believe? Each suspect had confessed to the murder, each claiming to be the sole person responsible. Which of them did it? Or had they collaborated in the assault and were now trying to shield each other?

The case was picked up by the national press which made the most of its sensational aspects. BOY CHAUFFEUR'S ORDEAL – STONER TOOK COCAINE – VORTEX OF ILLICIT LOVE – PYJAMAS AT 60/– A PAIR! screamed the headlines. And at the outset popular opinion was set firmly against Mrs Rattenbury. Alma was more than twice her lover's age, and seen both as adulteress and seducer. Stoner had been a perfectly normal, decent boy before he fell into her clutches. Perhaps the youth was only behaving chivalrously in confessing belatedly to his own guilt.

The trial was held at the Old Bailey, and the two accused were to be tried individually, but in the same court. This created problems in itself, since statements made in one could not necessarily be used as evidence in the other. Further confusion was caused by the fact that both Mrs Rattenbury and her lover ended up by pleading not guilty. But for the public, the ultimate puzzle was provided by the fact that Stoner never entered the witness box. This could be interpreted in one of two ways. Either his counsel considered that his appearance would damage his own case or the boy was nobly refusing to say anything in the box which might incriminate Mrs Rattenbury.

It was, in fact, a trial of either/ors. But one certainty did emerge. The police had found the murder weapon, with blood and hairs on it, hidden behind a trellis in the garden. It was Stoner who had obtained the mallet – he had borrowed it from the home of his grandparents at 20.00 on the fateful evening.

Unlike Stoner, Alma did enter the witness box, and she made an impressive figure. She spoke in a low, clear voice which gave every appearance of truthfulness. Moreover, she was perfectly frank about her adultery.

She said that shortly after she phoned Mr Jenks to arrange the Bridport trip, Stoner had approached her in a jealous rage and cornered her in the dining room. He was emphatic that she should not go to Bridport with her husband. He threatened to kill her if she did. He claimed to have seen her making love to her husband that very afternoon in her bedroom.

Alma denied his claim, and tried to soothe all his fears about Bridport. She thought she had succeeded in calming her lover, but he left the house not long afterwards. The timing implied that it was about then that Stoner went off to fetch the mallet.

That night, having said goodnight to her husband and had her chat with Irene, Alma retired to her bedroom. Stoner joined her soon afterwards in his pyjamas, looking 'a little queer'. She asked what the matter was, and after much prompting he explained. 'He told me that I was not going to Bridport the next day as he had hurt Ratz. It did not penetrate my head what he did say to me at all until I heard Ratz groan, and then my brain became alive and I jumped out of bed . . .'

Downstairs with Irene she tried to revive her wounded husband. She also started drinking whisky 'to block out the picture'. The last thing she remembered was putting a white towel round her husband's head, and the episode with the false teeth. She had trodden on them with her bare feet. They had made her hysterical.

All that followed was a blank to her. The records, the dancing, the babbling, the bribe and the flirting with policemen – all were erased from her mind. She only 'came to' about midday the following morning.

Mrs Rattenbury's statements coincided closely with Irene's. In truth, there was precious little evidence against her apart from her own hysterical and contradictory confessions. Her temporary amnesia was curious, true. But it was not hard to see how the shock of the discovery, the whisky and the morphia might have combined to 'blank her mind'.

As the trial progressed, things pointed more and more to the guilt of the jealous young chauffeur. In fact, his defence counsel was reduced to trying to limit the damage by elaborating on his cocaine addiction. This, it was implied (but never stated) might account for an unreasoned attack for which a verdict of manslaughter might be appropriate. Unfortunately for the youth who stood silent in the dock, serious doubts were raised as to whether he even knew what cocaine looked like. Interviewed by a medical officer at Brixton, Stoner had been asked to describe the drug's appearance. He replied that it was brown with black flecks in it. Cocaine, of course, is a white powder.

The jury took little more than an hour to consider their verdict. They found Alma Victoria Rattenbury not guilty; and they found George Percy Stoner guilty.

Mrs Rattenbury faltered forward, calling weakly 'Oh . . . oh, no,' and was ushered hurriedly from the dock. Stoner was left standing manfully before the judge, a lone figure bravely containing his emotion. The black cloth was brought out. Asked if he had anything to say before sentence was passed, Stoner answered 'Nothing at all, sir'. They were the only words he spoke during the trial.

Often, the acquittal of a woman on a hanging offence has been greeted with cheers by the crowd. But they booed Mrs Rattenbury as she was hurried away in a taxi. Cruel words had been spoken about her in court; the judge himself had severely censured her conduct. Freedom would be no easy burden to bear. Above all, there was her young lover, waiting in the death cell – how could she endure the day when the trap door would be sprung?

On Tuesday 4 June, three days after her acquittal, Alma

Rattenbury took a train on the London–Bournemouth line. But she did not reach the Villa Madeira. Instead, she alighted at Christchurch and wandered the backwaters of the River Avon. By a railway bridge (from which Stoner had once felt the impulse to hurl himself to his death), Mrs Rattenbury sat down in the grass and pencilled a few notes on the backs of envelopes taken from her handbag. 'One must be bold to do a thing like this. It is beautiful here, and I am alone. Thank God for peace at last . . .'

A farmworker nearby saw her walk into the lily-strewn water, a blade glinting in her hand. She gazed fixedly as she walked. He rushed towards her, but when he got there it was too late.

At the post mortem it was found that she had plunged the knife no fewer than six times into her chest. Three wounds had pierced her heart, one of them so severe that she must have worked the blade backwards and forwards before she withdrew it. Alma Rattenbury was dead before the water claimed her and carried her drifting from the bank.

George Stoner, at the death cell in Pentonville, collapsed sobbing when he heard the news. A petition for his reprieve was already being gathered, to which thousands put their names. And four days after Alma's death, his lawyers lodged a formal appeal.

For the first time, Stoner submitted his own version of the events. He was entirely innocent of any part in the murder, he said. He had fetched the mallet for perfectly ordinary reasons and left it in the coal shed. When he made his way into Mrs Rattenbury's room that night, she appeared terrified. When a groan was heard from the drawing room, she leapt out of bed and rushed downstairs . . .

This was a remarkable twist to the tale. Was Mrs Rattenbury guilty after all? In the event, the judges decided that there was no case for an appeal, nor would they accept Stoner's new statement. It appeared no more than a cynical strategy to start making claims now that he would not make while his mistress was alive.

Stoner did not, however, hang. On the day after the appeal was turned down the Home Secretary granted a reprieve, and his death sentence was commuted to penal servitude for life.

Does an element of mystery still longer about the affair? If Stoner was guilty, what was it about the trip to Bridport that provoked his murderous wrath? An exhaustive study of the case (*Tragedy in Three Voices*, 1980) points to a piece of information which only came to light over forty years after the events. A friend of Alma's stated in a 1978 interview that she had asked Mrs Rattenbury in Holloway what had made Stoner so unusually angry. Alma replied that the chauffeur had overheard her conversation with her husband about the proposed business trip. 'Ratz', it appeared, had suggested to her that she used her charm on the Bridport man so that financial arrangements for the flats would go through smoothly. She might even have an affair with him if necessary.

This, by implication, was too much for the jealous lover. He could tolerate Alma's affectionate companionship with her elderly husband. But to countenance his beloved being used in this way was quite impossible.

It is a theory which fits the known facts. Stoner has commonly been represented in crime writing rather as Mrs Rattenbury's counsel portrayed him – as a youth whose love turned him into a 'Frankenstein's monster' with passions his mistress could not control. But that view misses the essential decency of the boy which everyone noted at the time. It was his decency which was outraged by the Bridport proposal, as much as his jealousy was aroused.

George Percy Stoner served only seven years in penal servitude. Released with good conduct during World War Two, he took part in the D-Day landings and after the war settled down to a respectable married life. Alma was buried at a Bournemouth cemetery in June 1935. Her shroud, wreaths and draperies were pink, her favourite colour; she always had a horror of white.

The Kenya Scandal

It was January 1941. The Blitz had been raging over London for some six months, and in the sands of North Africa the see-saw struggle for Italy's desert colonies had begun. Kenya was then a British territory, and a mustering point for Allied forces planning the push on Mussolini's Ethiopia. At Nairobi, the Military Secretary was Josslyn Hay, Earl of Erroll and hereditary High Constable of Scotland.

During his brief career as an administrator, the 39-year-old Hay proved brilliant at his job. And his achievements came as something of a surprise to the settler community. For the Earl was chiefly notorious as a member of the Happy Valley Set, a permissive and pleasure-seeking section of the local white aristocracy.

Its centre was the Wanjohi river, cutting a declivity among the beautiful White Highlands of Kenya. One bastion of luxury was the exclusive Muthaiga Country Club, laid out with ballroom, golf course, squash courts and croquet lawns like something plucked from the land scape of the Home Counties. Cocaine circulated among the elite, and alcohol was consumed in great quantities: pink gins, sundowners, champagne and whisky among the favourite tipples. By night, a mood of drunken licentiousness prevailed, and the denizens played roaring hooligan games.

Another centre of the Set was a large mansion called Clouds, the home of Lady Idina Gordon. The weekend house parties held there were notorious for their shameless excesses. Wives and partners were regularly swapped in the guest bedrooms. Josslyn Hay had flourished in this setting. He had been Lady Idina's third husband, and a predator in the jungle of luxury.

Dismissed from Eton and named as a 'very bad blackguard' by the judge in an English divorce court, Hay was a specialist in seduction. For quarry he preferred the wives and girlfriends of his aristocratic companions; his motto was 'to hell with husbands'. And when, in the early hours of 24 January 1941, he was found shot through the head on the floor of his Buick, no one dwelled long on the possibility of a political murder. Predictably, the prime suspect was a husband: specifically, 57-year-old Sir Henry 'Jock' Delves Broughton.

The trial caused a sensation at the time. It was the scandal of Africa and followed with relish throughout the English-speaking world. The case came, no doubt, as a relief for a public weary with stories of bombings and evacuations. But it also provoked intense outrage, exposing an extravagant and dissolute way of life lived outside the cauldron of the war. The case continued to fascinate long after the fighting was over, and the question 'Who Killed Lord Erroll?' provided one of the world's classic unsolved mysteries.

Sir Henry Delves Broughton was a devotee of horse-racing and a member of a great English land-owning family. In November 1940, he had married the glamorous Diana Caldwell, a blue-eyed ash-blonde who was young enough to be his daughter. Sir Henry was recently divorced from his first wife, and acknowledged the difficulties his new marriage might face by entering an extraordinary contract with Diana. Six weeks before the wedding, he agreed with her that if she fell for a younger man and wanted a divorce he would not stand in her way. Moreover, he agreed to provide her with £5,000 annually for at least seven years after a divorce.

The couple never shared a bedroom. And the contract

implied no confidence in the durability of their relationship. But even Sir Henry cannot have anticipated how quickly his marriage was to come into jeopardy.

A week after the wedding, the Broughtons emigrated to Kenya. And on 30 November, at the Muthaiga Club, Diana met Lord Erroll for the first time. They fell for each other immediately. Diana later recalled that on the very first moment they found each other alone, Erroll said: 'Well, who's going to tell Jock? You or I?'

Erroll himself was free at the time: his first marriage to Idina Gordon had ended in divorce; his second wife, also a Countess, had died of drink and drugs in 1939. And he wasted no time in establishing his new liaison; but no one told 'Jock' – not yet.

Soon, Broughton, Diana and Erroll were dining regularly together at the Club. The two men got on well together, for Broughton, like Erroll, was an Old Etonian. At his trial, the injured husband was to call his wife's lover 'one of the most amusing men I have ever met'. Broughton added that, 'if you can make a great friend in two months, then Joss Erroll I should describe as a great friend'.

It was not long before the passion shared by Diana and Erroll became conspicuous. At a party at the Club on 22 December, they could be seen dancing together locked in embrace. In the first week in January they shared a weekend along together at the house of a discreet friend. And if Broughton had not guessed by now what was going on, there were alert eyes and ears all around. On Monday 6 January he found an anonymous note in the pigeon-hole at the Club. It read:

You seemed like a cat on hot bricks at the club last night. What about the eternal triangle? What are you going to do about it?

What was he going to do about it? Broughton made light of the note with Diana, but the problem would not go away. At a party the following week, Broughton sat watching his wife dance with her lover. Lady Delamere, a mutual friend, said, 'Do you know that Joss is wildly in love with Diana?' By his own admission, Broughton became rather distrait: 'It confirmed my worst suspicions.' He did not try to break up the liaison, but he did talk over the situation subsequently with Diana: 'I think you are going out rather too much with Joss.'

This meek reprimand was ignored; the affair continued and Broughton took to drinking more heavily than usual. Seeking advice from a friend, he was told that he should ask Erroll if he was really in love with Diana. 'If he says no, tell him to buzz off. If they are in love with each other, cut your losses. Pack your boxes and get off back to England.'

The pressure was mounting. Not long after his conversation, Broughton received a second anonymous note:

Do you know that your wife and Lord Erroll have been staying alone at the Carberrys' house at Nyeri together?

On that same afternoon, 18 January, Diana broke the ice and said she was in love with Erroll. The Broughtons had been married barely two months.

Broughton tried to stall. He had been planning a three-month trip to Ceylon and suggested that she should come with him to see how her feelings were affected. He also saw Erroll, proposing that Diana should accompany him on the Ceylon trip, and that Erroll might leave Kenya for a while.

Erroll, of course, was an old hand at dealing with injured husbands. He said he could not possibly go away – after all, 'there was a *war* on'.

The situation had reached an impasse. That night, Broughton went home alone while Diana and Erroll dined out with friends at the Muthaiga Club. She came back wearing a new set of pearls – a gift to her from her lover.

The following sequence of events had immense importance in the coming trial. The next day, Diana declared that she could not remain in her husband's house under the circumstances, and went off with a friend to stay at Erroll's. On 21 January, while she was away, Broughton reported a burglary to the police. He said that two revolvers, a cigarette case and a small sum of money had been stolen from his living room.

Also on the 21st, Broughton and Erroll both saw their lawyers about a divorce. On the surface at least, Sir Henry appeared ready to capitulate, for he wrote to a friend, 'They say they are in love with each other and mean to get married. It is a hopeless position and I'm going to cut my losses. I think I'll go to Ceylon. There's nothing for me to live in Kenya for.' He also received a third anonymous note:

There's no fool like an old fool. What are you going to do about it?

The 23 January was a fateful day for all of the parties concerned. The three principals in the drama lunched with a fourth friend, Mrs Carberry, at the Muthaiga Club. Erroll told a colleague, 'Jock could not have been nicer. He has agreed to go away. As a matter of fact, he has been so nice it smells bad.'

There was a celebration dinner at the Club that night. And there, Broughton astonished everyone by proposing a toast to the lovers: 'I wish them every happiness,' he said, 'and may their union be blessed with an heir. To Diana and Joss.'

Erroll took Diana dancing that night, having agreed to bring her back by 03.00. Broughton was driven home at about 02.00, apparently tired and somewhat drunk. June Carberry helped him upstairs, and they said goodnight before she retired to her room.

Erroll's Buick turned up some 15 minutes later. There was laughter in the hall, the car door was heard slamming, and Diana came upstairs.

Around 03.00 that morning, two African labourers saw

the Buick off the main Nairobi-Ngong road. It had travelled only 2½ miles from the Broughtons' home, and though its lights were blazing the vehicle had plunged steeply into a pit off the wrong side of the road, 150 yards ahead of an intersection. Crouching under the dashboard was the body of Lord Erroll. His hands were clasped in front of his head. When police examined the corpse, it was found that he had been shot through the head at point-blank range with a .32 calibre revolver.

Much about the circumstances was perplexing. For example, the car had armslings which, it was known, had been in place on the day before the murder. These had been removed – wrenched off or unscrewed – and lay on the floor of the car. The position of the fatal wound suggested that Erroll had been shot either by someone sitting on the seat beside him, or through the open window from the running board. Had the murderer flagged Erroll down on the road, or been in the car with him all the time? And how did the body of a full-grown man get to be crowded down into the footwell? Had it slipped there as the car lurched – or been crammed under the wheel on purpose?

Precisely *how* the murder was accomplished remains a complete mystery to this day. But it did not take the police long to establish a prime suspect. Enquiries quickly revealed that Sir Henry had both the motive and the opportunity. The fact of murder was hushed up for 24 hours, and the Broughtons were first led to believe that Erroll had broken his neck in a motor accident. When the police arrived to take statements that morning, Diana was hysterical and not pressed for questioning. Broughton's immediate reaction was to ask 'Is he all right? Is he all right?'

Before noon, Broughton drove into Nairobi. He said that Diana wanted a handkerchief placed on the dead man's body: 'My wife was very much in love with Lord Erroll,' he explained. He seemed very nervous as he made the request, and was not permitted to enter the mortuary.

A policeman, however, took the handkerchief and performed the office.

Returning home just after midday, Broughton immediately made a big bonfire in the rubbish pit in the grounds.
He ordered his head boy to bring petrol for the blaze; it
was a curious act under the circumstances. Broughton
explained it at the trial by saying that he just liked making
bonfires, and always had, ever since childhood. The
charred remains of a golf stocking were all that were
retrieved from the site. That stocking, however, was bloodstained – with the blood of his victim? The police began to
assemble their case.

Erroll's funeral was held on 25 January. Broughton
arrived late, and dropped a letter from his wife onto the
coffin of the Earl. Ever watchful, the police had the scrap
of paper exhumed. It turned out to be a simple love-note.
On one side, Diana had written 'I love you desperately',
and on the back Erroll had replied, 'and I love you forever'.

When the fact of murder was publicly announced,
Diana loudly accused her husband of the crime.
Broughton made no reply. But on 10 March, when her
husband was arrested, her mood softened. It was Diana
who went to Johannesburg to hire the most brilliant
advocate in Africa. His name was H.H. Morris, K.C., and
he specialised in winning difficult murder cases.

The prosecution had its motive. And it had much more
besides. There was the business of the burglary, for
example. One of the guns 'stolen' on that occasion had
been a .32 calibre weapon. Broughton had done some
target practice with it when he first arrived in Kenya. And,
searching the informal practice ground, the police found
four .32 calibre bullets which, it was alleged, exactly
matched two discovered at the scene of the crime. The
murder weapon, in other words, was Broughton's own
gun – and the 'burglary' had been a pure invention.

To confirm its thesis, the prosecution went on to point

out that all six bullets had been fired with an old-fashioned 'black powder' propellant. This had been unobtainable in Kenya for more than 25 years. A ballistics expert testified that the chances of two people using black powder bullets were remote in the extreme.

Could the elderly Broughton have made it to and from the murder point in the time available to him? According to Mrs Carberry, he knocked on the door of her room at about 03.30 to ask 'if she needed anything'. This, according to the prosecution, was 'a most peculiar thing to do'. But it made sense as an attempt to establish an alibi. Imagine the scenario: Broughton slips out of the house when the couple return. Then he furtively enters the car – or runs to the road junction – and murders his rival out of earshot. Hastening back to his home, he knocks on Mrs Carberry's door solely to give the impression that he never left the house.

There was the mysterious bonfire, and the bloodstained golf stocking – all suggesting a carefully premeditated plot and a subsequent cover-up. Presumably, the planning began with the fake theft of the revolvers and included the magnanimous champagne toast at the Club. Of course, it implied a considerable deviousness on the part of the murderer. But this was an era when Agatha Christie was all the rage: the case against Sir Henry looked formidable.

Yet from the outset of the trial, the defence counsel, Harry Morris, had made it known that he had something up his sleeve. It was something simple, he said, 'so simple that I almost mistrust it'. But he would not divulge what that secret was – not even to the defendant.

The bombshell burst during cross-examination on the ballistics evidence. The experts had testified that all six bullets came from the same .32 calibre revolver, with five grooves and a right-hand twist. Morris asked innocently whether these were features of Colt revolvers. No, came the reply, all Colts had six grooves and a twist to the left. So the murder bullets could not have been fired from a

Colt? The expert agreed that they could not.

Now Morris played his trump. He let it be known that Broughton's two stolen revolvers were registered as Colts – the firearms certificates confirmed it. Erroll, then, could not have been shot with one of the stolen guns!

For a *coup de grâce*, Morris pointed out that the murder weapon had not been recovered. And its barrel was needed to positively identify the practice bullets Broughton had fired with the two found at the scene of the crime. He pressed the ballistics expert: 'The claim that all six bullets were fired from the same weapon cannot be proved. Is that not so, Mr Harwich?'

'It is.'

Suddenly, the prosecution's case against Sir Henry began to look terribly shaky. The 'black powder' issue became practically irrelevant. And with nothing to connect Broughton in any way with the murder weapon, what did remain as hard evidence against him? The motive? Yet even before his marriage Sir Henry had indicated by the contract that he was the least possessive of husbands. He made a dignified and impressive figure in the witness box: a little forgetful it is true on some points of detail (he did not recall knocking on Mrs Carberry's door, for example). But he was quite candid about being cuckolded. Once, for example, he had invited Erroll to stay the night in full knowledge of his wife's adultery: 'She could ask whom she liked. I should not have tried to stop her in any event. I see no point in it. We met every day at the club and I cannot see it makes any difference if a man comes to stay the night. It would be extremely bad strategy. In my experience of life, if you try and stop a woman doing anything she wants to do it all the more. With a young wife the only thing to do is keep her amused.'

As to the famous toast to Diana and Joss, was that sincere on his part? 'Certainly it was. The whole party was very happy and everybody on top form. I was resigned to losing my wife and I cut my loss.'

Broughton was masterful during this three days of cross-examination. He came across as a bluff old racing man who had known when he was beaten. Could the deviousness implied by the prosecution really be imputed to him? Harry Morris did not think so, for he returned to Johannesburg without even bothering to wait for the verdict. When it came, on 1 July 1941, Broughton was found not guilty, and he walked from the court a free man.

Did he really do it? And if not, who did? Rumour was rife in Kenya's white community. There were other injured husbands to consider; there was talk of hired native assassins. Then there were the women of the Happy Valley Set: those who plumped for a female killer tended to opt for the chic, exquisite and faintly mad Alice de Janzé, a one-time lover of Erroll's. She was no stranger to firearms – she had once shot herself and an earlier lover on the platform of the Paris Gare du Nord; both had survived and she was acquitted of attempted murder on the grounds of *crime passionnel*. In Kenya at the time of the Erroll murder, Alice visited the Earl in the mortuary where she placed the branch of a tree on his body. According to a friend, she also kissed his body saying 'Now you're mine forever'. Later that year she committed suicide in a flower-filled room asking (in true Happy Valley style) that a cocktail party be held over her grave.

In truth, however, she was just one among Kenya's élite whose name was linked with the affair. There were so many loose ends: who, for example, had written the anonymous letters to Broughton?

The Happy Valley Set never survived the scandal, and Broughton never recovered from the stigma of the trial. He did take Diana on the long-projected trip to Ceylon, but there suffered a back injury which partially paralysed him. On 5 December 1942, he died in Liverpool having taken massive overdoses of Medinal. He left two suicide notes referring to the strain of the trial and the pain of his recent injury. He did not, in the text, declare himself guilty of murder, however.

Forty years after the events described, the case continued to fascinate and torment. Through painstaking research and interviews with survivors, reporter James Fox produced a brilliant study of the Erroll affair (*White Mischief*, Jonathan Cape, 1982). The book arrives at a firmly implied conclusion about the murderer's identity. It would be invidious to betray the last pages of this account of a real-life Whodunnit. But it is fair to comment that Sir Henry Delves Broughton's background included some shady episodes. Suspicions of devious insurance fraud and blackmail attach to the memory of the reasonable old cove who walked free from the Kenya courtroom.

Saved by a Judge's Blunder

It probably qualifies as the World's Easiest Murder Mystery. Everyone knew who killed Rose Pender in the early hours of 21 August 1911. The suspect's name, his motive and his murder weapon were clearly established at the trial. But because of a judicial blunder, the murderer walked free from the Court of Criminal Appeal. Officially, the case remains open.

It was a seedy affair, people with wretched and depraved characters from the London underworld. Thieves, pimps and prostitutes filed into the witness box to give evidence at the Old Bailey. At the outset, no one could have imagined that the case would become an historic one, marking a watershed in British legal history.

Charles Ellsome, who described himself as a labourer, was brought to the dock in September 1911, for the murder of Rose Pender, his mistress. She was a prostitute, 19 years of age, and Ellsome had lived on her immoral earnings.

And when she eventually left him for an Italian boy, Ellsome publicly threatened vengeance.

A few days before the fateful night, Ellsome borrowed a shilling from a friend and with it bought a long-bladed chef's knife. He told the same friend, 'I am going to do that Italian in for taking Rosie away'. In the small hours of the 21st, a man on his way to work in Clerkenwell heard a girl's voice crying, 'Don't, Charles! Don't!' Later, a milk-man found Rose's dead body in the street, bloodstained with multiple stab wounds.

Police enquiries quickly revealed Ellsome to be the prime suspect. Prostitute friends of the victim confirmed that for some time her ex-lover had been threatening to do Rosie in. To one witness he had even confided, 'A fortune-teller told me the gallows were in my cards, and that she was the girl I should swing for'.

On the 22nd Ellsome was tracked down and arrested. He gave his name as 'Brown' to police, but he said, 'It's me you want'. And a thief named Fletcher supplied damning evidence by describing how, shortly after the body was found, Ellsome had come to his house in a breathless condition and confessed the murder to him.

The case came to trial at Court No. 1 at the Old Bailey. The curious procession of miscreants was brought into the box to give evidence. And Mr Justice Avory, a usually meticulous judge, presided over all. In fairness to him it should be said that he had endured a very heavy week. The court agenda was crowded, and only that morning he had summed up at the end of a wife-murderer's trial. The Ellsome case came up after lunch – it lasted only for one extended afternoon session.

Formidable evidence was heard against the accused, the chief prosecution witness being the thief, Jack Fletcher. He lived with two ladies of the streets, and testified that when Ellsome arrived at his house on the murder night, he announced, 'I have killed her stone dead'.

Fletcher asked who he had killed, and Ellsome replied, 'Rosie, my missus. I killed her stone dead, Jack. She drove me to it.'

Ellsome had then produced the knife and showed it to his friend. He said he had met the girl by chance in the street and explained exactly how things happened: 'I asked her to come back to me, but she said she liked her Italian boy best. Then I lost my temper, pulled out the knife, showed it to her and said, "I'll kill you first". She said, "Here you are then; I don't care" – and bared her breasts. I plunged the knife in. She cried, "Don't, Charlie, don't," and I knew I had done the damage, so I stabbed her eight or nine times afterwards.'

Fletcher's two women had been in the house at the time, and they corroborated his account. When interviewed by the police, Fletcher himself had made further statements, filling in additional details but in no way departing from his original story.

For the defence, it was a hopeless case. The accused had no alibi, and the best that the defence counsel could do was to try and cast aspersions on the character of the various witnesses. Fletcher, in particular, came in for a grilling, and emerged as a rather flash character. It was learned that he carried a police whistle in his pocket (it came in handy when danger threatened in some of his low-life locales). And it was clear that he knew the court-room ropes. At one point the defence counsel asked:

'You are very nicely dressed; where did you get the clothes from?'

'Singing outside theatres.'

'May I suggest that it was by thieving?'

'This is a case of murder, and not felony, and I refuse to answer.'

'I must ask you, however?'

'Well, then, I thieve for my living and am proud of it.'

The judge began his summing up in the most impeccable

way. He started by explaining that if the character of a witness was questionable, then corroboration was of vital importance. Then he made his blunder. He suggested that there was no discrepancy between the thief's first statement to police and his evidence in the witness box.

This was perfectly true. But the first statement (which had been produced at the police court trial) had never been put in evidence at the Old Bailey. Technically, it was quite improper to direct the jury that Fletcher's evidence was corroborated by his first statement. The jury had not seen the document in question.

Did the jury even notice the slip? It took them less than an hour to bring in their verdict of guilty. Asked if the prisoner had anything to say, Ellsome replied: 'No, sir. I have only one Judge.'

Mr Justice Avory brought out the black cap, and Ellsome was sentenced to death. But he never went to the gallows. His defence counsel, A. S. Carr, was quick to pounce on the judge's error. It had come like a gift from the gods, and while his client awaited the end in the condemned cell, Carr took the case to the Court of Criminal Appeal.

This was a newly founded institution, set up in 1907 after considerable public pressure. Behind it lay a humane concern for victims of miscarried justice. The court might allow an appeal if it considered that the verdict of a jury was unreasonable, or could not be supported by the evidence – or that the judgement should be set aside on a point of law.

Until the Ellsome affair, no appeal in a murder case had succeeded. But on the issue in hand, Mr Justice Darling ruled that there was really no option. Indisputably, the Old Bailey judge had misdirected the jury by introducing a statement which was not in evidence. Darling regretted that the Court had no power to order a new trial. He declared that the Court could not express any view as to whether Ellsome was guilty or not. But he quashed the conviction – and Ellsome walked out of the Appeal Court a free man.

There was a tremendous irony in the ruling. The Court had been established to protect the innocent; a guilty man was acquitted on the first successful appeal. In the event, the Court survived as a valued institution – but it was 20 years before another convicted murderer was to make a successful appeal.

Death in the House of Cards

There are 52 cards in a deck. And when the famous bridge and whist expert Joseph Elwell was found murdered at his New York home, the police quickly came up with a list of suspects. Elwell had so many mistresses that he had to keep records of their names and addresses. In his desk was found a card index containing a host of entries, with pet names and telephone numbers. In all, 53 women were recorded. You could call it a full deck of suspects – and perhaps the extra card was the maverick Joker that brought his outstanding career to an end.

Joseph B. Elwell had started his working life as a Brooklyn hardware salesman. But from adolescence onwards, he had excelled at card-playing. Bridge and whist were his favoured games, and in his early twenties he was already winning big stakes at the fashionable New York gambling clubs. It was not long before he gave up selling hardware to teach bridge to wealthy socialites. And he also wrote two authoritative books about the game. *Elwell on Bridge* and *Elwell's Advanced Bridge* were classics in their day.

He married in 1904, and had a son the following year. With his winnings, his royalties and tutoring fees he was soon able to set up home in Manhattan. By 1916, when

Elwell separated from his wife, he was already a wealthy man. For his estranged spouse he set aside $2,400 a year, as well as paying all his son's expenses. The sums involved were trifling. From his book sales alone, Elwell was said to be receiving some $10,000 per annum, and this was a fraction of his total income.

Bridge is more of a science than a game – it is no diversion for reckless gamblers. Elwell invested his earnings wisely. Apart from following up financial tips offered by his wealthy pupils, he diversified into horse-racing. Not by betting, of course: Elwell set up the Beach Racing Stable, supplied from a Kentucky stud farm where he owned some two score thoroughbreds. His partner in the enterprise was William H. Pendleton, a prominent man of the turf.

By 1920, the year of his murder, Elwell had a yacht, an art collection and three separate cottage retreats. In New York, he lived in a three-storey house in West Seventieth Street. Apart from his own bachelor suite, there was a special guest boudoir for female visitors. This was luxuriously furnished, and the ladies came in exotic succession: wealthy wives, fashionable divorcees, glamorous show girls, titled women and many others. His appetite is attested by his card index file – and by other material found in the house. The police discovered dozens of love letters, photographs, and even a kind of pension list recording sums paid monthly to discarded mistresses.

On the evening of 10 June 1920, Elwell went to dine at the Ritz-Carlton Club. His female escort on that occasion was Viola Kraus, a woman divorced that very day. Her sister, Mrs Lewisohn, was present with her husband Walter Lewisohn, a businessman connected with the show world.

By a curious coincidence, the foursome ran into Viola's ex-husband at the Club. His name was Victor von Schlegell, and he was dining with a young lady singer.

There seems to have been no rancour between the recently divorced couple, and all laughed heartily over the encounter. They were to laugh again later that night. For Elwell's party went on to the New Amsterdam Theatre where *Midnight Frolics* was playing. Who should be sitting at an almost adjacent table but von Schlegell and his young singer? Victor quipped at the time, 'I can't keep away from Vi even if the judge said today that we needn't be together again.'

The evening's entertainment ended at 02.00. The Lewisohns offered Elwell a lift home in their taxi, but the card-player claimed it was too crowded. He had also had a slight tiff with Viola, which may account for the refusal. Instead, he stopped a cab for himself and was driven home alone. The driver was to testify that, having received a tip from him, he saw Elwell enter the door of his house at 02.30.

Elwell employed three people as domestic staff: a valet, a chauffeur and a housekeeper. But none of them lived on the premises. To find out what happened behind the locked doors that night, the police were to consult telephone company records.

Shortly after his arrival, Viola phoned him, perhaps to patch up the quarrel. As a card-player, Elwell was something of a night-hawk and does not seem to have slept much afterwards. At 04.39 he rang his racing colleague, Pendleton, but received no reply and put the phone down after five minutes. At 06.09, Elwell telephoned a Long Island number. Whom he called is still not known to this day.

Dawn light broke over New York and the milkman deposited his bottles at the house. At 07.10 the postman delivered the mail. Elwell was still alive at that time. For when the housekeeper arrived at 08.10, she found her employer sitting in his pyjamas in a living-room armchair. The morning mail was on the floor before him, an open letter was in his lap. And exactly between his eyes was the hole left by a .45 calibre bullet.

Blood from the wound stained carpet and pyjamas, spattering the wall behind the chair. Elwell was still breathing, though unconscious – he died in hospital some two hours later.

The case was perfectly baffling. The two side-doors into the house were firmly locked, and the housekeeper had found the front door locked too. All the windows were fastened from the inside, except Elwell's own inaccessible window on the third floor. Murder by an intruding burglar appeared to be deeply improbable. There was no sign of a break-in, no sign of a struggle. Assorted items of jewellery as well as $400 in notes lay untouched about the house. Besides, what self-respecting burglar would still be on the premises so late into the morning?

The front door lock had recently been changed. Only Elwell and the housekeeper, Mrs Larsen, possessed keys. Everything pointed to the conclusion that the victim himself had admitted someone into the house. And the circumstantial detail suggested that, if the murderer was a woman, he must have known her very intimately.

The bridge expert was a vain man. Aged 45, he customarily wore a plate of false teeth to fill the gaps in his smile. He was balding, too, and wore a toupé (he had 40 of them in all). When Elwell was found barefoot and dying in his pyjamas, he was wearing neither wig nor denture. Those accessories were found neatly placed on the dresser. It was unlikely he would have invited a lady in, unless on sufficiently intimate terms to have seen him like that before.

Elwell was shot between 07.10 (when the post arrived) and 08.10 (when the housekeeper found him dying). Medical experts further determined that he had been hit at least 45 minutes before Mrs Larsen arrived. That meant that the shot had been fired between 07.10 and 07.25. But of course, it was possible that the killer had been with

Elwell in the house for hours beforehand – especially if the murderer was a bedroom companion.

Had he entertained a woman that night? It seemed unlikely, for his own bed appeared to have been only lightly laid upon. The cover was turned back and the pillow slightly dented, as if he had relaxed there on the sultry June night. The pillow beside his was undented; and in the guest boudoir, the bed was perfectly made. A pink silk kimono was, however, found hanging in the wardrobe. Given the number of his mistresses, the possibility of a female killer could not be entirely discounted.

Of course, the bewildering variety of his bedmates all had their attendant lovers, husbands or relations. Ballistic evidence did tend to suggest a male murderer. Elwell had been shot with a heavy .45 calibre army automatic pistol; hardly an obvious choice of weapon for a woman. The U.S. service cartridge was found, and the shot was a clean one fired from some 3–4 feet. Close range, certainly – but not point blank. The gun, moreover, seemed to have been fired from the hip, or from a crouching position. The bullet had followed an upward trajectory, entering the forehead, exiting an inch higher at the back and going on upwards to smash against the wall. By a macabre chance it had then ricocheted back to land quite neatly on the side table right by the victim's elbow.

The murderer had disturbed nothing, left no fingerprint. The only remaining clue was one cigarette stub (of a brand other than Elwell used) found on the living-room mantle-piece.

Hazily, the picture suggested a brief visit, probably made after the mail arrived. Elwell admitted the murderer and was so unconcerned in his or her presence that he went on rifling through his letters. He had permitted the gun to be drawn and the murderer to approach within little more than a yard before firing.

It might, of course, have been a business associate. But

Elwell had no special rivals: his racing-stable partner was among those questioned and he was fully exonerated. For the police, however, the bridge expert's love life opened up a Pandora's Box of possibilities. All 53 women named in the card index were investigated and closely questioned, along with others, men and women, discovered through the letters. Husbands, lovers and relations were also explored – everyone appeared to have an alibi. One by one the suspects were ticked off – the valet, the chauffeur, the housekeeper's husband, a Polish countess, an Egyptian princess . . . the list of possibilities appeared endless.

Names that featured repeatedly in the press stories included three prominent suspects:

Mrs Elwell The estranged wife had learned some time before the murder that her husband had struck her out of his will. But she had a cast-iron alibi. Moreover, she stood to lose by Elwell's death, for her son's expenses and the $2,400 a year would be cut off.

Viola Kraus She had been with Elwell on the murder night, they had quarrelled and she had phoned him at his home. It was also established that she was the owner of the pink silk kimono in the boudoir. However, the Lewis-ohns testified that she was with them at their home over-night and through the murder period.

Victor von Schlegell Did Viola's husband, so recently divorced, still feel possessive about her? Victor had break-fasted with his young singer on the following morning, but went out early to pick up his car from a garage. He arrived there at 08.00, and might *just* have had time to kill Elwell before arriving at the garage. However, nothing indicates that he had any jealous feelings about Viola (he married his singer in due course).

No solution was ever found. But in the realm of pure speculation it is interesting to consider the enigma of 'Annie'.

One of the letters found in Elwell's desk had been sent

by a 16-year-old Kentucky girl. She signed herself simply 'Annie' and complained to Elwell that she was going to get 'into trouble'. She begged him to 'do the right thing' by her.

Sidney Sutherland, a writer of the 1920s, toyed with the idea that her father, or brother, may have come to New York to persuade Elwell to 'do the right thing', and plugged him between the eyes when he refused. It is as plausible a theory as any: you can imagine Annie's seduction on one of Elwell's trips to the stud farm. You can picture the straight-shootin' Kentucky man with his old service pistol. He arrives by dawn light and puts his proposition fair and square to the rich northern city slicker. Toothless and balding in his expensive pyjamas, Elwell brushes him off and returns petulantly to his armchair and his mail. One shot (it has to be from the hip) sees off the card player. The avenger nonchalantly stubs out his cigarette and goes back to Kentucky, never speaking of the episode again.

Plausible – but pure hypothesis. The fact is that the Elwell murder remains a complete and utter mystery; and every theory is as insubstantial as a house of cards.

'Are You Going to Sleep All Day?'

At 14.30 in the afternoon of Sunday 24 October 1943, the nanny at Patricia Lonergan's apartment knocked at the door of her mistress's bedroom. 'Young woman,' she cried, 'are you going to sleep all day?'

There was no reply. The heiress had returned from a late-night party in the small hours of the morning, and the nanny took the 18-month-old baby out. She did not return with the child until seven in the evening when she tried the door again. It was still locked, and still there was no reply. Disturbed now by the ominous silence, the nanny sent for help. The door could not be broken down – it had to be removed bodily from its frame. And when the helpers finally attained the bedroom they discovered a grim tableau.

The nude body of the 22-year-old heiress was sprawled out across her wide bed, overlooked by its bronzed figures of Winged Victory. Blood had seeped from her head wounds through the sheets and blankets, down through the mattress and on to the floor where it formed a large dark stain. Mrs Patricia Burton Lonergan, heiress to a seven million dollar brewing fortune, would not be awakening that evening or ever again. She was dead: strangled and bludgeoned, police were to establish, by the pair of antique onyx-inlaid brass candlesticks that lay discarded on the floor.

The assailant had evidently fled via a second, automatically sprung door. It did not look like the work of a thief, for there was cash and jewellery in the suite as well as the victim's mink jacket neatly folded at the foot of the bed. But the struggle had been a violent one in which the heiress had scratched her attacker: traces of scraped skin were found under her manicured fingernails. In due course, the police were to establish that the time of death was about 09.00. Patricia Lonergan had been a corpse all day.

In the investigation which followed, police brought in her escort of the night before. He was Mario Gabelline, a 40-year-old Italian man-about-town. He stated that he had brought the heiress back to her apartment at 06.15 in the morning, but had left her in the lobby and returned immediately to his waiting cab. The taxi-driver was traced and confirmed his story. Gabelline was held on bail as a material witness, but he made an unlikely suspect.

More suspicion attached to Wayne Lonergan, 27-year-old former husband of the victim. He had been separated from the heiress only two months before the murder and had gone to live in Canada. Having no private means, he enlisted as a serviceman in the Royal Canadian Air Force. Though he lived in Toronto, it was discovered that Lonergan had been in New York on the weekend of the murder, staying in a friend's apartment.

Some curious facts were discovered about Wayne Lonergan's movements. On the Saturday evening he had gone to his ex-wife's apartment. He found that she was out, but was admitted by staff and played with his child for a while. That night he had taken an attractive blonde on a tour of New York night clubs before leaving her at her home at 03.00. Then (so it seemed) he retired to the friend's apartment where he wakened at about 10.30. He had called loudly for coffee and scrambled eggs, and phoned to make a lunch date with the blonde. When he turned up for the meal, he was not wearing his blue serviceman's uniform as he had done before. Instead, he was wearing a grey suit that ill-fitted his 6 ft 2 in frame. An explanation for his garb was discovered in the friend's apartment, in the form of a hastily written note:

John: Thank you so much for the use of your flat. Due to a slight case of mistaken trust, I lost my uniform and so borrowed a jacket and trousers from you. I shall return these on my arrival in Toronto.

Yours,

Wayne.

PS – I will call and tell you about it.

Another discovery was made at the apartment too: in the drawer of the owner's desk was the plate of scrambled eggs that he had ordered for his Sunday breakfast.

Apprehended in Toronto, Lonergan appeared not to know what fate had befallen his ex-wife. He explained the business of the missing uniform by saying that after taking the blonde home early on the fateful Sunday morning, he had gone for a short stroll and met a US soldier waiting for a bus. They fell into conversation and Lonergan offered to put him up. On waking, he discovered not only his uniform but also some money had gone. The soldier's name, he said was Murray Worcester and he was stationed somewhere on the East Coast. As for the enigmatic scrambled eggs, he had ordered them for the dog that his friend kept in the apartment. When the dog failed to show up, Lonergan hid the eggs not wanting to appear wasteful.

When first approached in Toronto, Lonergan had scratch marks on his chin. He claimed that he had recently cut himself shaving. To detectives who regarded him as the prime suspect, there came baffling confirmation: not only the blonde, but other witnesses too had seen him during the course of the Sunday. They were emphatic in declaring that his chin at the time was unmarked.

Nor had Lonergan appeared in any way to be in an excitable state. In fact, prior to the lunch, he had gone round to his ex-wife's apartment taking with him a 3 ft toy elephant for his son. He arrived some time after eleven, and receiving no answer left the toy with the note: 'For Master Billy Lonergan.'

The case aroused intense interest in the press. Patricia Lonergan, the beautiful socialite, had been immensely rich, living on an annual income of $25,000. Lonergan, in contrast, had lived a chequered life and had been a tie salesman on Madison Avenue when first introduced to the heiress. The couple had eloped to marry in Las Vegas in July 1941, and when Patricia bore a child it seems that she wanted to settle down. Lonergan, though, had enjoyed the life of luxurious irresponsibility. Only two months before the murder, the couple had separated and Mrs Lonergan had cut him out of her will.

While the newspapers speculated about the murder and its motives, Lonergan was persuaded to return to New York where he faced a severe grilling by detectives. At one stage he was confronted with a tall thin man that he said he had never seen before in his life. The man was Mr Maurice Worcester, a former US soldier, traced through searches of army records. The police were to claim that Lonergan had simply plucked the man's name out of thin air in seeking to explain the theft of the missing uniform. It was purely by chance that a real Maurice Worcester existed – and hardly surprising that Lonergan failed to recognize him.

After 84 hours of questioning, Lonergan made a confession which was leaked to the press. He said that he had slipped out of his friend's apartment on the murder morning, and arrived at Patricia's apartment shortly before 09.00. She was in bed and they quarrelled over Lonergan's intention to have lunch with the blonde. In a jealous rage, Patricia shoved him from her, shouting, 'Stay out of here, don't ever come back. You will never see the baby again!'

This, in Lonergan's version, provoked his fatal assault. Afterwards, at his friend's apartment, he rang for breakfast but found that he could not eat and so hid the plate of scrambled eggs, not wanting to arouse suspicion. He packed his bloodstained uniform in a duffel bag and dropped it, weighted with a dumbbell, into the East River.

As for the scratch marks missing from his chin at the lunch date, police found a simple explanation. A powder compact containing Max Factor Suntan No. 2 was discovered in the friend's apartment. It was contended that Lonergan had bought this at a drugstore shortly after fleeing the scene of the crime. Careful application of the heavy cream was all that was needed to camouflage evidence of the fight.

Wayne Lonergan was indicted for first degree murder, and after a mistrial in February 1944, was tried again in March. Effectively, through the leaked confession, the press had found him guilty already. But some irregularities emerged in the courtroom.

Lonergan pleaded not guilty. His defence contended that he had been offered the lower plea of second degree murder if he would confess. In fact, the confession was not signed or authenticated by him. It was never shown that Lonergan had visited the apartment at the time of the murder, nor that he had handled the onyx candlesticks. Above all, he had no motive for deliberately killing his ex-wife. He was not jealous of her Italian escort, nor did he stand to gain financially by her death. The prosecution's case left room for reasonable doubt: a panic-stricken intruder might have been responsible.

In the event, the jury was out for more than nine hours, and returned with a verdict of guilty to murder in the second degree (murder without premeditation). On 17 April 1944, the prisoner was sentenced to 35 years to life imprisonment.

Wayne Lonergan served 22 years in Sing Sing, and was paroled in 1965.

We'll Never Know

The Black Hole of Calcutta

It was an inauspicious beginning to the British occupation of India, but an important one. Perhaps for some deep Freudian reason, the Black Hole of Calcutta is the stuff that myths are made of. It was the myth of the atrocity purportedly committed against innocent English men and women by the Nawab of Bengal in 1756 that allowed Britain to take over Bengal and, eventually, the whole of India.

The Seven Years War had spilled over both into North America and India where both Britain and France had trading concessions. The French held Hyderabad while the British held Calcutta and Madras, ceded by the French under the Treaty of Aix-la-Chapelle in 1748 in return for Cape Breton Island.

However, the old Nawab – or governor – of Bengal died in 1756. He was succeeded by his grandson who was both headstrong and vacillating. When he heard exaggerated reports that the British were fortifying Calcutta, he besieged the city. After four days, on 20 June 1756, it fell.

The foreign settlers were quite unprepared for the attack. Governor Drake and the majority of the English residents fled to the river and escaped on board ships. John Holwell, a council member of the East India Company, and 170 others retreated to the Company's headquarters' Fort William, which had been built in the early part of the century.

Accounts of what happened next are confused. A truce may have been called but, fearing treachery, Holwell opened fire on the Bengalis. The outraged Bengalis then took the fort, with some loss of life. Holwell was captured. The Nawab entered Fort William and ordered that the principal inhabitants be held overnight.

In all, 146 people were held. There were talks and the

Nawab promised the captives his protection and good treatment. However, it seems that a drunken soldier killed one of the Nawab's men. When he found out about it, the Nawab asked where miscreants were usually held. He was told of the fort's guardroom which was known as the Black Hole – a small room just 18 feet by 14 feet, between two arches of the outer wall. It was completely bricked in, except for two small barred windows that opened onto the courtyard. Usually, drunken soldiers were imprisoned in there until they sobered up.

At eight o'clock, when it was already dark, the Nawab ordered that all 146 captives, including one woman named Mary Carey, be jailed there. It is possible that the Nawab was unaware of the size of the jail.

It was a sultry Bengali night and Holwell and his companions were crammed in like sardines. The heat was intense and they took their clothes off – hats were waved around in an attempt to circulate the air. The guards passed them water, which they fought over. There were cries and groans from those at the back who were suffocating; some pleaded with the guards to be shot. Holwell sucked on his sleeve to keep his mouth wet. He later thought of drinking his own urine and considered slashing his wrists with a knife he had in his pocket.

By 11.30, Holwell noted that nearly everyone was delirious. He witnessed the death of the carpenter named Leech and the Reverend Gervase Bellamy who died hand in hand with his son. Holwell eventually collapsed and was pulled out from under a pile of corpses by Henry Lushington, a clerk, and John Cooke, a company secretary. They carried him to the window, where he recovered.

At 6 a.m., the doors were opened and they were let out. The 23 survivors included Holwell, Lushington, Cooke and Mary Carey. A total of 123 were dead. Their bodies were thrown in a ditch outside the east gate and covered with earth. Later, Holwell would erect an obelisk on the spot.

Cooke and Lushington made off to catch up with the English ships that were waiting down the river. Others stayed on but, after another incident involving a drunken soldier, all the British were ordered out on pain of having their noses cut off. Only Holwell and some of the soldiers stayed, held in irons. That, at least, is Holwell's story, which he wrote down in a letter to a friend on board the ship that took him back to England in 1757.

However, when Lushington and Cooke reached the English ships and reported to Governor Drake, they said nothing of what happened in the Black Hole. The soldiers held by the Nawab talked to some Frenchmen, but none of them mentioned the Black Hole either. The source of the story was Holwell's letters home; his story is full of inconsistencies and many doubted its authenticity.

Robert Clive – Clive of India – was in Madras at the time, but on 2 January 1757, he retook Calcutta. Clive defeated the Nawab's army, even though it vastly outnumbered his own, at Plassey in June 1757, then installed his own Nawab. This led to the virtual annexation of Bengal in 1765. In Clive's account of the conquest of Bengal, there is no mention of the Black Hole. He even referred to the Nawab as 'a man of courage and humanity', which was the general view. The Black Hole was certainly not used as an excuse for making war on him.

In 1773, Cooke testified to the Select Committee. Up until this time, he had remained silent on the subject of the Black Hole. To the Committee, he confirmed Holwell's story; but then, he was not an unbiased witness – Cooke and Holwell had been friends long before the fall of Fort William. On one occasion, Cooke had put up bail for Holwell. The spoils of the Battle of Plassey had made Cooke a rich man, and by then, the story of the Black Hole of Calcutta had become the principal justification for British rule in India.

So if official versions of what atrocity took place in the

Black Hole of Calcutta are not true, what did happen? It seems likely that, during the bungled truce, Holwell had ordered that the gate to the Fort be opened before he fired on the Bengalis. This prompted a massacre. A much smaller number of people than the 146 Holwell claimed were held in the Black Hole and some of them may have died there. But as the huge loss of life was plainly Holwell's fault, he exaggerated its significance, contending that many of the men who had died defending the Fort's walls had died in the prison. By the time his story circulated, it was in everyone's interests to go along with it.

Reign of Terror

After the French Revolution, the government of the fledgling republic found itself embroiled in a civil war and under attack externally from Britain, Austria, Spain, Portugal, Prussia, Russia, Sardinia and Naples. In response, on 5 September 1793 – 9 Thermidor, Year I on the Revolutionary calendar – the republic issued a decree making 'terror' the order of the day. The enemies of the Revolution – nobles, churchmen and those suspected of hoarding food and private property – were to be eliminated. There followed a wave of atrocities known as the Reign of Terror.

The first plan was to send the revolutionary army from Paris out into the countryside with a mobile guillotine. Robespierre, who headed the all-powerful Committee of Public Safety, wanted an army of 500,000 men to do the job and so introduced conscription.

On 17 September, the Committee passed the Law of Suspects, allowing them to arrest and execute anyone suspected of harbouring anti-revolutionary views.

'A river of blood will now divide France from its

enemies,' rejoiced Robespierre.

The Revolution was a product of the age of reason and organised religion was seen as the enemy. In line with this argument, the Committee sent agents out across the country to de-christianise the population. Churches and cemeteries were vandalised; the Bishop of Paris was forced to resign and Notre Dame was deconsecrated and renamed the Temple of Reason.

Lyon had rebelled against the Jacobins, but on 9 October, after a bloody bombardment, the revolutionaries retook the city and renamed it Ville Affranchie 'Liberated Town'. The houses of the rich were demolished and 20-30 rebels executed. Suspecting that the locals were being too lenient on their own, a revolutionary zealot named Mathieu Parein was sent to handle the situation. He ordered that those who had an income of 30,000 livres or more must hand it over immediately and that all vestiges of religion should be obliterated. Houses were searched and mass executions began.

The guillotine became overworked. On the eleventh of Nivôse, according to the scrupulous accounts the Jacobins kept, 32 heads were severed in 25 minutes. A week later, 12 heads were severed in just five minutes. This was a messy way to dispose of political enemies; the residents of the Rue Lafont where the guillotine was set up kept complaining about the blood overflowing from the drainage ditch that ran under the scaffold.

As an alternative, mass shootings took place. As many as 60 prisoners were tied together in a line and shot with cannon. Those who were not killed outright were finished of with bayonets, sabres and rifles. The chief butcher, an actor named Dorfeuille, wrote to Paris boasting that he had killed 113 Lyonnais in a single day. Three days later he butchered 209 and promised that another 400-500 would 'expiate their crimes with fire and shot'. This was an underestimate: by the time the killing had stopped, 1,905 were dead – and the victims were not restricted to the rich, the aristocratic and the clergy. The unemployed were also liquidated, along with anyone the Revolutionary Tribunal decided was a *'fanatique'*.

Marseilles – now Ville-Sans-Nom ('Town Without Name') – was similarly purged. After the insurrection in the Vendé, the local agent wrote to the Committee of Public Safety in Paris describing their reprisals.

'There is no more Vendée, citizens,' he said. 'It has just perished under our free sword along with its women and children. I have just buried it in the marshes and mud of Savenay. Following the orders you gave me I have crushed children under the feet of horses and massacred women who at least will give birth to no more brigands. I have no prisoners with which to reproach myself.'

The name Vendée was changed to Vengé – 'Avenged'.

A total of 200 prisoners were executed in Angers in December alone, 2000 at Saint-Florent. At Pont-de-Cé and Avrillé, 3000-4000 were shot in one long, relentless slaughter. At Nantes the guillotine was so overworked that a new method of execution, known as 'vertical deportation', was developed. A flat-bottomed barrage would be holed below the waterline, then a plank nailed over the hole to keep the boat temporarily afloat; prisoners were put on the barge with their hands and feet tied. The barge would be taken out into the middle of the Loire where the executioner would pull out the plank and jump to safety on board a boat alongside. The barge would then go down, taking the prisoners with it. Anyone attempting to escape drowning would be sabred.

At first this form of execution was reserved for clerics and was known as a 'republican baptism'. Later the 'national bath' was more widely used. Prisoners were often stripped of their clothes first. Young men and young women were sometimes tied together naked and given a 'republican marriage'.

The revolutionary army spread out across the country, looking for sedition. They would slaughter men, women and children they suspected of harbouring anti-Jacobin sympathies. Crops were burned, farm animals slaughtered, barns and cottages demolished and woods torched; any town or village that had entertained anti-jacobin troops would be razed. Terrorists planned to put arsenic in wells and enquiries were made of a wellknown chemist about the possibility of developing poison gas.

Next, 12 infernal columns were sent to 'pacify the countryside' by killing everyone in their path. Women were raped, children killed, both mutilated. Entire families were found swimming in their own blood: one impeccable republican lost three of his sons plus his son-in-law on the first visit of the Jacobins. They returned to massacre his remaining son, his wife and their 15-year-old daughter. To save ammunition, General Cordeffier ordered his men to use the sabre instead of a gun.

At Gonnord, General Crouzat forced 200 elderly people, along with mothers and children, to kneel in front of a pit they had dug; they were shot so that they fell into the grave. Some tried to make a break for it, but were struck down by the hammer of a local mason – 30 children and two women were buried alive when earth was shovelled into the pit.

In the Loire Valley, around 250,000 people were killed – a third of the population of the region – and that figure does not include those who lost their lives in the revolution or during the subsequent wars, fighting on the republican side.

In Paris, thanks to the Law of Suspects, the prisons were full to overflowing. The rich were made to pay for their board and lodging – the guillotine was being overworked too. A prostitute was executed for expressing royalist sentiments, trade had dropped off after the Revolution. Following her to the scaffold was the one-time playmate of Mozart, Marie-Antoinette, Queen of France. When one prisoner stabbed himself to death in front of the Revolutionary Tribunal, the court ordered that his corpse be guillotined anyway – revolutionary justice was not to be cheated.

The Revolution then began to consume its own. Anyone who opposed Robespierre was sentenced to 'look through the republican window' – that is, put his head through the frame of the guillotine. When the great hero of the Revolution, Georges Danton, tried to call a halt to the Terror, he too was arrested and sent to be shaved by the national razor. Entire families were guillotined, the older members being forced to watch the younger being executed while awaiting their turn.

Robespierre was a prig. He saw himself as a missionary of virtue and believed he was using the guillotine as an instrument for the moral improvement of the nation. The dechristianisers, whom Robespierre viewed as immoral, paid for his views with their lives. He then instituted the Festival of the Supreme Being, in which he took the leading role. This was not a return to believing in God, he explained: nature was the 'Supreme Being'. However, many people wondered whether Robespierre really thought the Supreme Being was himself.

The new crimes of 'slandering patriotism, 'seeking to inspire discouragement', 'spreading false news', 'depraving morals', 'corrupting the public conscience' and 'impairing the purity and energy of the revolutionary government' were introduced. To speed up the course of justice, those accused were allowed no defence counsel and no witnesses would be called. The jury was made up of good citizens who were more than capable of coming to a fair and unbiased judgement without being distracted by such trifles. There were only two outcomes: acquittal or death. Given that Robespierre himself coined the slogan, 'Clemency is parricide,' this usually meant death.

Executions jumped from five a day in the new revolutionary month of Germinal to 26 in Messidor.

However, things had been going well for the French army and the danger from abroad had eased. Some Republicans began to doubt the need for such Draconian measures. Anyone against this new Revolutionary Justice must have something to hide, Robespierre argued, and promptly investigated them. He was so busy organising the persecution he did not realise that, behind his back, leading Revolutionaries were mocking his cult of the Supreme Being.

On 26 July 1794 (8 Thermidor, Year III), Robespierre made a speech calling for 'more virtue' and his supporters called for his enemies to be sent *'à la guillotine.'* The next day, critics pointed out that Robespierre had departed from protocol: instead of speaking for the collective leadership, he had made a speech in his own name. Robespierre was lost for words at this accusation. In the silence a voice piped up, 'See, the blood of Danton chokes him.'

Quickly, his opponents moved against him. They knew if they did not, they would soon face the guillotine. Robespierre and his supporters were arrested. He could hardly ask for clemency. After a failed suicide attempt which left him bloodied, and his jaw shattered, Robespierre and 17 of his followers were guillotined. A fastidious little man, he went to the scaffold covered in blood. To give the blade an unimpeded fall, the executioner pulled off the paper bandage that was holding his jaw together. He yelped in pain, only to be silence by the falling blade.

During the Reign of Terror, over and above those who were slaughtered in the countryside, at least 300,000 people were arrested; 17,000 were officially executed. Many more died in prison or without trial. No one is able to lay a figure on officially how many died and how many were 'unofficially' executed. The world will never know.

The Death of the Romanovs

The Romanovs had ruled Russia for 400 years. By the end of the nineteenth century, their empire stretched from the borders of Poland to the Sea of Japan. But even that was not enough for Nicholas II. He tried to extend his empire further in the east, aiming to seize China, Tibet and Persia. His ambitions were thwarted by defeat in the Russo-Japanese War of 1904-05.

This weakened him at home and he was forced to give up his autocratic power to become a constitutional monarch answerable, in theory, to a parliament or Duma. However, this did not suit him, so he allied himself with right-wing extremists and, in 1907, dissolved the Duma. His ambitions to extend his Empire into the Balkans led, in some measure, to World War I – though, when it broke out, he did try and stop the confrontation between the great powers. He took control of the war effort while his wife Alexandra handled domestic government. She fell under the influence of the mad monk Rasputin, who became so unpopular he was assassinated. Nicholas's mishandling of the war led to riots in 1917, following which, his government lost control in St Petersburg, then Russia's capital. Politicians from the Duma formed a provisional government. Meanwhile, Bolshevik workers and soldiers began to form themselves into committees known as Soviets.

The generals had lost confidence in Nicholas. When the Duma insisted that he abdicate, they concurred, seeing it as the only way to prevent civil war. On 15 March 1917, Nicholas abdicated in favour of his brother the Grand Duke Michael. The 13-year-old Tsarevich Aleksei was too young to take over and suffered from haemophilia.

However, on 16 March, the Duma decided the formation of the Soviets meant that the continuation of the monarchy in any form was impossible and they persuaded Grand Duke Michael not to assume the throne.

On 21 March, Nicholas was arrested, as were Alexandra and the rest of the family. Although they were allowed to stay in their palace, they were guarded by soldiers, who had suffered because of Nicholas's incompetent leadership at the front.

The provisional government arranged for the Tsar and his family to go into exile in Britain. The British government agreed, but King George V, the Tsar's cousin, stepped in, asking how the Tsar intended to support himself in Britain. The socialist movement was strong in the UK; the war was dragging on and George feared giving sanctuary to the hated Tsar might bring the British monarchy down too.

In August, the provisional government moved the Tsar and his family to Tobolsk, a provincial backwater between the Urals and western Siberia. There they would be safe from the turbulent politics of St Petersburg.

The people in Tobolsk were courteous to the Romanovs, as were most of the troops that guarded them there. They would even play cards with Nicholas and the children. However, in November 1917, the royal family's fate was sealed when the Bolsheviks overthrew the provisional government. In January 1918, they closed the Duma, as they only controlled a quarter of the votes there. Furthermore, in March, they signed a peace treaty with the Germans, ending Russia's involvement in World War I.

With no voice in the Duma, non-communists had no way to oppose Bolshevism. Civil war was therefore inevitable, and it broke out in spring 1918. The Bolsheviks had already shown they were ruthless. Many of them had suffered under Nicholas's repressive regime – it seemed unlikely that he could survive.

Bolshevism was not widespread in Siberia, except for in one place – Yekaterinburg – the capital of the 'Red Urals'. The Soviets there had nationalised the mines even before Moscow had fallen to the Bolsheviks. The Yekaterinburg commissars were determined that the Romanovs would not escape.

The party leadership in Moscow sent for the Tsar, but on his way there he was intercepted by an armed detachment of Bolsheviks from Yekaterinburg, who seized the royal family and took them there. They were greeted by a large crowd shouting insults and the Bolshevik authorities had to threaten the use of force before the crowd would let them through safely. The Romanovs were taken to a house that had been confiscated from a wealthy merchant called Ipatiev, which was now known as the House of Special Purpose. A number of royal aides were taken and shot on suspicion of being involved with counter-revolutionary plots to free the royal family from there.

Instead of being guarded by soldiers, the Romanovs were watched day and night by a special Red Guard recruited from the local factories. The Tsar and his family were not permitted to talk to their guards, who were rude and abusive and pilfered their belongings. Nicholas was denounced as a bloodsucker. Female members of the royal family were not allowed to the lavatory by themselves but had to be escorted by a male guard. The walls of the house were covered with lewd graffiti, a lot of it showing Rasputin and Alexandra having sex in various positions while Nicholas looked on. One piece of doggerel went:

Our Russian Tsar called Nick

Was dragged off the throne by his prick.

As the war against the counter-revolutionaries heated up, the language of Lenin and the other leading Bolsheviks turned increasingly to class war and violence. The words 'purge' and 'cleansing' were soon being used to justify murder. In Yekaterinburg, local anarchists demanded that the Bolsheviks hand over the Tsar so they could kill him. There was at least one-armed attempt to abduct Nicholas and assassinate him. After that, the anarchists were rounded up.

The Tsar received several letters from army officers who said that they were organising an escape. These may have been part of a plot that would allow the guards to kill the Romanovs while they were fleeing; but they built up the family's hopes. On more than one occasion, they stayed up all night fully clothed, believing they were about to be saved. Fearing that there may indeed be plots to free the Tsar, the deputy head of the Yekaterinburg Cheka – or secret police – Yalov Yurovsky, was appointed head of the Romanovs' guard. He was a convinced communist and a cruel man. He brought with him Grigori Nikulin, who Yurovsky described as his 'son' and who was certainly the executor of his will. Nikulin was an experienced killer; his first act when he arrived at the House of Special Purpose was to shoot Prince Dolgorukov, Nicholas's trusted aide-de-camp.

As soon as Yurovsky arrived, he fired the men who were pilfering from the Romanovs and brought in his own men from the Cheka. These men were not known to the locals and were referred to as Latvians, not surprising, as ethnic Latvians played an important role in the Cheka. In fact, they were Germans, Austrians, Hungarian Magyars and Russians. Discipline was tightened.

In Moscow, Lenin was making plans to put Nicholas on trial. He wanted the proceedings broadcast on radio across Russia, with Leon Trotsky as prosecutor. But things were turning against the Bolsheviks: many people saw their peace treaty with Germany as an act of treason – cowardly at the very least – and there began to be strikes against Bolshevik rule. Even the revolutionary writer Maxim Corky was condemning Lenin and Trotsky for having betrayed socialism.

There were other threats too. Allied troops had arrived at Murmansk; the Japanese had taken Vladivostok and 30,000 Czech soldiers rebelled when the communists tried to disarm them. The Czech Legion moved eastwards down the trans-Siberian railway in the hope that ships would pick them up from Vladivostok and deliver them to the Western Front. They took Samara, while an anti-Bolshevik government was formed in Omsk. Yekaterinburg was midway between Samara and Omsk, and looked set to fall – a trial would now be impossible.

It is not known who gave the order for the execution. It could have come from the leadership in Moscow – the communists in Yekaterinburg still talked of arranging a trial, but that may have been a bluff. 'Trial' could simply have been a code word for 'execution'. Nevertheless, in the House of Special Purpose, preparations were made for the killings. An orthodox priest was allowed to visit the Romanovs; the family sang hymns together and prayed.

Yurovsky claimed that an order came at 6 p.m. on 16 July 1918 telling him to 'exterminate the Romanovs', though he said it came from Perm, not Moscow. Yurovsky was none too fussy, though. He already referred to his Cheka guards as 'the execution squad', and had told his chief of staff, P.Z. Medvedev, to bring revolvers that morning as he planned to execute the whole family that night.

The family was told that they were going to be moved so they should not go to bed that night. At 2 a.m., they were summoned to the basement – there was some disorder in the town and they would be safer down there.

Once they were safely in the basement, Yurovsky, Nikulin and ten other men entered. Yurovsky read a death warrant. The lorry that was going to carry away their bodies revved outside to cover the sound of shooting. Yurovsky pulled a revolver and shot the Tsar at point-blank range. With a second revolver he shot the Tsarevich Aleksei, who had just turned 14. The boy groaned in pain and Yurovsky emptied the rest of the bullets into him.

Alexandra and her four daughters fell to their knees while the other mèn opened up on them, although two Hungarians refused to shoot the women. The Tsar's doctor was also shot, along with his manservant Trup. The Tsarina's maid Demidova was not hit by the first volley, so the men came at her with bayonets which she sought to parry with a cushion. She died in agony. The children's spaniel, Jimmy, was also killed, his head smashed in with a rifle butt.

The Tsar's daughters did not die immediately – they had sewn valuable jewellery inside their corsets to give them money in case they escaped, and the bullets ricocheted off it, leaving the girls in agony. The political commissar, P.Z. Ermakov, stood on the arms of the Grand Duchess Anastasia and stabbed her repeatedly with a bayonet. During the 1930s, he was wheeled out as a hero of the revolution, a role model for Soviet youth.

The bodies were loaded onto the lorry and Ermakov took them to some mine shafts nearby. The drunken guards there stripped the Grand Duchesses to gloat over the young girls' naked bodies. When they burnt the women's clothes, to their surprise and delight, they found the jewellery. Then they threw the bodies down the mine, followed by grenades.

Yurovsky was furious when he discovered that the guards had told the whole town where the Tsar and his family lay buried. The White Russians would take Yekaterinburg in a matter of days and he had promised Moscow that the bodies would never be found.

The next night, Yurovsky went back to the mine shaft with his most trusted men and recovered the Romanovs,' bodies. The plan was to dump them down another, deeper shaft; but the lorry got stuck in the mud on the way, so they buried them where they were, just in case the Whites discovered the corpses, the bodies of the Tsarevich Aleksei and one of the women were buried separately. In addition, the faces of all the corpses were smashed and disfigured. This proved unnecessary and it was not until 1976 that anyone suspected where the Romanovs were buried.

Yurovsky reported to Moscow that the deed was done. However, the Bolsheviks only announced that Nicholas had been killed. Alexandra and Aleksei had been moved to a safe place, the official announcement said – the authorities were not sure how the people would react to the murder of women and children.

Immediately after the atrocity, witnesses came forward to say that Alexandra and her children were seen on a train on their way to Perm. More often, witnesses spoke of a young woman alone, clearly injured and traumatised. She was thought to be the Grand Duchess Anastasia. Soon after, reports said, she was arrested by the Cheka, raped and murdered. Nevertheless, several young women turned up in the West claiming to have been Anastasia, though none managed to substantiate her claim. A man claiming to be Aleksei and bearing some of the distinguishing marks of the Tsarevich turned up in Baghdad, but he soon disappeared into obscurity.

After the Tsar and his immediate family were murdered, the rest of their entourage, including their servants, who had remained behind at Tobolsk, were killed. The Grand Duke Michael had already been shot in Perm on 12 June; the rest of the Grand Ducal party had been taken to Alapayevsk where, on the day after the Tsar was killed, they too were murdered. They were taken by cart to nearby mine shafts and thrown in. The Grand Duke Sergius put up a fight and was shot dead first; the rest were thrown in alive. Afterwards, planks and dynamite were thrown in. When the bodies were recovered, they all had grave head wounds. Some died instantly, but some may have lived on for hours.

The Czechs captured Yekaterinburg on 25 July. Almost

immediately, they found the charred remains of the Romanovs' clothes and other possessions, and began an investigation. They quickly concluded that the entire family had been massacred. Or had they? Anastasia's remains were never found. Her whereabouts remain unknown, and what happened to her is much speculated upon. As the years pass by, the less likely it becomes that she will be found. The Anastasia mystery may remain unsolved forever.

Massacre in the Katyn Forest

After Nazi Germany and the Soviet Union signed a non-aggression pact in 1939, Hitler was free to invade Poland, beginning World War II. Yet at the same time as Germany seized the western part of the country, the Soviet Union seized the east. As a result, 250,000 Polish military personnel fell into Russian hands.

When Germany attacked the Soviet Union in June 1941, the government in Moscow found itself allied to Great Britain and the Polish government in exile in London. Stalin agreed to let a Polish army be formed on Soviet territory under General Wladyslaw Anders, who asked the Soviets to hand over the 15,000 Polish officers they had once held in camps at Smolensk to form the nucleus of his command. After an embarrassed silence, the Soviets could not hand them over. They told Anders that, in December 1941, most of the prisoners had escaped to Manchuria and could not be located. Their whereabouts was a mystery.

However, on 13 April 1943, the Germans announced that they had discovered mass graves containing Polish officers in the Katyn forest near Smolensk. A total of 4,443 corpses were unearthed. They had been shot from behind, piled in stacks and buried. Investigators determined that they were General Anders' missing officers who, the

Germans claimed, had been executed by the Soviets in 1940.

A propaganda war ensued. The Soviets said that the Polish officers had been engaged in construction work to the west of Smolensk when the Germans arrived in August 1941 and that they had killed them. But both German and Red Cross investigators produced evidence that they had been killed in 1940.

The Polish government in exile asked the International Committee of the Red Cross to provide official reports on the fate of the Polish prisoners that they had held. The Soviet government refused to co-operate and, on 25 April 1943, broke off diplomatic relations with the Polish government in London. The Soviets then established a rival Polish government in exile, comprised entirely of communists.

After the war the Katyn massacre remained a thorn in the side of Polish-Soviet relations. The Soviet Union continued to insist that the Polish officers had been killed by the Germans and the communist government in Warsaw had no choice but to accept this. However, when a non-communist coalition came to power in Poland in 1989, they shifted the blame to the Soviets. Finally, in April 1990, Soviet President Mikhail Gorbachev admitted that the Soviet secret police, the NKVD, was responsible for the massacre.

The following is an account of what happened. In the autumn of 1939, the Soviets assembled what they held of the Polish military in 138 camps. The officers were separated and imprisoned in the old Russian Orthodox monasteries at Kozelsk and Starobelsk. Each prisoner was interviewed and investigated. Next, those who had served in the Polish intelligence services, military policemen, border guards and even some local policemen were segregated and transferred to the monastery at Ostashkov. The Soviet authorities provided the prisoners with a meagre ration, just about enough to sustain a man. Generals were allowed to keep their batmen, though. The prisoners were allowed to run their own kitchen and organise work parties to clear snow, but anyone who showed real leadership qualities was arrested and held incommunicado.

The State Jewellery Trust visited the prisoners to buy their watches, fountain pens and jewellery from them. The money could be spent on additional food. Religious services were held surreptitiously. Nevertheless, morale remained high.

Unlike other prisoner-of-war camps, these three camps were run, not by military units, but by the dreaded NKVD, the forerunner of the KGB. The men were interrogated over and over again. NKVD officers tried to indoctrinate them... to little effect. Not only did the Polish prisoners refuse to embrace communist ideology openly among their fellow prisoners, they also refused to do so privately during interrogations. By March 1940, the NKVD had given up. They decided that there were only 448 of the 15,000 Poles they could use. Some of them were communists, who eventually formed the core of the Polish Red Army. Others were ethnic Germans, some of whom were handed over to the German authorities. The rest could be useful in some way or, in some way or another, could not be considered class enemies.

The Katyn forest lay to the west of Kozelsk. In April 1940, the men in the camp there were told they were being sent home. Lists were drawn up for those who were about to depart. The men picked then had to line up and return any equipment given to them by the camp authorities. In a second building their personal possessions were returned to them. Everything was checked carefully. By this time, the departing men were segregated from those waiting behind and were not allowed to communicate with them. The selected men were then given a good meal, and a ration of bread and three herrings wrapped in white paper for the trip. For the men from the camp it seemed like heaven; white paper alone was an unimaginable luxury.

The generals were the first to go. When they left the camp, the NKVD officers formed a guard of honour. At Starobelsk, a military band played up-tempo tunes. The other officers followed later in groups of 50 to 360 men. There was no discernible pattern as to who went in which group, though officers with leadership qualities tended to be sent first. When those who remained behind asked the NKVD privately why this was, they were told that they should count themselves lucky still to be in the camp.

From Ostashkov and Starobelsk, the men were taken in closed trucks to waiting trains. From Kozelsk, they were marched to the nearby railway station. The column was closely guarded by NKVD men with guns and dogs. Some Poles began to wonder why such security precautions were needed if they were really going home.

At the station, they were loaded into closed prison carriages and taken to the railway station at Gnezdovo, a mile and three-quarters from the Katyn graves. The first batch had no idea where they were going, but the shadows of the telegraph poles they could glimpse through the tiny windows near the roof of the carriage told them they were going north-west – towards Poland. Those that followed found messages concerning their destination scratched into the wooden walls of the carriages.

The journey took two or three days, depending on the rail traffic. When they disembarked at Gnezdovo, they were searched; money and valuables were confiscated. Groups of 20-30 at a time were taken in buses into the forest. They were gagged – their arms were tied behind their backs and the rope looped around their necks so that, if they struggled, they would choke themselves.

The mass graves had already been dug. The Polish officers were brought six at a time and forced to kneel on the edge of the grave. Below them were layers of dead bodies, stacked neatly head to toe. Two NKVD men then walked down the line. One shot each Pole in the back of the head; the other kicked the corpse in the small of the back so it fell into the grave. While the NKVD men went to get six more prisoners, Russian peasants standing on the corpses below pushed the fresh ones into place. This went on hour after hour, day after day until finally the pits were full – then they were covered over.

It was a well-oiled killing machine run by NKVD specialists. Each prisoner was shot through the occipital bone in the back of the head and the bullet emerged from the forehead, extinguishing life instantly. It is therefore all the more amazing that one Polish officer taken to the Katyn forest survived and escaped.

His name was Lieutenant-Colonel Eugenjusz Andrei Komorowski. In September 1939, escaping from the invading Germans, he had ridden with some trepidation towards the Russian lines. He was with General Boleslaw Olszyna-Wilczynski, the Military Commander of Grodno who aimed to surrender to the Russians rather than the Germans. When he tried to do so, he was shot by the Russians while a Polish farmer and his wife looked on and laughed.

Eventually, Komorowski ended up in the camp at Kozelsk. He was scheduled to leave on 28 April 1940. As they marched out of the camp they were met by a huge force of NKVD men and warned that any man trying to escape would be shot. The NKVD kept up a constant barrage of insults at the Poles, whom they considered inferior.

It had rained the night before and the column had to ford a swollen stream. The banks were muddy and the men could not get a grip to stand up. As they slid around, the guards grew angry, causing the Poles to fear that they were going to be fired upon there and then.

One guard lashed out at a Pole with his rifle butt and someone shouted, 'Kill the guards! They're planning to murder us all.'

The Poles attacked the NKVD men, who responded with machine-gun fire. Many of the Poles were killed. Komorowski was hit in the right shoulder and right thigh – the bullets knocked him to the ground and he passed out.

When he came to, he felt a gentle rocking and heard the clack of wheel; he was on a train. He also smelt the overpowering smell of human excrement; warm liquid was dripping from above, onto his head and face; there was a weight on top of him and everything around him felt soft.

He realised that he was in a railway truck full of corpses. Blood was seeping out of the man stacked on top of him. The dead men had emptied their bowels, making the awful stench. Yet somehow he was alive. He could breathe and see just the tiniest shaft of light; then he slid back into unconsciousness.

Next time he awoke he could smell a new smell – rotting flesh. It was lighter this time and he could see among the corpses friends from the camp. This time he felt pain: his right shoulder was on fire; he felt sure he had broken bones; and pain was coming from his upper thigh. He prayed that no vital organ had been hit.

Afraid that he was going to die in this stinking compartment, he turned his thoughts to life, to his wife and the other beautiful women he had known.

The train clacked to a stop. Outside he heard voices. The doors squeaked. He could hear men being ordered out and told to get on the buses. Later, he heard the door of his compartment being opened.

'Drag the bastards out,' a voice demanded. 'The truck is

coming.'

Komorowski played dead. As they lifted him out, two Russians discussed whether to steal his smart Polish army boots.

'Do you want to be shot?' said one of them. 'They're to be buried in Katyn with boots and papers so that no trace of them will ever be found.'

Outside it was cold. They dragged him along like a rag doll and lay him on the ground. After a while a truck arrived and the corpses were flung onto it. Komorowski counted fourteen thuds as they landed. Luckily, he was the last.

The truck bumped up a hill and through a gate. Komorowski saw barbed wire and started to shiver in the cold air. But he managed to get the tremble under control by the time they reached a wooden lodge. Beyond it he saw a group of Polish officers. The truck slowed. An NKVD officer examined the corpses and directed the truck to the right, deeper into the forest.

It came to a halt by a mass grave, where Komorowski could see Russian peasants walking on the corpses; there were more bodies than he could count. He lay still and watched while his brother officers were murdered and saw how they were stacked so that the grave would hold the maximum number of bodies. Weak from loss of blood and the horror of what had happened to him, Komorowski could not fully take in what he was seeing. Suddenly, a wave of nausea swept over him; he struggled not to vomit.

He closed eyes and tried to block out what he had seen; he struggled to keep the smell of rotting flesh out of his nostrils. The grave must have been open for days. Somehow, he resisted vomiting; somehow, he resisted screaming; somehow, he resisted weeping. He lay there silently until the NKVD mass murderers had finished their day's work. Then the peasants came to unload the truck. Komorowski was lucky again – he was thrown face down on top of the last man to be killed. His body was still warm. No one was put on top of him.

It was late and the peasants decided to cover the corpses with earth the next day. Then they drove off in the truck. He heard other cars, buses and trucks drive off; the forest fell silent. Komorowski lay there on top of layer upon layer of his dead comrades and wept.

A cold wind ruffled the back of his hair. Gingerly, he raised his head. Then he realised, suddenly, that he did not have to lie still and play dead. Why would the NKVD leave anyone to guard the dead?

He thought of his wife again. In his imagination, she told him to muster all his strength to get out of there before the Russians came back again. Somehow he pulled himself out of the grave and stumbled towards some trees. He looked for the North Star. He reckoned the station was to the south, so he would go north until he was out of the area, then turn west and head for Poland.

His progress was slow: he was in considerable pain. In the darkness, with tears in his eyes, he kept bumping into trees; but every so often, he found a clearing, checked the position of the pole star and continued his halting journey.

Eventually he reached a river and waded through its freezing water. Cold, hungry and weak from loss of sleep, he kept blacking out. Eventually, he snagged his coat on a barbed wire fence. He cut his hands trying to free himself and eventually gave up and fell asleep. When he awoke there was a fog. He climbed the fence and, looking back, the fog was lifting and he could see the peasants turning up for work at the lodge. This stirred him on.

His situation seemed hopeless. Nevertheless, in his pocket he found a bar of chocolate and a can of herring he had bought from the camp shop with the money from his watch. He ate the chocolate, then smashed the tin open with a rock. Some of the oil splashed on some leaves, but he picked them up and licked it off. The food gave him renewed strength and he hobbled on.

The sun came out and dried off his clothes; it also helped him navigate. He reached a barn where he washed his wounds in a pail of water. He was lucky that the two bullets that had hit him had passed right through. He drank some milk direct from the teat of a cow and found an old smock and some baggy trousers, which he changed into.

Out in the forest again, he made a fire, burnt his uniform and papers, and buried his boot. He travelled on barefoot foraging for food. A few days later, he found a pair of old boots in a barn, and stole them.

Avoiding houses, he entered barns only to sleep in at night. However, soon he realised that he would need other people's help if he were to survive. One evening, he climbed up on to the porch of a remote house and begged the people inside for help. Eventually, they let him in, fed him, tended his wounds and said they would let him sleep in the loft for one night; but once he had gone to sleep, they went to fetch the police. Fortunately, Komorowski was a light sleeper. He heard the man of the house saddle his horse and he escaped.

He made his way across Russia, stealing food wherever he could. Then one day, he heard people speaking Polish. He was back in Poland, but that was not the end of his troubles: if he stopped and asked people for help, he could endanger their lives; and there was always a possibility that the people he spoke to would be Russian Poles whose sympathies were with the occupying forces.

Eventually, he reached the farmhouse where General Boleslaw Olszyna-Wilczynski had been shot and went in to see the couple who had ingratiated themselves with the Russians by laughing. They were not pleased to see him there was a violent row and Komorowski killed them both. He felt no remorse and left the bodies on the kitchen floor as he helped himself to their food. Then he blew out the light and went to bed.

In the morning, he stole the man's papers and a suit, then headed on to Grodno. Presenting the papers at the sentry post outside town, he distracted the guard with a few words of Russian. When he reached home he received the worst shock of all: he found another couple living his apartment who told him that his wife had been shot by the Russians. The grief drove him temporarily insane, before he decided he wanted revenge. He determined to leave Poland so that he could fight. Most of all, he wanted to tell the world what had happened to his comrades in the Katyn forest.

He headed for Rumania with the idea of travelling on to Paris, but by the time he got there, Paris had fallen to the Germans. So, he headed for Switzerland, crossing Hungary and Czechoslovakia by hoboing on trains. In his numbed mental state, he took incredible risks, but the fact that he had exhibited no fear seemed to help him. Komorowski rode freight trains across Austria, then walked across the border into Switzerland. There he gave himself up to a policeman who took him to the Red Cross. They fattened him up and informed the Polish authorities. When two Polish officers turned up, they did not believe that he had come all the way from Russia, preferring to believe that he had escaped from a German camp they flew him to London. By then, his mind had wiped all memory of the horrors of the Katyn forest. It was years before the full truth of the atrocity he had witnessed came back to him.

But a mystery still remains. The Germans only found 4,443 bodies in the mass graves at Katyn. The men in the mass graves were all from the camp at Kozelsk. What had happened to the other 10,000 or so who had been in the camps at Ostashkov and Starobelsk? Some witnesses say that at least 6,000 of them were taken to Archangel and put on barges, which were floated out into the White Sea. The barges were then sunk by artillery fire and the men drowned in the freezing water.

An NKVD document dated 10 June 1940 indicates that the men were murdered and buried in mass graves at Bologyne and Dergachi in the Ukraine. In 1991, a mass grave was found at Piatikhatki, near Kharkov, which was thought to contain the bodies of the men from Starobelsk; but the KGB only allowed the exhumation of 140 bodies there. Apparently, no one knows where the rest of the Polish officers were buried. They don't even know where the ones who were massacred in the Katyn forest are: in April 1944, Soviet earth moving machines were photographed at work in Katyn, removing the bodies and destroying the graves. However, Katyn is where the memorial to all 15,000 of the missing Polish officers stands.

Also unsolved is the mystery of what happened to the other 10,000 Poles who were transported to Russian labour camps. How many more Katyn massacres are yet to be exposed?

Sharpeville

South Africa has had a troubled history since the white settlers arrived. First the British fought the Zulus, then they fought the Boers. However, in the 1948 election, the Boers of the Nationalist Party took power. They stopped immigration from England and introduced the policy of apartheid, or separate development.

One major tool in ensuring the separation of the races were the pass book laws. Every black person who lived outside the bantustans – special areas set aside for African habitation – was to carry a pass book. This contained the bearer's name and address, sex, ethnic classification, the labour officer they were registered to, details of their offences against the pass laws, their employer's name and address (which had to be signed each week), tax receipts, drivers and weapons licenses, and a photograph. The system had been introduced by the British in the Cape in 1809. The African National Congress was formed in 1912 and held their first protest against the pass laws in 1919.

When the Nationalists took power they drastically tightened the passbook laws. Pass books had to be produced on demand; those who did not have one or whose pass book was not in order were fined heavily, jailed, forced into low-paid work or confined to the bantustans. During the 1950s, 1 million black people were moved out of the cities – which were designated white areas – and returned to the over-crowded, poverty-stricken parcels of land reserved for Africans.

In 1958, opposition to apartheid split and the Pan-African Congress was formed by 'Africanists' who demanded 'Africa for the African'. The ANC was a broader church: it was a coalition of Africans, largely English-speaking white liberals, communists, those of mixed race and Indians, and anyone else opposed to apartheid.

In 1959, both the ANC and PAC called for non-violent protests against the pass-book laws. The ANC's campaign was to start on 31 March 1960; the PAC began theirs on 18 March, and called for nationwide demonstrations on the 21st. Thousands responded in a small township in the Transvaal called Sharpeville.

Sharpeville had some 36,000 residents in 1960. At one o'clock around 10,000 of them turned up at the police station. This was not a single building but a compound, with a number of buildings and a big yard, surrounded by a wire fence. There were about 200 policemen – both white and African – inside. To the north was a large field; to the west was a square; and to the south a row of houses.

The protesters completely surrounded the police station. The commanding officer, Lieutenant Colonel Pienaar, turned up at around one o'clock with some reinforcements. A protester threw a rock at his car, which put him in a bad mood. Although there were batons and tear-gas canisters in the compound, his deputy, Major Van Zyl, had not tried to disperse the mob. By one o'clock, the crowd was too big and pressed too close to the fence to try that.

Pienaar had been expecting trouble. Nine policemen – four white, five black – had been killed when trying to close a beer hall in a township outside Durban a couple of months before. His men were heavily armed with Sten guns, rifles and revolvers, and there were six Saracen armoured cars in the compound.

The crowd outside was generally good tempered, but as more and more people turned up, they began shouting, 'Our land! Our Land!'

The rock that had hit Pienaar's car gave him the impression that the crowd had already been violent. Some of his officers were feeling tense; Pienaar himself was unnerved. Though peaceful, the demonstration was illegal – all protests by Africans were. It was his duty to break it up. At 1.30, Pienaar decided that what was needed was a show of force. He stationed the armoured cars along the north side of the compound, with their crews standing on the car roofs. Around 70 officers were positioned along the south and west, with rifles and machine-guns. Although most of them had already loaded their guns, Pienaar gave the order to load just five rounds – the idea was to intimidate the crowd. It was not clear what he intended to do next and he was under the impression that Major Van Zyl had tried threatening the crowd and firing over their heads – it had not worked.

Outside the compound were men from the South African Special Branch. A Colonel Spengler moved in to arrest the organisers of the demonstration and brought them into the compound. Although the gates had to be opened to do this, the crowd did not try to force their way in. According to Joshua Motha, who was standing in the crowd near the main entrance, the crowd was good humoured. They thought the police would make an announcement, addressing their grievances, then they would all go home.

A little later, a large grey police car, escorted by three Saracen armoured cars, arrived. The crowd let them into the compound and, again, did not try to rush in. Joshua Motha and the people around him thought that the man in the car was a spokesman for the government come to make the announcement. The car even bumped into one of the protesters, slightly injuring them, but the crowd did not react.

The armed policemen looked as though they were lined up as an honour guard for the man the protesters thought had come to make the announcement. The crowd pressed forward to hear what he had to say; two or three people at the front were arrested. Children began to shout slogans and throw stones. Lieutenant Colonel Pienaar said he thought they were in a state of frenzy; pictures taken by press photographers show that they were not.

No one is very sure what happened next. Some people close to the police station heard a loud noise. A newspaper photographer thought it was a shot, but no one was really sure. Others heard a voice saying, 'Fire!' Most heard neither. But for whatever reason, the police opened up with everything they had. Within seconds, 69 people were dead or dying and 180 wounded.

When Joshua Motha heard the shooting, he thought the police were firing blanks, until he saw a man lying on the ground. A bullet grazed his trousers, and as he turned to run, another caught him in the hip.

The shooting had not stopped when the crowd turned and ran. The policemen continued shooting protesters in the back. One young woman fell and her boyfriend went back to help her. When he turned her over, he saw that she was dead. The bullet had blown away her chest. One small boy put his coat over his head, as if it would protect him.

It was not just the policemen at the fence who shot – the men standing on the roofs of the Saracens blazed away from the hip. They sprayed bullets indiscriminately in broad arcs, stopping only to reload. In the 40 seconds or so that the shooting lasted for, 705 rounds were fired.

When the shooting stopped, nothing was moving – the crowd had gone. Bodies lay scattered across the field and square. A young mother rushing to the square to find her husband mistook the bodies for sheep that had been mysteriously slaughtered there. Only when she drew nearer did she realised that they were people.

Not all the victims had been protesters. Lechael Musibi was just an innocent passer-by, a teacher at a local school. None of his pupils had turned up that morning, so he left his keys with one of his students and set off on his bicycle to get them. His route took him past the police station. Suddenly the crowd was running at him; he fell off his bike. As he tried to get up, the shooting started again. He lay flat on the ground and watched as people fell. As soon as the shooting stopped, he picked himself up and made his way to the library nearby. When he arrived, a little girl said, 'Look, he's been shot.' Before that, he had not realised that he had been hit.

One man who had been delivering invoices for his company some way away died – a stray bullet had hit him and his head had been blown off.

The police came out of the compound to inspect their handy work, but did nothing to help the wounded. Trucks were brought to cart away the dead. Joshua Motha was ordered to get up and get out of the way; nothing was wrong with him, he was told. He tried to move but could not, so the police dragged him out of the way. It was only then that someone thought about calling an ambulance.

Reverend Robert Maja, the local Presbyterian minister, turned up. He brought water for the wounded and tried to cover them with clothing to protect them from the heat.

Demonstrations in South Africa back then were not often covered by the white-run press. However, Humphrey Taylor from the magazine The Drum happened to be there that day. He searched the bodies to see if anyone was carrying weapons. There were none. All he found abandoned among the bodies were shoes, hats and bicycles.

Two truckloads of bodies were taken to the mortuary and 11 ambulances ferried the wounded to hospital. The living and the dead were all gone by 2.30 p.m. The rains came at four and washed the blood away.

Taylor found that he could not get the story of the atrocity published in the newspapers in South Africa, so he sent it to England. The next day, the British papers were full of the massacre at Sharpeville. The leading British television commentator, Richard Dimbleby, compared it to Guernica. The Daily Herald called for a boycott of South African goods and by lunchtime over 600 people had gathered outside South Africa House in Trafalgar Square to protest. In the evening, a long protest march wound its way through the streets of London, as the massacre was condemned in parliament and around the world. The UN passed a resolution of condemnation. Even investors protested: within three days, £90 million was wiped off the Johannesburg stock market. The slide continued – with the beginning of the ANC campaign on 31 March, £70 million were wiped off share values in a single day.

The South African government was unrepentant, though. A few days later the South African police tried to stop a PAC protest meeting in the Western Cape. They charged the crowd and were met with a hail of stones, so they opened fire. Two Africans were killed and 49 injured.

Over the next few days, the South African government gave their account of what had happened at Sharpeville. On 22 March, the Prime Minister, Dr Verwoerd, said that the riots had nothing to do with pass books or apartheid. They were periodic outbursts that might happen anywhere. He praised the police for their courage; the government claimed that they had been attacked by 20,000 demonstrators, many of whom were armed. The Johannesburg Star reported that 80 per cent of the injured had been wounded below the belt, and that the police had merely been trying to wound the demonstrators, not kill them. The South African papers also reported that the demonstrators had been armed.

The Bishop of Johannesburg and white liberal organisations challenged this, raising money for lawyers to take statements from the injured and defend the protesters the police had arrested and charged with public order offences. An independent doctor was found to attend the postmortem examinations. He established that many of the dead had been shot in the back. Soon they had overwhelming evidence that the demonstrators had not been armed.

Lieutenant Colonel Pienaar said that this was beside the point. 'The native mentality does not allow them to gather for peaceful demonstration,'he said. For them, to gather means violence.'

On 26 March, ANC leader Chief Albert Luthuli publicly burnt his pass book and urged everyone to do the same. The ANC designated 28 March a day of mourning and many Africans stayed at home. Pass-book laws were suspended briefly. The PAC and ANC thought they had won, but on 30 March the South African government declared a state of emergency. Another 30 years passed before the pass-book laws and apartheid were finally laid to rest.

However, Sharpeville was the beginning of the end. After the massacre, South Africa was no longer viewed as a civilised nation. Eventually, the South African government was forced to set up a Commission of Enquiry. It found that:

'The officers made no attempt to persuade the crowd to disperse by nonviolent means.

'The officers failed to order the crowd to disperse.

'The officers failed to warn the crowd that if they did not disperse force would be used.

'The officers made no attempt to use any form of force less drastic than firearms.

'The officers failed to supervise and control the men under their command.

'The officers took no steps to ensure that if shooting started it would be limited and controlled and could be stopped.

'The constables started shooting without receiving an order to do so.

'Many of the constables shot to kill, not merely to wound.

'They did kill 69 people including eight women and ten children.

'The shooting was indiscriminate and continued long after the crowd had turned and fled.

'The 180 wounded included 31 women and 19 children.

'There was no justification for the police to open fire on the crowd and therefore no justification for the conduct of the police.'

The Commission of Enquiry failed to conclude that the system of apartheid was to blame for the atrocity. Officially, responsibility for it is unsolved. Frustratingly for world history, the blame rested upon no one.

Cambodia Year Zero

The war in Vietnam destabilised the whole of South-East Asia and in 1975 Phnom Penh, the capital of Cambodia, fell to the fanatical communist guerrillas, the Khmer Rouge. On 17 April, their peasant army marched down the once smart boulevards. The expressionless teenagers of this austere fighting force struck a note of terror in the hearts of the inhabitants.

It was well known that this guerrilla army was extraordinarily well disciplined. They were impervious to argument, bribery or sentiment. These young troops had not come to loot or rape; they would have no drunken victory celebration. The fate that awaited the inhabitants of Phnom Penh would be much worse. The city was to be evacuated.

The leaders of the Khmer Rouge were Paris-educated communist zealots. They had adapted Marxism for the Third World. Instead of putting the urban proletariat on a pedestal, as Karl Marx had, they believed that all goodness stemmed from the rural peasantry. Consequently the city dwellers were going to be turned into peasants – or would die in the process.

On the afternoon of the 17th, the whole population of Phnom Penh was ordered to leave for the countryside. There was no transport so they would have to go on foot, and there would be no exceptions – even the hospitals were emptied. The country had been at war for eight years and Phnom Penh had been under siege for fifteen months. Many people had been wounded by shelling fire or were suffering from disease and malnutrition. For them, it was a death march: as the great exodus stumbled out of the city into the unknown, under the watchful eyes of the impassive Khmer Rouge, the weak fell by the roadside and were left to die where they lay.

Meanwhile, the teenage soldiers looked for anyone appearing to be well-educated or enjoying wealth and power. They looked for people with soft hands, those who looked well fed or well dressed. They were pulled out of the human stream and interrogated. Anyone who admitted to being one of the urban elite – a bureaucrat, a businessman, a doctor, a teacher, a lawyer or an engineer – was taken away and shot. This was known as 'class vengeance', a favourite slogan of the Khmer Rouge.

The officials of the previous government and army officers were treated separately. A Khmer Rouge broadcast ordered them to present themselves at the Ministry of Information. Fearing that worse might happen to them if they did not, most turned up as ordered; all were killed.

By the evening of the 17th, the tree-lined avenues, the pavement cafés, the chic haute cuisine restaurants, the opium dens and the brothels of Cambodia's capital were empty. The city was silent, deserted. Only a handful of journalists remained behind, huddled in the French embassy. They were evacuated three weeks later.

The evacuation of Phnom Penh was not done on a whim. The decision had been made three months earlier. The leadership of the Khmer Rouge realised that they were not strong enough to run the country in a conventional sense. The communist cadres responsible for building the new society numbered only 14,000. Even their young peasant army was not big enough to control the population of the city which numbered over one million. The reasoning behind the evacuation was that if one took those city dwellers and dispersed them across the countryside, they would be too disorganised and disorientated to offer resistance leaving the Khmer Rouge with undisputed power.

Manpower was certainly needed in the countryside. The guerrilla war and American bombing had laid waste to much of the land. Rice stocks were perilously low but, being fanatically anti-colonialist, the Khmer Rouge would not accept any aid from abroad, as an article of faith. The economy would be rebuilt by Cambodians themselves. This would be done by turning Cambodia into one huge labour camp.

Fundamentally, the evacuation of Phnom Penh was seen as a great leap forward towards the ideal communist society. In one stroke the urban rich lost all their property and became peasants. Those who could not adapt or accept the change were not worthy of the communist paradise and would be killed. With urban corruption eradicated, a new – utopian – society could flourish. 1975 was to be Year Zero: Cambodia was to be built again on totally new foundations.

The seeds of this new society already existed in the 'liberated' areas that had been under Khmer Rouge control during the war. There, money and private property had already been abolished; the peasants had been organised in collective farms. For the meagre rations doled out by the Khmer Rouge leadership, they had worked from dawn to dusk to support the war effort.

These collectivised peasants were the communists' 'old people' and they would instruct the 'new people' from the cities on how to be good peasants and good communists. However, those who survived the forced march from the city arrived at the collectives to find that they did not receive a warm welcome. The peasants resented the easy life city folk had lived while they toiled in the paddy fields.

Once they got to work, the city people's incompetence in the fields earned them the contempt of the 'old people'. Those who were completely useless were 'eliminated' for 'economic sabotage'. Most just perished from 'natural causes', being unused to the privations the peasants suffered – backbreaking labour, starvation, disease and lack of medical care. The attitude of the Khmer Rouge was summed up in the slogan, 'If this man lives there is no profit. If he dies there is no great loss.'

The identity of the leaders behind the murderous policy remained a mystery for a long time. They were a small group of Paris-educated intellectuals that included the infamous Pol Pot, Ieng Sar, Ieng Thirith and Khieu Samphan. They had set up headquarters in the ghost city of Phnom Penh and ruled the country with a rod of iron. Cambodia was divided into zones, each of which had a party secretary directly answerable to the central authority in Phnom Perth. Below each party secretary was a central committee and, beyond the committee, no one had ever heard of Pol Pot and his merry men. Orders were issued simply in the name of Angka, the Organisation.

In March 1976, Cambodia was renamed the Democratic Republic of Kampuchea and Pol Pot and his henchmen pushed forward towards the establishment of their ideal society. Solitary eating was abolished – all food had to be consumed in communal canteens and came from stocks controlled by the Khmer Rouge. Any private enterprise such as picking wild fruit or vegetables to supplement the diet was punishable by death; even the consumption of lizards, toads and earthworms was outlawed.

Family ties were discouraged. Children in the co-operatives slept in dormitories away from their parents; youngsters were encouraged to spy on their parents and denounce them if their behaviour fell short of what was demanded by the Angka. Members of families were assigned to different work parties and sent to opposite ends of the country. With no telephones and no postal system, once contact had been broken between family members and friends they were unlikely ever to come across each other again.

The teachers and intellectuals had already been exterminated. Instead of education there was a brutal process of indoctrination. Executions were carried out either on the orders of the secret police or of the cooperative ruling committee and they were a discrete and mysterious as the Angka itself. People disappeared in the night; it was not advisable to ask where they had gone. Some were killed on pure whim. To possess thick-lensed glasses, for example, meant you had read too much, so you were the target of Pol Pot's butchers.

The favourite method of execution was a blow to the back of the head or neck with the base of an axe-head: bullets were in short supply. Disembowelling and burying alive were also popular – victims were usually required to dig their own grave first. Whole truckloads of people would suddenly disappear. Curiously, Khmer literature did not use the figurative struggle between good and evil that is the staple of Western stories. Rather, it stressed harmony and beauty. Cambodians were therefore completely unprepared for the mindless violence that their leaders had brought back with them from France. Many Cambodians would stand in line, awaiting their turn to be struck on the back of the head. A traditionally peaceful people, they had no intellectual defence against the Khmer Rouge's murderous strategy.

Keeping a firm grip on the reign of terror in the village was easy for the communists. Rotting human remains, scattered along the trails into the village, did the job. Rumours of grotesque tortures were spread victims were said to have had their throats cut open by razor-sharp reeds or serrated palm fronds. These accounts had a chilling effect.

After the 'class enemies' – anyone who had an education, anyone who had not been born a worker or a peasant – were eliminated, the Khmer Rouge targeted the ethnic minorities. The Chinese, the Vietnamese and Cham Muslims were 'liquidated'. Pol Pot believed in ethnic cleansing and racial purity along the lines of Hitler and his 'final solution'; minorities were systematically exterminated.

From the beginning of 1977, the Khmer Rouge executioners turned in on themselves. Those in the party from a 'bourgeois' background were the first to be picked out. They were blamed for the continuing failure of the economy – though everyone else saw that the real blame lay with the murderous system itself; they paid with their lives.

Food shortages continued, because agriculture was now in the hands of people who knew nothing about it. Irrigation projects and dams were build by hand without engineers and experts supervising the work. They were dead. When the first rain came, these massive civil-engineering projects that had cost thousands of lives in their construction were simply swept away.

As far as the party was concerned, these failures could not be the fault of the system – they were being sabotaged by enemies of the state. The Khmer Rouge became consumed by paranoia: torture centres were set up. The most notorious was Tuol Seng in Phnom Penh, where expert Khmer Rouge torturers 'uncovered' conspiracies that usually implicated more people who were about to suffer their tender mercies. Tens of thousands died a horrible death.

The killings became so indiscriminate and widespread that, by mid 1977, Pol Pot himself tried to call a halt. In September 1977, he went public for the first time, making clear his own dominant role in the Communist Party that was now running Kampuchea. In an address to the people, he claimed to have liberated them from 2000 years of 'despair and hopelessness'. However, most of his speech was devoted to the need to defend Kampuchea against foreign aggression.

The Khmer Rouge had always distrusted the Vietnamese who, in precolonial times, had dominated the region. There had been border clashes immediately after the fall of Phnom Penh back in 1975. In the autumn of 1977, the border conflicts flared up again. The Khmer Rouge central committee sent out a new instruction: purge all those who had contact with Hanoi. More party members died.

The Eastern Zone committee came under suspicion. Their region bordered Vietnamese territory. They were not doing enough to resist the highly efficient Vietnamese Army who had, after all, ousted the Americans. At the beginning of 1978, the Eastern Zone leadership was purged, but some escaped the Khmer Rouge executioners by fleeing across the border into Vietnam. One of those who fled was the man who would eventually replace Pol Pot; his name was Heng Samrin. With credible Vietnamese leadership in their territory, the Vietnamese took a hand. The excesses of Pol Pot and the Khmer Rouge were undermining their victory in Vietnam and inviting renewed foreign intervention. On 21 December 1978, Kampuchea was 'liberated' once more – this time by a full-scale Vietnamese invasion that installed Heng Samrin as head of a puppet government. Pol Pot's first wife, the ideologue whose crazy ideas underpinned Year Zero, went mad.

A mystery remains. No one knows how many people died in the killing fields of Pol Pot's Year Zero Kampuchea, or what proportion of deaths were due to malnutrition and disease – much of which was cause by ideology-led dislocation – as against deliberate execution. The accepted figure is that two million people died at the hands of their own countrymen – making Cambodia's Year Zero a greater human catastrophe, per capita, than Hitler 's Germany We cannot be sure though; the extent of these killings will always be a topic of much speculation. Pol Pot was captured in 1998; he was tried, but died of natural causes before he could be punished for the atrocities he had committed.

Lockerbie

At 6.25 p.m. on 21 December 1988, Pan Am Flight 103 took off from London's Heathrow Airport 25 minutes behind schedule. The Boeing 747 was carrying 246 passengers and ten crew members.

The plane, which was heading for New York, had on board both Britons and Americans heading for the States for the Christmas holiday, among them 35 of a party of 38 students from Syracuse University who had been studying abroad and were going home to spend Christmas with their families. Others were on more serious business: Brent Carisson, a Swede and chief administrative officer for the United Nations' Council for Namibia, was flying to New York to sign an accord on Namibia's independence.

At 37 minutes after take off, Flight 103 was cruising at 31,000 feet – six miles high – over the Scottish border. The plane was flying at 434 knots – 500 miles an hour. James MacQuarrie, the 55-year-old American pilot, and his 52-year-old co-pilot, Raymond Wagner, switched on the autopilot and settled down for a routine transatlantic journey. As they gave their instruments one final check, the air traffic controller at Shanwick gave them final radio clearance for their flight out over the Atlantic.

Outside it was cold and dark. Intermittent rain splattered against the cockpit's reinforced windscreen. The 115-knot jet stream was creating light turbulence. Below them, clouds at around 16,000 feet covered the Scottish landscape.

At precisely 7.02 and 50 seconds p.m., over the tiny village of Castlemilk three miles south of Lockerbie, a terrorist bomb planted in a radio-recorder in the plane's baggage hold exploded. It weighed less than a pound.

The baggage hold was in front of the plane's left wing.

The bomb went off just 25 inches from the skin of the fuselage. The shock wave punched a hole in the side of the plane, sending burning baggage out into the freezing air, and ripping through the jumbo's main electrical cables. MacQuarrie had no chance to make a Mayday call. The flight recorder only recorded the sound of the explosion before its power failed too.

Then came the blast itself. It stretched the fuselage skin. Within a second, it had blistered and busted. Around the five-foot hole, the edges 'petalled' outwards in a starburst. The blast was also channel upwards, causing the passenger compartment to buckle and break. Everyone on board had heard the explosion; shock waves travelled down the air-conditioning, reverberating through the cabin; and those in the forward section and those on the left-hand-side of first class on the upper deck suffered minor injuries from the blast.

People sitting directly over the left wing felt the plane disintegrating beneath them. The starburst around the hole was rapidly unzipping. One petal tore back as far as the wing; a second ripped forward 43 feet and a third tore around under the belly of the plane almost up to the windows on the starboard side. A passenger plane is only held together by its thin skin – it does not have a metal chassis like a car. With such severe damage, the forces on it will rip it apart.

Amid the sound of tearing aluminium and popping rivets, the aircraft nose-dived. The flight control cables had been severed by the explosion and it rolled to the left. The left side of the forward fuselage ripped open and the entire nose section twisted upwards and to the right. The cockpit turned all the way around until it was facing the back of the plane, then broke away. It hit the right wing, knocking the inner engine off its stanchion. The nose hit the tailplane, causing extensive damage. From there, the body of the plane travelled in an increasingly steep flight path until, by 19,000 feet, it was travelling vertically downwards.

On the way down, both the nose and the fuselage spilled their contents. The aerodynamic effects of the plane's steep dive tore the remaining three engines off the wings. At around 9,000 feet, the rear of the cabin broke away and disintegrated, scattering bits of the cabin floor, the rear baggage hold and the landing gear across the fields and houses below.

It was a quiet Wednesday evening in the small Scottish village of Lockerbie when Myra Bell looked out of the window of her flat. As she looked out at the southern edge of the village, she saw a huge black object falling from the sky, not realising that it was a passenger plane and all the people on board it were going to die.

A wing filled with more than 200,000 pounds of aviation fuel crashed into Sherwood Crescent at 200 miles an hour. It crashed into the houses at the end of the crescent, leaving a huge crater 100 feet long and 30 feet deep. The fireball could be seen six miles away, while those in the rest of the crescent felt the terrible heat and air being sucked out of their houses. The force of the blast sent Robert Jardine flying across his living room. When he looked out of the window he saw that the home of his neighbours, the Flannigan family, had disappeared completely. The body of ten-year-old Joanne Flannigan was found in the wreckage of their home, but those of her parents, 44-year-old Thomas and 41-year-old Kathleen, were never found. The home of John and Rosaleen Somerville and their children 13-year-old Paul and ten-year-old Lyndsey, had disappeared too; their bodies had been vaporised in the impact. In all, 11 residents of Lockerbie died in the disaster.

The main body of the fuselage landed 350 yards from the Townfoot service station, which went up in flames. The ball of fire that had been number three engine hit the town, while the nose section buried itself in a hilltop three miles from the east of the town. The other engines hit the Netherplace area; one hit the water main.

Nearby, the seismic station belonging to the British Geological Survey registered 1.6 on the Richter scale. The main impacts occurred at 19.03, 36.5 seconds and 46 seconds after the bomb had gone off. Some local residents believed that there had been an earthquake, others that two low-flying fighters had collided. Keith Paterson thought that the Chapelcross nuclear power station had exploded. He only discovered what had really happened when he grabbed a torch and went outside. In the dark, he saw two eyes looking up at him. They belonged to a dead body. All 257 people on board Flight 103 were dead – or soon would be. It was later discovered that some people had miraculously survived the crash and may have lived for some time after they hit the ground but, by the time they were found, it was too late.

The first fire engine arrived at 7.10 p.m., eight minutes after the bomb exploded. Rescuers were soon combing the area for survivors. It was an impossible task: wreckage from the plane was spread over an arc 80 miles long. All those they found were dead. Captain MacQuarrie's body was found on the grass outside the cockpit. Inside the nose section rescuers found another 15 bodies, nearly all of them cabin crew or first-class passengers.

Christine Copeland found the body of a young woman in her garden, which turned black before her eyes. The body of a young man landed on the front doorstep of Esther Galloway – for the next 3 days she had to step over it while the accident investigators went about their work. However, most of the bodies were not intact and the emergency forces had to set about the grim task of finding body parts.

Every body part had to be examined by a doctor, photographed, numbered and tagged before it could be removed. Some pieces had to be dug out of the rubble or cut out of the wreckage of the aircraft. This was a gruesome and laborious business – some bodies were not removed until five nights after the crash

The Lockerbie disaster was the worst air crash in British history, and the worst plane crash in the life of Pan Am. What made it an atrocity was that it was not an air accident at all – the bomb with a timing device had been planted deliberately. Furthermore, the authorities had been warned.

One week before Flight 103 was blown from the skies, the American Embassy in Finland received a message from an anonymous caller saying, 'There will be a bombing attempt against a PanAmerican aircraft flying from Frankfurt to the United States.'

Flight 103 had originated in Frankfurt. Passengers from Germany travelled on a 727 to London but the flight used the same number. At Heathrow, the passengers and luggage were transferred to the 747, along with more passengers from England and others on connecting flights from elsewhere.

This information was forwarded to the American embassy in Germany. Embassy staff cancelled their reservations on Flight 103, surveillance was stepped up, but no warning was given to the general public.

At first, two anti-Arafat Palestinian terrorist groups – the General Command of the Patriotic Front for the Liberation of Palestine and Abu Nidal's Fatah Revolutionary Council – were blamed. Later, Scotland Yard concluded that the bomb had been planted by Iranians or groups sympathetic to Iran.

In November 1990, it was discovered that the US Drug Enforcement Agency often used Flight 103 to fly informants and suitcases of heroin seized in the Middle East back to America. Pan Am staff were used to loading these cases without the usual security checks. One of the

DEA men involved in this operation, Detroit-resident Nazir Khalid Jafaar, was on board the downed flight and it was thought that he might have unwittingly put the bomb on board the plane.

In the end this theory was rejected. Eventually, the world's biggest murder investigation concluded that Libya was to blame. The attack, investigators said, was done in retaliation for the 1986 bombing of Libya by US planes that had taken off from bases in Britain. The United States and Britain asked the government in Tripoli for the extradition of two Libyans – Lamen Khalifa Fhimah and Abdelbasset Ali al-Megrahi. Colonel Qaddafi refused to hand them over for trial.

In 1992, the UK and US went to the United Nations and asked for economic sanctions to be imposed on Libya, if Qaddafi did not hand over the two men. In late March, the United Nations Security Council gave the Colonel two weeks to hand over the suspects, or flights in and out of Libya would be banned and the country would be shunned as a diplomatic pariah. In response, Qaddafi threatened to cut off oil supplies to those countries supporting the resolution. There was a surplus of oil on the world market at the time and no one took any notice. However, by 1998, Qaddafi was tired of being an international outcast. South Africa's President Nelson Mandela flew to Tripoli and brokered a deal. In 1999, the two men were sent to the Netherlands where they were detained in a special terrorist-proof military compound to be tried under Scottish law.

At the time of going to press, the three judges heading the trial had just delivered their verdict. Abdelbasset Ali al-Megrahi was found guilty and sentenced to 20 years in prison, whilst Lamen Khalifa Fhimah was acquitted. On his return to Libya, Fhimah was given a hero's welcome by both Qaddafi and the public.

Years after the tragedy occurred, the need for justice was

great. For the families who suffered for years without knowing the truth behind the loss of their loved ones, a decisive end to the court case was paramount. Whether the motive for the bombing was political retalliation or a personal act of terrorism, many issues remain unsolved. The residents of the small Scottish town where it happened have another cross to bear. The name Lockerbie will forever be associated with an air atrocity and send a shiver down the spine of anyone who sets foot on a plane.

Waco

On April 19, 1993 the world witnessed the fire that destroyed 'Mount Carmel', the Branch Davidian compound in Waco, Texas. Inside, the radical sect leader, David Koresh, along with about 80 of his devotees, perished. This event, along with the 51-day siege preceding it, is now simply known as 'Waco'.

David Koresh was the self-proclaimed leader of the small, obscure religious sect called 'Branch Dividians', a splinter group of the Seventh-Day Adventist Church. He joined the group in his teens, discarding his real name of Vernon Howell and assuming the more biblical 'David Koresh'.

Koresh rapidly established himself in the sect, had an affair with its then-leader, Lois Roden, and began to gain a string of personal followers. When Lois Roden died in 1987 Koresh vied for the leadership of the sect with Roden's son, George. A gun fight between the two men and their respective followers decided the outcome and Koresh emerged victorious.

In the late eighties and early nineties, Mount Carmel was home to just under 100 Branch Davidians. Koresh, a self-proclaimed prophet, had an undeniable skill for citing reams of biblical passages, and an even more convincing ability to interpret it in his own unique way.

This 'ability' was enough to convince his followers that he was the new Messiah. In this role he declared that all women belonged to him, believing himself to be responsible for creating a new race. Koresh convinced his female followers – girls as well as women – of their role in spreading his seed and bearing his children. Husbands and fathers were willing to hand over their wives and daughters to him for this purpose. In the three years prior to the siege, Koresh is believed to have 'married' a number of women and girls within the sect; between ten and fifteen children are thought to have been fathered by Koresh as a result of these 'relationships'. The outside world soon became aware of the goings-on inside Mount Carmel. Allegations of child abuse rapidly became widespread among the media; reports focused on the extent of Koresh's manipulation, and questionable misinterpretation, of the bible in pursuit of justification for his sexual deeds.

The allegations of abuse generated a large amount of media attention and speculation. But the Bureau of Alcohol, Tobacco and Firearms (ATF) realised a further irregularity with the Branch Davidians. ATF agents were steadily accumulating reports regarding the amount of illegal weapons, ranging from firearms to explosives, that the sect were hoarding in Mount Carmel. Mounting evidence led to a warrant being granted for Koresh's arrest.

The ATF launched a raid on Mount Carmel on February 28, 1993 in an attempt to execute the search and arrest warrant. A gun fight ensued between the ATF agents and Koresh's followers (who had been tipped off about the intended raid) and this clash resulted in the deaths of four ATF agents and six Branch Davidians.

This day marked the beginning of a fifty-one day siege of Mount Carmel. Shortly after the ATF's raid, the FBI became involved in the tense situation, in an attempt to regain authority and control. They were keen to find a peaceful solution to the incident, however they quickly drafted in their Hostage Rescue Team; little did they realise that this was the beginning of a seven-week standoff.

For 51 days, David Koresh refused to free any of his followers from Mount Carmel, effectively holding them as hostages. The weeks were filled with constant negotiation between federal agents, Koresh and some of his fellow Davidians. As time went on Koresh became increasingly difficult to negotiate with, frustrating the FBI with his unyielding approach. Koresh knew the world was watching him; he relished the attention and the opportunity to put the Branch Davidians on the world map. The FBI frequently drew blanks with their tactical negotiations; Koresh repeatedly broke promises claiming he was interpreting the words and wishes of God. He did though release a number of children from the compound; the rest, he claimed, were biologically his own and he would not surrender his own 'family'.

President Clinton was kept informed of the Waco incident throughout. He initially favoured a peaceful policy of negotiation to resolve the situation, but later leaned towards a more pro-active approach, endorsing the need for military presence.

Throughout the standoff, the armoured presence drew tighter and tighter around the Koresh compound. According to police and FBI reports, any movement from the armoured vehicles around Mount Carmel agitated Koresh considerably, the sect-leader becoming visibly irritable during negotiations.

By the end of seven weeks, all supplies and communication links (except for the ability to make outgoing calls to the negotiators) to and from Mount Carmel ceased. The tactical strategy employed by the FBI had reached a limit, and a stalemate ensued. A decision was taken by the US authorities to use CS gas on the compound – a decision which later caused the biggest debate of all in the aftermath of the Waco fire.

But the CS gas plan did not force Koresh and his captive followers to leave Mount Carmel. It is now believed that the Branch Davidians were in possession of gas masks which clearly would have helped against the effects of CS gas; the weather that day was extremely windy which would have dispersed the CS gas too quickly for it to have a profound effect. Still, David Koresh held his followers inside the compound.

Approximately six hours after the CS gas episode, three fires erupted simultaneously in the compound. Post-event evidence implies that the fires were ignited inside the compound – by hand. The compound, and its inhabitants, were rapidly destroyed. Just nine Davidians managed to flee from Mount Carmel and lived to tell the tale.

Once the fire was extinguished, FBI officers were able to enter the buildings. Inside, their fears were confirmed; approximately 80 bodies, including those of twenty children, were discovered. But not everyone had met their fate as a result of the fire. Although the FBI's medical personnel found many to have died as a result of asphyxiation, some were killed after debris had fallen on top of them as the building collapsed. The remainder had died from gun shot wounds – the result of suicides and mercy killings. Despite protests from remaining Branch Davidians after the event, the CS gas used by the FBI did not kill any of the people inside the compound (either through inhalation of the gas or from its byproduct from fire, cyanide).

David Koresh was considered by the world to be a murderer. His increasing arrogance with the FBI throughout the siege only made his case worse, forcing the FBI to use more powerful methods to deal with events.

In addition to the illegal weapons store that they knew Koresh held, FBI agents were particularly concerned about the physical and sexual abuse women and children would be suffering. Worsening sanitary conditions also added to their concerns.

For their part, the FBI were widely criticised in the path they chose to take. It was considered too passive and lacked initiative and instinct. The incident should have been under control in hours after the crossfire on 28 February and should not have extended into a 7-week standoff.

Many questions remain unanswered. Why was the incident dealt with so incompetently? Did the fire really start from within the compound? Who fired the first shots on 28 February? How many more like David Koresh are out there?

David Koresh and the massacre at Waco still remain in the minds of many world-wide. The media have played a large part in publicising his way of life, of emphasising the control he had over the lives of his followers. He is ultimately held responsible in the eyes of the world for the deaths of 80 men, women and children – disciples who had trusted in him and who had devoted their lives to him only to be callously sacrificed on the altar of Koresh's perverted religion.

The Zodiac Killer

A brutal assassin who styled himself the 'Zodiac Killer' stalked the Bay area around San Francisco for over ten years. Like Jack the Ripper, he taunted the police with letters and clues. Also in common with the Ripper, he, too, was never caught and may even have moved on, to kill again.

His reign of terror began on a chilly, moonlit night at

Christmas in 1968. A teenage couple had drawn up in their car in an open space next to a pump house on the Lake Herman road in the Vallejo hills overlooking San Francisco. This was the local lovers' lane and David Faraday and Bettilou Jensen were indifferent to the cold. Indeed, they were so wrapped up in each other that they did not notice another car pulling up about 10 feet (3 metres) away. Their amorous reverie was then rudely interrupted by gunfire, however. One bullet smashed through the back window, showering them with glass, while another thudded into the car's bodywork. Bettilou threw open the passenger door and leapt out. David, who was trying to follow her, had his hand on the door handle when the gunman leant in through the driver's window and shot him in the head, causing his body to slump across the front seat. Bettilou's attempt at flight was futile: as she ran screaming into the night the gunman ran after her; she had covered just 30 feet (9 metres) when he fired five shots at her. After she had collapsed and died the gunman walked calmly back to his car and drove away.

A few minutes later another car drove down the quiet road. Its driver, a woman, saw Bettilou's body sprawled on the ground, but did not stop, instead speeding on, towards the next town, Benica, to get help. On the way, she saw the flashing blue light of a police car approaching her and frantically switched her headlights on and off to try to attract the driver's attention. The car stopped and she told the patrolmen what she had seen. They then followed her back to the pump house arriving here about three minutes later. Although Bettilou was dead David was still alive, but because he was unconscious he could not give them any information about what had happened. He died shortly after his arrival at the hospital to which they had rushed him.

There was little for the police to go on: the victims had not been sexually assaulted and nothing was missing (the

money in David's wallet was still there). Detective
Sergeant Les Lundblatt, of the Vallejo-county police force,
investigated the possibility that they had been murdered
by a jealous rival, but there were found to be no jilted
lovers and no other amorous entanglements. The two
teenagers were ordinary students who lives were an open
book. Six months later Bettilou Jensen and David
Faraday's files had become just two of a huge number
relating to unsolved murders in the state of California.

On 4 July 1969 their killer struck again. At around
midnight at Blue Rock Park – another romantic spot, just
2 miles (3 kilometres) from where Bettilou and David were
murdered – Mike Mageau was sitting in his car with his
girlfriend, the 22-year-old waitress Darlene Ferrin. They
were not entirely alone because other courting couples
had also parked their cars there. Like Bettilou and David
before them, Mike and Darlene were too engrossed in
each other to notice when a white car pulled up beside
them. It stayed there for only a few minutes before driving
away, but then it returned and parked on the other side of
the road. A powerful spotlight was suddenly shone on
Mike's car, whereupon a figure approached them.
Thinking that it was a policeman, Mike reached for his
driver's licence. As he did so, however, he heard the
sound of gunfire and saw Darlene slump in her seat;
seconds later a bullet tore into Mike's neck. The gunman
then walked unhurriedly back to the white car, paused to
fire another four or five shots at them and then sped off,
leaving the smell of cordite and burning rubber in his
wake.

A few minutes later a man called the Vallejo Country
police station and reported a murder on Columbus
Parkway, telling the switchboard operator 'You will find
the kids in a brown car. They are shot with a 9 mm Luger.
I also killed those kids last year. Goodbye'. When the
police arrived Darlene was dead, and although Mike was

still alive the bullet had passed through his tongue and he was unable to speak.

There was another lead for the police to follow, however. Four months earlier Darlene's babysitter had noticed a white car parked outside Darlene's flat. Thinking that it looked suspicious, she asked Darlene about it. It was plain that the young mistress knew the driver: 'He's checking up on me again', she told the babysitter. 'He doesn't want anyone to know what I saw him do. I saw him murder someone.' The babysitter had had a good look at the man in the white car and told the police that he was middle-aged, with brown, wavy hair and a round face. When Mike could talk again he confirmed that the gunman had had brown hair and a round face. After that, however, the clues to the killer's identity petered out.

Then, on 1 August 1969 – almost two months after the shootings of Darlene and Mike, three local newspapers received handwritten letters. They all began: 'DEAR EDITOR, THIS IS THE MURDERER OF THE 2 TEENAGERS LAST CHRISTMAS AT LAKE HERMAN & THE GIRL ON THE 4TH OF JULY....' (Like David Berkowitz's letters, they went written in capital letters and contained basic errors in spelling and syntax.) The author gave details of the ammunition that he had used, leaving no one in any doubt that he was indeed the gunman. Each letter also contained a third of a sheet of paper covered with a strange code, which the writer demanded that the papers print on their front pages; if they did not, he warned, he would go on 'killing lone people in the night'. The letters were signed with another cipher – a circle with a cross inside it which looked ominously like a gun sight.

All three of the newspapers complied with the writer's demands and the coded message was also sent to Mare Island Naval Yard, where cryptographers tried to crack it. Although it appeared to be a simple substitution code the

USA Navy's experts could not break it. Dale Harden, a teacher at Alisal High School in Salinas, however, could. Having had the idea of looking for a group of ciphers that might spell the word 'kill', he managed to locate them and after ten hours' intense work he and his wife had decoded the whole of the message, which read: 'I like killing people because it is so much more fun than killing wild game in the forest (sic) because man is the most dangerous of all to kill ...' The killer then went on to boast that he had already murdered five people in the San Francisco Bay area and added that after he had been reborn in paradise his victims would become his slaves.

After the murderer's cryptic message was made public a tidal wave of information was offered by ordinary citizens: over 1,000 calls were received by the police, but none of them led anywhere. So the killer helpfully volunteered another clue, this time revealing a name; or rather a nickname, that he knew would attract the attention of the headline-writers. Writing again to the newspapers, he began his letters 'DEAR EDITOR, THIS IS ZODIAC SPEAKING ...' He again gave details of the slaying of Darlene Ferrin that only the killer could have known. Yet although the killer's strategy increased his publicity profile the police were still no nearer to catching him.

On 28 September 1969 the 20-year-old Bryan Hartnell and the 22-year-old Cecelia Shepard – both students at the nearby Seventh-day Adventists' Pacific Union College – went for a picnic on the shores of Lake Berryessa, some 13 miles (21 kilometres) north of Vallejo. At around 4.30 pm they had finished eating and were lying on a blanket, kissing, when they noticed a stocky man, with brown hair, walking towards them across the clearing. Having disappeared momentarily into a copse, when he re-emerged he was wearing a mask and carrying a gun. As he came closer Bryan saw that the mask had a symbol on it: a white cross within a circle.

The man was not particularly threatening in his manner and his voice was soft. 'I want your money and your car keys', he said. Bryan explained that he only had 76 cents, but said that the masked man was welcome to that. The gunman then began to chat, telling them that he was an escaped convict and that he was going to have to tie them up with the clothesline that he had brought with him. Having forced Cecelia to tie up Bryan, he then trussed her up himself.

The gunman talked some more before calmly announcing 'I am going to have a stab you people', whereupon Bryan begged to be stabbed first, saying 'I couldn't bear to see her stabbed'. Having quietly agreed to this, the gunman sank to his knees and stabbed Bryan repeatedly in the back with a hunting knife. Although he was feeling dizzy and sick, Bryan was still conscious when the masked man turned his attention to Cecelia. Having initially appeared calm, after the first stab he went berserk, plunging the hunting knife into her body again and again while she frantically twisted and turned beneath him in a futile attempt to escape the blows. When she was finally lying still the man regained his composure. He got up, walked to their car, pulled a felt-tie pen from his pocket and then drew something on the door before strolling away.

A fisherman who had heard their screams ran towards them, to find both Bryan and Cecelia still alive. Napa Valley police officers were already on their way, having been alerted by an anonymous phone call in which a man's gruff voice had said 'I want to report a double murder', then going on to give the precise location at which the bodies could be found before leaving the phone hanging from its cord.

When the police arrived Cecelia was in a coma; she died two days later, in hospital, without having regained consciousness. Bryan recovered slowly and was able to give a full description of their attacker, but the police had already guessed who he was, for the sign that the killer had drawn on the door of their car was a circle with a cross within it. The police also located the phone booth from which the killer had reported the murder, it was less than six streets away from the headquarters of the Napa Valley Police Department. They furthermore managed to lift three good-quality fingerprints from it, although their owner's details were unfortunately not found among the police's records.

On 11 October 1969, just two weeks later, a fourteen-year-old girl was looking out of a window of her home in San Francisco when she witnessed a crime in progress. A taxi was parked on the corner of Washington and Cherry streets and she could see a stocky man, who was sitting in the front passenger seat, going through the pockets of the driver, who appeared to be dead. She called to her brothers to come and watch what was happening and together they observed the man getting out of the taxi, leaving the cab driver lying slumped across the seat, and wiping the door handle with a piece of cloth before walking off in a northerly direction. Although the children promptly called the police they did not give their evidence very clearly and the telephone operator who took the call (which was logged at 10pm) made a note that the suspect was an 'NMA' – Negro male adult – even though he was, in fact, white. Indeed, after the police had put out a general alert a patrolman actually stopped a stocky man near the scene of the crime and asked whether he had seen anything unusual; the man replied in the negative and because he was furthermore white the patrolman waved him on his way.

A stocky man was later seen running into the nearby Presidio – a military compound that contains housing and a park – whereupon the flood-lights were switched on and the area was searched by patrolmen with dogs, but with no success. When they inspected the taxi the police found the driver, the 29-year-old Paul Stine, lying dead from a gunshot wound to the head. The motive for his killing, they thought, was robbery.

Three days later the San Francisco Chronicle received a letter from Zodiac. 'THIS IS THE ZODIAC SPEAKING', it said. 'I AM THE MURDERER OF THE TAXI DRIVER OVER BY WASHINGTON ST AND MALE ST (sic) LAST NIGHT, TO PROVE IT HERE IS A BLOOD STAINED PIECE OF HIS SHIRT.' (The piece of cloth enclosed with the letter was indeed found to match the shirt of the murder taxi-driver. The bullet that had killed Stine was also identified as a .22 that had been fired from the same gun that had been used to kill Bettilou Jensen and David Faraday). The letter went on to say: 'I AM THE SAME MAN WHO DID IN THE PEOPLE IN THE NORTH BAY AREA'. THE S.F. POLICE COULD HAVE CAUGHT ME LAST NIGHT', it taunted, before concluding: 'SCHOOL CHILDREN MAKE NICE TARGETS. I THINK I SHALL WIPE OUT A SCHOOL BUS SOME MORNING. JUST SHOOT OUT THE TIRES AND THEN PICK OFF ALL THE KIDDIES AS THEY COME BOUNCING OUT.' The letter was signed with the now familiar circle containing a cross.

The description of the man supplied by the children, as well as by the policeman who had stopped the stocky, white male as he was leaving the scene of the crime, matched those given by Darlene Ferrin's babysitter, Mike Mageau and Bryan Hartnell. A new composite image of the Zodiac Killer was now drawn up and issued to the public by San Francisco's chief of police, Thomas J Cahill. It depicted a white male, 35 to 45 years old, with short, brown hair, which possibly had a red tint; he was described as being around 5 feet 8 inches (1.75 metres) tall, heavily built and a wearer of glasses. This 'wanted' poster was plastered around San Francisco.

The Zodiac Killer's appetite for publicity seems to have been insatiable. At 2 am on 22 October 1969, 11 days after the murder of Paul Stine, a man with a gruff voice called the police department in Oakland just across the bay from San Francisco. After introducing himself as Zodiac he said: 'I want to get in touch with F Lee Bailey. If you can't come up with Bailey I'll settle for Mel Belli. I want one or other of them to appear on the Channel 7 talk show. I'll make contact by telephone'.

The men for whom he had asked were the USA's two leading criminal lawyers, and although F Lee Bailey was not available at such short notice Melvin Belli agreed to appear on Jim Dunbar's talk show at 6.30 on the following morning. At around 7.20 am a man called in and told Belli that he was Zodiac, although he preferred to be called Sam. Then he said 'I'm sick. I have headaches'. The mystery caller was eventually traced to Napa State Hospital and proved to be a psychiatric patient.

The actual Zodiac continued his correspondence, however, writing to Inspector David Toschi, of San Francisco's homicide squad, and threatening to commit more murders. In another letter he claimed to have killed seven people – two more than the Zodiac Killer's official body count up till then. He later said that he had murdered 10, taunting the San Francisco Police Department (SFPD) with the score line 'ZODIAC 10, SFPD 0'. He furthermore gave cryptic clues as to his real name and shared his fantasy of blowing up school children with a bomb with the recipients of his letters.

The following Christmas Melvin Belli received a card saying 'DEAR MELVIN, THIS IS THE ZODIAC SPEAKING. I WISH YOU A HAPPY CHRISTMAS. THE ONE THING I ASK OF YOU IS THIS, PLEASE HELP ME ... I AM AFRAID I WILL LOSE CONTROL AND TAKE MY NINTH AND POSSIBLY TENTH VICTIM'. Another piece of Paul Stine's bloodstained shirt was enclosed. Forensic handwriting experts feared that Zodiac's mental state was deteriorating.

On the 24 July 1970 the Zodiac Killer wrote a letter that included the words: 'THE WOEMAN (sic) AND HER BABY THAT I GAVE A RATHER INTERESTING RIDE FOR A COUPLE OF HOWERS (sic) ONE EVENING A FEW MONTHS BACK THAT ENDED IN MY BURNING HER CAR WHERE I FOUND THEM'. The afore-mentioned woman was Kathleen Johns. On the evening of 17 March 1970 she was driving in the Vallejo area, with her baby in the car with her, when a white Chevrolet drew up alongside her. The driver indicated that there was something wrong with her rear wheel, so she pulled over and the other driver also stopped; according to Kathleen he was a 'clean-shaven and neatly dressed man'. He told her that her wheel had been wobbling and offered to tighten the wheel nuts for her, which she gratefully agreed to. When she drove off, however, the wheel that he had said that he had fixed came off altogether, whereupon the driver of the Chevrolet offered her a lift to a nearby service station. She again accepted his offer of help, but when they reached the service station he drove straight past it, replying to her query as to why he had done so in a chillingly calm voice. 'You know I am going to kill you', he said.

Kathleen managed to keep her head, however, and when her abductor slowed down on the curve of a motorway ramp she jumped from the car while holding her baby in her arms, ran off and hid in an irrigation ditch. The driver then stopped the Chevrolet and started to search for her, using a torch that he taken out of the boot of the car. Fortunately for Kathleen, he was approaching the ditch in which she was cowering with her child when he was caught in the beam of a lorry's headlights. An hour later, having watched him drive off, Kathleen made her way to a police station to report what had happened to her. On seeing Zodiac's 'wanted' poster pinned to the wall of the police station she identified him as the man who had threatened to killer her. When the police drove her back to her car they found that it was now a burnt-out shell – it seemed that the Zodiac Killer had returned to set it alight.

Despite the new leads that Kathleen Johns had provided the police were still no nearer to catching the Zodiac Killer, although the Vallejo-county police believed that he was now the driver of a new, green Ford. The reason behind their suspicion was that the driver of such a car had once stopped and ostentatiously watched a highway patrolman who was parked on the other side of the motorway. After the patrolman had decided to ask him what he was doing and had driven through an underpass to reach him he had found the green Ford gone: it was now parked on the other side of the motorway, exactly where the squad car had been moments before. Zodiac subsequently played this cat-and-mouse game every day for two weeks.

Detective Sergeant Lundblatt was becoming increasingly convinced that the Zodiac Killer was a man named Andy Walker. Walker had known Darlene Ferrin and Darlene's sister had also identified him as the man who had waited outside Darlene's flat in the white car. He bore a marked resemblance, too, to the description of the man who was seen near Lake Berrylessa when Cecelia Shepard was stabbed to death. Walker was also known to suffer from bad headaches and to get on badly with the women with whom he worked. He had furthermore studied codes while in the army.

However, neither did his fingerprints match the one that had been left in Paul Stine's taxi nor did his handwriting equate to that on Zodiac's notes. The police then discovered that Walker was ambidextrous, which meant that his handwriting would change depending on which hand he used to write with. They also formulated the theory that the murder of Paul Staine had been so meticulously planned that the Zodiac Killer may have used the severed finger of an unknown victim to plant fingerprints in the taxi and thereby throw the police off his scent.

The police decided that they had to obtain Walker's palm prints in order to see if they matched those that had been found on the telephone that had been left dangling after the Paul Stine killing. An undercover policeman therefore asked Walker to help him to carry a goldfish bowl, but although Walker obliged the palm prints that he left were smudged. Walker soon realised that he was being targeted by the police, however, and approached a judge, who issued a court order which forced them to stop harassing Walker.

Letters from Zodiac threatening more murders were received; some were authenticated, but rendered few new clues. The only thing that the police could be sure of was that Zodiac was a fan of the comic operettas of Gilbert and Sullivan. He had taunted them with a parody of 'The Lord High Executioner', listing those people whom he intended to kill and using the refrain 'Titwillo, titwillo, titwillo', and there were furthermore no letters on killings during the entire run of San Francisco's Presentation Theater's 'The Mikado'.

The police also deduced that Zodiac had a curious connection with water. Not only did all of the names of his crime scenes have some association with water, but in one of his letters he had claimed that the body count would have been higher if had not been 'swamped by the rain we had a while back'. The police therefore reasoned that he lived in a low-lying area that was susceptible to flooding or that he perhaps had a basement to which he kept equipment for making his long-threatened bomb.

Next a K-mart shop in Santa Rossa, California, was evacuated following a bomb threat made by a man who identified himself as the Zodiac Killer. Two months later Zodiac wrote another letter to the *San Francisco Chronicle* claiming to have killed 12 people and enclosing a map with an 'X' marking the peak of a mountain in Contra Costa Country, across the bay from San Francisco, from which an observer, he said, would be able to see the entire panorama of the area in which the murders had taken place. When detectives examined the location more closely, however, the spot marked was found to be within the compound of a naval relay station, to which only service personnel with security clearance were granted access.

The letters, which continued to come, now demanded that everyone in the San Francisco area wear lapel badges bearing the Zodiac Killer's symbol. Whey they did not comply he threatened Paul Avery, the *San Francisco Chronicle's* crime writer who had been investigating the Zodiac story, whereupon journalists (including Avery), began wearing badges saying 'I am not Paul Avery'. Avery, who was a licensed private eye and a former war correspondent in Vietnam, also started carrying a .38 and practised shooting regularly at the police firing range.

An anonymous correspondent then tied the Zodiac slaying to the unsolved murder of Cheri Jo Bates, an 18-year-old college student who had been stabbed to death after leaving the college library in Riverside, California, on Hallowe'en in 1966. Although the police could not rule out a connection they could not prove a concrete link either. When Avery investigated it, however, he discovered that the police had received what they considered to be a crank letter 'Z'. In a series of typewritten letters the author furthermore gave details of the murder that only the killer could have known. He also threatened more killings and wrote of a 'game' that he was playing. Handwritten letters were received, too, whose writing matched that of Zodiac's. Armed with this evidence, Avery managed to persuade the police to re-open the Bates case in the light of the Zodiac murders.

During 1971 there were a number of murders which could have been committed by Zodiac. Indeed, letters purporting to have come from him confessed to them, but he could easily have been claiming the credit for other people's handiwork.

At around 9 pm on 7 April 1972 the 33-year-old Isobel Watson, who worked as a legal secretary in San Francisco, got off a bus in Tamalpais Valley. She had just begun walking home, up Pine Hill, when a white Chevrolet swerved across the road and nearly hit her. After the car had come to a halt the driver apologised and offered to give her a lift home; when Isobel declined he got out of the car, pulled out a knife and stabbed her in the back. Her screams alerted her neighbours, who came running out of their homes, whereupon the man jumped back into his car and sped off. After Isobel had recovered she have a description of her attacker: he was a white man in his early forties, around 5 feet 9 inches (1.78 metres) tall, and had been wearing black-rimmed reading glasses. The police believed that there was a better than 50-50 chance that he was the Zodiac Killer.

As time went by, many of the detectives working on the Zodiac case were reassigned, and eventually only Inspector David Toschi was left. Agents from the Federal Bureau of Investigation (FBI) looked at the files, but even they could take the case no further. Zodiac's correspondence now ceased for nearly four years, but although psychologists believed that he was the type to commit suicide Toschi was not convinced that he was dead. He reasoned that Zodiac got his kicks from the publicity that his murders generated rather than from the killings themselves and that he would therefore have left a note or some other clue that he was Zodiac if he had killed himself. Then, on 25 April 1978, Toschi received confirmation that Zodiac was still alive when the *San Francisco Chronicle* received a letter from him. It mentioned Toschi by name and said that the writer wanted the people of San Francisco to know that he was back.

Robert Graysmith, the author of the book *Zodiac*, deduced that the eponymous murderer was a film buff. In one of his cryptograms, for example, he had mentioned the 'most dangerous game', which is the title of a film, in another calling himself the 'Red Phantom', which is also the name of a film. He furthermore frequently mentioned going to the cinema to see *The Exorcist* or *Badlands*, the latter a fictionalised account of the murderous spree of the Nebraskan killer Charles Starkweather.

The police used the information supplied by Graysmith, as well as the Zodiac Killer's obvious love of publicity, to try to trap him. When a film about the Zodiac killing was shown in San Francisco a suggestion box was installed in the lobby of the cinema, into which the audience was invited to drop notes containing any information or theories that they may have had regarding the murders. Inside the huge box was hidden a detective, who read every note by torchlight as it fell through the slot; he had been ordered to raise the alarm if any looked as though they could have come from the Zodiac Killer, but none did.

The Oakland police though that they had captured the Zodiac Killer at one point. The suspect was a veteran of the Vietnam War who had seen the Zodiac film three times and had been apprehended while masturbating in the cinema's lavatory after a particularly violent scene. They were soon proved wrong, however, for his handwriting did not match Zodiac's. Amid a welter of recrimination Toschi was transferred from homicide following (baseless) accusations that he had forged the Zodiac letters for self-promotion. The police in the Bay area now began to believe that the Zodiac Killer was either dead or serving him for another crime in a prison outside the state. On the other hand, maybe he reckoned that his time was running out, having nearly been caught following the killing of Paul Stine.

Robert Graysmith was not convinced by these theories, however. He had managed to link the Zodiac killings with the unsolved murders of 14 young girls, usually students or hitchhikers, in the Santa Rosa area during the early 1970s. Although most of them had been found naked, with their clothes missing, they had generally not been sexually molested. Each had been killed in a different way, as if the murdered had been experimenting to ascertain which method was best. Graysmith now reckoned that Zodiac's body count could be as high as 40.

Graysmith believed that Zodiac's symbol – a cross within a circle – was not intended to represent a stylised gunsight, but rather the projectionist's guide that is shown on screen during the lead-in to a film. He traced a promising-sounding suspect through a cinema in San Francisco on whose ceiling the constellations were painted: the man, Graysmith was told, had filmed some murders and kept the gruesome footage in a booby-trapped can. Another suspect of Graysmith's was a former boyfriend of Darlene Ferrin, who had also been a resident of Riverside at the time when Cheri Jo Bates was murdered. He lived with his mother, whom he loathed, and dissected small mammals as a hobby. During the crucial 1975 to 1978 period, when the Zodiac Killer had been quiet, he had been in psychiatric institution after having been charged with molesting children at the school where he was employed. Graysmith could not pin the Zodiac murders on either of his suspects, however. He published the story of his investigation in 1955.

In 1990 a series of murders was perpetrated in New

York by someone who claimed to be Zodiac. Although descriptions of the New York killer did not match those given by the witnesses to the Zodiac murders in California, a man can change a lot over 20 years. Who can tell where he may strike next?

The Wests

Number 25 Cromwell Street, Gloucester: an ordinary house in an ordinary terrace. The man of the house, Fred West, was cheerful and hard-working. His wife, Rosemary, was a busy, lively mother. They were generally liked by their neighbours. Although there was some gossip about the number of men who visited the house late at night, and some said that they disciplined their children too harshly, it was nothing that they felt that they should tell the police or social services about. The Wests, however, had some minor legal problems: during the 1970s the upper floors of the house had been divided into cheap bedsits and Fred, a builder by trade, had added a single-storey extension to the rear of the property without obtaining planning permission for it.

The story of what was actually going on behind the façade of this apparently ordinary house began to unravel during the summer of 1992. Police Constable Steve Burnside was patrolling his Gloucester beat when a group of young people came up to him and told him that children were being abused at a house in Cromwell Street, which was owned by a man named 'Quest'. Although the young informants were unsure of the facts, it was enough to warrant further police attention and as a result social services eventually took the five of Wests' children who were under sixteen into care. Fred and Rosemary were charged with a number of sexual offences, including rape and buggery, but the case against them was dropped when two prosecution witnesses refused to testify. Fred and Rosemary hugged each other in the dock and then returned to their old ways as if nothing had happened.

Detective Constable Hazel Savage, however, who had investigated the initial allegations, remained convinced something terrible was going on in Cromwell Street. During quiet chats with the West children she had won their trust; they seemed particularly concerned about the disappearance of Fred and Rosemary's 16-year-old daughter, Heather, who had last been seen on 29 May 1987. Her parents had not even reported her as being missing, and when questioned had said that she had left home of her own accord 'with a lesbian in a blue Mini'. But the children said that Fred would often joke about Heather being 'under the patio' and Savage believed that these 'jokes' were made a little too often to be simply the product of poor taste. On 23 February 1994 she therefore obtained a search warrant enabling her gain access to the property at Cromwell Road and the following day the police started to dig up the garden.

A mechanical digger was brought in to remove the topsoil. Then, in the pouring rain, an 'archeological-type dig' began, under the aegis of the Home Office pathologist Professor Bernard Knight. Supervised by Detective Superintendent John Bennett, a team of 30 officers, working relays, began sifting shovelfuls of sodden earth through a sieve in the search for clues. At night the work continued under the glare of arc lights. On the second day a trowel hit something hard and the loose soil was scraped away to reveal a human skull. It was thought to be Heather's, and on 25 February 1994 Fred and Rosemary West were arrested. 'I didn't kill her' shouted Fred, as the couple was driven away in a police car.

After the police had interviewed her Rosemary was released without charge. By the time that her husband appeared in Gloucester magistrates' court a few days later to be formally charged with murder two more bodies had been found. Both were badly decomposed, having lain in the garden for 16 years.

One of the bodies was identified as being that of Shirley Ann Robinson, a lodger at 25 Cromwell Street who had last been seen in 1977. At the time of her death she had been 18 years old and heavily pregnant. According to Liz Brewer, another lodger, Fred West was the father of her child and Rosemary West had also been pregnant with another man's child at the time. 'The Wests had told Shirley they had an open marriage', said Liz. 'Fred didn't seem to mind his wife expecting by another man.' When Shirley had disappeared the Wests had informed Liz that Shirley could not cope with the growing tension between Fred and Rosemary and had gone to visit relatives in Germany. 'I was told she probably wasn't coming back'. she said.

Over the next five days the bodies of two more women were unearthed in the cellar of the house. The situation was becoming so gruesome that the police officers involved in the excavation were given stress counselling: 40 more policemen were also seconded to the investigation. The police now thought that there were five more bodies in the house and two further corpses buried in a field near Fred West's former home in Much Marcle. At 25 Cromwell Street the floorboards were lifted, fittings were ripped out and 200 tons of soil were excavated from the garden. In addition, the police opened up the chimney breast and broke up the bathroom floor using pneumatic drills. They furthermore discovered that the basement had been dug out to a depth of 5 feet (1.5 metres), which had undermined the foundations of the house.

Next a sixth body – again that of a young woman – was found buried under the cellar and it was then that the police brought in a ground-penetrating radar system. Developed during the Falklands Conflict to locate plastic landmines, it was the first time that this technology had been used in a murder investigation. The device cost £2,000 a day to rent. A seventh body was located under concrete in the cellar; the eighth was buried 4 feet (1.2 metres) beneath the bath on the ground floor (Fred's brother-in-law, Graham Letts, had helped him to lay the concrete floor there in 1987). The ninth, that of the 15-year-old Carol Ann Cooper, was discovered behind a false wall in the bathroom. Carol had last been seen on 10 November 1973; she had been in care at a children's home in Worcester at the time, but had been let out for the weekend to visit her grandmother.

The police also sealed off the nearby 25 Midland Road, the Wests' former home. Other bodies were thought to have been buried in a cornfield, known as Fingerpost Field, on the road between Much Marcle and Dymock. They decided that up to 3 properties at which Fred West had lived or worked would also have to be searched.

By 11 March 1994 Fred West had been charged with eight murders. Throughout the investigation he had been questioned by relays of detectives, who had found him to be co-operative 'some of the time'. From their interviews with him they had been able to piece together the bare bones of his life story.

Frederick Walter Stephen West was born on 29 September 1942 in Much Marcle. He lived with his parents and siblings at Moor Court Cottages and developed his powerful physique while working as a farm labourer. His mother's favourite son, Daisy was believed to have seduced him when he was 12. His father, Walter – also a farm labourer – enjoyed incestuous relationships, too, and regarded his daughters as sexual playthings; Fred would follow in his father's footsteps.

At the age of 19 Fred was arrested after having impregnated a 13-year-old girl. When questioned by the police he was unabashed and openly admitted to molesting young girls, asking 'Doesn't everyone do it?' Although West escaped a charge of statutory rape when his victim refused to give evidence in court, his mother threw him out of the house and he went to live nearby, with his Aunt Violet. He then started work as a lorry driver, soon afterwards meeting the woman who would become his first wife; a blonde, 18-year-old witness named Catherine 'Rena' Costello.

Rena was already five months pregnant by another when she married Fred on 17 November 1962. Fred gave the baby, Charmaine, his surname, and he and Rena then had a child of their own, Anne-Marie. They moved briefly to Lanarkshire and then to a caravan park in Bishop's Cleeve, near Cheltenham. The marriage was already in trouble because West wanted to play sadistic sex games, which Rena hated. When she subsequently disappeared West told his friends that she had taken up with an engineer and had returned to Lanarkshire. She was never seen again. Meanwhile, West had started seeing the 15-year-old Rosemary Letts.

Rosemary Pauline Letts was born on 29 November 1953 in Barnstaple. Her father, Williams Letts, was a steward in the Royal Navy who battered and bullied his wife and treated their seven children with appalling severity (he was later diagnosed as being schizophrenic). As the third-youngest of children, Rosemary escaped the worst of his father's attentions, however. When the family moved to Bishop's Cleeve her mother walked out, taking Rosemary and her two younger brothers with her. Later in the same year Rosemary met the 27-year-old Fred West at a bus stop and they soon began going steady. Fred had probably already committed one murder – maybe two – by this time, while the 15-year-old Rosemary was making a little pocket money from prostitution.

Rosemary's parents disapproved of the relationship and put Rosemary into care, but when Rosemary attained her independence at the age of 16 she moved in with West and his two daughters at the local caravan site. In 1970 they had a daughter of their own, Heather. Thereafter the Wests moved to a two-story, pebble-dash house in Midland Road, Gloucester, along with Fred's daughter, Anne-Marie. Charmaine had been put into care in 1969, but was later returned to Fred, going missing shortly afterwards. The Wests apparently abused her viciously, on the grounds that she was 'not of theirs', and at Rosemary's trial witnesses told of seeing Charmaine standing on a chair, her hands tied behind her back, while Rosemary beat her with a wooden spoon.

The police believed that Fred had killed Charmaine at around this time and that when Rena had come looking for her daughter he had killed her, too. Neither was reported missing and when Rosemary was asked where Charmaine was she replied 'She's gone off with her mother'. West certainly did not expect any problems to be caused by his first wife when he married Rosemary on 29 January 1972 at Gloucester Registry Office, for on the marriage certificate he entered his marital status as 'bachelor'. Three days later the Wests moved into 25 Cromwell Street. Here they would create their own fantasy world, a world in which Rosemary not only gave free reign to Fred's desire for sadistic sex, but actively indulged in it herself. The house in Cromwell Street was also home to a family of nine children, at least two of which were fathered by another man (West was furthermore said to have fathered as many as 24 children by different women). Because his wages were not enough to support such a large family the Wests supplemented their income by taking in lodgers and by Rosemary's prostitution under the working name of 'Mandy Mouse'.

Neighbours remembers Fred West as being a devoted father who loved taking his children to the seaside and worked hard for a number of local employers. Using his do-it-yourself skills he turned 25 Cromwell Street into a temple to Formica. The downstairs front room was turned into a bedroom for Rosemary; set into the floor was a trap door which led down to the cellar, which West converted into two rooms in which four of the children slept. There was another bedroom, with a lace-canopied bed, on the first floor, as well as a sitting room containing a fully stocked bar, television and video (this storey was out of bounds to the children). On the top floor was one more bedroom, which was kept locked. It contained a four poster bed that was fitted with spotlights and a concealed microphones; whips, chains, manacles and bondage gear were also to hand. It was here that they shot home-made, hardcore pornographic films starring the Wests and the punters who paid for Rosemary's services as a prostitute.

The coupled lived for sex and were both constantly on the lookout for young women whom they could use as sexual playthings. Rosemary played a key role in this, Fred later explaining that it was a lot easier to pick up girls when he had Rosemary in the car with him because their victims felt more secure with a woman being present. After the young women had been lured to Cromwell Street their faces were bound with sticky, brown parcel tape and plastic breathing tubes were stuffed into their nostrils. Then their limbs were tightly bound and they were repeatedly raped and tortured. After they had died their bodies were mutilated – some say cannibalised – and their remains were then tossed unceremoniously into pits that had been dug in the cellar or back garden. (No one thought it odd that Fred did a lot of do-it-yourself work around the house – after all, he was a builder.)

By 8 April 1994 the police had identified every one of the nine bodies that had been found at 25 Cromwell Street. They were all those of young women aged between 15 and 21. Four had last been seen waiting for buses.

Lynda Gough, a seamstress who worked at the Co-op

in Gloucester, had disappeared in April 1973 – just two weeks before her twentieth birthday – when she had left her parents' home to move into a flat in Gloucester. Her distraught parents had made enormous efforts to find her. The Swiss-born Thérèse Siegenthaler, a 21-year sociology student at Woolwich College in south London, had left Lewisham home for the Holyhead ferry on 15 April 1974 to hitchhike to Ireland. She had boasted that because she was a judo expert she could take care of herself. The third body found in the garden was that of the 17-year-old Alison Chambers, who had been placed with a firm of solicitors in Gloucester under the Youth Training Scheme. Alison had run away from her home in south Wales and had written to her mother saying that she was staying with a 'big family'.

The police team then moved to Letterbox Field, on Stonehouse Farm at Kempley. After a trench 135 feet (41 metres) long had been dug and 160 tons of soil removed the remains of West's first wife, Rena, were found She had gone missing at the age of 24 and her remains were identified on 14 April 1994, which would have been her fiftieth birthday. A quarter of a mile away, at Fingerpost Field, in Stonehouse Copice, police found the remains of Anna McFall, a nanny who had been employed by Rena who had vanished during the early 1970s at the age of 22. The remains of Charmaine West, who had disappeared in 1971 at the age of eight, were found under the kitchen floor at 25 Midland Road.

Up until this time it had been assumed that Fred West alone was responsible for the murders. On 21 April 1994, however, Rosemary West was jointly charged with a 67-year-old man with raping an 11-year-old girl and assaulting a 7-year-old boy, causing actual bodily harm. Although man was released on bail Rosemary continued to be held. Two days later she was charged with having sexual intercourse with the same girl without her consent.

After that she was charged with the murders of Lynda Gough, Carol Ann Cooper, Lucy Partington, Thérèse Seigenthaler, Shirley Hubbard, Juanita Mott, Shirley Robinson, Alison Chambers, and finally, on 26 May 1994, of her own daughter, Heather. Fred West had already been accused of all nine murders, as well as of the murders of two people whose remains had been found at Midland Road and Leterbox Field, but who had not yet been identified. His younger brother, John Charles Edward West, was accused of raping two underaged girls, along with Rosemary.

The most extraordinary thing about the West case was that they had got away with it for so long; for more than two decades the Wests' secret careers as sadistic sexual torturers and murderers of young women had flourished unchecked. West had killed his first victim – Anna McFall, from Sandhurst, Gloucestershire – before he had even met Rose. West had made Anna pregnant while she was working as a nanny for him and Rena in 1967 and had murdered her because she wanted him to leave Rena. The next two to die were Rena and little Charmaine. The police believed that West had killed his wife when she came looking for her daughter in 1971 and that Charmaine was strangled a few hours later.

Victim number four was the nineteen-year-old Lynda Gough. A local girl, she had become friendly with some of the Wests' lodgers at the Cromwell Street house and had moved in herself in March 1973. She had found herself becoming unwillingly involved in the Wests' twisted sex games and was dead within a matter of weeks. Her body had been buried under the bathroom floor; tape had been wound thickly around her head and her dismembered limbs had been piled on top of one another.

The fifth victim was the 15-year-old Carol Ann Cooper, who lived in a children's home in Worcester and was last seen boarding a bus on the way to her grandmother's on the night of 10 November 1973. Although West admitted killing her he said that Rosemary had not been involved. Number six was the twenty-one-year-old Lucy Partington. A devout religious student, she was studying medieval English at Exeter University when the Wests spotted her waiting at a bus stop in Cheltenham as they drove back from a Christmas visit to Rosemary's parents in Bishop's Cleeve on the night of 27 December 1973. At 25 Cromwell Street she endured a week-long ordeal of rape and torture. West did such a sloppy job dismembering her body that he cut his hand and had to go to hospital.

The next of the Wests' known victims was the Swiss-born Thérèse Siegenthaler. The 21-year-old had been hitchhiking to Ireland for a holiday when West had picked her up in his lorry near Chepstow. She was then taken to Cromwell Street, where she was imprisoned, tortured and raped. When the police unearthed her remains at Cromwell Street some of her body parts were found to be missing. Number eight was the fifteen-year-old Shirley Hubbard, a schoolgirl from Droitwich who had disappeared on 14 November 1974 while she was travelling by bus from Worcester to her parents' home. She, too, had been forced to wear one of West's 'mummy' style masks before being repeatedly raped.

The 18-year-old Juanita Mott was picked up as she hitch-hiked into Gloucester from her home in Newent on 11 April 1975. Lured to their home by the Wests, she was then trussed up with 17 feet (5 metres) of grey, plastic clothesline and her own stockings. After the Wests had finished with her Fred killed her with a blow from a hammer before decapitating her body and burying it in the cellar. Their tenth victim was Shirley Robinson. A bisexual, the eighteen-year-old had shared three-in-a-bed sex sessions with the Wests during early 1978 before becoming pregnant with West's child and falling in love with him (Rosemary had also been pregnant in 1978 with the child of a West Indian man). Rosemary had become jealous of Shirley and had put pressure on her husband to get rid of her. He had compiled: Shirley's body was found next to that of her unborn child in the garden of 25 Cromwell Street.

A few months after Shirley had disappeared the Wests had latched on to the 16-year-old Alison Chambers, who was living in a children's home in Gloucester at the time and was exactly the kind of vulnerable girl that they liked. One of her friends was a lodger at 25 Cromwell Street and she visited the house regularly. The Wests had asked her to become their nanny and shortly after she had moved in they had involved her in their sadistic sex play. The police found her body underneath the Wests' lawn.

Their last-known victim was Heather West. Born in 1970, Heather was thought to have been the product of an incestuous relationship between Bill Letts and his daughter, Rosemary. Fred had made her life a living hell: when she had refused to let him molest her he had beaten her viciously. When she vanished, on 17 June 1987, the Wests told friends that she had run away from home.

The Wests were reunited in the dock of Gloucester's magistrates' court on 30 June 1994. West brushed his wife's neck with his hand and bent down to speak a few words to her, but Rosemary ignored him and refused even to glance at him. As they rose to leave the court after the brief hearing West tried to touch his wife again, only to receive the same response. They appeared together again for one last time in December 1994, when Rosemary West again pointedly ignored her husband.

On New Year's Day, 1995, Fred West was found hanged in his cell in Winson Green Prison. He had made a rope by plaiting strips of sheet together. Standing on a chair, he had the tied his home-made rope to a ventilator shaft, put the noose around this neck and kicked away the chair. (Things had not gone to plan, however, for the fall had not broken his neck and he was slowly strangled to death instead.) His suicide left Rosemary to face ten murder charges alone, along with two counts of rape and two of indecent assault. Her trial, which was presided over by Mr Justice Mantell, opened at Winchester Crown Court on Tuesday, 3 October 1995.

An early witness was Caroline Owens, who had been picked up by the Wests while she was hitchhiking in 1972. They had bound, beaten and raped her, she said, further alleging that Fred West had threatened that he would murder her. A witness described as 'Miss A' also said that she had been abused by the Wests at 25 Cromwell Street. And Anne-Marie, Fred's daughter, described how she had been raped by Fred and Rosemary at the age of eight; West had told her that she 'should be grateful' and that all fathers did this to their daughters. She had become pregnant by her father at the age of 15, but he had arranged an abortion.

In her defence Rosemary West claimed that she was innocent. She said that her husband had manipulated her into participating in the assault on Caroline Owens, but stated that she did not know 'Miss A'. She furthermore denied all knowledge of the murders, as well as of the alleged assault on her stepdaughter, Ann-Marie. The defence played four of Fred West's taped interviewed with the police, in which he had admitted to committing the murders and had said that Rosemary had played no part in them. The prosecution then called Janet Leach as a rebuttal witness. She had sat in on the police interviews with West and testified that when she and West were along together after the interviews he had given a different version of his story, explaining that he had lied to the police in order to protect Rosemary, who had committed some of the murders. West had also told her that there were at least 20 more bodies that had not been discovered by the police.

The jury found Rosemary West guilty of all ten counts of murder. In passing sentence Mr Justice Mantell said 'Rosemary Pauline West, on each of the ten counts of murder of which you have been unanimously convicted by the jury the sentence is one of life imprisonment. If attention is paid to what I think you will never be released. Take her down'. He also ordered that the outstanding rape charges against her should be left on file.

On 19 March 1996 Rosemary West lost her appeal against her conviction. Meanwhile, the police continued their investigations into the deaths of nine other girls who had visited Cromwell Street and were never seen again

The Monster of Florence

In 1968 Antonio Io Bianci was making love to Barbara Locci in the front seat of his car when they were both shot dead, Barbara's husband being subsequently arrested and convicted of the murders. It would be six years before Signor Locci could prove his innocence and establish that the double murder was the first atrocity committed by a serial killer who preyed on counting couples in Tuscancy who later became known as the 'Monster of Florence'.

While Signor Locci was languishing in jail another courting couple was killed in a car. The police established that they had been shot with the same .22-calibre Beretta pistol that had been used in the Bianchi and Locci murders; the female victim had furthermore been mutilated. During the course of the next year two more people were killed in a similar manner. Although a German couple was murdered, too, neither of them was mutilated (they were homosexuals and their killing was probably a mistake).

Upon Signor Locci's release the Monster of Florence appeared to suspend his activities. He struck again in

1981, however, stabbing his female victim some 300 times. Four months later, in October 1981, another woman was murdered and mutilated. The Monster of Florence continued to wage his campaign of murder over the next four years. The slayings followed a rigid pattern: all of the men were shot through the driver's window before the women were killed, their bodies then being dragged from the car and mutilated with a knife (their left breasts were generally hacked off). Ballistics tests revealed that all of the 67 bullets that were fired in a total of 16 murders came from the same gun, all also being marked with the letter 'H'. The Monster of Florence's final attack, in 1985, differed slightly from the rest, however. He slaughtered his last victims – a French couple – in their tent, cutting off a section of the woman's genitalia (which he later posted to the police) during his grisly mutilation of her body.

The Florence police handled the case badly. Numerous false accusations were made and one man who had been named as the killer committed suicide by cutting his throat. Another five were jailed for the killings, three of whom were released when the Monster struck again while they were behind bars; because there was no evidence against a fourth a judge released him, while the fifth man remained the subject of controversy.

During the course of the Monster of Florence's bloody reign of terror the police received scores of anonymous notes identifying Petro Pacciani as the killer. Pacciani was a peasant farmer who had been convicted of murder in 1951 and jailed for 13 years for killing a rival in love. (Pacciani had followed his 16-year-old fiancée upon seeing her going into the woods with another man; when he could no longer stand the sight of them making love he had stabbed the man 19 times before raping the terrified girl next to the mutilated corpse.) The police speculated that if he was indeed the Monster of Florence the embittered Pacciani had sought to avenge himself on other couples. Key to their thinking was the theory that it had been the sight of his fiancés exposed left breast during her seduction that had triggered Pacciani's initial attack and that this was also why the Monster usually amputated the left breasts of his female victims. Pacciani had again come to the police's attention in 1987, subsequently being convicted of molesting his two daughters and accordingly being jailed.

His name was fed into a computer, along with those of more than 100,000 people who had the opportunity of carrying out the Monster of Florence's crimes. The computer identified just one suspect, however: Pacciani. Convinced that Pacciani was the perpetrator of the murders, the police searched his farm in minute detail for evidence, but nothing was found. They were on the point of giving up when a bullet was unearthed which was later found to match those that had been used in the murders.

Although a weapon was never recovered Pacciani was charged with murder. His trial dragged on for six months before the jury finally convicted him, whereupon he was jailed for life in 1994. Subsequently, however, a judicial review reassessed the flimsy evidence against him and after its ruling that his conviction was unsafe Pacciani was released from prison in 1996. As far as anyone knows the Monster of Florence is still at large.

Kurt Cobain

The tragic death of rock band Nirvana's Kurt Cobain on 5 April, 1994 sent shock waves around the world's music industry. His apparent suicide rocked the heart of youth culture, as his name was added to the list of stars to were too young to die.

Cobain's early life certainly influenced his later outlook on life and perspective of the world. Born on February 20,

1967 Kurt Cobain spent his early childhood years in the sleepy town of Aberdeen in the state of Washington. By nature a weak, often sickly child, Cobain's childhood memories were not, for the most part, happy ones, especially when his parents divorced around his seventh birthday. This, by his own account, was a turning point in his life. Gone were the ideal securities and united love of his family and Cobain reacted to this sadness by emerging an increasingly difficult and troublesome child. After the divorce, Cobain was passed around from relative to relative, effectively without a permanent address most of the time.

Cobain's teenage years in Aberdeen, like most young children, were heavily influenced by music. He and friend Krist Novoselic (who also later became a band-member of Nirvana) were enormous fans of the *Sex Pistols* and other similar punk bands whose aggressive lyrics and hardfast music fired the imagination of many at that time.

By 1985, Cobain was ready to move on. At 18, he moved to Olympia and began forming rock band after rock band of his own. Nirvana was formed in 1986 and consisted of Cobain, Novoselic and Dave Grohl. They performed strong, meaningful songs from the start, earning themselves early recognition. By 1988 Nirvana had produced their first album, *Bleach*.

Heavy promotional work led to them gaining rapid international fame, particularly across the Atlantic in Britain. When, in 1991 they released their second album, *Nevermind*, the band was propelled into mega stardom.

Cobain was the principal songwriter of the group. He confessed his lyrics came out of the anguish of his childhood years, and the anger that he needed to release after his parents all but rejected him. The tracks on *Nevermind* were musically and lyrically stronger than those on *Bleach*, and the first single which they released from the second album, *Smells Like Teen Spirit*, became an anthem for Nirvana fans around the world.

As an overnight millionaire and a critically acclaimed songwriter and musician, Cobain was pushed into the public eye under the microscopic gaze of the world's media. Still fundamentally an insecure and often sickly man, Cobain did not cope with the pressure well. Even today, many consider his disbelief at Nirvana's success did nothing to prepare him for the fame and fortune of rock'n'roll.

Cobain's passionate lyrics and his perpetual desire to relieve his angst through his music fuelled his surprise at the following Nirvana gained. The pressure of just how much his music influenced others, and how little he could control just whom it influenced, affected Cobain greatly. He was easily upset when his music was misinterpreted and began to rely heavily on heroin to deal with the pressures of rock star life, and also to overcome the pain of the continual medical problems he had been unable to leave behind with his childhood.

In the early nineties, Cobain found love in the form of fellow rock star, Courtney Love. They were married in Hawaii in February, 1992. Courtney Love was already pregnant when they were married, and gave birth to Frances Cobain later in the year. Their marriage from the start had huge ups and downs. Its endurance was reportedly often shaky, but they remained together, both unified in their love for their young daughter.

In early 1993, Nirvana released the well-received album *In Utero*, which contained material more personal and more passionate than Cobain had written before. Shortly after, Nirvana's *Unplugged* tour was to be the last recording the band made together. Cobain became increasingly wary of the influence his music had on people, and at the same time more dependent on heroin. An avid gun collector, Cobain had pursued an interest in handguns for some time, and possessed a collection of them.

Part-way through Nirvana's European tour in 1994, Cobain was taken ill and the band cancelled a number of scheduled performances. Whilst recovering from his illness, Cobain attempted suicide. He was rushed to hospital having consumed a large amount of strong painkillers, washed down with champagne. The suicide bid was covered up as an accident (so much so that close friends and relatives did not hear about it) and he soon returned home to Seattle. Courtney Love convinced Cobain to start a detox rehabilitation program upon his homecoming. Cobain did so, but checked himself out after only a few days into the program. This was the last time Cobain saw his family; after he checked himself out of the program, he was officially reported as missing.

An electrician who was visiting his mansion found his body on April 7, 1994. The workman simply wanted to install a new security system, and when no one answered the front door, he went around the back of the property. Peering in at the window of the annexe-room at the back of the mansion, the stunned electrician saw Cobain lying on the floor. He called the police who discovered Cobain's body crumpled on the floor with a shotgun pointing to his chin. Post-event medical reports state that Cobain killed himself two days earlier on April 5, by putting a shotgun in his mouth. Found near to the body was a suicide note addressed to his wife and his little girl.

Cobain's death came as shock to most. Distraught fans, his grieving family and the stunned music world all paid tribute alike to the talented musician and songwriter whose work had affected so many. Some fans took the death to heart. A memorial a couple of days after the discovery of Cobain's death was far from peaceful, and police were needed to cope with the angry and disbelieving crowd.

For some fans, the news of Cobain's death was too much. He had represented so much to so many and several cases of copy-cat suicides across the world were reported. Nirvana, Kurt Cobain and youth culture are still synonomous today. The impact their music had on fans was, and is still, overshadowed by the media's desire to highlight all that was bad about Cobain's heroin-filled existence and his angst-filled music.

For some, Kurt Cobain's 'suicide' never happened. They feel the circumstances surrounding the rock star's death are far from clear and a flawed police investigation, and a misrepresentation by the media have led to a debatable verdict. Was Kurt Cobain's tragic loss of life, and the end of so much talent, really the result of suicide or could it have been murder? Or was his tortured existence finally too much for Cobain to take, fuelling his death wish to its ultimate conclusion? His status as a rock legend enhanced and elevated in death like so many other "too fast to live, too young to die" icons of our time, the death of Kurt Cobain will remain an unsolved mystery forever.

Michael Hutchence

No superstar death in recent years has caused as much speculation as that of the INXS lead singer, Michael Hutchence. He left behind a web of mystery in the circumstances surrounding his death in a Sydney hotel room in November, 1997.

Born on January 22, 1960 in Australia, Michael Hutchence spent the early years of his life living in Sydney. However, as a result of his father's job, Hutchence's family left Sydney for Hong Kong when he was just four years old. For a child, Hong Kong was an exotic location in which to grow up, but more notably it was the place where a toy company gave Hutchence his first paid singing assignment.

The family moved back to Australia in 1972, settling in

Sydney once more. Hutchence's teenage years were spent in the city, growing up with Andrew Farris (later a band-member of INXS) as a best friend. But times were not all good. Hutchence's parents divorced when he was just fifteen; his father remained in Sydney while his mother relocated to America. Forced to choose a home, Hutchence went to the US with his mother. However Hutchence soon moved back, once more, to Sydney and took up residence with his father. Back at the same high school with his friends, Hutchence joined an extra-curricular band "The Farris Brothers" with Andrew, Tim and Jon Farris, along with Garry Beers and Kirk Pengilly. The boys took the band seriously, and, when the time came two years later to leave high school, they remained as a group, concentrating on writing new material and practising for small gigs in the city.

The group went from strength to strength and in 1980 they signed their first contract with a record company. The group also changed their name to the more marketable INXS. Over the next four years, INXS gained experience, record sales and more importantly, publicity.

In 1987, and six albums later, INXS were one of the most popular and marketable bands of the time. They had received increasing critical acclaim for their music and Michael Hutchence was recognised as an international superstar in his own right. The late 1980's were without doubt the peak of INXS's pop life. But fame and fortune had its drawbacks. Hutchence, like many similar pop stars cum superstars of the time, threw himself into the arms of the world that encapsulated sex, drugs and rock'n'roll. He became famous for his prolific drug taking and supposedly wild sex life as he did for his music. He had a string of beautiful and famous girl friends, most notably the Australian singer Kylie Minogue and the Danish supermodel Helena Christensen.

As a superstar in his own right, Hutchence considered

leaving INXS to pursue a solo career, but soon rejoined the band to record their seventh album, *X*, a successful album by any standards but not as popular as their previous album had been. The resounding success of the group's late eighties music had become their benchmark, and new material, although selling extremely well, was not quite as popular as it had once been. The early nineties was an increasingly difficult period for Hutchence, knowing that INXS had had their heyday. In 1995, his personal fortunes changed when he met Paula Yates and entered into an affair with the then-wife of Sir Bob Geldof. The affair rapidly became public knowledge and Geldof wasted no time in filing for divorce. The courts granted this but a more involved question remained – who would retain custody of Yates' three children by Geldof?

In what became a much-publicised and fought out custody battle, the future of the three children was for the time being undecided. Yates and Hutchence had a child of their own – Heavenly Hiraani Tiger Lily in July 1996. The couple lived together with their child in London, with the custody battle continuing in the meantime. In 1998, the band members celebrated 20 years of INXS by undertaking a world tour, the final leg of which was in Australia. The last two days of Hutchence's life, November 21 and 22, were spent in Sydney at the end of the tour. But they are two days which have been greatly scrutinised and speculated upon as no one, it seems, can comprehend why Michael Hutchence died there and then.

On the evening of the 21st, Hutchence spent time with his father, who has since stated that his son seemed fine that evening and certainly did not show any cause for concern. Back in his hotel room later that evening, Hutchence was contacted by Yates with the news that she and the four children could not come out to Australia to visit him due to restrictions of the court case. The events of the remainder of the evening have been pieced together from the telephone calls that Hutchence made and also from the recollections of two friends who spent the evening in the hotel room with the singer until the early hours of the following day.

The following morning, Hutchence's naked, lifeless body was found crumpled behind the door of his hotel room. He had seemingly died as the result of hanging. A coroner ruled a verdict of suicide.

The coroner's report, for the most part, should be taken as read and accepted as an end to what is a sad, tragic and wasteful loss of a talented life. Hutchence had been on medication for depression and there was speculation that his marriage to Paula Yates was hitting a rocky patch, especially with the pressure of the custody battle. The news that his wife and the children would not be able to fly out to Australia probably added to the cloud of sadness that Hutchence was apparently under.

But even the coroner had to base his opinion and verdict on a set of circumstances which he chose to interpret in his own, ultimately partially subjective way. So if another person were to consider the same circumstances, reports and evidence, would they have arrived at the same conclusion?

It was even suggested that Hutchence may have died as a result of a wild sexual act that went wrong. Two people – Kym Wilson and Andrew Rayment – spent most of the night of the 21st with Hutchence in his hotel room, and remained there until the early hours of the following morning, leaving just hours before Hutchence's body was discovered. Both stated that Hutchence had seemed worried about the court case, but otherwise nothing else appeared different about his character. All three consumed a variety of drinks that evening.

Several close associates received calls from Hutchence on the evening of the 21st and on the morning of the 22nd. One was Michelle Bennet, who actually came round to the hotel to visit Hutchence on the morning of the 22nd, anxious to make sure he was OK after he had seemed "upset" during the conversation they had had earlier that morning. Despite knocking loudly on the hotel room door and phoning him, Bennet was unable to see Hutchence at all. Little did she know at the time why this was so. Hutchence's personal manager, Martha Troup, and Bob Geldof were also contacted by Hutchence. Both, like Michelle Bennet, expressed concern with the sound of his voice on the telephone.

A medical report of Hutchence's body showed that alcohol, cocaine and prescription drugs were present in his bloodstream at the time of death. Some of the prescription drugs were those given to him for the treatment of his depression, which, incidentally, was considered 'minor' by his doctor.

Hutchence was discovered by the chamber maid slumped behind the door in his hotel room. A belt had been used for the purpose of hanging, but this had eventually snapped under the weight of the body, hence the discovery of Hutchence on the floor.

Since no one can link together the pieces of the jigsaw surrounding Hutchence's troubled death with absolute certainty, his death is still shrouded in mystery. The coroner's report has laid to rest much of the speculation and suggestions that the media put forward, but the coroner's opinion is still ultimately open to subjection.

Diana, Princess of Wales

The whole world went into shock and mourning following the news of the early morning French car crash in which Princess Diana was tragically killed. Thousands of mourners gathered to pay tribute to the Princess in both England and France.

Diana's marriage to Prince Charles did not end up the

fairy tale marriage it had seemed intended. The marriage was unhappy and eventually ended in divorce. Diana lost the title 'Her Royal Highness' and was relegated to the fringes of the British royal family.

Princess Diana was the most photographed woman in the world who had given a style and panache to the royal family. She was well loved by the public and devoted a great deal of time to charity work, becoming known as the 'Queen of Hearts'. After she and Prince Charles split up she was just as popular and remained in the limelight. Diana was attractive and wore stylish clothes which were admired and copied by many. It was thought that Diana, 36, had at last found happiness with her new love Dodi al Fayed and that she was thinking of settling down in France to avoid such intense media attention.

On 31 August 1997, Princess Diana left the Ritz, on the Place Vendôme, with her boyfriend Dodi al Fayed. In an attempt to escape the photographers a decoy convey of cars left the hotel led by Fayed's Range Rover. The Princess left the Ritz slightly later at a quarter past midnight in a black Mercedes limousine. She was accompanied by Dodi and one of his bodyguards, with a security official from the Ritz driving. This change of vehicle was not enough to shake off all the photographers as some of them stayed to follow the Mercedes.

The Mercedes accelerated to an estimated 90 mph along a straight heading from the Place de la Concorde, in an attempt to avoid the pursuing motorcycles. Apparently only the drivers with the best motorcycles were able to keep up with the car. At high speed the driver appeared to have lost control when entering a bend at the entrance to the underpass at Alma bridge. The car then smashed headlong into a pillar forcing the bonnet to cave in and pushing the engine into the passenger compartment. The vehicle slammed into the walls of the underpass. At 27 minutes past midnight passing drivers alerted the police.

Fayed and the driver were both killed instantly. It took 90 minutes for the firemen to cut through the roof of the limousine and extract Diana and her bodyguard from the wreckage. The Princess was found to have head injuries and was bleeding heavily from her chest. Attempts were made on the spot to massage her failing heart back to life, and after 30 minutes she was taken to Pitie Salpetriere hospital, where a team fought in vain to save her life. She was pronounced dead at 4am after no effective circulation could be established. The only survivor of the crash was bodyguard Trevor Rees-Jones.

Initial investigations suggested the driver lost control of the car whilst driving at high speed to try to avoid the chasing paparazzi. Police were holding seven photographers in connection with the crash. There is a law in France which protects people against invasion of privacy which the paparazzi were clearly violating. At the scene of the incident unscrupulous photographers were snapping away rather than following French law by providing aid to the injured.

Authorities revealed that Henri Paul, the driver of the Mercedes, had at the time of the crash a blood-alcohol limit of almost four times the French legal limit, therefore was legally drunk. It was claimed that Paul had been called to drive the car at the last minute. This was disputed by Mohammed al Fayed, father of Dodi and employer of Henri Paul. He also denied that the car was speeding, he claimed the speedometer needle was pointing to zero rather than as the police report suggested was stuck at 196 kilometres (121 mph). The stuck speedometer is a strong indication of the car's speed at impact. The speed limit on the highway is 30 mph and all eyewitness reports claim that the car was speeding. The stretch of road has been the scene of at least two fatal accidents in recent years.

It was later revealed that Paul had taken anti-depressant

drugs, including Prozac, before driving the Mercedes, which could have boosted the damaging effects of the alcohol. Apparently photos from a film seized at the crash site had shown Paul looking startled by a camera flash, the bodyguard pulling down his sun visor and the Princess looking back at motorcycle headlights. These photos were obviously taken from the front of the Mercedes but it is not known when they were taken during the short journey of only 1.8 miles. Some witness accounts suggest that a car or motorcycle was directly in front of Diana's car before it crashed. Other accounts suggest that a car and motorcycle were working together, with the car trying to slow down the Mercedes to allow the motorcyclist to get along-side it and take photographs. Although it is known that the car was being followed by the Paparazzi it is not known how closely they were to the car, some reports suggest they were 500-600 yards away.

Tests on pieces of headlight and car paint traces found at the scene were shown not to have come from the Mercedes, this suggests that another car was involved in the incident. Scientists determined that the pieces of tail light belonged to a Fiat but were unsure of the year or model. It was confirmed that these pieces of tail light were found in the same place as pieces of the Mercedes' right headlight, yards behind the spot the Mercedes crashed into the pillar. A witness reported hearing a loud screeching noise of a car slamming on its brakes just prior to the sound of the crash. Police ruled out the possibility that the second car belonged to any of the paparazzi.

Unfortunately the only survivor of the incident, Trevor Rees-Jones was unable to remember much about the incident and could not shed any light on what had caused the crash or how the Paparazzi were behaving. He could only remember getting into the Mercedes at the Ritz hotel and recalled that the driver had "seemed fine"at the time.

A French doctor who was the first person to treat

Princess Diana claims that she was unconscious and was moaning and gesturing in every direction. *Time* magazine suggested that Diana was six weeks pregnant at the time of the crash. They claim that an associate at the scene said that Diana was drifting in and out of consciousness, and that she had said she was six weeks pregnant whilst making a rubbing gesture on her belly. The evidence from the French Doctor contradicts this as Diana was given an oxygen mask to help her breathe whilst being unconscious.

Members of the royal family receive round-the-clock police protection but since her divorce Diana decided to break away from this constant surveillance. She knew that there would be risks to be without such protection but wanted to try and live a normal life. It is said that this was a factor in why she died.

It is not yet known which of the many factors was responsible for the tragic death of Diana. Was it due to the constant press harassment which finally killed her? Was it Henri Paul's fault for driving too fast and being under the influence of drink and anti-depressant drugs? Was another car involved in the crash? What is known is that the Paparazzi should not have been harassing the Princess and Henri Paul should not have been driving the car whilst being over the drink drive limit.

Ghostly
Mysteries

Noose for a Strangler

George Gaffney was a petty thief. He operated from London's seedy Soho red light district in the early years of this century. His crimes were all minor, except for one – and that was the most serious of all.

On the first day of March 1910, Gaffney saw on a streetseller's cart a strange three-foot length of woven silk rope which he recognised as a 'thuggee cord', used by the Hindu assassins' sect in the Middle East to dispatch their victims.

Gaffney bought it. Two weeks later, he used it . . .

The cheap thief had been having problems with a girl named Bessie Graves, who expected him to marry her because she was pregnant. But Gaffney had wooed her under the alias of Arthur Eames. Now he had found a much more promising opportunity – an elderly rich widow, named Stella Fortney.

Called by an hysterical landlady, Scotland Yard detectives found Bessie Graves with the strangler's cord drawn so tightly around her throat it was embedded in the flesh. Their only clue was that the probable strangler was a man who called himself Arthur Eames.

It was little for the Yard to go on, and three weeks later Gaffney was still at large pursuing his romance with the widow.

It occurred to him one night that he would make a more impressive appearance if he called on the lady in a hansom cab. A second later he was screaming. In the half-light of the closed vehicle, George found Bessie Graves sharing the seat with him. The dead girl's eyes stared glassily into his, and the swollen tongue lolled from her mouth.

For more than a week Gaffney drank steadily, then he went to see Stella. She was far from friendly that evening, but melted when Gaffney gave her a stolen diamond ring.

They shared a bottle of champagne, after which she sent him to the cellar for another. Bearing a kerosene lamp, Gaffney was halfway down the steps when Bessie Graves climbed out of the darkness to meet him.

She had succeeded in loosening the strangler's cord, which swung from her throat like a necklace. But the staring eyes were worse. Screaming Gaffney threw the lamp at her and crashed headlong to the bottom of the stairs.

Gaffney spent three weeks in hospital. And when he left he decided that he had only one chance of throwing off the ghost who would not leave him alone. If he put England behind him forever, perhaps Bessie Graves would remain there, too. He booked passage on the liner *Montrose*, for Quebec.

With renewed hope he checked into a small hotel on the eve of the voyage. In the semi-gloom of the room, he saw Bessie again.

This time she had freed herself from the silken noose and was holding it out to him. Feebly, he took it from her clawlike fingers. When he lifted his eyes again, Bessie had vanished. But the message was obvious. Gaffney sat down and began to scrawl his confession.

He told in detail of Bessie's murder and of her successive visits from the tomb. And now, he said, there was no possible escape.

Called by hotel staff, men from the Yard broke into Gaffney's room. They found the thief hanging from a beam. They read his confession and agreed at once that the case of the Soho strangler was closed.

Yet there was one element of the case that puzzled them. For the first time, a vital piece of evidence had vanished from the Yard's thief-proof vaults. It was the thuggee cord – the same cord that Gaffney used to hang himself in the closet.

Murder on the Menu
How Lazio cooked up a lethal plot

Innkeeper Lazio Kronberg and his wife Susi faced a bleak future in the little Hungarian town of Tisakurt. It was 1919 and the couple had spent their savings trying to keep the inn going throughout the Great War. Now they had hardly enough to buy food.

There were other tragedies. Their only daughter had run away to Budapest, where she was said to be a prostitute. Their eldest son Nicholas had also run away, fleeing the house at the age of nine after Lazio whipped him for failing at school. Their other two sons had died in the war.

Night after night the old couple would sit and discuss the hopeless years ahead. At last they came to the grim decision that there was only one hope – murder for profit.

Carefully, they prepared for the killings. Lazio dug a long trench six feet deep in the woods. He filled it with quicklime, prepared to tell anyone who asked that he was planning to build new out-houses. From the village store, Susi brought home a small brown sack filled with strychnine crystals. She told the storekeeper they were going to use it to poison wolves.

Between 1919 and 1921, ten people breathed their last in the Kronberg inn. In all cases, there had been good wine with dinner and an even more remarkable vintage afterwards . . . heavily laced with strychnine. The couple grew more cautious as their stolen wealth increased. There must be only one more victim, and then the quicklime pit would be sealed forever.

He came on August 14, 1922; a genial fat man in his mid-thirties, with a suitcase so heavy that it must surely contain gold coins. He had been a salesman for years, and was now looking for good land in which to invest his money.

When Susi cooked the evening meal and Lazio served it, the visitor insisted that they must be his guests for supper. And they must call him by his nickname Lucky.

Throughout the festive two-hour meal, the guest talked about his travels and was so friendly that the Kronbergs were reluctant to kill him. But it had to be done, and at last Susi brought in the 'special' wine.

Their fat guest died as he drained his glass, convulsing his lips curled back from his teeth in the final spasm of strychnine poisoning.

In Lucky's bedroom, they searched his bag and saw at once they had been right. There was a fortune in gold coins. His hands shaking, Lazio pawed through the dead man's clothes and then saw something else – a snapshot of the Kronbergs themselves!

The couple looked at each other with dawning horror and grief. They had murdered their long-lost son. They left the gold and went back to the dining-room, where Nicholas was slouched at the table. They wrote a short confession and then sat down with him.

Three days later, the villagers found them, all dead from strychnine poisoning.

During the years that followed, few ventured inside the house. Those daring to stay two or three nights with a view to buying the place were always frightened off by the same grisly apparition: the sight of 13 ghostly figures from the 1920s, seated around the dining table. Each had its lips peeled back in a ghastly strychnine grin.

Another world war came and went, the house became dilapidated, but still no one would spend a night inside or even near it. Then on September 23, 1980, flames licking at the evening sky told the village that an arsonist had been at work. The old inn was reduced to ashes. No one tried to find the culprit. No one cared.

Tisakurt was at last free of its house of horror.

490

Murder, by a Dead Woman

Police have never solved one of the most bizarre murders in criminal history – for the killer was a dead woman. The roots of the crime go back to the 1870s, when Miss Ada Danforth and her little ward, Fanchon Moncare, regularly cruised between France and New York.

Miss Danforth explained that Fanchon was an orphan whose parents had died in a fire. On her 18th birthday she would inherit a fortune, but meanwhile Ada was her legal guardian.

Fanchon would curtsy adorably to any inquiring passenger and skip away with her doll. But back in their stateroom, the child masquerade ended. Fanchon's cherubic face would twist into a mask of evil. She would flay her 'guardian' with the gutter language acquired from 43 years of hard living . . . from her early days as a circus midget to her present career as a thief and smuggler.

In spite of the quarrels, the partnership was successful. While Ada attended to the baggage, little Fanchon – whose real name was Estelle Ridley – would dance through customs barriers still cradling her cherished doll. And no one ever dreamed of stopping her.

Afterwards, the pair would take a cab to New York's Chinatown, where Wing To, an elderly friend, waited to receive them. In the back room, the head of the doll was unscrewed and a fortune in gems spilled out – the harvest of several months' larceny on the Continent.

The business might have gone on for years but for one thing – Fanchon entered into a deadly feud with a beautiful rival, Magda Hamilton. According to police records, both women were vying for the affections of Dartney Crawley, a high stakes gambler.

Magda violated all the underworld taboos by going to the police as an informer, and the partners in crime found a reception committee waiting for them when they next docked in New York. For the first time ever, little Fanchon's doll was inspected, and minutes later the pair were en route to the notorious Tombs prison.

The midget, who had an impressive criminal record, was sentenced to life imprisonment. Ada, 10 years younger, was jailed as an accessory for 20 years.

It was Fanchon who provided the most dramatic moment of the trial. When she saw the gloating Magda sitting in the packed courtroom the midget sprang to her feet and made a shrill vow that she would one day kill her betrayer.

Triumphantly, Magda married Dartney Crawley. He deserted her six months later to try his luck in a California mining venture. But the divorce settlement was generous, and Magda was very comfortably off. Her prosperity grew through shrewd investments, and she became a prominent figure in New York café society.

Fanchon was all but forgotten by everyone . . . but Magda Hamilton. One morning she burst into police headquarters and viciously cursed the officers for not letting her know that Fanchon had escaped.

She had awakened from a heavy sleep, she said, to find the midget in her bedroom. Fanchon still wore her childish finery and clutched a big china doll. But she was now a bent and withered hag, grinning with toothless gums.

Magda screamed and fled into the bathroom where she locked the door and cowered for the rest of the night.

The hysterical Magda now insisted on adequate police protection until the little monster was recaptured.

A bemused police sergeant produced a week-old copy of the *New York Sun*. He pointed to a short item on the back page reporting that Fanchon Moncare had hanged herself in her cell.

That afternoon, Magda Hamilton booked passage for Europe on a Cunard liner. Since the ship was to leave the next day, she had a farewell dinner with a friend and then went home.

Next day the servants found her trunks neatly packed. But there would be no ocean voyage for Magda. The woman was sprawled half-naked on the bed, her eyes protruded and there was congealed blood at the corners of her mouth. According to the medical examiner, she literally drowned in her own blood. The membrane of her throat was ruptured as if some heavy object had been rammed into it with savage force.

The murder weapon was never found. But there was a clue of sorts. Lodged in Magda's bloody mouth were several hairs – similar to those found on the head of a child's china doll.

The Mummy's Hand

Count Louis Hamon was famed as an occultist and psychic healer. He was often given exotic presents by grateful clients he had cured. But the oddest gift of all brought him nothing but trouble.

On a visit to Luxor in 1890, Hamon cured a prominent sheik of malaria. The sheik insisted that the healer accept a gruesome gift, the mummified right hand of a long-dead Egyptian princess.

Count Hamon's wife disliked the dry, shrivelled hand from the first. But her dislike turned to horror and revulsion when she heard the story behind it. In the seventeenth and last year of his reign, King Akhnaton of Egypt – the heretical father-in-law of Tutankhamen – quarrelled over religious matters with his daughter. And the king's vengeance was ghastly.

In 1357 BC, he had the girl raped and murdered by his priests. Afterwards they cut off her right hand and buried it secretly in the Valley of the Kings. The people of Egypt were appalled, for the girl would be barred from paradise because her body was not intact at burial.

Hamon would have turned the relic over to a museum, but could not find a curator willing to accept it. He locked it away in an empty safe in the wall of his London home.

In October 1922, he and his wife reopened the safe – and stood back in horror. The murdered girl's hand had changed. Shrivelled and mummified for 3,200 years, it had begun to soften with new flesh. The Countess screamed that it must be destroyed. Although he had never before been afraid of the unknown, Hamon agreed with her.

He insisted on only one thing; that the hand of the princess must have the best funeral they could give it. They were ready on the night of October 31, 1922. Halloween.

In a letter to his life-long friend, the archaeologist Lord Carnarvon, Hamon wrote that he laid the hand gently in the fireplace and read aloud a passage from the Egyptian Book of the Dead. As he closed the book there was a blast of thunder that rocked the house into total darkness. The door flew open with a sudden wind.

Hamon and his wife fell to the floor and lay there in the sudden glacial cold. Lifting their eyes, they saw the figure of a woman. In Hamon's account, 'she wore the royal apparel of old Egypt, with the serpent of the House of Pharaohs glittering on her tall headdress'. The woman's right arm ended in a raw stump.

The apparition bent over the fire and then was gone as suddenly as it had appeared. The severed hand had vanished with it, and was never seen again.

Four days later, Hamon read that the Carnarvon expedition had discovered Tutankhamen's tomb and that they would enter it in spite of the ancient warning emblazoned at the threshold.

From the room in the hospital where he and his wife were under treatment for severe shock, Hamon sent his old friend a letter begging him to reconsider.

He wrote, 'I know now the ancient Egyptians had knowledge and power of which today we have no comprehension. In the name of God, I beg you to take care'.

Carnarvon ignored the letter and soon afterwards he was dead from an infected mosquito bite. One by one, members of the expedition followed him to the grave in what became known as the Curse of the Pharaohs.

Skyway to Doom

Has the ghost of an American construction worker put a curse on the Sunshine Skyway Bridge? That was the theory put forward by a Florida fisherman after nearly 60 people died in four separate shipping disasters at the Tampa Bay bridge during the first five months of 1980.

In January, 23 coastguards were killed when their cutter collided with an oil tanker. The following month, a freighter smashed into one of the main bridge supports, and ten days later a tanker ran out of control, and slammed into the main span.

But the worst accident to hit the jinxed bridge came on May 9. Possibly blinded by the wind-lashed rain of a violent storm, the skipper of a 10,000-ton Liberian freighter, *Summit Venture*, misjudged his approach to the bridge. Instead of passing under the middle of it, the ship ploughed into one of the main supports, and a huge section of the road running over it collapsed.

Cars, trucks, and a Greyhound bus plunged 150 feet into the water; 32 people died, 23 of them on the bus. Other drivers missed death by inches, slamming on their brakes just in time as the yawning gap opened up in front of them.

The Florida House of Representatives stood for a moment's silence as news of the tragedy reached them during a meeting. One member blamed the Tampa Bay harbour pilot system, and called for an inquiry.

But a local fisherman, 27-year-old Charlie Williams, said later: 'When the bridge was being built, a construction worker fell into some wet concrete. He's still there, in the structure. The Skyway has been cursed ever since.'

The bridge, which is four miles long, was opened in September 1954. More than 40 people have committed suicide by leaping from it.

Torment of Calvados

Diaries written by a French aristocrat who lived in a gloomy mediaeval castle set among the apple orchards of Normandy tell the story of one of the most violent hauntings ever recorded. Known simply as X, he recorded in vivid detail the extraordinary events that turned his historic home into a nightmare in the year 1875.

They began without warning. Everyone in Calvados Castle had settled down for the night when they were disturbed by ghostly wailing and weeping and rapping on the walls. The noises were heard by the entire household – X himself, his wife, his son, his son's tutor who was an abbé, Emile the coachman, and servants Auguste, Amelina and Celina.

After several nights of ever-increasing noise and disturbance, the aristocrat instructed that fine threads were to be strung across every entrance to the castle. He hoped, of course, that in the morning they would be broken, proving that someone had entered and was trying to terrorise them.

But the threads remained intact. There was no escaping the fact that the forces existed within the castle walls.

On Wednesday, October 13, 1875, X began keeping a diary. That night the abbé was alone in his room when he heard a series of sharp taps on the wall and a candlestick on the mantlepiece was lifted by an unseen hand.

The terror-stricken priest rang for X who found that not only had the candlestick been moved, but also an armchair which was normally fixed to the floor.

For the next two days, pounding on the walls, footsteps on the stairs and other un-nerving phenomena continued unabated. X and the abbé armed themselves with sticks and searched the castle from top to bottom. They could find no human explanation.

By October 31 the castle was hardly ever at peace. X recorded in his diary, 'A very disturbed night. It sounded as if someone went up the stairs with superhuman speed from the ground floor, stamping his feet.

'Arriving on the landing, he gave five heavy blows so strong that objects rattled in their places. Then it seemed as if a heavy anvil or a big log had been thrown at the wall so as to shake the house.

'Nobody could say where the blows came from, but everyone got up and assembled in the hall. The house only settled down at about three in the morning . . .'

The following night everyone was awakened by what sounded like a heavy body rolling downstairs followed by blows so ferocious they seemed to rock the castle. Over the next few days, the haunting had become so violent the family felt it could not possibly get any worse. But greater ordeals were to come.

On the night of November 10, X wrote in his diary, 'Everyone heard a long shriek and then another as of a woman outside calling for help. At 1.45 we suddenly heard three or four loud cries in the hall and then on the staircase.'

Cries, screams and moans which 'sounded like the cries of the damned' seemed to fill the whole castle. Heavy furniture was moved, windows flung open and – more terrifying – Bibles were torn and desecrated. The family began to wonder if the powers of darkness had taken over.

X's wife suddenly became the focus of attention. Hearing a noise in the abbé's room, she crept up the stairs and put out a hand to press down the latch on the door. Before she could touch it she saw the key turn in the lock then remove itself, hitting her left hand with a sharp blow. The abbé, who had run up the stairs after her, saw it happen and afterwards testified that madame's hand was bruised for two days. That night something hammered on her door so furiously she thought it would break down.

The New Year brought only fresh terrors to the wretched family: louder knocking, more persistent voices. The worst day of all was January 26 when the noise was thunderous. 'It sounded as if demons were driving herds of wild cattle through the rooms.' Peals of demonic laughter rang through the ancient walls. The family had had enough.

Next day a priest was called in to exorcise the evil spirit and the family saw to it that every religious medallion and relic they possessed was placed in full view. The treatment was effective and at last the hideous uproar ceased.

To the family, who believed they would be forced to abandon their home, the peace that followed came as a blessed relief.

But the ghostly tormentors of Calvados had not quite finished. Shortly after the exorcism, all the religious relics disappeared and could not be found. Then, one morning, as the lady of the house sat writing at her desk an unseen hand dropped them one by one in front of her. There was one short burst of violent sound, then silence.

The Haunting of Willington Mill

When Joseph Procter and his family moved into the mill house in 1835 they paid little attention to rumours that the place was haunted. The house was a pleasant, comparatively new building set by a tidal stream in the Northumberland village of Willington, in England's rugged north-east. The Procters were a highly-respected, devoutly Quaker family. Mr Procter was said to be a man of high intelligence and common sense, good and kind to his family and employees.

Yet after little more than a decade, the Procters were driven to leave in distress, unable to stand any more of the weird and ghostly happenings that plagued them from the day they first arrived at Willington Mill.

Only much later were they to learn that their home had been built on the site of an old cottage, that a terrible crime had been committed there years before . . . and that a priest had refused to hear the confession of a woman who desperately wanted to unburden her conscience.

So prolific was the haunting of Willington Mill while the Procters lived there that when W T Stead, the writer and ghost hunter, first pieced together the story in the 1890s, there were still 40 people alive who had actually seen the ghosts.

The hauntings began one night in January 1835. A nursemaid was putting the children to bed in the second-floor nursery when she heard heavy footsteps coming from a room immediately above. It was an empty room, never used by the family. At first the girl took little notice, thinking it must be one of the handymen with a job to do. But they went on night after night, getting louder and louder.

Other servants and members of the family also heard them, but when they burst into the room to surprise the 'intruder', no one was there. They sprinkled meal over the floor, but there were no footprints.

One morning, as Mr Procter was conducting family prayers, the heavy steps were heard coming down the stairs, past the parlour and along the hall to the front door. The family heard the bar removed, two bolts drawn back and the lock turned.

Mr Procter rushed into the hall to find the door open. The footsteps went on down the path.

Poor Mrs Procter fainted.

It became increasingly difficult to get servants to stay in the house. Only one girl, Mary Young, whom the family had brought with them from their previous home in North Shields, loyally refused to leave.

There was a period when it seemed as though the whole house had been taken over by unseen people. There were sounds of doors opening, people entering and leaving rooms, thumps and blows and laboured breathing, the steps of a child, chairs being moved and rustling sounds as if a woman in a silk dress was hurrying by.

Until a certain Whit Monday, the haunting remained entirely by sound. On that day, Mary Young was washing dishes in the kitchen when she heard footsteps in the passage. Looking up she saw a woman in a lavender silk dress go upstairs and enter one of the rooms. That night the noises in the house were worse than anybody had heard before.

Two of Mrs Procter's sisters arrived for a visit. The first night, sleeping together in the same four-poster bed, they felt it lift up. Their first thought was that a thief had hidden there, so they rang the alarm and the men of the house came running. No one was found.

On another night their bed was violently shaken and the curtains suddenly hoisted up then let down again several times.

They had the curtains removed, but the experience that

followed was even more terrifying. They lay awake half-expecting something to happen when a misty, bluish figure of a woman drifted out of the wall and leaned over them in an almost horizontal position. Both women saw the figure quite clearly and lay there, speechless with terror, as it retreated and passed back into the wall.

Neither would sleep in the room another night and one of them even left the house to take lodgings with the mill foreman Thomas Mann and his wife.

One dark, moonless night the Manns, their daughter and their visitor were walking past the mill house after paying a call on neighbours. All four saw the luminous figure of what appeared to be a priest in a surplice gliding back and forth at the height of the second floor. It seemed to go through the wall of the house and stand looking out of the window.

The focus of the hauntings seemed to be what the Procters called The Blue Room and in the summer of 1840 they agreed to allow Edward Drury, who specialised in supernatural investigation, to spend a night there. He took with him a friend who refused to get into bed, but dozed off in a chair.

Drury later wrote a letter describing what happened. 'I took out my watch to ascertain the time and found that it was ten minutes to one,' he said. 'In taking my eyes off the watch they became riveted upon a closet door, which I distinctly saw open, and saw also the figure of a female attired in greyish garments, with the head inclining downwards and one hand pressed upon the chest as if in pain. It advanced with an apparently cautious step across the floor towards me. Immediately, it approached my friend, who was slumbering, its right hand extended towards him. I then rushed at it . . .'

It was three hours before Drury could recollect anything more. He had been carried downstairs in a state of terror by Mr Procter. Drury had shrieked, 'There she is. Keep her off. For God's sake, keep her off!'

The grey lady was seen by others. So were unearthly animals and other startling apparitions. The Procters tried to shield their children from the worst of the haunting, but eventually they became involved. One day a daughter told Mary Young, 'There's a lady sitting on the bed in mama's room. She has eyeholes, but no eyes, and she looked hard at me.'

Then another daughter reported that in the night a lady had come out of the wall and looked into the mirror . . . 'She had eyeholes, but no eyes.'

Another child saw the figure of a man enter his room, push up the sash window, lower it again, then leave.

In 1847 Joseph Procter decided his family could endure no more. They moved away to another part of Northumberland and were never again troubled by ghosts.

The house was later divided into two dwellings and eventually deteriorated into a slum. People continued to hear and see strange things from time to time. But Willington Mill House was never again to know the terrifying days and nights that afflicted the pious Quaker family.

John Wesley's Nightmare

The servant who answered a knock on the door of a Lincolnshire parsonage was mildly annoyed to find no one there when he opened it. He blamed playful youngsters, but when, only hours later, he watched a corngrinding handmill turning without human help, he realised that something beyond his understanding was happening.

The events of that December day in 1716 heralded a two-month nightmare for the devout household at Epworth. Their ordeal was chronicled by one of the family's children

– John Wesley, who was to become founder of the Methodist Church.

His sister Molly was the next person to notice something strange. As she sat reading in the library, the door opened on its own, and she heard footsteps walking round her chair, accompanied by the rustling of petticoats.

One by one, the rest of the family told of their own eerie experiences: rappings on a table, mysterious footsteps on the stairs, bangs in the hall and kitchen, the sound of an invisible cradle rocking in the nursery.

At 9.45 each evening, a man's steps were heard plodding down the north-east corner of the house. The Wesley's christened him Old Jeffrey.

John's father Samuel became convinced that the spirit was an agent of evil testing the faith of the family. Finally he challenged it to leave the children alone, and meet him alone in the study for a showdown. It was to be a spectacular confrontation.

When Mr Wesley tried to enter the room, a powerful force pushed the door back in his face. He struggled through and began asking the phantom to identify itself. His questions were answered only by furious knocking from each wall in turn, building to a terrifying crescendo.

But the parson's faith and nerve were unshakable. Gradually the spirit's apparent anger subsided, the sounds faded, and the house was left in peace.

The Epworth haunting is one of the best-documented cases of poltergeists, ghosts that are heard but not seen. They are more common than spirits that materialise, and in many ways even more frightening.

The word poltergeist is derived from German, where the earliest cases were reported. In 355 AD, people in the village of Bingen-am-Rhein were hauled from their beds by unseen hands, and subjected to an onslaught of stones and strange noises. Five centuries later, the same thing happened at nearby Kembden, when a disembodied voice accused the local priest and some of the villagers of misdeeds.

In 1721, the Groben home of German Oriental scholar Professor Schupart was invaded by an invisible terror which threw furniture about. His wife was bitten, pinched and knocked down, and the professor was violently assaulted by an invisible attacker. Incredulous neighbours witnessed the incident.

Since then, poltergeists have been reported all over the world. In 1762, eminent men of letters such as Dr Samuel Johnson, Horace Walpole and Oliver Goldsmith were among those who investigated strange rappings and scratching at a house in London's Cock Lane.

And at Syderstone Rectory, in Norfolk, curious groans, slamming doors, running footsteps in corridors, and knocking that shook the whole house were reported by several families in a 40-year period that ended in 1833.

In 1890, Cesare Lombroso, a leading Italian psychiatrist was called in by the owners of a small inn at Turin. He watched bottles of wine smash and shoes fly through the air.

In 1937, stones and other missiles rained down for almost a week on a family in Port Louis, Mauritius – even when all doors and windows were bolted shut.

One of the most terrifying poltergeists on record struck in 1878 at Amherst, Nova Scotia. Terrible crashes under the bed of 19-year-old Esther Cox were followed by lighted matches tumbling from the ceiling. Mystery fires flared up in the cellar of her home, and a dress went up in flames.

A doctor treating the girl for shock was pelted with plaster and planks of wood, and saw bedclothes being ripped off her bed. The family fled after a wall was daubed with the message: 'Esther Cox, you are mine to kill.'

Today, the invisible spirits are still getting up to mischief, often in the most unlikely places. In 1963, the day after motor cycle dealer Sid Mularney knocked down a wall in his workshops at Leighton Buzzard, Bedfordshire, he found three of his bikes damaged.

He then watched spanners fly off their hooks and tarpaulin rise from a scooter and shoot across the room. Petrol tanks were mysteriously moved, and neighbours complained of weird nocturnal noises from the building.

A West German lawyer's office in Rosenheim, Bavaria, was suddenly plunged into chaos in November, 1967. Light bulbs started smashing for no reason and lamp shades tumbled to the ground. One day all four phones on the man's desk rang simultaneously, but there were no callers when he lifted the receivers. Experts who checked his premises reported sudden strange surges in the electricity current.

An American family found a quilt in a box when they moved into their new home in Poy Sippi, Wisconsin, in 1972, and decided to use it on their spare bed. But guests seldom slept soundly under it. They told their hostess, Mrs Dora Monroe, that someone kept tugging it off the bed during the night.

Mrs Monroe's daughter Florence said she was awakened at midnight, and during a battle to keep the quilt covering her, she heard a voice say: 'Give me back my Christmas present'.

The Foundation for Research into the Nature of Man, set up at Duke University, Carolina, in 1964, noted that poltergeist activity often stops when a teenager leaves the home or office. Some experts believe the manifestations may be caused by psychokinesis, an energy released during puberty which gives young minds power over matter.

The Defiant Spirit

A ghost which defied a priest's effort to exorcise it finally drove a young couple from their home.

Andy Ralph, his wife Julie and their seven-month-old baby Charlene quit the Victorian house in Sheerness, Kent. In Andy's words, 'Our nerves finally cracked. Nothing would drive the spirit away.'

Julie said, 'We were horrified one evening when coins started flying into the room. They were coming from the stairwell and bouncing off the floor and walls of the sitting room. There was no explanation for it.'

Apart from the case of the flying coins, the couple claimed that doors mysteriously slammed, light bulbs flicked on and off without anybody touching a switch, Julie felt a strangling sensation as she relaxed in an armchair, and sounds of someone gasping for breath, heavy footsteps and scraping noises were heard.

Andy and Julie, both aged 19, put up with the eerie incidents for five months. Eventually the phenomena became too alarming and they sought the help of a priest, who exorcised the old house. The exorcism failed, and within days the persistent spook was back.

If the ghost wouldn't budge, the Ralphs would, and in 1981 they quit, leaving a mystery that has not yet been solved.

Locals had one theory – Harry Morgan, a kindly man who had died alone in the house six years earlier and whose body had gone undiscovered for several days, may have been getting his own back on his 'uncaring' neighbours.

Riddle of the Rectory

A dark gloomy mansion on the border between the English counties of Essex and Suffolk has been described as the world's most haunted house. And even though the building, Borley Rectory, burned down mysteriously in 1939, its legend lives on in strange happenings near the spot where it once stood.

The 23-room red-brick house was built in 1863 for the Reverend Henry Dawson Ellis Bull. As soon as he and his family moved in, they heard puzzling sounds at night. Footsteps and tappings were followed by bells ringing and voices answering. Ghostly chanting was heard from the nearby village church.

Soon the disturbances took on a more physical form. One of the 14 children in the family was awakened one day by a slap in the face. Another claimed to have seen a man in old-fashioned clothes standing by her bed. A nun, a phantom coach and horses, a headless man and a woman in white were all reported in the grounds by passers-by or servants.

In 1929 poltergeist activity began. Pebbles, keys and mementoes flew through the air for no apparent reason, and a cook told her master that a kitchen door locked each evening was inexplicably open when she arrived for work the following morning.

Just before the Bull family moved out, newspaper reporters kept vigil one night, and noted an eerie light in a deserted wing of the building.

The Reverend Lionel Algernon Foyster and his wife Marrianne moved into the Rectory in 1930, and the baffling incidents continued. Curious messages started appearing on walls or scraps of paper, urging: 'Marrianne get help.'

Mrs Foyster also heard a disembodied voice call her

name, and she was later attacked by an invisible assailant. Soon after that, the couple fled for a more peaceful home.

Ghost investigator Harry Price, founder of Britain's National Laboratory of Psychical Research, recruited a team of volunteers to document exactly what was happening at Borley. They reported sudden drops in temperature of up to ten degrees, curious incense-like smells, stones and cakes of soap thrown across rooms, and books moving as if of their own accord. A Benedictine monk trying to hold an exorcism in the Rectory was hit by flying pebbles.

When Captain W H Gregson bought the building, he renamed it Borley Priory. But the new name brought the jinxed home no better luck. In 1939 it was wrecked by fire. Several people claimed that, as the flames raged, they saw a young girl at an upstairs window. Witnesses told the village policeman a grey-clad nun had been sighted slipping away from the inferno.

Even though the Rectory was destroyed, arguments about its ghosts raged on. Some said they were the spirits of a monk and a nun who had eloped from nearby Bures centuries before, but had suffered the traditional punishment when caught – decapitation for him, being buried alive for her.

But London medium Helen Glanville claimed that during a 1937 seance at her home in Streatham, she was told that the Borley ghost was that of Marie Lairre, a nun induced to leave her convent at Le Havre, France, to marry one of the Waldergrave family from Borley Manor. She was strangled by him in May, 1667 – on the site where the Rectory was built.

In 1943, excavations of the ruins revealed fragments of a woman's skull and skeleton four feet below ground, together with a number of religious pendants. Were they the bones of unhappy Marie, or were they, as some suggested, the remains of a plague victim from even earlier times?

The Rectory may be long gone, but its supernatural residents outlasted it for many years. Chauffeur Herbert Mayes heard the thunder of invisible hooves as he drove past the shell of the building. During World War Two, air raid wardens were called to the ruins several times when lights were reported at windows. And as late as 1961, car headlights, cameras and torches all inexplicably failed to work during investigations at the site.

Only a few miles north of Borley lies the Suffolk village of Polstead. There, too, the Rectory is said to be haunted. And when a young Irish vicar moved out after only five nights in his new parish, the church put the 350-year-old building on the market claiming it was 'much too large and expensive to maintain'.

The Reverend Hayden Foster, 35, arrived in Polstead from Dublin with his wife Margo and son Gerard in April 1978, and for four nights they all slept soundly at their new 16-room home.

On the fifth, the couple moved to another bedroom to accommodate guests who had travelled for Mr Foster's induction ceremony next day. What happened that night was enough to make the family pack their bags in the morning, and move back to Ireland.

Mr Foster told a reporter from the local newspaper, 'At about 3 a.m., we were lying half awake when Margo saw the walls of the room change from being freshly-painted to peeling, damp old wallpaper – just as it might have looked 20 or 30 years ago.

'She heard screaming like a child's, but it wasn't Gerard. Then she felt as if she was being strangled or suffocated. She was trying to say the Lord's Prayer, but she couldn't get it out because of this overwhelming force. I felt too that there was real danger in that room. There is a definite feeling of evil in that place.'

Villagers in Polstead were not surprised when the Fosters left. They knew the legends about the Rectory.

Some said they had seen a procession of monks crossing the road outside its gates, their sandals six feet above the ground.

Others recalled that the Reverend John Whitmore, vicar from 1795 to 1840, had held an exorcism service in the house.

But the Diocese Bishop, Leslie Brown, had not been told the stories.

He said, 'I knew nothing about the Rectory's reputation when the Fosters arrived. If I had, I certainly would never have moved them in.

'The previous vicar had said nothing to me at all, and when I asked his wife about it afterwards, she said, 'Oh well, we got quite used to hearing footsteps going upstairs.'

The Renishaw Coffin

In the Sitwell family it was always known as the Renishaw Coffin. The famous literary trio – Osbert, Edith and Sacheverell – heard about it when they were children and the stories of it and its ghost became part of their upbringing.

Their famous Renishaw Hall, a gloomy Derbyshire mansion dating from 1625, was always thought to be haunted. But it was not until their eccentric father, Sir George Sitwell, decided to improve the house by altering and enlarging the central staircase that the coffin came to light.

In order to carry out the work, two small rooms had to be demolished, one on the ground floor, one a first-floor bedroom. Sir George, who was fanatically proud of his family history, asked the clerk of works to take note of anything interesting he came across, hoping that some traces of ancient building might be found.

The coffin was discovered between the joists of the bedroom floor. From its construction, and the fact that it had nails rather than screws, it was presumed that it dated from the 17th century. It was firmly attached to the joists with iron clamps. Because of lack of space, it had never been fitted with a lid, the floorboards above it serving the purpose. The coffin contained no skeleton, but certain marks proved that there had once been a body in it.

The discovery threw new light on the frightening experiences of two women who had slept in that bedroom when they were guests at Renishaw. The first was a Miss Tait, daughter of Archibald Campbell Tait, the Archbishop of Canterbury. She had been invited to Derbyshire in 1885 to join the house party celebrating Sir George's coming of age.

In the middle of the night she was awakened by someone kissing her three times. The kisses were ice cold. The room was empty.

She ran to the room where Sir George's sister was sleeping and told her what had happened. Miss Sitwell made up a bed for her friend on her sofa, explaining that nothing would induce her to sleep in that room as she had once had exactly the same experience.

After the party, Sir George's agent, Mr Turnbull, came to see him about some business and during the conversation Sir George jokingly told the story of Miss Tait's phantom kisses.

Far from being amused, the agent looked shocked. Apparently, when Sir George had generously lent him Renishaw for his honeymoon, a friend of the agent's bride had come to stay. She had slept in that same bedroom and had had the same experience. She left next morning, obviously frightened, but the Turnbulls had simply credited her with an on over-active imagination.

One autumn evening, a few years after Miss Tait's haunting, Lady Sitwell was entertaining a few guests in the upstairs drawing room after dinner. The room was brightly lit and the door stood open onto a passage. She was chatting to a friend who sat on her left when she became conscious of a figure in the passage outside. Friends noticed that she seemed to be following something with her eyes. She wrote later, 'I saw the figure with such distinctness that I had no doubt at all that I was looking at a real person.'

The figure was that of a woman, apparently a servant, with grey hair done up in a bun under a white cap. Her dress was blue with a full dark skirt. She moved with a furtive, gliding motion as though wishing to escape notice, but her arms were stretched out in front of her and the hands clasped. She moved towards the head of the staircase on which Sir George had worked 20 years before – and disappeared.

Lady Sitwell called out: 'Who's that?' When no one answered, she urged her friends to find her the mystery visitor, and everyone present joined in the search for the unknown guest.

They were on the point of giving up when a young woman, looking down into the well-lit hall below, suddenly cried out, 'I do believe that's the ghost!'

Just where the door of the old room used to be, she saw a woman with dark hair and dress obviously distressed and in deep thought. Her figure, though opaque, cast no shadow. It moved in a gentle glide, full of sadness, and melted away. What happened in the two rooms that Sir George demolished has never been discovered and the empty coffin has kept its secret.

Stroll to Oblivion

David Lang vanished from the face of the earth on September 23, 1880, and, has never been heard of since – apart from his ghostly voice. His disappearance, on a sunny afternoon and in front of five witnesses, remains one of the most baffling mysteries of all time.

During his last moments, Lang, a prosperous farmer, was strolling across a field in front of his home near Gallatin, Tennessee. His children, George, eight, and Sarah, 11, were playing in the front of the house. His wife had just walked out of the house to greet an approaching buggy carrying Judge August Peck and his brother-in-law.

David smiled, waved at the visitors and started walking toward the group at the farmhouse. He took a dozen steps, then Mrs Lang's horrified scream shattered the afternoon. Judge Peck dropped the buggy reins. The two men sprinted across the field to join Mrs Lang and the children at the spot where David Lang had last been seen.

There was no trace of the farmer. In full view of five witnesses, he had simply vanished.

His wife fell to her knees and began to beat frantically at the ground. Judge Peck lifted her to her feet and the five fanned out in a frantic search of the pasture. The search yielded no sign of the missing man.

The judge summoned help. Neighbours began to arrive and search parties were formed. Far into the night, lanterns were swinging across the farm and through the woods beyond.

The next morning the county surveyor arrived and inspected the area where Lang had vanished. He announced that it was firmly supported by thick strata of limestone. There were no potholes or caves into which a man could fall.

Mrs Lang was by now numb with shock and under her

doctor's care. As the search continued through days, weeks and eventually months, she stoutly resisted any suggestion of a funeral or even a memorial service for David Lang. She asked only that all churches pray for his return.

The shock of the experience had deeply affected the two Lang children – particularly Sarah. She turned into a shy, withdrawn child who spent long hours daydreaming. Finally there was an outstanding incident that prompted Mrs Lang to take her children away from the farm.

On an April evening in 1881, Sarah ran sobbing into the house to report that there was a 'ring' around the spot where her father had vanished. When Mrs Lang went to investigate, the child said she could clearly hear her father calling. He was begging for help in a tortured voice, but it faded away into silence.

Mrs Lang did not hear her husband's ghostly voice, but in the pasture she made a strange discovery. Where her husband had last been seen, there was a perfect circle of withered yellow grass some 20 feet in diameter.

The Race to Eternity

The day 'marathon man' James Worson accepted a sporting challenge was the day he disappeared from the face of the earth. The proud, athletic, English shoemaker screamed once, and vanished forever.

On September 3, 1873, Worson boasted of his athletic prowess to two fellow townsfolk of Leamington, Warwickshire. He said that on more than one occasion he had raced from one town to another in record time.

The people of Leamington knew Worson's talents as a footracer, but his friends were sceptical. He might he as good as he thought, they told him, but could he prove it? Worson happily accepted the challenge. He would show them, he said, with a 20-mile run from Leamington to Coventry.

They began the test in high spirits. Worson put on his running clothes and set out. His friends, Hammerson Burns and Barham Wise, trailed close behind him in a horse-drawn gig, Burns carrying a camera.

The mood of the three was still festive a quarter of the way to Coventry. Worson appeared as tireless as he had claimed, running with ease and turning occasionally to exchange words with his friends.

The runner was never out of their sight. Running in the middle of the dirt road, Worson suddenly appeared to stumble. He pitched forward in a headlong fall and had time for only one piercing scream. Wise said later, 'It was the most ghastly sound either of us had ever heard.'

That terrible cry was their last memory of him. Worson's body never struck the ground – he vanished in the middle of his fall without touching the earth.

The road itself provided tangible evidence of what they had witnessed. Burns' pictures of the long-distance runner's tracks – clear footprints in the soft dirt, faltering and ending as abruptly as if Worson had crashed into a stone wall.

When the men returned to Leamington a massive hunt began. Searchers combed every inch of the terrain between Leamington and Coventry without success. Bloodhounds were strangely reluctant to approach the spot where Worson's footprints ended. And for years after his disappearance there were reports of a ghostly green runner on the empty night road from Leamington to Coventry.

Mystery of the Planter's Tomb

The riddle of the Barbados coffins is one of the most baffling supernatural mysteries of all time. For 12 years, unseen forces repeatedly desecrated a sealed tomb on the Caribbean island. Eventually the family which owned the crypt was forced to abandon it. Only then did the bodies of their departed rest in peace.

The Chase family, slave-owning sugar planters, acquired the tomb in 1808. It was built of stone, recessed into the cliffs above Oistin's Bay, and sealed with a marble slab. When the family took it over, it already held one wooden coffin, that of a Mrs Thomasina Goddard.

Twice within a year, the slab guarding the only entrance was rolled aside as the family buried two of their children, Mary Ann and Dorcas. In 1812, their father Thomas also died. Eight men carried the lead coffin up to the headland, but when the tomb was opened, the mourners gasped in horror.

Mrs Goddard's body still lay in its proper place, but the caskets containing the children were standing on end against one of the walls. There was no sign of a break-in.

Pallbearers gently restored the two tiny coffins to their positions, then lugged in the box containing Mr Chase. It was laid beside the others. Stonemasons carefully cemented the marble slab securely across the entrance.

Four years later, they returned to bury a boy relative, and found the seals were intact. But again there was torment for the tragic family. The same sight of desecration met their grieving gaze when the slab was removed.

Order was restored, with eight men struggling to life Mr Chase's coffin back to its place, but by now, the tomb was the talking point of the entire island. Two months later, new coffins were added – and the same chaos was discovered. And the same happened in 1819 when the next burial took place.

Each time, Mrs Goddard's casket was undisturbed, which seemed to rule out flooding or earth tremors. The stone walls and ceilings were checked, but no faults found. There was only one way in, and each time the cement seals around the slab were unbroken. Fear of sacred places ruled out interference by the islanders, even if it had been physically possible.

Lord Combermere, Governor of Barbados, was among the stunned funeral party in 1819. As the family wept, he personally supervised the orderly arrangement of the coffins, which now totalled six, and sprinkled fine sand around them. When the entrance slab was again cemented in place, he added his seal to the joint.

On April 18 the following year, he unexpectedly asked the rector of the nearby church to open the tomb. The six coffins which had been laid in a neat line, the three smaller ones resting on top of those containing adults. Now they were again scattered around the cave.

Mr Chase's casket was once more standing upright, with only Mrs Goddard lying where she had been left. There were no marks in the sand, and Lord Combermere's seal was intact.

The Chases could no longer stand the notoriety the tomb was bringing them. All their family coffins were carried to Christ Church graveyard, and buried in a joint funeral ceremony.

Sir Arthur Conan Doyle, creator of Sherlock Holmes and an avid investigator of the paranormal, took an interest in the story. He put forward the theory that supernatural forces played havoc with the coffins because they were made of lead, and so delayed the decomposition of the bodies. He also believed that Thomas Chase committed suicide.

But for all this theorising, the abandoned tomb has kept its secret and may do so forever

The Hell Hounds

Dogs, cats and horses have always been associated with the spirit world. They are said to sense, even see, ghosts which are invisible to the human eye. But some animals exist as four-legged phantoms themselves. The most terrifying are the giant black hounds of hell.

Almost every part of Britain has such legends: fiendish harbingers of doom with blazing eyes and snarling teeth. The Yorkshire version, the Padfoot, is said to be as big as a donkey. The Welsh call theirs Gwyllgi, and the Lancashire dog is known as Trash or Shriker. On the Isle of Man, the Mauthe or Moddey Dhoo is said to haunt Peel Castle, and soldiers once refused to patrol the battlements there alone.

One sentry who dared to serve solo was found gibbering next morning, and died three days later.

The most frequently documented hell hound is Black Shuck, whose name is derived from Scucca, the Saxon word for the Devil. Hundreds of people claim to have seen him at night in the lonely fenlands of East Anglia, the one eye in the centre of his head blazing scarlet or yellow.

He has been reported on the coast near Cromer, loping along lanes near the Norfolk Broads at Neatishead, and at Wicken Fen, near Newmarket. In Suffolk, people living near the heathland of Walberswick and Dunwich call him the Galley Trot. And it was in this area, during World War Two, that he gave an American airman and his wife a night they would never forget.

The couple had rented a flat-topped hut on the edge of Walberswick Marsh while the husband served at a nearby air base. One stormy evening they were startled by a violent pounding on the door. The airman peeped through a window and saw a huge black beast battering their home.

The terrified couple piled what little furniture they had against the door, then cowered as the attacker hurled his body against first one wall, then another, then leapt on to the roof. The ordeal lasted several hours before the noise faded away. The couple waited anxiously for daylight, and at dawn crept outside to inspect the damage. There was no sign of the attack, and no paw or claw marks in the soft mud around the hut.

The West Country is said to have a pack of wild black dogs, whose blood-curdling howls have been heard several times across the vast wastes of Dartmoor.

But a different phantom beast worried hundreds of people in five Devon towns when they woke one winter's morning in February, 1855. Clearly visible in the heavy overnight snow were animal footprints four inches long and almost three inches wide – footprints which, it was later discovered, stretched in a zig-zag trail for nearly 100 miles from Totnes to Littleham.

Dogs brought in to track the mystery creature through undergrowth at Dawlish backed off, howling dismally. Baffled investigators found that at one stage, the trail went into a shed through a six-inch hole. In another place, the prints indicated that the animal had squeezed through a long narrow drainpipe. Next night, local people bolted their doors and refused to venture outside. They were convinced the Devil himself had walked through Devon.

Journalist and ghost-collector W T Stead told of a letter sent to him in 1902 by an Englishman who went hunting in the South African Transvaal. The man claimed he was riding back to camp when an eerie white horse carrying an unearthly rider emerged from a thicket of trees, and pursued him. That night, one of the hunter's guides told him of an earlier safari, when an Englishman shot seven elephants in the thicket.

He returned next morning to collect the ivory tusks – and was never seen again. His white horse returned to camp alone, but died 24 hours later. The guide added, 'I would not go into that bush for all the ivory in the land.'

Gisele's Burning Memories

From the moment he saw the old house, Paul Fortier knew it would be an appropriate setting for the good years ahead. That they were going to be good years, he had no doubt.

His first novel, *Fields of Amaranth*, was doing well, and he was at work on a second that promised to be even better. What was more, he had a beautiful young wife and a five-year-old daughter who was the image of her mother.

Denise Fortier also liked the house in Montreal, Canada – but with reservations. After they bought it in 1905, she began to wish that Paul had looked into its history as carefully as he had checked the foundations.

From neighbours she was to learn that the house had been involved in some of Montreal's most blood-chilling crimes.

Built in 1805 as a detention home for 'wayward children', it was wrecked by fire after two of the children had murdered the owner and his wife. In spite of their age, the children were hanged.

The house was rebuilt, but for more than a century was plagued by disasters. They included arson, murder, and inexplicable double suicides. And there were 'cold spots' – pockets of numbingly cold air that seemed to move from room to room.

Denise became increasingly apprehensive about their new home, and Paul began to look at her with growing doubt and pity. In desperation, Denise went to her priest. Though the good man listened sympathetically as she urged him to exorcise the house, she thought that his face mirrored some of Paul's scepticism. Denise went home that evening with the certainty that something frightful was going to happen.

Looking at her husband that evening, she was sure that Paul had changed. He drank too much wine at the dinner table and became morose. Something in their mood seemed to communicate itself to five-year-old daughter Gisele. Sensing that the little girl was frightened, Denise carried her off to bed.

The child whispered, 'Can we leave here sometime soon?'

'I don't know, dear. Why?'

'Those cold spots you tried to show daddy – I think there was one in my bed last night. I woke up with my teeth chattering even though the room was hot.'

Trying to conceal her own fear, Denise bent and kissed her. 'It was probably just a bad dream,' she said.

They were the last words the little girl heard from her mother's lips.

That night the child again woke to a nightmare. It began with a suffocating odour of smoke in the house. Screaming, she ran to her parents' bedroom and flung open the door. The walls and ceiling of the room were ablaze, but there were infinitely worse horrors.

Her father's body lay close to the bed with a pair of scissors driven into his throat. And in the deep, soft bed her mother was struggling with two naked boys scarcely bigger than Gisele. Denise's lips yawned in a silent scream as the giggling children pummelled her body.

But when Gisele returned from next door with help, the room had changed to inexplicably that the little girl's story would always be doubted.

There was no fire in the room, and no evidence that there had been one. The vicious children had vanished. Beaten almost beyond recognition, there was only her mother's unconscious body and the corpse of Paul Fortier.

Police concluded that Gisele's story was pure fantasy subconsciously devised to conceal the facts. Obviously there had been a savage family quarrel in which she had seen her battered mother kill her father in self-defence.

It was a theory Denise herself could neither confirm nor deny. In a catatonic state, she was taken to a hospital where she died three months later. The orphaned child went to live with her grandparents in Seattle.

Because of fear of its ghostly inhabitants, the Fortier house was never again occupied. It burned to the ground in 1906.

A Rover's Return

Cecil Bathe had just driven past a wrecked German tank during World War Two when a sandstorm struck. The Royal Air Force mechanic, returning to his Libyan base after a supply trip, decided to wait it out. He sat reading a dog-eared magazine and drinking beer given to him earlier by some Australian pals.

As a gust of wind shook his three-ton truck, Cecil looked up, and saw a lone un-uniformed figure in the whirling dust. He beckoned the man to the lorry and told him to jump in. Both sheltered from the lashing sand outside, chatting and swigging beer.

The stranger, wearing a khaki uniform without any insignia, spoke in a clipped, rather stilted accent. But after two years of desert warfare, Cecil paid no heed to the rather ragged look, and put the accent down to either South African or Dutch, both fighting alongside the Allies.

As they drank, the Englishman noticed his stranded companion had a raw burn on his right hand and arm. He urged the stranger to get medical attention, but the only response was a chilling laugh and the words, 'It's a bit late for that. Anyway, it doesn't matter.'

But Cecil did discover that he and his eerie companion had something in common. Before the war both had been

Rover Scouts and had attended an international jamboree in southern England.

Daylight had begun to fade as the wind dropped and the RAF man decided to try to make a run for his camp. He offered the stranger a lift, but he shook his head. 'I'm going in the other direction,' he said. 'Thank you for the beer.'

The man stepped down from the truck and they shook hands. 'God watch over you, Tommy,' said the stranger. Cecil felt that the hand he was shaking was cold and stiff.

Cecil drove away, but there was no trace of the uniformed figure in the rearview mirror. He got out to look, but all he could see was the wrecked shell of the enemy tank.

Later that week Cecil returned to the airfield by motorbike just as a recovery crew was hauling the tank wreck onto a transporter.

He stopped to look and the corporal in charge told him that the tank driver had died at the controls a month before when the tank was hit in the turret by a shell. They had laid the body out under canvas.

Cecil lifted the makeshift shroud.

There, with decaying skin and dead eyes, was his beer-drinking desert companion of a few days earlier.

Shaken, Cecil dropped the groundsheet. He clambered onto the tank wreck and peered into the half-light. Glinting in the sunlight he could see an Australian beer bottle.

Spirit of the Deep

If there are ghosts of people who die, can ships also become spirits too? Captain Dusty Miller came close to answering that question, but he took his knowledge to a watery grave when his yacht, the *Joyita*, sank in 1955. For in the months before his last voyage in the South Seas, something unknown had stalked him and his ship.

Passengers reported that another ship was following in their wake, moving along mysteriously through the darkness with no lights or sound. The ghostly ship had a high superstructure aft, they said, but otherwise could describe her only as looking like an ancient galleon, 'from the time of Columbus.'

When Captain Miller glimpsed her in his binoculars on a voyage to Pago Pago, his faced turned deathly white.

He ordered the running lights turned off and took over the helm himself, heading the *Joyita* into a squall. When the weather cleared there was no sign of the ghostly galleon.

The *Joyita* had the reputation of being an unlucky yacht, and Dusty knew this when he bought her.

Roland West, a film producer with RKO studios, had built her in the first blaze of Hollywood's glory and named her *Joyita* – Spanish for little jewel – in honour of his actress sweetheart Jewel Carmen. The romance fizzled and bad luck began to haunt the yacht even before her launching in 1931.

Workmen fell from the rigging and died. The Portuguese widow of one victim publicly laid a curse on the yacht and owner.

On her maiden voyage, to Catalina Island, the ship was towed back into port after a disastrous engine room fire.

The *Joyita* was sold and went into charter service. The great stars of the screen were among those who sailed in her. But when a passenger mysteriously vanished, nobody wanted to know the boat any more.

The United States Navy took her over in World War Two, but put her back in dry dock when she kept running aground. Even out of service, her record was grim; a caretaker died from battery acid fumes, there was a series of unexplained fires, and two men were killed in a fight aboard her.

Sold as war surplus, the now shabby yacht went from owner to owner. Dusty Miller bought her with his last few dollars.

On October 3, 1955, the *Joyita* put to sea for the last time from Apia Harbor in Western Samoa. Held in port by order of unhappy creditors, she had almost rusted away for months before Miller could persuade them to let him take her out.

The *Joyita* carried desperately needed food and medical supplies for the islanders of Fakaofo 200 miles north, and she was to bring back 70 tons of copra. Besides the crew of 16, there were nine passengers.

Samoans living on the waterfront later claimed that, minutes after her departure, they saw a huge, dark vessel gliding in the *Joyita*'s wake. She was enormously high aft, and unlike any ship seen in those waters. She was travelling without lights and with no sound of motors, but she moved at an incredible speed.

Nothing was heard of the *Joyita* until November 10, 1955, when another freighter found her lying abandoned 90 miles north of Fiji. She had a 55-degree list to port and one rail was awash. Radio gear was smashed, the logbook was missing and there was no recognisable message – but carefully-placed signal flags in the rigging spelled out the letters WNQV. To this day investigators have not been able to discover what this may have meant.

No bodies were found in the flooded compartments, and the fate of the 25 persons aboard is still unknown.

In Suva, where the wreck was pumped out, marine inspectors found no answers. The tale of the mysterious ship was put down to native superstition, although it had been government men aboard the *Joyita* who had first reported the ghostly vessel.

But the sailors of the South Sea ports still have no doubts. They still see a clear link between the doomed *Joyita* and the strange, dark galleon from another age.

The Phantom 'Dutchman'

'At 4 a.m. *The Flying Dutchman* crossed our bows. She emitted a strange phosphorescent light as of a phantom ship all aglow, in the midst of which light the masts, spars and sails of a brig 200 yards distant stood out in strong relief as she came up on the port bow, where the officer watch from the bridge saw her, as did the quarter-deck midshipman, who was sent forward at once to the forecastle, but on arriving there no vestige nor any sign whatever of any material ship was to be seen either near or right away to the horizon, the night being clear and the sea calm.'

This unsettling apparition was reported in those words by a 16-year-old Royal Navy midshipman aboard the British warship *Inconstant* steaming off the coast of Australia on July 11, 1881. The report might have been put down to the lad's age, inexperience and a youthful imagination – except for one thing. The midshipman was none other than Prince George, later to become King George V of England.

The vision was also seen by 13 other men aboard the *Inconstant* and two sister ships. Later that day the seaman who had first sighted her fell to his death from a mast-top. Some weeks later the Admiral of the Fleet died.

Over the years, the seagoing belief that bad fortune will dog anyone who sights the *Flying Dutchman* has often been fulfilled. So what – or perhaps who – was the *Flying Dutchman*?

The name originates from the 17th century when an unscrupulously greedy Dutch captain, Hendrik van der Decken, set sail from Amsterdam to seek his fortune in the East Indies. The voyage went smoothly until the Dutch East-Indiaman was rounding the Cape of Good Hope. A fierce storm blew up, ripping the ship's sails to shreds and battering her creaking timbers. But the determined captain pressed on, ignoring the pleas of his crew.

What became of him and his ship is not known, but legend has it that the Devil appeared to the captain and urged him to challenge God's will and sail straight into the storm. The Dutchman agreed and brought upon himself and the curse of the Almighty – that he and his ship of living dead should roam the seas without ever making landfall until the Day of Judgement.

Most sightings of the *Flying Dutchman* have been made in the area where legend says she vanished, around the Cape of Good Hope. The phantom vessel has even been spotted from shore.

In March 1939, some 100 people saw the phantom East-Indiaman. They were all sunbathing on Glencairn Beach in False Bay, south-east of Capetown, when a fully rigged sailing ship appeared out of the heat haze. It passed across the bay with its sails full, although there was not a breath of wind. The ship seemed to be heading for a distant, isolated beach. But, as the crowd of excited witnesses looked on, the mysterious *Flying Dutchman* vanished as suddenly as it had appeared.

In September 1942, four people were relaxing on the terrace of their home at Mouille Point, Capetown, when they spotted an ancient sailing ship heading into Table Bay. They followed its progress for about 15 minutes before it disappeared from view behind Robben Island.

The story of the *Flying Dutchman* is fanciful enough. It inspired Wagner's famous opera. But when witnesses of the ghost ship include a future King of England, the sea's best-loved legend becomes difficult to dismiss as just another sailors' yarn.

Fishermen's Fear

For hundreds of years fishermen on the east and southeast coasts of England have kept a watchful eye for a phantom schooner, the *Lady Lovibond*. They wonder how many sailors who met their deaths on the notorious Goodwin Sands had first spied the ghost of the three-master.

The *Lady Lovibond* ran aground on the Goodwins and sank with all hands on February 13, 1748. Captain Simon Peel, his bride and some of their wedding guests were on board. Legend has it that the first mate, who was in love with the bride himself, killed Peel out of jealousy and steered the ship to its doom on the Goodwins.

Fifty years later to the day, a three-masted schooner identical to the *Lady Lovibond* was seen heading for the Goodwins. The crew of a fishing boat followed her and heard the sounds of a celebration and women's voices. The schooner hit the sands, broke up – and vanished.

The same apparition appeared to another ship's crew exactly 50 years later and was next seen by a group of watchers near Deal, Kent, on February 13, 1898.

Does the phantom appear every 50 years? Watchers were on the lookout on February 13, 1948, but visibility was poor and they saw nothing.

North America also has a famous phantom ship lurking off Rhode Island. The *Palatine* left Holland in 1752, packed with colonists bound for Philadelphia. A fierce winter storm blew her off course and, when the captain was lost overboard, the panicking crew mutinied.

The passengers spent Christmas Day in confusion and terror. Two days later, the *Palatine* ran aground on rocks off Block Island and began to break up. As the storm abated, the doomed ship began to slip back off the rocks, drawn out to sea again by the tide. But before she could do so, dozens of local fishermen descended on the *Palatine*, took off the passengers and looted the ship.

When their frenzied rampage had ended and they had stripped the *Palatine* of everything in value, the fishermen set it on fire and watched it drift, ablaze from bow to stern, out to the open sea.

They watched in horror when they saw a woman appear from her hiding place on the *Palatine* and stand on the deck screaming for help until the flames swallowed her.

There have been sightings of the ghostly vessel off the New England coast ever since, blood-red flames rising from a wrecked hulk.

Terror Aboard UB65

Night was falling at the end of a bitterly cold day in January, 1918, as the German submarine UB65 slid into the English Channel looking for action. She was 15 miles off Portland Bill as the grey winter twilight deepened. The sea was rough and sheets of spray drenched the conning tower.

The U-boat's starboard lookout, screwing up his eyes as he peered over the bridge, was astonished to see an officer standing just below him on the heaving deck.

What in God's name was he doing there? He must be mad. Come to that, how on earth did he get there anyway? All the hatches save that on the conning tower had been firmly battened down.

He was about to hail the officer to warn him that he was in great danger when the figure on the deck turned and gazed up at the bridge. Even in the twilight, the lookout recognised the face, and his blood froze.

It was the ship's former second officers, killed in an explosion on the maiden voyage, his body buried in the military cemetery at Wilhelmshaven.

It seemed hours before he could move his lips. 'It's the ghost,' he yelled. The U-boat's captain rushed to his side, and he too saw the upturned face, before the figure melted into the gathering darkness.

This was not the first time that the phantom of UB65 had appeared to strike terror into the hearts of the men who sailed in her. They had begun to dread the ghost as a harbinger of doom.

Ever since her keel was laid, disaster had followed disaster until UB65 became known as a jinxed ship. The submarine had been built in 1916, one of a fleet designed to operate off the coast of Flanders and create havoc in the Channel. Her crew was made up of three officers and 31 ratings.

Only a week after work started on her, things began to go wrong. A girder being swung into position slipped from its chains and crashed down killing one workman outright and pinning another to the ground. He could not be released for an hour and then died in agony.

Before the submarine was finished there was another accident, this time in the engine room. Three men, overcome by fumes, died before they could be rescued.

On her trial run UB65 ran into a fierce storm and a man was washed overboard. While she was on diving tests, one of the tanks developed a leak and it was 12 hours before she could be brought to the surface. The atmosphere was thick with poisonous fumes and when at last the hatches were opened officers and men staggered out half dead with suffocation.

But it was on her return from her maiden voyage that the UB65 suffered her most violent shock. As she was taking in torpedoes a warhead exploded and in the terrible explosion that followed the second officer was killed and several men badly injured. The officer was buried with full naval honours and the submarine had to go into the dockyard for repairs.

Some weeks later, just before the vessel was due to sail, a member of the crew crashed unceremoniously into the wardroom. Chalk white with shock, he gasped out, 'Herr Ober-Lieutenant, the dead officer is on board.' The captain accused him of being drunk, but he swore that not only he but another rating had seen the dead officer walk up the gangplank.

The captain and other officers ran to the deck where they found the second seaman crouched against the conning tower. He explained in a voice barely above a whisper that the dead officer had come on board, walked towards the bows and stood there with folded arms. After a few seconds, he vanished.

The captain, fully aware of the impact such an incident would have on his superstitious crew, circulated the rumour that the whole thing had been a practical joke. Nobody believed him. Everyone knew the ship was haunted.

On each tour of duty the U-boat carried its ghostly second officer. Men on watch jumped at every shadow. Word spread throughout the German navy that the UB65 was haunted and nobody was anxious to serve on her.

Eventually, the authorities felt it was time such nonsense was stopped and sent a commodore to investigate. The high-ranking officer questioned the entire company. At first he could hardly conceal his impatience with what he believed was superstitious fancy. After hearing all the evidence, he was so impressed that he admitted he could understand the request by almost every member of the crew to transfer to another ship. Officially, the requests were never granted, but one by one men were switched.

The UB65 was withdrawn from active service and, while in dock at the Belgian port of Bruges, a Lutheran pastor was quietly taken aboard to carry out the rite of exorcism. When she went to sea again the U-boat had a new captain and crew. This captain refused to tolerate what he called 'damn nonsense' and threatened any man who spoke of ghosts with severe penalties. Strangely enough, the ship carried out two tours of duty without trouble, but when the unbeliever was replaced, the spirit reappeared. But the next trip was worst of all.

During May of 1918, the UB65 cruised in the Channel and later off the coast of Spain. The ghost was seen three times. A young petty officer swore he saw an unfamiliar officer walk into the torpedo room. He never came out again. After two more sightings, the torpedo gunner went mad, screaming that the ghost would not leave him alone. He threw himself over the side and his body was never recovered.

In spite of her terrible history, the UB65 managed to escape the massive onslaught on the U-boats which came in the final months of war. On July 10, an American submarine patrolling at periscope depth spotted her on the surface. The Americans prepared to attack and were on the point of firing when the UB65 blew up. The explosion was 'tremendous, almost unbelievable,' said eye witnesses. When the smoke cleared all that was left was debris.

Many rational theories were put forward to explain what had happened. It was suggested that the submarine had been rammed by another German sub or perhaps the UB65 herself had fired a torpedo that ran wild. But spectators admitted that none of them quite accounted for the force of the explosion.

The nearest anyone could guess was that by some means the mouth of a torpedo tube had been damaged so that when one was fired it fouled and detonated the rest of the torpedoes in the craft.

The company of 34 men went down with the UB65 – or

maybe it was 35, for the ghost of the second officer was never seen again.

Perhaps he had finished the terrible job he had stayed on earth to do.

The Ghost Ship Ourang Medan

A dozen ships picked up the SOS, which read, 'Captain and all officers dead. Entire crew dead or dying.' And later, 'Now I am also near death.' The the airwaves went dead.

It was a perfect day in February 1948, and, of all the vessels that heard the strange message, only one was able to identify the ship in trouble and pinpoint her position. The ship was named as the Dutch freighter *Ourang Medan*, bound for Djakarta, Indonesia, through the Malacca Strait.

Within three hours, the first rescue vessel was alongside the *Ourang Medan*. A crewman said later, 'Sharks were surging around the hull, and it looked like every shark in the Bay of Bengal had homed in on her knowing there was death aboard.'

When there was no response to flag or radio signals, a boat was launched and the rescue party climbed aboard. They found all the ship's officers massed in the chartroom as if their skipper had called them to a council of war against some unknown disaster. All had died there.

They seemed to have died within seconds of each other; their eyes stared in horror and their bodies were already locked in rigor mortis, some with their arms pointed to the heavens.

The dead seamen littering the decks had died in the same way. A doctor who boarded with the party later reported no signs of poisoning, asphyxiation or disease, but all seemed to have known that death was coming – even the ship's dog. They found it below decks with paws in the air, fangs bared in a silent snarl. In the radio shack, the telegrapher had fallen over his silent key.

The rescue ship tried to take the Dutch ship in tow to the nearest port, but when tackle had been readied and a towline rigged, there was a gush of oily smoke from one of the holds. Knowing they could not contain the blaze without flushing pumps and steam for the fire, the salvage crew fled to their own ship. They had only time enough to cut the towline before the stricken freighter exploded.

The blast scattered wreckage for a quarter of a mile and even killed some of the hungry sharks. What was left of the *Ourang Medan* sank.

In the short inquiry that followed, the doctor reported that something unknown had killed the seamen. Although the official verdict was 'death by misadventure', the mystery of the ghost ship *Ourang Medan* has never been solved.

The Mystery of the Mary Celeste

The most famous ghost ship of all time is the *Mary Celeste*. More than a century after her bizarre discovery, drifting and devoid of life in the middle of the Atlantic, no one is any nearer solving the mystery.

Mary Celeste, a square-rigged brigantine, pointed her bows out of New York's East River on November 4, 1872, bound for Genoa, in Italy, with a cargo of crude alcohol. Aboard were her 37-year-old American master, Benjamin Spooner Briggs, her first mate, Albert Richardson, and a crew of seven. Also tucked safely below decks were the captain's wife, Sarah, and their two-year-old daughter Sophia.

On November 24, Briggs recorded in his log that he had sighted the Azores. The weather was stormy and some of the sails were furled. The following morning the ship's bearings were noted in the log.

It was the last entry ever made.

Ten days later the British brigantine, the *Dei Gratia*, sighted the *Mary Celeste* drifting aimlessly. Captain David Morehouse ordered a longboat to be launched to investigate. The three crewmen who rowed across to the mysterious ship found not a single man, woman or child aboard – living or dead.

In the captain's cabin was Mrs Briggs' rosewood melodeon with a sheet of music still on it as if someone had left in a hurry halfway through a piece. The sewing machine was on a table. Little Sophia's toys were neatly stowed. In the crew's quarters washing hung on a line. Clothing lay on bunks, dry and undisturbed. In the galley, preparations seemed to have been made for breakfast, although only half of it appeared to have been served.

Captain Morehouse, mindful of the salvage value of the vessel, took the *Mary Celeste* in tow. As they headed for Gibraltar, he had time to ponder on his mysterious discovery. As he put forward theories for the riddle of the *Mary Celeste*, so he found arguments for dismissing them.

Morehouse first thought that the ship must have been abandoned in a storm. But why then was there an open and unspilled bottle of cough medicine along with the unbroken plates and ornaments in the captain's cabin?

A mutiny, perhaps? There was no sign of a struggle – and why should the mutineers abandon ship along with their victims?

Perhaps the ship had been taking water? There was three feet of water in the hold, but this would be the normal intake over ten days for any old timber-hulled ship.

Nine of the casks of alcohol were found to be dry, but a further cask had been breached. Could the crew have gone on a drunken rampage? Yet below decks the ship had been in perfect order. In fact, there was no sign of panic or alarm. One of the last acts of Captain Briggs had been to cut the top neatly off his boiled egg before leaving it uneaten on his plate.

The most baffling question of all was this: How was the *Mary Celeste* able to remain on course without a crew for ten days and 500 miles? When the *Dei Gratia* caught up with the mystery ship, Captain Morehouse was sailing on a port tack. The *Mary Celeste* was on a starboard tack. It was inconceivable that the mystery ship could have travelled the course she did with her sails set that way. Someone must have been aboard her for several days after her last log entry.

Captain Morehouse towed the *Mary Celeste* into Gibraltar harbour on December 13. After an inconclusive public inquiry, he and his men were awarded the salvage money they had sought.

The ship was refitted and sold. But she remained ill-fated. Sailors refused to sail in her, believing the vessel to be cursed. She changed hands 17 times before finally running aground and sinking on a coral reef off Haiti in 1884.

The Devil's Triangle

A startling theory to explain the mysterious disappearance of ships and planes in the notorious Bermuda Triangle is that the strange happenings in that region are caused by tormented souls from the spirit world.

The claim is made by two leading exorcists who believe that the 'spirits' in the area known as the Triangle of Death, the Devil's Triangle and the Hoodoo Sea are from ten million negros who were dumped or thrown overboard during the slave trade period. Their troubled souls can 'take over' the minds of pilots and sailors, just as people on land are said to be possessed by spirits.

In a unique experiment, special prayers were held in the Bermuda Triangle to lay at peace these tormented souls who supposedly haunt the Atlantic graveyard of 140 ships and planes and more than 1,000 people who over the years have disappeared without trace.

Backing this extraordinary theory is British surgeon and psychiatrist Dr Kenneth McCall. He said, 'We call it the Possession Syndrome in patients who are mentally disturbed.

'It may be multiple or single, in a family or haunted place. The spirits have got to express themselves, so they possess us and control our minds.'

'Just as in our world here, one or two people can cause torment or haunting disturbances. This can happen with the crew of a ship or plane – and on a very large scale in the Bermuda Triangle. It seems the spirits are trying to draw attention to their state. They are not concerned with destroying the other people.

'There is no such thing as time and space to the spirits. They are wandering and lost and possess people to draw attention to their own plight, just as a lost child will do to an adult.

'These unhappy lost spirits are in purgatory. Because they did not die naturally and were not committed to God, they are causing disturbance.'

Dr McCall, at the age of 67, wrote a special service to be said over the troubled waters and this included the Requiem Mass and the Anglican Eucharist of Remembrance.

He said, 'I think this will lessen the number of planes and ships that disappear there.'

Dr McCall carried out 600 cases of exorcism, or laying on of hands, in the United States, Canada, Holland, Germany and Switzerland. He was a member of a Church of England Commission on Exorcism in Britain. He made many visits to America and with 12 American professors wrote a book on the subject.

537

It was after working as a missionary in China, where he was imprisoned, that he found he could cure other prisoners through the power of prayer.

He said, 'When I returned to Britain in 1946 and learnt all about psychiatry, I realised that the same results occurred in mental hospitals. The patients were disturbed because they were possessed by a spirit.'

His theory that millions of disturbed spirits are in the Bermuda Triangle – the area bounded roughly by Bermuda in the north to Miami and beyond Puerto Rico – came to him when he was becalmed on a small banana boat in the Sargasso Sea.

He said, 'I had been on a lecture tour in the States and visiting relatives. The ship's boiler burst and we were drifting. It was calm and peaceful and I heard singing. I though it was the coloured crew, but I couldn't think why they were singing all the time.'

Dr McCall checked and found that none of the crew was singing and there was not even a record player aboard. 'Then I realised it was a negro dirge, like a moaning chant. It went on and on solidly for five days and nights before we got moving again. My wife Frances also heard it. What we heard fitted all my other theories.'

He believes that during the slave trade years, about ten million slaves went overboard. 'They used to push them over because they got more money from insurance that way. Those who were pregnant or diseased were thrown to the sharks. Others preferred to jump over the side rather than die in slavery.'

Of the many mysteries of the Bermuda Triangle, the most famous is that of the missing warplanes. It is also the case that first aroused widespread public curiosity and gave the area its name.

On December 5, 1945, a flight of five Grumann United States Navy bombers took off from Fort Lauderdale, Florida, for a training flight in perfect weather. Shortly afterwards, the pilots radioed that they were on course, although they were actually flying in the opposite direction. Two hours after take-off, all contact with the aircraft was lost.

A Martin bomber was immediately sent to search for the missing planes. Within 20 minutes, radio contact with it had also been lost. No trace of any of the aircraft was ever found. In all, six planes and 27 men simply vanished into thin air.

In Dr McCall's view, the leader of the training flight believed to the last that he was heading in the right direction, but that his judgement was distorted by spirits.

The spirit theory had been current among seamen for many years before the world heard of the Triangle. The greatest disaster in the area had taken place 27 years earlier, in March 1918. That was the month in which the US supply vessel *Cyclops* vanished from the face of the earth without making a single distress call. No wreckage or any of the crew of 309 was ever found.

The service and prayers aimed at ending such disasters were carried out in the Bermuda Triangle by exorcist Donald Omand, a 74-year-old retired Church of England vicar and expert on the occult, who described himself as a spiritual surgeon. In previous exorcisms, he had driven spirits from people, buildings and animals.

Dr McCall was unable to go with him to the Triangle, but Omand was accompanied by an English doctor and writer Marc Alexander, who said, 'The Rev Omand often works with medical men and psychiatrists. Nearly all his cases are referred to him by doctors.

'This is a sensational subject and my eyes were opened by a lot of the things he did.'

Omand's work of laying spirits at rest has been supported by Peter Mumford, the Bishop of Hertford, who said, 'He was a member of a church commission which reported a few years ago on exorcism. He is a recognised exorcist and an expert in this field. He is a very experienced and well regarded and has contributed to our understanding of this field.'

But whether he has placated the 'spirits' of the Bermuda Triangle, only time will reveal.

'Help Me in the Name of God'

A woman's ghostly cries for help are the only clues to the disappearance of a Mississippi riverboat that vanished 106 years ago. The strange voice was first reported on the evening of May 28, 1875. Picnicking near the riverbank, more than 50 Vicksburgh high school students told police they had heard a woman screaming for help somewhere on the river.

The police decided it was a prank. They made a thorough search of the waters, but there was no such woman. There has been no such woman in 106 years, though hundreds of different people have reported the same eerie cries. The reports have come from Vicksburgh, Natchez, St Joseph and other points along the Mississippi.

In most documented cases, the chilling screams are followed by words in French, *'Aidez-moi au nom de Dieu, les hommes me blessent!'* ('Help me in the name of God, the men are hurting me!')

No one can explain the disembodied voice or its message, but there are fishermen and residents of the riverbank communities who believe it is linked to a darker mystery that still haunts the 'father of waters'.

On a clear blue day in June, 1874, the riverboat, *Iron Mountain* set out from Vicksburgh for New Orleans carrying 57 passengers and towing a string of barges. The big paddle-wheel steamer was famous in her time, plying the Ohio and Mississippi rivers to every port between New Orleans and Pittsburgh.

But on this voyage, she was sailing into history, for after rounding a bend in the river, she vanished.

Not long after her departure, the string of barges was found bobbing in the water. The towropes had been slashed in two – something that would be done only in an emergency. But no emergency had been reported, and rescue craft converging on the scene could find no evidence of one.

Hundreds of miles of river bottom were dragged, but the waters yielded no trace of wreckage or bodies.

Of the many explanations advanced at the time, one has often reappeared through the years. In that troubled period after the Civil War, riverboat pirates still operated on some parts of the Mississippi, and there was tempting cargo of wealth and beauty aboard the *Iron Mountain*.

On the passenger list were several Creole women who spoke French. Could the big steamboat have been sacked by pirates who dismantled her and concealed the sections after a ghastly carnival of rape and murder?

Voyage of the Frozen Dead

The Yankee whaling ship *Herald* was cruising off the west coast of Greenland, inside the Arctic Circle. From the bridge, Captain Warren peered ahead at a three-masted schooner drifting through the ice floes like a ghost ship. Warren took eight men in a longboat and rowed to the silent vessel. Through the encrusted ice, they could make out the schooner's name: *Octavius*.

Warren and four of the sailors boarded the schooner. They crossed the silent, moss-covered decks, opened a hatch and descended to the crew's quarters. There they found the bodies of 28 men, all lying on their bunks and wrapped in heavy blankets.

They fumbled their way aft to the captain's cabin,

where the nightmare continued. The master of the *Octavius* slumped over the ship's log, a pen close to his right hand as if he had dozed at work. On a bed against one wall of the cabin, a blonde woman lay frozen to death under piles of blankets. And in a corner there were a sailor and a small boy whose bodies told a tragic story.

The sailor sat with his flint and steel clutched in frozen hands. In front of him was a tiny heap of shavings, silent evidence of a fire that had failed to ignite. The little boy crouched close to him, his face buried in the seaman's jacket as if he had huddled there in pathetic search for warmth.

The men from the *Herald* clambered back onto the deck, taking with them the schooner's log book as proof of what they had found. Back aboard the whaler, they could only watch helplessly while the derelict schooner drifted away from them among the icebergs, never to be seen again.

It was well they had taken the log book. The world would not be ready to accept their story, which remains one of the strangest tales of the sea.

The last log entry was dated November 11, 1762. The dying captain wrote that the *Octavius* had been frozen for 17 days. The fire had gone out and they could not restart it. The location of the ship at this time, said the captain was Longitude 160W, Latitude 75N.

Captain Warren looked at the charts in disbelief. In those last hours of human life, the ship had been locked in the Arctic Ocean north of Point Barrow, Alaska – thousands of miles from where the whaler had found her. Guided by some unknown force, year after year the battered schooner had crept steadily eastward through the vast ice fields until she entered the North Atlantic. In doing so she had then achieved the dream of all mariners.

For centuries men had sought the legendary Northwest Passage – a navigable route around the Arctic Ocean between the Atlantic and the Pacific. On that historic

13-year voyage, the ghost ship *Octavius* with her crew of frozen dead had been the first to find it.

The Lonely Lighthouse

On the night the Eilean Mor Lighthouse went dark, two sailors on the brigantine *Fairwind* saw a strange sight. Cutting diagonally across their bow a longboat with a huddle of men aboard was bearing toward the lighthouse on the rocky Flannan Islands off the west coast of Scotland.

The sailors called, but there was no answer. The boatmen wore foul weather gear and when moonlight slashed through a rift in the clouds, their faces shone like bone. One of the would-be rescuers testified later, 'Our first thought was that they were floating dead from some shipwreck. But then we heard the oarlocks and saw the movement of their arms.'

Later on that night of December 15, 1900, a squall broke. Without the guardian light ships were in dire peril. There was one angry question from the skippers: Why was the lighthouse dark?

On the day after Christmas, the supply vessel *Hesperus* hove to off the islands to investigate. When there was no answer to repeated signals, crewmen set out in a small boat to the landing dock. Tying up, they were chilled by the strange silence.

The lighthouse had been staffed by three men, but no one was there to welcome the *Hesperus*. There were no signs of violence and the larders were well stocked. Lamps were all trimmed and ready, the beds made, the dishes and kitchen utensils shining.

As the searchers climbed through the empty lighthouse, they found only two things that struck them as unusual. On the stairway and in a cubbyhole office where the log was kept, there were shreds of seaweed unknown to them.

There were no oilskins or seaboots in the building, which seemed to imply that all three men had left the lighthouse together.

No lighthouse keeper had ever been known to abandon his post, even in the worst weather, and this was a point repeatedly made during the inquiry which followed – an inquiry which was hushed to silence by the reading of the log book kept by keeper Thomas Marshall:

'December 12: Gale north by northwest. Sea lashed to fury. Never seen such a storm. Waves very high. Tearing at lighthouse. Everything shipshape. James Ducat irritable.' and later that day: 'Storm still raging, wind steady. Stormbound. Cannot go out. Ship passing sounding foghorn. Could see light of cabins. Ducat quiet. Donal McArthur crying.

'December 13: Storm continued through night. Wind shifted west by north. Ducat quiet. McArthur praying.' And later: 'Noon, grey daylight. Me, Ducat and McArthur prayed.'

Inexplicably, there was no entry for December 14. The final line in the log read: 'December 15, 1 p.m. Storm ended, sea calm. God is over all.'

No explanation could be offered but that the men had been seeing visions. While the log entries had reported gales lashing in Flannan Isles, there had been none at all 20 miles away on the island of Lewis.

Locals pointed to an even more mysterious cause of the disappearance of the lighthouse men. For centuries, the Flannan Isles had been haunted. Hebridean farmers might sail there during daylight to check on their sheep – but few except the 'foolish sassenachs' at the lighthouse dared stay overnight.

Final 'proof', if the locals needed any, was the evidence of the sailors of the *Fairwind* – of the longboat crowded with ghosts.

Legend of the Hairy Hands

Holidaymaker Florence Warwick had never heard of the ghostly hands that are supposed to terrify victims on Dartmoor in Devon, but she discovered all she would ever want to know when her car broke down on the moor one evening.

Florence, aged 28, was driving along the lonely road from Postbridge to Two Bridges after a sightseeing tour. When the car started to judder she pulled over to the side of the road to look at the handbook.

She recalled: 'As I was reading in the failing light, a cold feeling suddenly came over me. I felt as if I was being watched. I looked up and saw a pair of huge, hairy hands pressed against the windscreen. I tried to scream, but couldn't. I was frozen with fear.'

She watched wide-eyed as the disembodied hands that are said to have haunted this desolate place for 60 years began to crawl across the windscreen. 'It was horrible, they were just inches away,' she said. 'After what seemed a lifetime, I heard myself cry out and the hands seemed to vanish.'

Florence was so shaken she hardly noticed that her car started first time. By the time she had driven the 20 miles back to Torbay, where she was staying with friends, she began to think she had imagined the whole incident. But then her friends told her the legend of the hands.

The 'curse' on the road began to be felt in the early 1920s. Pony traps were overturned, a cyclist felt his handlebars wrenched from his grasp and ran full tilt into a stone wall, horses shied and bolted. A doctor travelling on a motor-cycle with two children in the sidecar was nearly killed when the engine literally detached itself from the machine. An Army officer reported an enormous pair of hands covered in long dark hairs taking charge of this steering wheel, covering his own.

Things reached a head in 1921 when a newspaper sent investigators to the spot and the local authority had the camber of the road altered. But the hands refused to be deterred.

Not long after the road improvements a young couple were visiting the area with their caravan. As is common on Dartmoor, a heavy fog suddenly fell one evening as they were driving towards Plymouth. Rather than drive on and risk losing their way, the couple decided to park in a lay-by along the Postbridge road. They cooked themselves a snack and settled down to sleep.

The woman had only been asleep for a short time when she was awakened by a strange scratching noise which seemed to be coming from outside the caravan. Thinking it might be a dog wandering lost on the moors, she got out of bed to take a look. Suddenly a strange chill came over her and she turned to look at the window above her husband's bunk.

There, slowly crawling across glass right above her sleeping husband, was an enormous pair of hairy hands. The woman was too stunned even to cry out, but for some inexplicable reason, as she sat rigid with fear staring at the gruesome apparition, she made the sign of the cross and the hands vanished.

The incident was the talk of the county, and it gave rise to the inevitable jokes and hoaxes. Soon enough the local police began to ignore reports that came in, attributing many of the sightings to an over-indulgence in the local cider. But in 1960 a fatal accident on the lonely stretch of road raised again the spectre of the hands.

A motorist driving from Plymouth to Chagford was found dead beneath the wreckage of his overturned car. No other car was involved and there seemed to be no reason, other than a fault in the car itself, that could have caused the vehicle to career off the road. But when police experts examined the wreckage they could find no mechanical fault in the car. It is a mystery which has never been solved.

Motorists are not the only ones to have suffered the attentions of this unusual manifestation. Walkers making their way along the stretch of road have reported strange experiences and sensations even though they have never heard of the legend of the hands.

One hiker enjoying the rugged beauty of the scenery got carried away during his walk and found himself making his way along the road at dusk. Suddenly he was overcome by an inexplicable feeling of panic, he was rooted to the spot, yet he could see no reason for his sense of fear. Minutes later the feeling passed and he carried on his way puzzling over his strange experience. Only later did he hear the story of the hauntings.

Nobody has been able to explain the strange happenings on this lonely stretch of highway. The only clue to the appearance of the hairy disembodied hands is that in the far distant past a Bronze Age village stood along the once-busy but now-sinister Dartmoor road.

Cursed Car of Sarajevo

Archduke Franz Ferdinand wanted a car that would impress the public when he and his wife, the lovely Duchess of Hohenburgh, toured the tiny Bosnian capital of Sarajevo. There were reasons for putting on a brave show. Europe seethed with political unrest, and the Archduke's good-will trip could be hazardous.

The royal couple arrived at Sarajevo on June 28, 1914, in a blood-red, six-seat open tourer. It made a splendid target. A young fanatic armed with a pistol leaped onto the running board of the car. Laughing in the faces of the Archduke and Duchess, he fired shot after shot into their bodies.

The double assassination was the spark that touched off the Great War, with its casualty list of 20 million.

After the Armistice, the newly appointed Governor of Yugoslavia had the car restored to first-class condition, but after four accidents and the loss of his right arm, he felt the vehicle should be destroyed.

His friend Dr Srikis disagreed. Scoffing at the notion that a car could be cursed, he drove it happily for six months – till the overturned vehicle was found on the highway with the doctor's crushed body beneath it.

Another doctor became the next owner, but when his superstitious patients began to desert him, he hastily sold it to a Swiss racing driver. In a road race in the Dolomites, the car threw him over a stone wall and he died of a broken neck.

A well-to-do farmer then acquired the car, which stalled one day. While another farmer was towing it in for repairs, the vehicle suddenly growled into full power and knocked the tow-car aside, killing both farmers.

Tiber Hirshfield, the car's last private owner, decided that all the old vehicle needed was a less sinister colour scheme. He had it repainted in a cheerful blue and invited five friends to accompany him to a wedding. Hirshfield and four of his guests died in a head-on smash as they drove to the festivities.

Finally the rebuilt car was shipped to a Vienna museum where it was lovingly cared for by attendant Karl Brunner, who revelled in the stories about the car's 'curse' and forbade any visitor to sit in it.

During World War Two, bombs reduced the museum to rubble. Nothing was found of the car – or Karl Brunner.

Horseman of Bottlebush Down

Ghosts and spirits have come back across hundreds of years. But none have come further than the mystery horseman who rides the north Dorset countryside.

The horseman of Bottlebush Down is thought to date back to the Bronze Age, which makes him and his mount around 2,500 years old.

His appearances are nearly always close to the A3081 road which runs between Cranborne and Sixpenny Handley in Britain's beautiful West Country. Although the area is today mainly quiet and devoted to agriculture, it was thought to have been a hive of activity thousands of years ago.

The fields are dotted with low, round burial mounds. A strange earthwork, known locally as the Cursus, runs for some six miles across the fields. It consists of two parallel ditches about 80 yards apart and it is here that the horseman is usually seen.

The horseman's ghostly rides have become legend in this part of the West Country. Farmworkers and shepherds have reported seeing him galloping across the fields towards the Cursus and in one incident in the 1920s two young girls were terrified as they cycled one night from Handley to Cranborne.

The wide-eyed girls told police that they were cycling along the road when suddenly a horseman appeared from nowhere and rode alongside them for some distance before disappearing.

But it was a few years earlier that the most documented sighting was made, and one that put the time stamp on the horseman.

Archaeologist R C Clay had such a close encounter with the rider that he was able to date the apparition by his clothes. Clay, leader of a team excavating a Bronze Age settlement near Christchurch, in Dorset, came face to face with the horseman in 1924 as he was driving home from the excavations to Salisbury, in Wiltshire.

As he passed the spot where an old Roman road crossed the modern highway, he saw a horseman galloping across the fields ahead of him. The horseman was riding full tilt towards the road, but as Clay slowed down to let him cross, the rider swung his horse round and galloped parallel with the vehicle some 40 yards away.

For some 100 yards or more, the horseman kept pace with the car while Clay watched fascinated. In spite of his surprise, the archaeologist managed to take in a great deal of detail about horse and rider.

He said later, 'The horse was smallish with a long tail and mane. It had neither bridle nor stirrups. The rider had bare legs, a long flowing cloak and was holding some sort of weapon over his head.'

As suddenly as he had appeared, the horseman disappeared. Clay stopped his car and tried to gather his thoughts. His first instinct was to get out and look round, but as it was getting dark he decided to press on home.

The next morning he was back to see if he could discover anything which would help explain his ghostly encounter of the previous evening. He searched the road and the surrounding area for several hundred yards on either side of the spot but found nothing – except a low burial mound almost exactly where the horseman disappeared.

For weeks afterwards he tried to find an explanation for what he saw. He drove along the section of road at the same time, evening after evening to see if in the gathering dusk he might have mistaken an overhanging tree or bank or anything for his galloping horseman. There was nothing.

His one encounter with the horseman, coupled with his expert knowledge, enabled him to date the figure as from the late Bronze Age – somewhere between 700 and 600 BC.

The Grief of Henry Watts

At the edge of a quiet Wiltshire road stands a small stone cross. Travellers hurrying along the road, between Marlborough and Hungerford, could be excused if they missed the tiny memorial to the 14-year-old boy who died tragically at the spot just over a century ago.

Grass and country flowers almost hide the cross, on which are inscribed the simple words 'A H P Watts, May 12, 1879'.

But four people driving home from the cinema on a quiet autumn night in 1956 will never forget the memorial. For they came face to face with the grieving ghost of the boy's father.

Little Alfie Watts worked for a carter in the village of Axford, and it was here in 1879 that he met his death. Alfie and the carter were at the head of a team of three horses which suddenly bolted. The man and the lad ran alongside the heavily-laden cart, struggling to halt the runaway team. But as the cart clattered through a steep-sided cutting, Alfie was thrown to the ground.

The boy fell beneath the wheels and died of his injuries two hours later. Morning villagers erected a memorial to him at that spot.

Years passed and memories dimmed. Occasionally someone remembered the stone cross, and the brambles and grass were cleared away. Then, in October 1956, Frederick Moss and three friends were driving home from the movies to Marlborough when the headlights picked out a tall, thin, clean-shaven man standing in the middle of the road.

He was dressed in a long brown coat and stood with his back to where the cross was almost hidden in the grass.

As the car swept on he made no attempt to get out of the way. Moss blew his horn, but still the figure stayed where

551

it was. It did not even look up.

The driver slammed on the brakes and stopped a few yards short of the figure, but as he got out to investigate, it disappeared.

Moss and his friends searched the area with torches, but found nothing. With the cutting walls rising steeply nine feet on either side, it was impossible for anyone to have climbed up without being seen.

When Moss arrived home shaken, he told his wife what he had seen. As she heard the full description of the mystery man, something clicked in her memory.

She was a native of the area and was born about 20 years after the accident. She said she clearly remembered the boy's father, Henry Pounds Watts, who died in 1907. He was a tall, thin man who dressed in a long brown coat and, unusually for those times, had neither beard nor whiskers.

The Mosses were in no doubt that this was the man on the road – a road which at that time was due to be widened, destroying the little cross. Perhaps Henry wanted to make sure that someone remembered his son's modest memorial before the road was widened.

If that was his aim, it succeeded. The road was widened but the cross was lovingly replaced nearby.

Dead Man's Quest for Justice

A row in Britain's House of Commons during the First World War may have been responsible for the mysterious reappearance of a long-dead pilot. The flier returned to haunt an airbase – three years after the crash that killed him.

Member of Parliament Pemberton Billing, head of the Southampton company which later developed the Spitfire aircraft, accused the Government in 1916 of doing nothing while certain Royal Flying Corps men were 'murdered rather than killed by the carelessness, incompetence or ignorance of their senior officers or of the technical side of the service'.

One of the examples he cited was that of Desmond Arthur, an Irish Lieutenant with No 2 Squadron, who died in a crash over the Scottish airbase of Montrose on May 27, 1913. Arthur was gliding down from 4,000 feet, preparing to land, when the starboard wing of the BE2 biplane folded in mid-air. As the tiny aircraft plunged, the pilot's seatbelt snapped, and he was thrown out of the cockpit. Ground staff watched him fall to his death, arms and legs flailing helplessly. There were no parachutes in 1913.

The Royal Aero Club's accidents investigation committee began a probe immediately, and concluded that an unauthorised repair job on the plane's right wing had been botched, then covered up. Someone had broken a wing span near the tip, repaired it with a crude splice, then concealed the work by stretching new fabric over the affected area. To Arthur's friends in the Royal Flying Corps, it added up to murder, but the offender could not be pinpointed.

Billing used the Aero Club's findings as a basis for his 1916 onslaught in Parliament. He was as astonished as anyone when the Government, anxious to avoid any scandal that might undermine public faith in its war effort, issued its own report on the crash. It said the wing repair explanation was based on the evidence of only one of 23 witnesses, and was completely without foundation. In other words, Arthur had only himself to blame for his death.

The interim report was issued on August 3, 1916, and a detailed version was promised before Christmas. In September, airmen based at Montrose began to notice curious things. Twice one officer followed a figure in full flying kit towards the mess, only to see him vanish before reaching the door. A flying instructor woke one night to find a strange man sitting in a chair beside the fire in his bedroom. When he challenged the intruder, the chair was suddenly empty. Two other men woke simultaneously one night, convinced a third person was in their room.

Was Desmond Arthur trying to rally his old friends in the Royal Flying Corps to clear his name? As the story of the hauntings spread around Britain's other airbases, two of the Government's committee of inquiry revealed that they had not even seen the Royal Aero Club findings that their interim report had denigrated.

After studying the results of the earlier investigations, Sir Charles Bright, an engineer, and a lawyer called Butcher added an amendment to the final report when it was issued at Christmas.

They declared, 'It appears probable that the machine had been damaged accidentally, and that the man (or men) responsible for the damage had repaired it as best he (or they) could to evade detection and punishment.'

The ghost of the dead pilot appeared to settle for that as vindication of his innocence in causing the crash. After one last appearance in January 1917, phantom flier Desmond Arthur was never seen again.

The Headless Cyclist

George Dobbs was determined that the bitter weather and shortages of wartime Britain were not going to get him down. It was 1940 and the country was in the grip of one of its worst winters for years. Snow covered the countryside and, to make matters worse, the war news was gloomy.

George wrapped himself up against the hostile night and set out from his home near Northampton to walk to the Fox and Hounds pub for a few beers to cheer himself up.

With his hands deep in his pockets, he struggled up the

slippery slope past the cemetery when he noticed the dim headlights of a car slowly approaching, its wheels running in and out of the icy ruts. Framed against the lights of the car, George saw a cyclist pedalling towards him. He too was having difficulty in steering his machine because of the snow and ice.

At first George thought that the cyclist had no head, but he quickly dismissed the idea as being a trick of the light or the fact that the rider had muffled himself up against the cold.

The next time George glanced up, the cyclist was still fighting for control of his machine, completely unaware of the approaching car. But before George had a chance to cry out, the car drew level with him and chugged past towards Market Harborough.

George could not believe it. The car must have hit the cyclist, he thought. He ran through the snow as fast as he could to the spot where he had last seen the cyclist – expecting to find the result of a terrible accident.

There was nothing. No cyclist, no cycle and no accident. George searched both sides of the road in vain.

He fled as quick as his legs could take him to the Fox and Hounds pub at nearby Kingsthorpe. As he thawed out in the pub, he told his story.

When George finished there was silence – until Lid Green, who was for many years the local gravedigger, leaned across the bar.

He said, 'That sounds just like the chap I buried 25 years ago. He was knocked off his bike in deep snow outside the cemetery gates.

'His head was torn off in the crash.'

Spirit of the Disused Aerodrome

A young collector of military souvenirs knew who to blame when he found his tailor's dummy in SS uniform hurled from its regular place in the hall of his home.

Only days earlier, both the man and his wife had been given the shock of their lives when an RAF pilot, complete with World War Two leather jacket, helmet and oxygen mask, appeared in their home in Croydon, south London. Clearly the ghost did not appreciate finding reminders of an enemy in his new haunt.

The young couple asked to remain anonymous when in 1978, after a series of odd happenings, they called in the Society for Psychic Research.

They told investigator Brian Nisbet that the pilot had appeared four times, first in the wife's bedroom as she prepared for a dinner party, then in the lounge as the husband watched TV, and twice more in the bedroom, once when the wife was ironing, once when the couple were together.

After that, they saw him no more – but his invisible spirit began playing tricks on them and their guests. First he hurled the offending tailor's dummy ten feet across the hall. Then he turned up in the spare bedroom, where a young married couple were staying there as guests. In the middle of the night, the man got up to go to the bathroom. While he was away, the wife suddenly felt the bedclothes being wrenched from her naked body.

It was the last straw for their hosts – they called in a local clergyman. Even during the exorcism ceremony, the phantom flier could not resist a prank. The wife felt the strap of her bra being plucked, though nobody was standing near her.

Investigator Nisbet discovered that the couple's house was on an estate built on the site of the old Croydon airport.

But he said, 'I have not been able to explain any of the things that have happened to these people.'

Phantoms of the Highways
The hiker, the jaywalker and the hunchbacked postman

The darts match ended early for Roy Fulton. It had not been a lively night. A pint and a half of lager and not much company in the little pub at Leighton Buzzard. Roy, 26, decided to drive to another pub, The Glider, nearer his home, at Dunstable, Bedfordshire.

It was a dark night and foggy patches hung over the flat, open countryside. Roy started up and drove his little van towards the village of Stanbridge. As he neared the first houses, the headlights picked out the dark figure of a youth standing at the roadside, thumbing a lift.

Roy pulled up past the young man and waited for him to catch up. He looked up at the stranger's face. It was pale and drawn and framed by short, dark, curly hair. The young man was probably about 20. The only unusual thing about him was the white shirt he was wearing with an old-fashioned round collar.

Roy opened the door. The young man said nothing. 'I'm going into Dunstable, where are you for?' Roy asked. The young man pointed towards Totternoe, a village beyond Stanbridge. He got in and shut the passenger door. Roy passed Stanbridge and drove on down the Totternoe road at a steady 45 miles an hour. The hitch-hiker sat silently. As the road neared Tatternoe, it was lit by streetlights. Roy slowed down and took a cigarette from his pocket. 'Cigarette?' he asked, flipping open the packet and holding it out to his passenger. There was no reply. Roy shook the packet and turned to his companion . . .

There was no one there. The passenger seat was empty. Roy slammed on the brakes and looked all around him. He stared through the side window at the road stretching into the empty darkness.

A cold draught blew across his neck and a chill gripped his stomach. His left hand edged across to the passenger seat. It was warm.

Roy reasoned that the hiker could not possibly have got out of the car at the speed of 45 mph. And, even if he had, he would have had to open the door and that would have automatically switched on the courtesy light, but no light had come on, and the passenger door was firmly shut.

Shaken, Roy drove on to The Glider. He ordered a large scotch and downed it in one gulp. Ashen-faced, he said, 'I've just seen a ghost.'

Lorry-driver Laurie Newman spotted what looked like the figure of a nun walking beside the A4 as he drove from Chippenham to Bath at 2.30 one morning. He slowed down to pull out and pass her, but as he did so, the figure turned and sprang, clutching the side of his cab, and leering through the side window. Shocked, Laurie stared back . . . into the face of a grinning skull.

Sebastian Cliffe also experienced a highway haunting as he drove from Bath to Warminster. As he approached a bend at Limpley Stoke, all his dashboard gauges stopped functioning and he felt a sudden chill. Then a ghostly face appeared at his windscreen. As it slowly faded, the gauges began to work again.

Spooky jay-walkers have startled drivers in the West Country. An old gipsy woman staggers across the Bath to Bradford-on-Avon road at Sally-in-the-Wood, a spot notorious for vehicles plunging off the road. And at Barrow Gurney, on the A38 south west of Bristol, several drivers have skidded to a halt to avoid a woman in a white coat who suddenly appears, and then vanishes.

Police at Frome, Somerset, report that at least three

motorists say they have been victims of a phantom hitch-hiker. The man, aged between 30 and 40, and wearing a check sports jacket, stops cars between the villages of Nunney and Critchill, and asks to be dropped at Nunney Catch. But when the cars reach the village he has disappeared. One driver was so shocked, he needed hospital treatment.

Has the ghost of a hunchback postman who died in 1899 returned as a 20th century killer? That was one theory being investigated by police in East Anglia after three people died on a lonely country road.

The first victim on the A12 between Great Yarmouth, Norfolk, and Lowestoft, Suffolk, was a lorry-driver who knew the route well. For no apparent reason, his vehicle careered off the road and smashed into trees in 1960. The coroner reported an open verdict.

Twenty years later a car driver who was also familiar with the road drove crazily into the trees. Within a year, a cyclist unaccountably swerved into the path of a car.

Survivors of accidents on the same stretch of road have also claimed that a 'shadowy figure' forced them to swerve. Andrew Cutajar, aged 19, of Lowestoft, said, 'The spectre of an old man was standing in the slow lane, just looking at me. I slammed on the brakes and skidded, expecting a thud. The car went straight through him and hit the kerb.'

There was no sign of the old man when Andrew got out to investigate.

Former policeman Frank Colby, also of Lowestoft, claims he has seen a hunchback figure with long straggly hair on the A12. 'He just walked across the carriageway and disappeared,' he said.

Psychic researcher Ivan Bunn, of nearby Oulton Broad, believes the figure may be the ghost of William Balls, a postman whose body was found in the area during the winter of 1899. Could it be that he is still trying to deliver a message . . . about his death?

Phantom Bride

A lady dressed in brown has haunted Raynham Hall, a magnificent mansion near Fakenham, Norfolk, for more than 250 years. She has been seen by a king, shot at by a famous author – and even captured by a camera.

The lady is believed to be Dorothy Walpole, sister of Sir Robert Walpole, who became Britain's Prime Minister in 1721. And her unhappy spirit is said to return because of a tragic love life.

Dorothy's father, also a member of Parliament, and also called Robert, became guardian to a young viscount, Charles Townshend, when the lad was 13. As he and Dorothy grew up together, the fell in love, but they were denied permission to marry. Dorothy's father feared people would think the Walpoles were after the Townshend fortunes.

Charles left to find consolation in the arms of a baron's daughter, and later married her. Dorothy drifted first to London, then Paris, drowning her sorrows in a reckless whirl of parties, and eventually scandalising high society by setting up home with a rakish French lord.

Then, in 1711, news reached her that Charles's wife had died. She hurried home to Raynham, and 12 months later the childhood lovers were married. For a while they were blissfully happy. Then the bride's past caught up with her. Her husband was told of how she had lived in Paris. In a rage, he confined her to her rooms, and ordered the servants to let no-one in – or out.

When Dorothy died, aged 40, ten years later, in 1726 the official cause was given as smallpox. But local rumour said she had been pushed from behind at the top of the hall's great staircase. Such gossip gained credence when servants from Raynham revealed that her ghost was soon seen wandering the corridors of her old home.

In 1786, the Prince Regent – later to become King George IV – was a guest at the hall. He woke one night to find a woman wearing brown standing beside his bed. Her hair was dishevelled, her face ashen white. The royal visitor fled the room in his nightgown and nightcap, and stormed through the house, rousing everyone with his wrath. He refused to stay an hour longer.

Alarmed at upsetting such an honoured guest, the Townshends ordered a nightly watch by servants and gamekeepers. A few nights later, the patrols sighted the lady in brown. But when one of the men moved into her path to challenge her, she walked straight through him. He felt an icy cloud pass into his bones and out again.

The brown-clad spectre cut short Christmas merrymaking at Raynham in 1835. Several guests left early after seeing her. Colonel Loftus, brother of the then Lady Townshend, bumped into her on consecutive nights. He described her as a stately woman in a rich brocade dress and a cap. Her face was clearly defined, but she had black hollows instead of eyes.

Dorothy's fame spread. Captain Frederick Marryat, the tough, sea-going author of *Mr Midshipman Easy* and *The Children Of The New Forest*, was invited to meet her for himself when he scoffed at the ghost stories. When he arrived at the hall, he was given a room where a portrait of Dorothy hung. It helped him recognise her late that night when he and two friends spotted her walking towards them down a corridor. They darted into a side room, but the lady stopped opposite the door, and gave them a wicked grin. Marryat was holding his pistol, and fired a shot at the shape. It went straight through the still-smiling spectre and smashed into the wooden door behind.

In 1936, two professional photographers arrived at Raynham Hall to take pictures of the house for Lady Townshend. On the afternoon of 19 September they were setting up their cameras at the foot of the staircase when one of them saw what seemed to be a cloud of vapour taking human shape. He shouted instructions to his colleague, who exposed the photographic plate without knowing why. When it was developed, the misty outline of a woman in a white gown and veil could be seen halfway down the stairs, and experts were convinced the picture was not a fake.

Had Dorothy Walpole decided to let the world see what she looked like on her wedding day 224 years earlier – on the steps where, some say, she was pushed to her death?

Phantoms of the Stage

All the world's a stage for the haunting performances of ghosts, but they seem particularly fond of theatres. Often they are connected with real dramas as strange as any fictional play.

William Terriss was a colourful adventurer turned actor. In December, 1897, he was playing the lead in a thriller called *Secret Service* at the Adelphi Theatre in The Strand. One night, as he left the stage door, he was stabbed to death and ever since his restless spirit has been blamed for a series of inexplicable happenings.

Actors have heard curious tappings, and the sound of footsteps. Mechanical lifts have been moved by invisible forces, and lights mysteriously switched on and off. In 1928, a comedy actress felt the couch in her dressing room lurch under her, as if someone was trying to move it. Then her arm was seized, leaving a bruise. The startled woman had not heard of the ghost until her dresser arrived, and explained that she was using the dressing room which had belonged to Terriss.

The phantom star's strangest performance came in 1955. Jack Hayden, foreman ticket collector at Covent Garden Tube station, noticed a distinguished figure in a grey suit and white gloves who looked as if he was lost. But when Hayden asked if he could help, the man vanished into thin air. Four days later, the same figure returned and put his hands on the head of 19-year-old porter Victor Locker.

Pictures of Terriss were shown to both men, and they instantly recognised him as their ghost. Both also asked to be transferred. Other London Transport staff on the Piccadilly Line have spoken of a strange presence at Covent Garden, and in 1972 a station-master, signalman and engineer all reported seeing the man in grey.

More than 50 cleaners at London's Drury Lane theatre claim to have seen a phantom wandering the dress circle in a long grey coat. The 18th century dandy in a powdered wig has also been spotted from the stage during rehearsals, and actors regard the sightings as a good omen they usually herald a successful run for a play. The eerie visitor could be linked with a macabre discovery by workmen in 1860. Inside a hollow brick wall, they found a skeleton with a dagger between its ribs.

A publicity gimmick that backfired introduced actress Judy Carne to the ghost of the Theatre Royal, Bath. A mock seance was arranged to promote her appearance in a production of the Noel Coward play, *Blithe Spirit*. But the light-hearted stunt became serious when the medium hired to host the proceedings started to receive real messages.

Judy, the 'sock-it-to-me' star of the TV *Laugh-In* show, said: 'We were all absolutely spellbound, including two cynical newspaper reporters. The voice of a woman told us she had been an actress who had starred at the theatre. She had been married, but had fallen in love with someone else.

'Here husband and lover fought a duel, and her lover was killed. Heartbroken, she hanged herself in the dressing room. As I listened, I became very emotional and felt real pain. I tried to talk to her, and ask if she was still unhappy, but the table we were sitting round rattled, and I heard weeping. I often went back to the theatre to try to contact her again, but she never re-appeared.'

Could the heartbroken 18th century actress be the phantom lady in grey who haunts the theatre and the buildings on either side of it? She has often been seen by actors, sitting alone in a box. She was there on August 23, 1975, when the curtain went up on a performance of *The Dame Of Sark*, starring Dame Anna Neagle. Theatre staff have also noted a strong smell of jasmine whenever she is near – a scent also familiar to a succession of landlords at the Garrick's Head public house next door.

Bill Loud, Peter Welch and Peter Smith all sniffed it in the cellars during their tenancies, and all also reported tricks by unseen hands – phantom tapping on doors, cuff-links and pound notes disappearing, only to turn up later in rooms where nobody had been for days, candles flying across the bar, cupboard doors rattling, and a fridge being mysteriously switched off.

On the other side of the other side of the Theatre Royal is the house once occupied by Regency buck Beau Nash and his last mistress, Juliana Popjoy. Today it is a restaurant called Popjoy's. One would-be diner got more than he bargained for when he called just before Christmas, 1975.

He ordered his meal, then went upstairs to the bar while the dishes were being prepared. As he sat on a green settee, enjoying an aperitif, a lady in old-fashioned clothes approached, sat down beside him, and vanished. The terrified man rushed downstairs, blurted his story to a waiter, and fled, still hungry, into the night.

The jasmine lady may have been responsible for an un-expected drama on the Theatre Royal stage in June, 1963. One of the props for the production was a clock. When its hands reached 12.30, it chimed loudly three times. But stagehands had removed the chime mechanism before the performance began.

A lady in grey also haunts the Theatre Royal in York. Actress Julie Dawn Cole, best known as a nurse in the long-running British TV series *Angels*, is one of many who claim to have seen her. Julie said, 'We were rehearsing on stage one Christmas when I saw her wearing a cloak and a hood. Her outline was irridescent, like gossamer, but I was left with a warm, happy feeling. I consider myself lucky to have seen her.'

British actress Thora Hird does not have such fond memories of her brush with the supernatural. The popular TV comedy star was appearing on stage in London in a play set in Victorian times. She found a bolero-type jacket in a trunk of theatrical jumble, and at first it seemed ideal for her role, fitting her perfectly, but at each subsequent performance, it grew tighter, until it had to be let out.

Thora said, 'One day, my understudy had to wear the jacket. That night, at home after the show, she saw the ghost of a young Victorian woman wearing the same jacket. Later, the wife of the director of the play tried the jacket on, and felt nothing. But when she took it off, there were red weals on her throat as if someone had tried to strangle her. We decided to get rid of the jacket.

'A few days after we did, three mediums held a seance on the stage of the theatre. One had a vision of a girl struggling violently with a man who was tearing at her clothes.'

The site of a former theatre in Yorkshire is haunted by a woman who did not really exist. Old Mother Riley was a comedy favourite with British film, radio and music hall fans in the Forties and Fifties. She was the creation of comedian Arthur Lucan, who died in his dressing room at the old Tivoli Theatre, Hull, in 1966, a week before he was due to attend a meeting with local tax inspectors.

Ironically, when the theatre was demolished, a tax office was built in its place, and Lucan may be having the last laugh on the staff.

An Inland Revue official said, 'We do not like to say too much about what Old Mother Riley is up to in Hull, but people do stay away from a storeroom on the ground floor. There is a strange atmosphere and it is said that the ghost of Mother Riley has been seen.'